D1561542

THE CHRISTIAN COLLEGE
PHENOMENON

THE CHRISTIAN COLLEGE
PHENOMENON

Inside America's Fastest Growing Institutions of Higher Learning

Samuel Joeckel and Thomas Chesnes, editors

Abilene Christian University Press

THE CHRISTIAN COLLEGE PHENOMENON

Inside America's Fastest Growing Institutions of Higher Learning

ACU
PRESS

Copyright 2012 by Samuel Joeckel and Thomas Chesnes

ISBN 978-0-89112-549-5
LCCN 2011023411

Printed in the United States of America

Scripture quotations, unless otherwise noted, are from The Holy Bible, New International Version. Copyright 1984, International Bible Society. Used by permission of Zondervan Publishers.

LIBRARY OF CONGRESS CATALOGING-IN-PUBLICATION DATA
The Christian college phenomenon : inside America's fastest growing institutions of higher learning / Samuel Joeckel and Thomas Chesnes, editors.
    p. cm.
 Includes bibliographical references.
 ISBN 978-0-89112-284-5
 1. Christian universities and colleges--United States. 2. Higher education and state--United States. 3. Christian college students--Religious life--United States. 4. College students--Religious life--United States. 5. College students--Conduct of life. I. Joeckel, Samuel. II. Chesnes, Thomas.
 LC427.C47 2011
 378.1'982827--dc23
                                                                                        2011023411

Cover design by Rick Gibson
Interior text design by Sandy Armstrong

Abilene Christian University Press
1626 Campus Court
Abilene, Texas 79601

1-877-816-4455 toll free
For current information about all ACU Press titles, visit our Website:
www.abilenechristianuniversitypress.com

11 12 13 14 15 16 / 7 6 5 4 3 2 1

CONTENTS

ACKNOWLEDGMENTS

We express appreciation to the many who helped make this volume possible. Palm Beach Atlantic University awarded us with Quality Initiative grants in 2007 and 2008, funds that enabled us to create our surveys and to attend conferences around the country where we received valuable feedback. Mimi Barnard, Vice President for Professional Development and Research at the Council for Christian Colleges and Universities (CCCU), offered us encouragement during the project's embryonic stage. The academic and student life officers who distributed the survey to their students greatly enriched the dataset. Joshua Firestone, our student assistant in 2007 and 2008, collected data and helped shape ideas. Tory Joeckel assisted with data collection. Nerolie Ceus, Collection Management Technician at the PBAU library, processed hundreds of interlibrary-loan requests for us. Don McCulloch and Pamela Wiener offered useful feedback on early drafts of the surveys. Jim Swick shared his expertise in statistical analysis. Marjorie Joeckel, Chris Jensen, Jenifer Elmore, and Larry Shrier proofread essays. We are grateful to those who joined us for lunch over the years in the PBAU cafeteria; may you continue to follow the arguments wherever they may lead. Most importantly, we appreciate the nearly 4,300 participants who took the survey and shared their perspectives on Christian higher education; this volume would not be possible without them. Finally, we thank our contributors for engaging our data with rigor and insight.

INTRODUCTION

Rival Viewpoints of One Reality

Christian higher education is at once sublime and ridiculous. It possesses the opportunities for learning and service that elude secular institutions. It likewise grapples with problems that could only befall institutions that call themselves Christian.

For instance, on the one hand, institutions uncompromisingly committed to Christianity—what Robert Benne calls "orthodox schools"—embrace a belief system that unifies their students' course of study around a shared interpretive lens.[1] Typically referred to as a component of faith/learning integration, this shared perspective gives direction to critical inquiry by encouraging students to pose the same question in every course offered on campus, regardless of its material: How might a Christian understand this? To employ Nicholas Wolterstorff's nomenclature, Christianity serves as a "control belief," shaping students' approach to any subject.[2] In addition, learning within the context of Christian higher education is often energized by the credo, "all truth is God's truth," an apothegm that is of course indebted to the venerable Reformed tradition. (Indeed, during our travels to various Christian institutions, we detected what we came to call "Calvin envy," a reference to the intellectual rigor often associated with Calvin College in Grand Rapids, Michigan.) Once conceived under the auspices of God's sovereignty, truth—whether in philosophy, literature, fine arts, or science—becomes the single-minded object of passionate pursuit for many Christian faculty and students, creating an ideal Christian learning environment.

On the other hand, these institutions can create the conditions that permit what Mark Noll refers to as modern-day Manichaeism, a heresy Noll locates in evangelical culture. "Evangelicals," Noll explains, "have often promoted a Manichaean attitude by assuming that we, and only we, have the truth, while nonbelievers, or Christian believers who are not evangelicals, practice only error."[3] Such an assumption sanctions intellectual arrogance and yields dishonest—not to mention just plain wrong—understandings of differing viewpoints. Our colleague David Horkott gives a name to inquiries motivated by these forms of arrogance and dishonesty: the "inoculation analysis." According to the principles of the inoculation analysis, a student learns just enough about differing perspectives in order to reject them. And, of course, the perspectives in question are usually

---

1 Robert Benne, *Quality with Soul: How Six Premier Colleges and Universities Keep Faith with Their Religious Traditions* (Grand Rapids, Mich.: Eerdmans, 2001), 50.

2 Nicholas Wolterstorff, *Reason Within the Bounds of Religion* (Grand Rapids, Mich.: Eerdmans, 1984), 67.

3 Mark Noll, *The Scandal of the Evangelical Mind* (Grand Rapids, Mich.: Eerdmans, 1994), 52.

perceived as challenges to Christianity in some way; typical objects of the inoculation analysis include postmodernism and the theory of evolution.

Consider another dichotomy. On the one hand, administrators at Christian institutions profess to perform their duties in accord with the tenets of their faith. Their creation of policies and interactions with faculty, staff, and students are informed by the gospel and guided by the Holy Spirit. Members of such a Christian community are more than mere professors, registrars, cafeteria workers, and students; they are souls of eternal worth. Such high estimation of the individual forges a caring and compassionate community, one in which administrators heed a divinely inspired injunction to love their employees as they love themselves.

On the other hand, carrying out administrative tasks within such a Christian framework can mitigate personal responsibility in the name of divine will. Administrators, for instance, might claim that they are not leading their institution; God is. This acknowledgment of God's role in the shaping of the institution may convey a sense of personal humility. However, it might also endow any or all of the administrators' decisions with divine authority. Administrators, in short, might too easily equate their decisions with the Almighty's will. When this is the case, how can the dissenting opinion justify its beliefs? How does one argue against the will of God? Employing religious rhetoric from a leadership position can be dangerous. In some respects, the Christian college or university operates as a theocracy. And any overview of history shows that most theocracies have damaged the cause of Christ as well as those who call themselves Christians.

The sublime-and-ridiculous dichotomy also applies to students at Christian institutions. Again, on the one hand, a predominately Christian student body practices a love modeled by Jesus Christ and abides by moral principles that have guided individuals for millennia. On the other hand, social pressure to live up to Christian standards can result in hypocritical religiosity and showy pietism. Indeed, the cliques into which students often become acculturated on secular campuses—jocks, nerds, frat boys, hippies, etc.—assume unique identities at Christian schools: witness what has been referred to on our campus as the "God Squad," described by some as displaying overt piety, imposing a Scripture verse upon every situation, and rendering judgment on those on the outside. And with the plethora of religious activities on campus, it is no wonder that some experience what one student in one of our surveys identified as "God overload."[4]

The subtitle of this edited volume captures these diametric frames of reference and underscores what we believe to be its unique perspective. An analysis from the inside implies the existence of a contrasting analysis from the outside: rival viewpoints of one reality. This project began with such considerations in mind; indeed, in its incipient stages, the project was tentatively entitled, "The Expectations and Realities of the Christian College Experience," a formulation that likewise underscores dueling perspectives and disparate viewpoints of the same reality.

---

4   See Carol Woodfin's essay, "Faith and Campus Culture: Are Faculty and Students on the Same Page?" (Part Two, Essay Two).

The Genesis of This Volume

We trace the origins of this project to conversations around a table with faculty colleagues at the school cafeteria. As often happens during such gatherings, the conversation was enlivened by a spirit of both camaraderie and confidentiality, a conversation not intended to be heard by students and definitely not intended to be heard by administration. The subject revolved around the two poles of Christian higher education: strengths and weaknesses, triumphs and disasters, and, yes, sublimity and ridiculousness. As claims and counterclaims ricocheted around the table, we wondered how faculty at other Christian schools *really* felt about our topics of discussion, how they would respond honestly and candidly, without fear of repercussions from their administration, and independently of their institution's party line.

Unfortunately, survey instruments distributed by university administration do not always encourage honesty and candidness. We would want to ask probing questions that could potentially put employees at odds with their employers. We therefore made the decision to distribute a faculty survey "under the radar" to faculty employed by institutions within the Council for Christian Colleges and Universities (CCCU); that is, we distributed our survey without the prior knowledge of the CCCU or its member institutions. To accomplish this, we began the tedious and laborious task of compiling email addresses of individual faculty from university websites. The two of us, along with our student research assistant, Joshua Firestone, and some help from Tory Joeckel (Samuel's wife) created a list of 9,594 faculty email addresses. In 2007, we sent the survey to every one of them.

As expected, we were not under the radar for very long. We received a number of responses from participants and non-participants alike: ranging from validations of the importance of the study to outright expressions of suspicion and hostility. The survey itself generated the honest answers we were seeking, enabling us to gain a clearer insight into the lives and beliefs of faculty nationwide. A few months later, we distributed a survey to students of the CCCU. This time, however, we went through the official channels and gained the blessing of the CCCU. Of the 105 requests sent to CCCU chief academic and student-development officials, we received *no* response from sixty-eight institutions. Only thirty-seven institutions had the courtesy to respond with a yes, no, or maybe. While we were pleased with participation in the student survey, we realized at that point the value of the faculty data and the prudence in our decision to distribute the faculty survey under the radar. Although they made some institutions nervous, these data, we realized, needed to be explored and analyzed from the diverse perspectives of an array of competent scholars, for we found it more urgent than ever to know what CCCU faculty *really* think.

This urgency intensified when we considered the skyrocketing popularity of Christian higher education. Institutions affiliated with the CCCU have experienced phenomenal growth in the last twenty years. In fact, whereas public institutions of higher learning in the United States experienced a 3 percent growth in enrollment from

1990-1996, CCCU institutions witnessed a 36.9 percent growth during that same period.[5] And in 2006, enrollment at CCCU institutions rose by 70.6 percent over the previous year, while other private colleges grew by 28 percent and public universities increased by 13 percent during the same period.[6] In July 2008, the CCCU approved five more institutions for full membership, raising the total number of member institutions to 110.[7] We believe this growth signals a phenomenon in higher education, what we call the Christian college phenomenon.

The Survey

We do not hide the fact that neither one of us is a social scientist. While both of us have research experience in the field of higher education, we have little experience in developing and administering surveys. From the beginning, we appropriated G. K. Chesterton's *bon mot* as our motto: "that if a thing is worth doing, it is worth doing badly."[8]

The first task was to develop questions for the survey instruments. The current set of questions underwent extensive revision. Some were included for the purpose of collecting demographics; others were driven by hypotheses. And many were exploratory, adopting a scattergun approach in which the target revealed itself only after it was hit. We decided that the student survey needed to be much shorter to ensure adequate participation. Although various drawbacks are associated with internet-based surveys[9], we decided that this medium would best serve the scope of our project. Using the web gave us the advantage of decreased costs, reduced human error, and the ability to reach a large number of people over a wide geographic area in a short period of time.

Of the 9,594 email requests to faculty, 741 were rejected as bad addresses, faculty who were no longer employed at the institution, or non-faculty employees. Of the remaining 8,853 requests, 1,907 at ninety-five of the then 105 members of the CCCU participated, a nearly 22% response rate (Table 1). Through the cooperation of student development and academic institutional officers, 2,389 students from nineteen different schools also participated in this study (Table 2). Institutions with low representation were those sent directly by our student assistant to peers enrolled at these schools (and thus without institutional cooperation).

The student response rate was difficult to determine. Since the invitations were sent through various methods, including institutional list-serves, it is unknown exactly how many students were reached. It is safe to assume that the student response rate was considerably less than the faculty rate. These response rates could be an issue of concern,

---

5   Leo Reisberg, "Enrollments Surge at Christian Colleges," *Chronicle of Higher Education* 45.26 (1999): A42.

6   Dalia Hatuqa, "Evangelical Colleges Gaining Popularity," April 9, 2006. http://nwitimes.com/articles/2006/04/09/news/illiana/a17a1d5ed1a3f9528625714a0078e17d.prt

7   See the CCCU website at <http://www.cccu.org/news/cccu_news/cccu_welcomes_five_new_members_two_new_affiliates>

8   G. K. Chesterton, "Folly and Female Education," in *What's Wrong with the World* (San Francisco: Ignatius Press, 1994), 175.

9   See Matthias Schonlau, Ronald Fricker, and Marc Elliot, *Conducting Research Surveys via E-mail and the Web*, Document MR-1480-RC (Rand Publications, 2002) for a thorough review of strengths and weaknesses of web-based surveys.

but not a surprise considering that the faculty survey was unsanctioned—not to mention the fact that the faculty survey consisted of over a hundred questions and the student survey of over fifty. Nevertheless, the two surveys produced over 300,000 data points originating from nearly 4,300 participants.

Shortly after the initial survey deployment and throughout this study, we recognized that our survey instrument had a number of weaknesses. For example, a number of questions could have been more direct or worded more clearly. Some topics begged for more exploration (such as on race and ethnicity). Of course, readers should keep in mind the obvious fact that we did not design this survey to analyze any *one* topic, thus the wide-ranging—and not subject-intensive—questions. Other questions were framed by the biases of the implementers. Many of these issues are discussed in the subsequent chapters and are fairly dealt with by our contributors. Despite these and other issues, the data collected in this study serve as an effective catalyst for discussion (especially in light of the professional expertise and experiences of our contributors) as well as springboards for future research on Christian higher education.

Keep in mind that there are many ways to interpret data. This volume represents a first look at the trends embedded within the dataset. In many of the essays of this volume, data filtering and cross tabulations were employed to illustrate key differences between groups of respondents and often depicted and cited in the essays' tables. Those with advanced statistical training may find this overly simplistic; however, to many readers of this volume, a heavy reliance on statistical parameters (such as an r, F, t, or p) would be neither useful nor meaningful. After all, one of the goals of this project is to make the trends embodied in these data accessible and understandable to a wide audience, including those with little background in statistics and analysis. Many of the contributors have little statistical training; however, their interpretations based on experience are more valuable than a miniscule p-value or a strong r. A few other authors in this volume employed more sophisticated analyses of the data; specific methods and notes are included within the appropriate sections.

Each contributor to this volume had unfettered access to this unprecedented data set as he or she explored one of the seven different subjects assigned to the seven parts of the book: Faith, Learning, and Scholarly Rigor; Faith and Campus Culture; Assessing the *In-Loco-Parentis* Model; Academic Freedom; Racial/Ethnic Diversity; Gender Equity, and Evolution and the Science Classroom. In addition, essays were composed in chronological order so that second and third contributors to each section could respond to the prior essay(s) in that section; in this way, the volume sustains a dialogic character. Adopting an empirical approach, contributors marshaled arguments on their subjects rooted in the real experiences of CCCU faculty and students, enabling them (and their readers) to put their fingers on the pulse of the Christian college phenomenon, its strengths and weaknesses, its sublimity and ridiculousness.

Overview of Each Section

Part One: Faith, Learning, and Scholarly Rigor

Incorporating reason and faith into the academic project lies at the heart of Christian higher education. Although employing various models, this project is typically referred to as the integration of faith and learning. Professors at CCCU institutions model to their students various ways in which a Christian perspective bears on their subjects, from biology to literature. In addition, these professors engage their scholarly research from Christian vantage points. Various obstacles stand in the way of this enterprise. Pragmatically speaking, the heavy teaching loads typical of most CCCU institutions make the production of quality research difficult. Moreover, the secular academy can be dismissive of distinctly Christian scholarship, casting faith as antithetical to reason as well as the religious neutrality that should govern intellectual inquiries. In contrast, upholding intellectual rigor alongside committed Christianity, professors at CCCU institutions seek a synthesis of reason and faith, a harmony that prevents either one from drowning out the other. Such a synthesis charts a course between the Scylla of secularization and the Charybdis of anti-intellectualism.

In the first essay of this section, entitled, "A Slippery Slope to Secularization? The Worthwhile Risk of Christian Higher Education," **Samuel Joeckel** and **Thomas Chesnes** explore whether secularization threatens institutions belonging to the Council for Christian Colleges and Universities. Joeckel and Chesnes' data analysis shows that, though vigilance should still be exercised, these institutions are hardly descending a slippery slope to secularization. In fact, as the second part of the essay argues, overzealous vigilance against secularization proves counterproductive, resulting in a theological and political homogeneity and defensiveness that militate against important aims of higher education such as the free exchange of ideas and a charitable understanding of diversity of thought.

Susan Van Zanten contributes the second essay, "Christian Scholarship: Opportunities, Realities, and Challenges." After providing an overview of the renaissance of Christian scholarship that occurred after the 1980s, VanZanten examines the scholarly activity of faculty at CCCU institutions. Due primarily to heavy course loads and inadequate institutional support, CCCU faculty lag behind their counterparts at other four-year institutions with respect to scholarly and creative production. VanZanten concludes that improved personal practices and institutional structures can help faculty overcome these hindrances to scholarly output.

In "A Coda on Faith, Learning, and Scholarly Rigor," **David L. Weeks** and **Donald G. Isaak** offer qualified assent to the thesis of Joeckel and Chesnes' essay. While agreeing that the faith identity of CCCU institutions appears to be solid, they remain concerned about "uncertainties." For instance, the majority of survey respondents claim to know what faith/learning integration is and how to practice it; however, Weeks and Isaak contend that faith/learning integration and its praxis can mean different things to different people. CCCU institutions would benefit, therefore, from "initiatives that provide clear, uniform definitions" of faith/learning integration and its practice for each discipline. The same uncertainties apply to the theological beliefs of faculty. The elasticity of the term "evangelical" allows for various emphases of belief, complicating what lies at the core of an institution's identity. One strategy for overcoming this ambiguity in the classroom is to allow faculty "advocacy on those matters with which everyone explicitly agrees upon (namely, those doctrinal beliefs that historically define Christianity)" but to expect impartial—yet fair—presentations of matters that lie on the periphery. Negotiating between essentials and inessentials of belief requires humility and commitment.

Part Two: Faith and Campus Culture

CCCU institutions strive not only to enlighten the minds but to nourish the souls of their students. Various activities outside the classroom on Christian campuses ensure that students are exposed to Christian doctrine and nurtured in Christian spirituality. Paramount among these activities are chapel services, which are mandatory for students and faculty at some institutions within the CCCU. In addition, all faculty at all CCCU institutions are required to sign some type of faith statement, affirming their adherence to their institutions' theological beliefs and practices, insuring that students receive an education consistent with their institutions' core principles. Such a faith-filled campus culture is not without its challenges. Hypocrisy among faculty and students, for instance, may adversely affect the spiritual climate of the institution; repulsion at what might pass for Christianity on campus can weaken faith. In other cases, a campus that abides by exacting moral scruples can create an environment that produces guilt in those with moral struggles. Ideally, the CCCU campus fosters a culture characterized by vibrant and authentic spiritual activity and instills confidence in its members that the institution is charting a course directed by God.

In "Thick Ecumenism: The Possibility of Enlarging Our Circles at Christian Colleges and Universities," **Phillip Irving Mitchell** notes the survey's finding that most CCCU professors favor the inclusion of Roman Catholics within their faculty ranks, using this piece of data as the springboard for an analysis of commitment and denominational diversity within the faith community of CCCU institutions. Drawing from Alasdair MacIntyre's model of tradition and appropriating Steven R. Harmon's notion of "thick ecumenism," Mitchell considers ways in which CCCU institutions might adopt more inclusive measures in hiring practices while simultaneously respecting their faith traditions, thus enriching faith and campus culture.

In "Faith and Campus Culture: Are Faculty and Students on the Same Page?" **Carol Woodfin** suggests that the faith culture at CCCU institutions might be counterproductive: that the ubiquitous presence of faith activities on campus—chapel, Bible studies, Christian fellowship activities, etc.—can produce what one student respondent called "God overload." Woodfin mines the qualitative data of the student survey to defend this claim, showing how many students experience spiritual stasis, on the one hand, or spiritual suffusion, on the other, as a result of this environment. Concomitantly, despite faculty fears about teaching controversial faith issues, Woodfin shows from the data that students strongly desire to be challenged: to engage ideas with honesty and openness.

Wayne Barnard identifies some strengths of Christian higher education in the final essay in this section. The sovereignty of God leaves no subject out-of-bounds for exploration and analysis. However, Barnard also pinpoints problems related to faith and campus culture: An overemphasis on campus rules and regulations—curfew, dress code, etc.—creates a culture animated by constraint, suspicion, and legalism. Barnard instead advocates what he calls an "ethos of freedom," which establishes optimal conditions for thinking, questioning, challenging, and exploring within the framework of faith. An ethos of freedom also enables faculty to expose "places of vulnerability," from which they can reach out both to God and to the other. Barnard points to the 2006 Soul Force visit to Abilene Christian University as an illustration of this ethos. Although Soul Force, a group of lesbian/gay/bisexual/transgender/queer activists, endorses a lifestyle opposed to the values of ACU, Barnard describes the meaningful conversations and valuable friendships borne out of love and compassion, and emboldened by an ethos of freedom.

Part Three: Assessing the In-Loco-Parentis Model

In addition to enlightening minds and nourishing souls, CCCU institutions seek to build the moral character of their students. To accomplish this goal, many Christian schools adopt an *in-loco-parentis* model. Assuming some parental responsibilities, these schools enforce moral rules and behavioral codes that students are expected to observe upon penalties such as academic probation or expulsion. From one perspective, the *in-loco-parentis* model amounts to an overprotective paternalism, infantilizing and inoculating students within a Christian bubble that can create an environment, on the one hand, of repression or, on the other, rebellion. From another perspective, the *in-loco-parentis* model mitigates the temptations that can compromise moral integrity; this model thus enforces rules against sex and alcohol, the abuse of which remains common in secular colleges and universities. As Robert Benne writes, "There is good reason to believe that college-age persons need a protected shelter for the formation of—perhaps even indoctrination into—the Christian vision and ethos. The world has changed. Youth are no longer shaped by a coherent culture that gives them a firm identity as young people." Benne continues, "Few of the Calvin or Wheaton graduates seem terribly wounded by their longer time in a Christian incubator."[10] Whether conceived as protection, shelter, or incubation, the *in-loco-parentis* model attempts to harmonize student behavior and the spiritual ideals to which the institution adheres.

This section begins with an essay written by **C. Eric Jones** and **April L. Cunion** entitled, "*In Loco Parentis*: Strengths, Weaknesses, and Future Directions." They argue that the *in-loco-parentis* model is successful insofar as it limits behavior proscribed by most CCCU institutions, primarily alcohol consumption and pre-marital sexual intercourse. Nevertheless, Jones and Cunion also show that the *in-loco-parentis* model is not

---

10 Benne, 200.

without challenges: moral codes, for instance, can prevent students from experiencing the sort of moral crises that are necessary for full identity achievement; in addition, the application of *in loco parentis* to spiritual development can be counterproductive, for as Jones and Cunion maintain, faith matures most when it is intrinsically oriented, self-motivated, and not monitored externally. To meet these challenges, Jones and Cunion offer future directions for the *in-loco-parentis* model: upper classmen should explain the rationale for campus rules to lower classman, thereby enabling the newer students to understand the rules as they take ownership of them from their classmates. In addition, students should be given more freedom with respect to moral rules as they mature during the course of their college careers.

Edee M. Schulze and **Paul Blezien** write the second essay, "*In Loco Parentis*: An Evolving Concept." They contend that the premises undergirding the Joeckel/Chesnes survey with respect to student development are fundamentally flawed, betraying a mis-understanding of the purpose of student-conduct codes. Maintaining that both public and Christian colleges and universities have long abandoned the *in-loco-parentis* model, Schulze and Blezien flesh out what has taken its place: what they call a "developmental and community-based approach" focusing on "holistic development." Within such a framework, conduct codes operate under the service of the traditions and beliefs of the institution. Thus, conduct codes should never constitute legalistic rules, but should instead contribute to the formation of a nurturing and challenging campus community devoted to the moral and spiritual growth of students.

In the final essay of Part Three, "*In Loco Parentis* from a Student and Faculty Perspective," **Allison Sanders** and **Samuel Joeckel** challenge Schulze and Blezien's contention that the *in-loco-parentis* model has been abandoned by CCCU institutions, drawing from scholars in the field and evidence from the survey to show that it is still operational. Sanders and Joeckel argue that the *in-loco-parentis* model produces shel-tered students, a phrase that not only signifies moral insularity—a Miltonic "cloistered virtue"—but fosters a culture detrimental to intellectual rigor and inhospitable to alter-ity (the marginalized groups on campus). Sanders and Joeckel conclude by standing together with Schulze and Blezien in their call for a community-based approach to the holistic development of students.

Part Four: Academic Freedom

Among its many aims, higher education encourages students to question and assess ideas and beliefs, to think critically as they cultivate a worldview that they can claim as their own. Martha Nussbaum traces this aim back to the Greeks, specifically Socrates, who praised the merits of an "examined life." According to Nussbaum, "This means a life that accepts no belief as authoritative simply because it has been handed down by tradition or become familiar through habit, a life that questions all beliefs and accepts only those that survive reason's demand for consistency and for justification."[11] Nussbaum's gloss on Socrates' phrase establishes a pedagogy that can easily compromise the mission of Christian higher education. Many strains of Christian thought value the role of tradition, especially as it is embodied in the creeds of the early church as well as in the writings of the Church Fathers and other Christians who have followed in their wake through the centuries. In addition, much Christian thought acknowledges limitations to reason and its role in finding truth. Nevertheless, some Christian professors, as they help their students claim a worldview of their own and as they pursue scholarly work in their own fields, challenge tradition and employ reason in ways that create tension with their institution's mission statement and core beliefs. Such tension raises issues of academic freedom. Are Christian universities ever warranted in limiting academic freedom in cases in which professors either say or write something contrary to the beliefs and values of their institutions? On the one hand, professors are expected to be loyal to the beliefs and values of their universities; on the other hand, following the long-established tradition of liberal arts education, they are expected to think critically, rigorously analyze their subject, and follow the argument or the data wherever they may lead. Performing the latter at the expense of the former can constitute grounds for termination, making the issue of academic freedom particularly important for Christian educators.

Joe Ricke contributes an essay entitled, "The Hesitants among Us: The Tightrope Act of Christian Scholarship." While pleased with the survey evidence suggesting that most CCCU professors enjoy academic freedom, Ricke attends to the significant minority who demur, what he calls the "hesitants among us." Ricke shows that faculty who do not believe they possess academic freedom (what he calls the AF group) on their campuses differ most significantly from all other survey respondents with respect to two categories he calls "religiosity" and "administrative concerns." The AF group, for instance, is less likely than the total group to experience faith growth at their institutions. Ricke theorizes that the AF group may perceive the religious culture of campus as being too dominant, exerting undue influence on the way theological formulations are framed as well as on the way religious beliefs are practiced, thereby compromising perceptions of academic freedom. In addition, university administration shapes perceptions of academic freedom in obvious ways. Consequently, Ricke warns against adopting a triumphalist attitude toward the issue of academic freedom, advocating instead a more sober approach that honestly recognizes the unique and formidable challenges for Christian schools and that incorporates full faculty involvement in drafting statements that attempt to define the slippery concept of academic freedom.

Like Ricke, **Dan Russ** acknowledges the survey evidence that suggests that the majority of CCCU professors claim to possess academic freedom. However, in "Fear Not: Security, Risk, and Academic Freedom," Russ finds other restrictions that threaten academic freedom: a deep distrust between a significant percentage of faculty and

---

11   Martha Nussbaum, *Cultivating Humanity: A Classical Defense of Reform in Liberal Education* (Cambridge: Harvard University Press, 1997), 10.

administration as well as distrust among faculty themselves; a heavy teaching load that discourages serious scholarship, thus precluding faculty from even exercising their academic freedom; the secular academy's dismissive attitude toward Christian scholarship; and profound differences of opinion among faculty concerning the core values of their institutions. Russ offers various strategies for overcoming these instructions, including a wholehearted embrace of the Pauline dictum "to speak the truth in love."

David Hoekema finds encouragement in survey data showing that 98% of CCCU faculty support their institutions' Christian mission. Like Russ, he finds faculty distrust toward administration to be detrimental in the pursuit of academic freedom. As he explains, "CCCU faculty members overwhelmingly affirm the central values and mission of their institutions, but a significant minority lack confidence in the individuals entrusted with implementing them." Like Ricke, Hoekema believes that in some respects Christian colleges and universities afford more academic freedom than their secular counterparts and less freedom in other respects. As he explains, "Matters of faith and personal conviction arise frequently and naturally in a Christian academic community, in ways that are less frequent and can be more problematic at a state university. Yet too often the very same convictions that should facilitate an atmosphere of openness and honesty are employed as bludgeons against critics."

Part Five: Racial/Ethnic Diversity

In 1991, Nicholas Wolterstorff wrote: "The Christian church is probably the most ethnically diverse grouping on earth; very few ethnic groups are not represented in Christ's body. Yet of almost all those ethnic groups it is true that if a member of the group attended one of the colleges belonging to the Christian College Coalition [now CCCU], he or she would feel alien—and worse, would typically experience discrimination." Wolterstorff added, "If you are not a white of West European stock who speaks English fluently, the chances are very high that you will not feel at home in these colleges."[12] In the years since Wolterstorff painted this bleak picture, the CCCU has taken steps to redress this problem. For instance, in 1991, the Coalition of Christian Colleges formed the Minority Concerns Project, which created networks for minority faculty and students and also co-sponsored conferences and workshops. In 1994, however, this venture fizzled and died. In addition, at its 2000 retreat the CCCU board charged then CCCU president Robert Andringa with "developing new ways to make racial harmony a more urgent priority in Christian education."[13] Progress has been made: According to the *Journal for Blacks in Higher Education*, twenty-nine member institutions of the CCCU now have black enrollments of 10% or more, more than triple the number of member institutions with the same black enrollment as reported in a *JBHE* survey in 1997.[14] Drawing from a

---

12 Nicholas Wolterstorff, Foreword to *Ethnic-Minorities and Evangelical Christian Colleges*, ed. D. John Lee (New York: University Press of America, 1991), ix.

13 See James Patterson, *Shining Lights: A History of the Council for Christian Colleges & Universities* (Grand Rapids, Mich.: Baker Academic, 2001), 72-94.

14 "Black Enrollments at Christian Colleges Are on the Rise," August 7, 2008, http://www.jbhe.com/latest/index080708.html

survey he conducted of minority faculty at Christian colleges and universities, Alvaro Nieves illustrates how racial harmony remains an urgent priority in Christian education: "There was a recurring sense of alienation and loneliness on the part of minority faculty. The sense of alienation appeared to be tied to the perception of prejudice on the part of both colleagues, students, and others, with little corresponding support. In addition, there was a sense of pressure to perform at exceptional professional levels and, at the same time, be the ideal minority professional."[15] In order to promote racial/ethnic diversity and justice, CCCU institutions must assess their own operating principles on institutional, theological, social, and philosophical levels.

In "Race and Ethnicity in CCCU Schools: Rhetoric and Reality," **Alvaro Nieves** confirms that faculty and students at CCCU institutions have become more ethnically and racially diverse over the past twenty years. Nevertheless, much work remains to be done. Minority faculty and students are still underrepresented and misunderstood, leading to frustration and disappointment, as Nieves shows through his analysis of qualitative data from the surveys. Nieves offers advice for improving the situation, including the following strategies (among others): active recruitment of faculty and students from underrepresented groups; development of mentorship systems for minority faculty; and strong leadership from student-life departments in showing sensitivity to the needs and concerns of minority students.

Jenell Williams Paris and **Michelle Knights** contribute an essay entitled, "Understanding CCCU Faculty of Color." Their analysis of the survey uncovers the following data: that minority faculty complete more scholarly projects while simultaneously teaching and advising more students than their majority colleagues. Consequently, policies should be put in place that ensure equality in course and advising loads. Minority faculty are also less likely than their peers to affirm that they chose to profess at a Christian institution because of a commitment to Christian higher education. Williams Paris and Knights contend that this ambivalence may be due to weak support of multiculturalism on some Christian campuses.

In "Biblical Multiculturalism: Moving Forward in Deed and Truth," **Terriel Byrd** and **Olga Rybalkina** offer theological and cultural reflections on what they consider to be the most promising avenue for creating diverse campus communities: biblical multiculturalism. According to Byrd and Rybalkina, multiculturalism pursued for its own sake will not succeed for a number of reasons. First, it is linked by many Christians to postmodernism (and thus relativism). Second, it eventuates too often in the politicization of race and ethnicity. And third, it too easily leads to tribalism, creating lines of division between people. *Biblical* multiculturalism, on the other hand, upholds the authority of Scripture and its truths, embraces the biblical mandate of unity and oneness, and incorporates all into the body of Christ. Realizing this ideal requires more than grass-roots

---

15   Alvaro Nieves, "The Minority Experience in Evangelical Colleges," in *Ethnic-Minorities and Evangelical Christian Colleges*, 10.

efforts; top administration must commit to this vision, helping all constituencies within the CCCU to move forward in deed and in truth.

Part Six: Gender Equity

In addition to facing a lack of racial/ethnic diversity, CCCU institutions must also confront the issue of gender diversity and equity. In fact, no significant empirical analysis exists that specifically examines gender relations within a representative sample of institutions belonging to the CCCU. Nevertheless, former Council President Robert Andringa identified gender inequity as a challenge for member institutions. "We are behind," he wrote. "We are behind in offering females the same opportunities to teach and administer as men."[16] As with the issue of racial/ethnic diversity, exploring the issue of gender equity requires an analysis of institutions' operating principles on institutional, theological, social, and philosophical levels.

M. Elizabeth Hall begins the conversation on the challenge of gender equity with an essay entitled, "Finding a Home in Academia: Gender Equity at CCCU Institutions." Marshaling copious evidence, she shows that gender inequities are realities in secular higher education and are even more acute in Christian higher education. Her analysis of the survey reveals that women faculty at CCCU institutions often do not experience a good fit with the evangelical subculture that exists at their institutions. Hall thus recommends the formation of institutional peers to ameliorate a sense of alienation that women faculty may experience; she also advocates the implementation of a "small-wins" approach whereby incremental changes might eliminate the "micro-inequities" that are often almost invisibly institutionalized within Christian higher education.

In their provocatively entitled essay, "Are We Doomed?: Why Christian Colleges and Universities Must Lead on the Issue of Gender Equity and Why They Don't," **Bettina Tate Pederson** and **Allyson Jule** acknowledge that a majority of survey respondents are happy with the status quo. Exploring open-ended responses, however, Tate Pederson and Jule piece together a "counter-narrative" that challenges this status quo. One thread of this counter-narrative registers concern regarding traditional biblical interpretations, which can create a campus climate unfavorable to gender equity; indeed, the authors contend that unless theology is subject to reexamination, gender equity is doomed. In addition to this reexamination, Tate Pedersen and Jule recommend that the CCCU take a larger role in promoting gender equity, including the creation of an office of gender issues at the national headquarters in Washington, DC.

In "Holding on to the Traditions of Men: Christianity, Gender, and the Academy," **Jennifer McKinney** locates gender inequities within the tendency of American Christianity to appropriate and enshrine as sacred unbiblical cultural norms that derive from the 1950s; these norms value men as breadwinners and women as homemakers. Christians within higher education likewise appropriate norms of secular academia:

---

16   Robert Andringa, Foreword to *The Future of Christian Higher Education*, ed. David Dockery and David Gushee (Nashville: Broadman & Holman, 1999), xvii.

thus, while CCCU schools may have policies against sexual harassment, they perpetuate gender inequities through operational assumptions that weave sexism (often invisibly) into their very structure. McKinney analyzes survey data that evidence ways in which believers adopt sexist, secular constructs—both from American culture and secular higher education—and then baptize them as Christian. McKinney urges the CCCU "to create models of higher education and gender that reflect the glory of a risen and redeeming Christ," a process that requires us to admit that much of what we currently believe about gender—and pass off as biblical truth—is little more than a cultural construction. Unless that admission serves as a foundation for redressing gender inequities, McKinney believes that Tate Pedersen and Jule's dire prognosis may prove true: we are doomed.

Part Seven: Evolution and the Science Classroom

Despite widespread acceptance and refinement of the modern evolutionary synthesis, the subject of evolution remains a contentious subject among many Christians. The theory of evolution underlies all sub-disciplines of the biological sciences, yet is often met with suspicion, hostility, or outright rejection. This resistance to the concept is often based not on scientific deficiencies, but as a perceived threat to Christian faith. If students see the acceptance of evolution as being incompatible with Christianity, as well as having the preconception of evolution as a "false theory," students of the CCCU may be less likely to critically evaluate the scientific evidence.

The belief that the theory of evolution is incompatible with Christianity is often described as the "second pillar" of antievolutionism. In "Deconstructing the Second Pillar of Antievolutionism in Christian Higher Education," **Thomas Chesnes** focuses on the adherence to this notion among faculty and students in CCCU institutions. Students are more likely to perceive the incompatibility than faculty, but are more accommodating as they mature. Further, differences were seen in the views between disciplines and theological orientations. A proper treatment of evolutionary theory in the Christian academy can reduce the potential of negative pastoral and professional consequences. In order to do so, the philosophical extensions of the theory need to be separated from its scientific basis.

In "Inherited Beliefs and Evolved Brains: A CCCU Challenge," **Howard Van Till** explores the criteria necessary to find compatibility between Christianity and biological evolution as well as the possible sources leading to an incompatibility judgment, including Intelligent Design Theory. Goals are given for CCCU science faculty to help students develop well-informed points of view on science and well-reasoned positions on the relationship between evolution and faith. He concludes the essay with an introduction to what he believes to be the next challenge facing science and religion—the phenomenon of religious belief in an evolutionary context.

Richard G. Colling delineates perhaps one of the greatest challenges for the Christian community in "Evolution and Christian Faith." The challenge is that if evolution is real, and if Christians truly believe the Bible, then "the only logical and viable faith-preserving position for Christians is that evolution must be seen as part of God's creative plan." He describes the leadership potential of CCCU institutions in showing the compatibility between evolution and Christianity, and in doing so potentially establishing a permanent place for the Christian faith in the intellectual and scientific discussions of the culture. This task, however, would require courageous and knowledgeable administrators, board members, and faculty.

Conclusion

In "Moving Up the Slippery Slope," **George M. Marsden** focuses on the theme of secularization, which threads its way through this volume. He argues that CCCU institutions are largely immune to the process of secularization outlined in his seminal book, *The Soul of the American University: From Protestant Establishment to Established Disbelief* (1994). He explains that historical conditions as well as significant differences between the now secularized, once mainline Protestant schools and CCCU institutions make the fate of the former unlikely for the latter: "chances of any extended slide or free fall [down the slippery slope] are slight." While conceding that academic freedom is more limited at CCCU schools than at secular institutions, he maintains that the CCCU has by and large moved from a "defender of the faith" model to a covenantal model. That is, issues of academic freedom no longer fall under the surveillance of theological watchdogs but are instead based upon cooperation and trust within the academic community. The covenantal model allows for a "moving up the slippery slope," away from secularization and toward a maturing and richer faith. He concludes by exploring what he considers to be one of the greatest challenges facing the CCCU: the vital and occasionally problematic relationship between individual CCCU institutions and their supporting church community.

Like George Marsden, **Martin E. Marty** maintains that the threat of secularization within the CCCU should not be overstated. Marty explains that the so-called secularization thesis is no longer as compelling as it once was. As a self-proclaimed CCCU outsider, Marty also calls attention to what he considers to be "the most troubling issue raised" by the essays in this volume: resistance to the theory of evolution. Marty insists that a failure to deal responsibly with evolution, which is fundamental to all the branches of science, and to teach it unhesitatingly will produce a generation of Christians unprepared to engage science in the twenty-first century. Likewise speaking from his outsider status, Marty believes that CCCU administrators and faculty "might be underselling their own achievements." Committed to rigorous Christian higher education, the best CCCU schools provide the training grounds for scholars who have come to lead their disciplines.

Table 1: Faculty Participation by institution

Institution	Count	Institution	Count
Abilene Christian University	42	Howard Payne University	18
Anderson University	30	Huntington University	22
Asbury College	29	Indiana Wesleyan University	35
Azusa Pacific University	47	John Brown University	18
Belhaven College	16	Judson College—Alabama	3
Bethel College--IN	19	Judson College—Illinois	18
Bethel University	25	Kentucky Christian University	10
Biola University	0	King College	8
Bluffton University	0	King's University College, The	0
Bryan College	0	Lee University	15
California Baptist University	27	LeTourneau University	8
Calvin College	72	Lipscomb University	12
Campbellsville University	14	Louisiana College	11
Carson-Newman College	21	Malone College	24
Cedarville University	2	Master's College & Seminary, The	19
College of the Ozarks	28	Messiah College	14
Colorado Christian University	14	MidAmerica Nazarene University	29
Corban College	12	Milligan College	14
Cornerstone University	16	Mississippi College	3
Covenant College	9	Missouri Baptist University	11
Crichton College	10	Montreat College	6
Crown College	10	Mount Vernon Nazarene University	0
Dallas Baptist University	0	North Greenville University	1
Dordt College	30	North Park University	1
East Texas Baptist University	23	Northwest Christian College	1
Eastern Mennonite University	20	Northwest Nazarene University	1
Eastern Nazarene College	15	Northwest University	16
Eastern University	25	Northwestern College—Iowa	21
Erskine College	11	Northwestern College—Minnesota	20
Evangel University	28	Nyack College	15
Fresno Pacific University	7	Oklahoma Baptist University	19
Geneva College	22	Oklahoma Christian University	22
George Fox University	53	Oklahoma Wesleyan University	8
Gordon College	16	Olivet Nazarene University	32
Goshen College	16	Oral Roberts University	15
Grace College & Seminary	21	Palm Beach Atlantic University	54
Greenville College	19	Point Loma Nazarene University	26
Hardin-Simmons University	29	Redeemer University College	8
Hope International University	0	Roberts Wesleyan College	17
Houghton College	18	Seattle Pacific University	43
Houston Baptist University	17	Simpson University	9

Southeastern University	30	Vanguard University of Southern California	26
Southern Nazarene University	25	Warner Pacific College	6
Southern Wesleyan University	9	Warner Southern College	6
Southwest Baptist University	34	Wayland Baptist University	21
Spring Arbor University	19	Waynesburg College	0
Sterling College	0	Westmont College	19
Tabor College	14	Wheaton College	36
Taylor University	26	Whitworth College	17
Trevecca Nazarene University	10	Williams Baptist College	13
Trinity Christian College	19	Unknown institution	44
Trinity International University	10	Total	1907
Trinity Western University	20		
Union University	41		
University of Sioux Falls	22		

Table 2: Student participation by institution

Azusa Pacific University	4	Palm Beach Atlantic University	235
Bethel University	525	Southeastern University	204
Bluffton University	10	Southern Wesleyan University	69
California Baptist University	339	Trinity Christian College	172
Cedarville University	10	Warner Pacific College	23
Corban College	146	Warner Southern College	104
Grace College & Seminary	1	Wayland Baptist University	81
Howard Payne University	87	Unknown	7
Huntington University	145	Total	2389
Malone College	191		
MidAmerica Nazarene University	1		
Northwest Christian College	35		

PART ONE

FAITH, LEARNING, AND SCHOLARLY RIGOR

A SLIPPERY SLOPE TO SECULARIZATION?

The Worthwhile Risk of Christian Higher Education[1]

SAMUEL JOECKEL AND THOMAS CHESNES

Faith, learning, and scholarly rigor exist in tension due to a fear variously named among those committed to Christian higher education: the declension thesis, the slippery slope to secularization, the loss of Christian identity. Michael S. Hamilton provides an example of how such fear generates alarmist rhetoric: "One moment of relaxed vigilance—one twitch or stumble in a secular direction—and down slides the college into the tar pits of apostasy. The only thing left of its former faith would be a stately chapel building—a fossilized artifact of the college's Christian past. The process started with Harvard—once the pride of Puritanism—and has since claimed almost every once-Christian college."[2] Hamilton's clarion call for refocused vigilance against secularization certainly has as one impetus the publication over the last fifteen years of a number of cogently argued books that document the loss of Christian distinctiveness in American higher education. Commenting on these books, Mark Noll notes that "although they move in different directions for different purposes, almost all of the important studies of which I am aware are narratives in one form or another of decline."[3]

In this essay, we explore the intersections between faith, learning, and scholarly rigor by examining how seriously the dangers of decline threaten institutions belonging to the Council for Christian Colleges and Universities (CCCU).[4] We show that, though vigilance

---

1 A version of this essay appeared previously as "A Slippery Slope to Secularization? An Empirical Analysis of the Council for Christian Colleges and Universities," *Christian Scholar's Review* 39:2 (Winter 2010): 177-196. Copyright 2010 by *Christian Scholar's Review*.

2 Michael S. Hamilton, "A Higher Education," *Christianity Today*, June 2005, 31.

3 Mark A. Noll, "The Future of the Religious College," in *The Future of Religious Colleges: The Proceedings of the Harvard Conference on the Future of Religious Colleges*, ed. Paul J. Dovre (Grand Rapids, Mich.: Eerdmans, 2002), 74.

4 The Council for Christian Colleges and Universities is, as its website explains, "an international association of intentionally Christian colleges and universities." The CCCU currently includes 110 members, though at the time we conducted our empirical research, the CCCU had 105 members. See http://www.cccu.org/.

should still be exercised, these institutions are hardly descending the slippery slope to secularization. Faculty participants in the Joeckel/Chesnes survey demonstrated a strong dedication to maintaining the Christian character of their colleges and universities; participants also showed overwhelming commitment to a seminal component of Christian higher education, the integration of faith and learning, all of which suggests that CCCU institutions need not summon their ideological forces in a last stand against the encroaching forces of secularization. In fact, as the second part of our essay argues, overzealous vigilance against secularization proves counterproductive, resulting in a theological and political homogeneity and defensiveness that militate against important aims of higher education such as the free exchange of ideas, a charitable understanding of diversity of thought, and scholarly rigor.

Context for Analysis

Much of the slippery-slope discourse over the past fifteen years has as its subtext George Marsden's magisterial *The Soul of the American University: From Protestant Establishment to Established Non-Belief*. (It should be noted, however, that Marsden himself does not use the phrase, "slippery slope.") Tracing the "relegation of religion to the periphery of American universities" during the early twentieth century, eventuating by the 1960s in an academic life "largely freed from religious perspectives," Marsden's analysis raised awareness of the intellectual and sociological force of secularization, inspiring a host of other studies that explored the intersections between faith and learning.[5]

A quick overview of secularization theory highlights the various ways in which Christianity has lost its unifying power within the halls of academe. Reflecting on events in the nineteenth century, Nicholas Wolterstorff, for instance, points to "two mighty hammer blows that caused the reassuring edifice [of faith and scholarship] to totter and sway": Darwin's theory of evolution and German higher criticism. As a result of these events, continues Wolterstorff, evangelical colleges went "underground," emphasizing "personal piety" and evangelism.[6] Jon H. Roberts and James Turner describe how, after about 1830, science became invested with increased explanatory power, thereby marginalizing supernatural accounts of phenomena through the establishment of methodological naturalism.[7] Roberts and Turner also connect the rise of academic specialization to secularization. Specialization created the compartmentalization of knowledge, with religion beating a "retreat to ceremonial occasions and the extra-curriculum": "Hence the new specialization worked, along with other forces, to exclude religious belief as an *intellectual* tool within the university."[8] Finally, Robert Benne offers a succinct theory

---

5   George M. Marsden, *The Soul of the American University: From Protestant Establishment to Established Nonbelief* (Oxford: Oxford University Press, 1994), 430.

6   Nicholas Wolterstorff, "The Mission of the Christian College at the End of the Twentieth Century," in *Educating for Shalom: Essays on Christian Higher Education*, eds. Clarence W. Joldersma and Gloria Goris Stronks (Grand Rapids, Mich.: Eerdmans, 2004), 27-28.

7   Jon H. Roberts and James Turner. *The Sacred and the Secular University* (Princeton: Princeton University Press, 2000), 53.

8   Ibid., 88.

of secularization: "Why did the bulk of church-related colleges and universities finally disengage from their sponsoring traditions? Fundamentally, it seems to me, that disengagement took place because both parties, the school and the church, lost confidence in the Christian account of reality. At bottom this matter was a crisis of faith, or at least in faith's confidence in its own intellectual and moral potency."[9]

What safeguards are in place to ensure that institutions belonging to the CCCU do not fall victim to the protean forms of secularization sketched above? To respond, we appeal to the words of Robert B. Sloan, Jr.: "If I were to offer only one (there are many) proposition for how to preserve distinctively Christian higher education, or how to preserve the character of a distinctively Christian institution, I would maintain that it is through the faculty of that institution. The faculty members," continues Sloan, "carry the intellectual freight . . . . Thus to preserve distinctively Christian higher education, there must be at any Christian institution a critical mass of faculty members who are committed to the proposition of Christian higher education."[10]

Our analysis has as its context the historical awareness (and reality) of secularization, raised by such books as Marsden's as well as those that follow in its wake, and the proposition that faculty constitute an integral component in the preservation of any educational institution's Christian identity. In an article in *Christian Scholar's Review*, Larry Lyon and Michael Beaty brought a similar context to bear on their empirical analysis of secularization at Baylor University, the University of Notre Dame, and Georgetown College. Employing a faculty survey (as well as a regent and student survey), Lyon and Beaty conclude "that as religious universities and colleges become stronger academically, they become weaker religiously."[11] Their data corroborate the secularization model.

Lyon and Beaty also claim that their "findings are relevant to virtually all institutions of higher education in the United States who attempt to take their religious identity seriously. This is so because many of the intellectual and social forces that affect Baylor are not unique to Texas and to Baptists."[12] While the constituencies of the CCCU are well-advised to study carefully the findings of Lyon and Beaty's analysis and consider the implications those findings bear on CCCU institutions, we find the claim concerning relevance to be tenuous with respect to secularization. Unlike Baylor, member institutions of the CCCU must meet two criteria, among others: a Christ-centered mission, evident in the institution's purpose statement, and an employment policy in which only those who profess faith in Jesus Christ can be hired.[13] Though Lyon and Beaty's analysis has *some* application to CCCU institutions, that application is limited. Our empirical analysis

---

9   Robert Benne, *Quality with Soul: How Six Premier Colleges and Universities Keep Faith with Their Religious Traditions* (Grand Rapids, Mich.: Eerdmans, 2001), 47.

10   Robert B. Sloan, "Preserving Distinctively Christian Higher Education," in *The Future of Christian Higher Education*, eds. David S. Dockery and David P. Gushee (Nashville: Broadman & Holman, 1999), 33.

11   Larry Lyon and Michael Beaty, "Integration, Secularization, and the Two-Spheres View at Religious Colleges: Comparing Baylor University with the University of Notre Dame and Georgetown College," *Christian Scholar's Review* 29:1 (1999): 99.

12   Ibid., 76.

13   See the CCCU website: http://www.cccu.org/about.

will explore how the secularization model specifically influences the unique character and identity that make up the 110 institutions in the CCCU.

Assessing the CCCU on the Slippery Slope

Data from the Joeckel/Chesnes survey suggest that faculty at CCCU institutions are firmly committed to Christian higher education. Ninety-eight percent of survey partici-pants either strongly or somewhat agreed that their college/university should maintain its Christian identity (FSQ 25). In addition, 94 percent of participants either strongly or somewhat agreed that they have a good idea of what is meant by the phrase "the inte-gration of faith and learning" (FSQ 18). More, 84 percent either strongly or somewhat agreed that it is not difficult for them to integrate faith and learning in their discipline (FSQ 19). According to these data, member institutions of the CCCU are places that succeed in cultivating faith and integrating that faith with learning. Our research cor-roborates James Patterson in his 2001 history of the CCCU when he writes, "Indeed, the twenty-five-year history of the CCCU reveals that its membership has consistently carried the torch for Christ-centered higher education."[14] Forty-five percent of our survey respondents said they took a job at a Christian college/university because of their com-mitment to Christian higher education; 29 percent did so because of the opportunity to integrate faith and learning (FSQ 21).

The data also suggest that CCCU institutions are places where faith is nurtured and strengthened. Seventy-nine percent of respondents stated that, as a result of the time spent at their college/university, their faith has either become much or somewhat stronger (FSQ 17). We find it significant that of three possible sources of faith growth—chapel, classes taught, and other faculty—classes taught and other faculty wield the greatest influence in fostering spiritual development (FSQs 14-16)). Like the data on faith/learning integration, this finding indicates that faith growth occurs at the very heart of CCCU institutions: in the classrooms and among faculty. An authentic faith commitment thus seems to operate organically within the basic and fundamental opera-tions of CCCU institutions.

Nevertheless, the survey also showed that, though the majority of respondents either somewhat or strongly disagreed that their college/university has been negatively influenced by secularism, 28 percent felt the opposite. More than one in four either strongly or somewhat agreed that their institution *has* been negatively influenced by secularism (FSQ 20). These numbers indicate that secularism perhaps exerts some pres-sure on the faith identity of CCCU institutions, thus the need to maintain some degree of vigilance against such pressure. To delve more deeply into this statistic, we isolated for purposes of analysis all of those who either strongly or somewhat agreed that their college/university has been negatively influenced by secularism. Who are these faculty

---

14 James Patterson, *Shining Lights: A History of the Council for Christian Colleges & Universities* (Grand Rapids, Mich.: Baker Academic, 2001), 11.

and, based upon their survey profile, what conclusions can we draw about perceptions of secularization?

Perceptions of Secularization

We discovered three different sets of characteristics among those who either strongly or somewhat agreed that their college/university has been negatively influenced by secularism. We found these respondents to be more theologically conservative, more politically conservative, and more epistemologically conservative (a phrase that will become clear below).

These respondents were more likely to self-identify as theologically conservative than all survey participants as a whole. These respondents were more likely to agree that the Bible is the only authoritative source of information about God. They were significantly more likely to believe in biblical inerrancy. They were less likely to agree that practicing homosexuals should be allowed membership in a Christian church. Finally, these respondents were less likely to wish that their college's/university's statement of faith were more generic and more broadly defined Christianity (Table 1).

Politically, survey participants who felt their institutions were negatively influenced by secularism were more conservative as well. They were more likely to self-identify as Republican and less likely to self-identify as Democrat than all other respondents. They were less likely to agree that the evidence for human-induced climate change is convincing. They were more likely to express moral opposition to embryonic stem-cell research. They were more likely to favor the criminalization of abortion. They were more likely to support the military campaign in Iraq. And they were more likely to support abstinence-only sex education (Table 2).

Those who found evidence of secularism in their institutions also registered responses that suggest a more conservative epistemological stance. These respondents were more likely to agree that answers to moral questions are primarily black and white, not shades of gray. They were more likely to agree that truth is absolute. And they were less likely to agree that postmodernism can be compatible with Christianity (Table 3).

Those who believe their college/university has been negatively influenced by secularism are thus more likely to share certain characteristics. Their conservatism—theological, political, and epistemological—shapes their heightened wariness of secularization.

The Dangers of Vigilance Against Secularization

Based upon the data concerning those who believe their college/university has been negatively shaped by secularism, we argue in this section that vigilance against secularization, fueled solely by the conservative orientation discussed above, leads to an ideological overcorrection, a defensive mentality standing guard against the promulgation of ideas that do not toe the conservative party line. The result is a loss of scholarly rigor. Years ago Arthur Holmes warned against the danger of a defensive mentality, explaining that "many suppose that the Christian college exists to protect young people against sin and heresy in other institutions. The idea there is not so much to educate as to indoctrinate, to provide a safe environment plus all the answers to all the problems posed by all critics of orthodoxy and virtue."[15] As we shall see, the "safe environment" Holmes describes might lead to a well-armored albeit shallow faith, but it also commits academic fraud.

For now, we emphasize that our argument in this section should not be taken as an indictment of conservatism, theological, political, epistemological, or otherwise. Instead, our argument should be read as an admonition against the creation of a homogenous academic culture that intimidates into silence those who disagree. When such a culture mobilizes the vigilance against secularization, intimidation and silence become more likely, threatening to stifle a thriving academic environment founded on open and honest conversation.[16]

This argument, of course, is not original. Anthony Campolo observes that one reason for the growth of what he calls "sectarian schools" is the "homogenous nature of their constituencies." He continues: "Their students are all of the same socioeconomic and cultural background. They hold similar beliefs in politics and theology. Their concepts of personal morality are strikingly uniform. Indeed, sociological research shows that institutions with homogenous traits grow fastest. They project no ambiguities and relate well to specific constituencies."[17] Paul R. Spickard, a former professor of history and Asian-American studies at Bethel College and now at the University of California Santa Barbara, states the following about Christian institutions: "It's a very closed intellectual and social environment where there's not much room for variety of experience or expression or gentle exploration around the edges. Anyone who didn't fit the mold ended up leaving sooner or later."[18] Leo Reisberg strikes a similar chord: "To be sure, Christian colleges will always appeal to a relatively narrow segment of the population. Students and faculty members at most of the colleges are more homogenous than they are throughout the rest of higher education."[19] Noll offers a reading of Christian schools that helps us better understand this homogeneity as well as the dangers of overzealous vigilance against secularization—a reading that harmonizes with our thesis:

> A sectarian strategy for those who . . . read the past as a relatively simple set of
> overwhelming secular forces and who wish to retain or restore meaningful reli-
> gious convictions at a college or university would seem to be straightforward:

---

15   Arthur Holmes, *The Idea of a Christian College* (Grand Rapids, Mich.: Eerdmans, 1975), 4.

16   Secular colleges and universities face a similar, though inverted threat. Rothman, Lichter, and Nevitte (2005) observe that, "over the course of 15 years, self-described liberals grew from a slight plurality to a 5 to 1 majority on [public] college faculties" ("Politics and Professional Advancement Among College Faculty," *The Forum* 3.1: 4). Secular institutions simply struggle with a different sort of homogeneity that threatens by intimidation.

17   Anthony Campolo, "The Challenge of Radical Christianity for the Christian College," in *Faithful Learning and the Christian Scholarly Vocation*, eds. Douglas V. Henry and Bob R. Agee (Grand Rapids, Mich.: Eerdmans, 2003), 144. Campolo claims that sectarian schools are recognizable by certain key characteristics: a "doctrinal statement in which they clearly delineate a strong commitment to the authority of Scripture, to the belief in miracles, to the virgin birth, and to the visible second coming of Christ. These schools also put a strong emphasis on the integration of faith and knowledge" (141).

18   Quoted in Beth McMurtrie, "Do Professors Lose Academic Freedom by Signing Statements of Faith?" *Academe*, May 24, 2002, A12.

19   Leo Reisberg, "Enrollments Surge at Christian Colleges," *Chronicle of Higher Education*, March 5, 1999, A44.

Hire only faculty who do not question any significant aspect of the community's system of values. Raise as much money as possible from private sources in order to avoid government funds and government interference. Above all, present your college or university to prospective students and their parents as a safe place, where body, soul, and spirit can be protected through the dangerous years of adulthood.[20]

Noll acknowledges that "such a strategy is not without merit, but it also has its limits, especially where it is most successful." He explains,

Bob Jones University possesses a wonderful art gallery, but no one outside of the immediate Bob Jones constituency attends the university or looks to Bob Jones faculty for learned guidance in art history or theories of representation. Regent University enjoys state-of-the-art media facilities, but almost no one outside of Pat Robertson's circle of influence attends Regent or looks to Regent faculty for learned guidance in communication theory or the cultural meaning of television.[21]

As Noll and these other scholars observe, institutional homogeneity compromises diversity of thought, free exchange of ideas, scholarly rigor, and thus academic credibility. We restate our claim: when calls for vigilance against secularization arise within such a homogenous culture, the compromises can easily snowball.

Consider now some other findings from the survey, first those concerning the issue of free exchange of ideas. Though the majority of our survey respondents (54 percent) agreed that professors at Christian institutions have more freedom to discuss issues and ask questions than do professors at secular institutions, 27 percent somewhat or strongly disagreed. Twenty-four percent strongly or somewhat agreed that they were hesitant to address certain important issues in class because they teach at a Christian college/university. These two survey questions provided us with a window into the issue of intellectual rigor. We isolated for the purpose of analysis the 30 percent of survey respondents who either disagreed or were neutral toward the idea that their college/university is a place of rigorous intellectual activity. We discovered that 39 percent of these respondents disagreed that professors at Christian institutions have more freedom to discuss issues and ask questions than do professors at secular institutions (compared with 27 percent of all respondents). We also found that 36 percent of these respondents also agreed that they were hesitant to address certain important issues in class because they teach at a Christian college/university (compared with 24 percent of all respondents; Table 4). These data suggest that one cause for perceived substandard intellectual rigor is the inability to speak freely in the classroom on important issues.

Consider now some of our qualitative data. One question of the survey asked, "What is the most difficult part about being a professor at a Christian university?" When

---

20   Mark Noll, "The Future of the Religious College," 89.
21   Ibid., 90.

collecting these data, we organized responses into categories. The largest category was 'heavy workload,' a category that totaled 344. A category we labeled 'compromised intellectual rigor' numbered 128. Here are some samplings from this category: "I think that at a Christian University students can be less open to new ideas, especially when it challenges their belief system." "It can be a challenge to escape the spiritual smugness that sometimes arises in the classroom or campus atmosphere: a spirit of 'we have it all figured out and don't need anything more.'" "The homogeneity of the students and their life experiences which brings a great deal of confidence in the 'rightness' of their own lives and actions and an unwillingness to question, think deeper, or try to imagine the goals and values and meanings of the lives of others." "Enabling students, many of whom are from socially and religiously conservative backgrounds, to expand their horizons in such a way as to make informed and honest evaluations of the alternatives (and their likely consequences) from the perspective of a well-considered values orientation." "Opening closed minds and filling them with a love of learning—be it from a bad conservative background that discourages free inquiry or from the lack of curiosity and the utterly pragmatic bent bred into today's coddled youth." "Sometimes there is a feeling that everything needs to be taught in line with a specific, possibly narrow-minded, interpretation of what Christianity is and is not." "The parochialism, close-mindedness, and lack of curiosity displayed by many students. Their unwillingness to engage the difficult questions, either out of laziness or out of fear that their faith will be weakened." "Making sure that honest inquiry or disagreement does not get covered up by Christian superficiality." "Some ideas, concepts, events are 'outside' the religious box and don't nicely fit into any kind of integration attempt. There is an expectation of some faculty and students that everything should have a verse to support it or it's bad, or secular, which means it is not to be discussed. The environment here can be too sheltered from the real world to the detriment of the student's education." "While I am free to discuss anything in the classroom I am not free to take a strong position on several politically related issues. We have freedom to discuss, but not freedom to voice dissenting opinion."

This response registers a fear for job security, a fear mentioned by a number of respondents as well. For example: "The most difficult part about being a professor at a Christian University is always having to hide any beliefs that are a little more liberal than is official policy at the institution, for example re: abortion, homosexuality, dancing." "Being afraid that at some point, the denominational convention and our convention-appointed trustees will decide some of us are not Christian enough for them, and will try to shove us out." "The feeling that I cannot address some very 'real' world problems, topics in the classroom for fear of losing my job." "Inability to freely express my liberal (and vital) faith to students and colleagues without fear of harsh scrutiny and dire consequences." And finally, this response: "The narrow and rigid ideological framework—suspicious of the world and even ideas themselves—that most students bring to their university education makes the difficult task of teaching them even more difficult. It becomes a delicate and high-stakes balance of helping them maintain/preserve their faith while simultaneously helping them open their worldview up to new ideas and ways of thinking as educated persons."

Conclusion

Based upon these data, we conclude that the dangers of secularization, insofar as they apply to the CCCU, have been overstated. Survey participants overwhelmingly endorse the Christian identity of their institutions; participants also understand and practice the integration of faith and learning. In short, survey respondents are committed to Christian higher education in both theory and practice, even experiencing faith growth as a result of their work. We therefore resonate with the words of Rodney J. Sawatsky, who, in the prologue to the 2004 edited volume entitled, *Scholarship and Christian Faith: Enlarging the Conversation*, contends that "this myth of declension has cramped our thinking and narrowed our reflection on the nature and character of Christian scholarship."[22] As the data suggest, the nature and character of Christian scholarship—and here we use the term "scholarship" in an expansive sense, including both research and teaching—are often too narrowly defined, resulting in an academic environment that can compromise intellectual inquiry and frustrate Christian scholars. When calls for vigilance against secularization originate from such an environment, fostered by a homogenous culture, those outside the culture—though equally committed to Christian higher education— can too easily be marginalized.

Calls for vigilance against secularization should therefore be tempered by an awareness of its often exaggerated imminence and danger. More, when the calls are issued, they should rise from a plurality of diverse voices: diversity with respect to theology, politics, and epistemology. Of course, such diversity must respect the faith and mission statements of individual institutions, though we believe these statements should be open to revision. Nevertheless, most faith and mission statements have some degree of flexibility built into them, enabling relatively diverse theological orientations and even more diverse political and epistemological positions. According to its website, the CCCU has

---

22 Rodney J. Sawatsky, "Prologue: The Virtue of Scholarly Hope," in *Scholarship and Christian Faith: Enlarging the Conversation*, eds. Douglas Jacobsen and Rhonda Hustedt Jacobsen (Oxford: Oxford University Press, 2004), 13. There exist other reasons to believe that the secularization thesis has been overstated. For instance, the conditions that enabled the secularization of Christian institutions in the last century—a narrative richly told in tomes by Marsden, James Burtchaell, and others—no longer obtain. Obviously we must simplify those narratives here, but in the early twentieth century, many colleges with Christian identities hitched a ride on intellectual juggernauts known as logical positivism and scientific progressivism. As we now know, the hubristic confidence in these intellectual movements was ill-placed. But for those Christians who followed their path, these movements rendered their faith untenable. However, as Marsden explains, the nails have been firmly driven into the coffins of these intellectual movements: "Perhaps it is true that traditionally religious schools will lose their distinctive identities. We should not underestimate the forces that push for a more standardized and secularized culture . . . . Much the same thing could happen, of course, but there is one very large difference that might make us hope otherwise. We now live in the aftermath of an era that began with the Enlightenment of the eighteenth century and ended with the decline of progressive scientific humanism in the last third of the twentieth century. For the first time in three centuries, the ideal that human progress will be achieved by ever-wider applications of scientific models to almost all of life seems passé" ("Beyond Progressive Scientific Humanism," in *The Future of Religious Colleges: The Proceedings of the Harvard Conference on the Future of Religious Colleges*, ed. Paul J. Dovre, 37-38.)
Additionally, over the last twenty years or so, Christian scholarship has blossomed into increasing sophistication and academic legitimacy. In short, Christian scholars possess a much larger understanding of the intersections of faith and reason, an understanding that would, at the least, make difficult the widespread fall into the "pits of apostasy" witnessed in the twentieth century.

as its mission statement the following: "To advance the cause of Christ-centered higher education and to help our institutions transform lives by faithfully relating scholarship and service to biblical truth."[23] Those on both sides of the theological, political, and epistemological spectrum can unite in supporting this mission, realizing that the ways of wedding scholarship and service to biblical truth are multifarious.

United behind a commitment to Christian higher education, CCCU institutions as well as professors with diverse views will undoubtedly disagree. But as Harold Heie explains, "The tragedy is not that Christians disagree with each other on some critical issues. In fact, such disagreement can be the bedrock of good education. The tragedy is that we find it increasingly difficult to talk to each other about our disagreements, so that we can learn from each other."[24] The contours of the academic community that our data sketch can too easily lead to the tragedy that Heie describes; we miss too many learning opportunities through the preemptive silencing of disagreements often due to the fear of recrimination. In addition, the cultivation of an academic community in which professors with diverse views can freely exchange ideas might also lead not only to disagreements but also to few instances of consensus. Theological, political, and epistemological diversity, along with the disagreements that it creates, fosters an academic environment in which truth is not so easily perceived, testifying to its complexity—in contrast to a community in which disagreements are risky, in which agreements are therefore encouraged or coerced, and subsequently a community in which facile, yet intellectually dishonest, justifications of truth claims are almost algorithmic. In the former community, intellectual inquiry proceeds with humility and provisionality; the endpoint of the inquiry is not always clear. Such an inquiry stands in stark contrast to what Parker Palmer identifies as the detrimental effects of a "spirituality of ends":

> A spirituality of ends wants to dictate the desirable outcomes of education in the life of the student. It uses the spiritual tradition as a template against which the ideas, beliefs, and behaviors of the student are to be measured. The goal is to shape the student to the template by the time that his or her formal education concludes. But that sort of education never gets started; it is no education at all. Authentic spirituality wants to open us to truth—whatever truth may be, wherever truth may take us. Such a spirituality does not dictate where we must go, but trusts that any path walked with integrity will take us to a place of knowledge. Such a spirituality encourages us to welcome diversity and conflict, to tolerate ambiguity, and to embrace paradox.[25]

---

23 See http://www.cccu.org/about.

24 Harold Heie, "Integration and Conversation," in *The University Through the Eyes of Faith*, ed. Steve Moore (Indianapolis, Ind.: Light and Life Communications, 1998), 69.

25 Parker J. Palmer, *To Know as We Are Known: Education as Spiritual Journey* (San Francisco, Ca.: Harper San Francisco, 1993), xi.

To state the matter more succinctly in the words of Arthur Holmes, the Christian world-view is an "open-ended exploration."[26] Holmes adds that Christianity is "not a closed system, worked out once and for all but an endless undertaking that is still but the vision of a possibility."[27] Christian higher education conceived as "authentic spirituality" or an "open-ended exploration" can be risky, but do we not admit that the risk is worthwhile? Providing what we consider to be a good model for Christian scholarship, Nicholas Wolterstorff explains how faith serves as the control beliefs that shape our theorizing. But Wolterstorff is also bold enough to admit that our theories might influence our beliefs. He writes, "The scholar never fully knows in advance where his line of thought will lead him. For the Christian to undertake scholarship is to undertake a course of action that may lead him into the painful process of revising his actual Christian commitment, sorting through his beliefs, and discarding some from a position where they can no longer function as control. It may, indeed, even lead him to a point where his authentic commitment has undergone change. We are all profoundly *historical* creatures."[28]

The open-ended inquiries to which these scholars allude are not possible when the outcomes of those inquiries are foregone conclusions. Consequently, though the stentorian exhortations against slipping down the slope to secularism have long echoed across CCCU campuses, perhaps it is time to sound warnings against a different, inverse danger: the formation of a university so vigilant against secularization that it stifles the spirit of open inquiry and underestimates the value of diversity of thought. If exhortations against secularization persist, the Christian institution of higher learning will have avoided what our research suggests is a minor threat, though at a major cost.

---

26 Holmes, *The Idea of a Christian College*, 4.

27 Ibid., 58.

28 Wolterstorff, *Reason within the Bounds of Religion* (Grand Rapids, Mich.: Eerdmans, 1984), 97.

Table 1: Responses in percent to questions regarding theological issues.
The NEGSEC group are those who believe their institution has been negatively influenced by secularism.

Would you consider yourself to be theologically conservative or liberal? (+/- 2.2 percent)		
	NEGSEC (528)	ALL (1907)
Strongly conservative	35	22.4
Somewhat conservative	48.7	46.5
Neutral	8.3	10.8
Somewhat liberal	7.8	17.1
Strongly liberal	0.8	3.7
The Bible is the only authoritative source of information about God. (+/- 2.3 percent)		
	NEGSEC (523)	ALL (1833)
Strongly agree	48.2	38
Somewhat agree	18.5	18.2
Neutral	2.9	5.2
Somewhat disagree	19.3	21.8
Strongly disagree	11.1	16.7
I believe in biblical inerrancy (+/- 2.3 percent)		
	NEGSEC (522)	ALL (1825)
Strongly agree	51.3	39.5
Somewhat agree	19.2	18.6
Neutral	11.9	13.6
Somewhat disagree	9	12.6
Strongly disagree	8.6	15.7
Practicing homosexuals should be allowed membership in a Christian church. (+/- 2.3 percent)		
	NEGSEC (509)	ALL (1755)
Strongly agree	9	19.4
Somewhat agree	11	14.9
Neutral	9.2	10.5
Somewhat disagree	16.9	16.6
Strongly disagree	53.8	38.6
I wish my college's/university's faith statement were more generic and more broadly defined Christianity (+/- 2.2 percent)		
	NEGSEC (509)	ALL (1854)
Strongly agree	4.6	8
Somewhat agree	12.1	16.2
Neutral	14.8	18.9
Somewhat disagree	27.3	23.9
Strongly disagree	41.2	33

Table 2: Responses in percent to questions regarding political issues.

The NEGSEC group are those who believe their institution has been negatively influenced by secularism.

What is your political affiliation? (+/- 2.2 percent)		
	NEGSEC (528)	ALL (1907)
Democrat	11.6	21.6
Republican	56.8	46.1
Independent	24.4	24.8
Other	7.2	7.7
The evidence for human-induced climate change is convincing (+/- 2.3 percent)		
	NEGSEC (514)	ALL (1795)
Strongly agree	24.9	36.2
Somewhat agree	28.6	28.5
Neutral	14.4	14
Somewhat disagree	18.1	12.5
Strongly disagree	14	8.8
I am morally opposed to embryonic stem cell research. (+/- 2.3 percent)		
	NEGSEC (512)	ALL (1783)
Strongly agree	49.4	32.5
Somewhat agree	15.2	13.9
Neutral	10.4	17
Somewhat disagree	18	19.4
Strongly disagree	7	17.2
Abortion should be made illegal in the United States (+/- 2.3 percent)		
	NEGSEC (509)	ALL (1760)
Strongly agree	47.7	35.1
Somewhat agree	24.6	22.3
Neutral	8.3	9.8
Somewhat disagree	10.2	15.5
Strongly disagree	9.2	17.4
I support the military campaign in Iraq (+/- 2.3 percent)		
	NEGSEC (509)	ALL (1757)
Strongly agree	24	15.8
Somewhat agree	28.5	24.2
Neutral	10	11.1
Somewhat disagree	12.6	13.9
Strongly disagree	25	35.1

I support abstinence-only sex education. (+/- 2.3 percent)		
	NEGSEC (508)	ALL (1755)
Strongly agree	47.4	33.4
Somewhat agree	26.6	23.5
Neutral	5.9	9.1
Somewhat disagree	13.4	16.8
Strongly disagree	6.7	17.2

Table 3: Responses in percent to questions regarding epistemological issues.

The NEGSEC group are those who believe their institution has been negatively influenced by secularism.

Answers to moral questions are primarily black and white, not shades of gray. (+/- 2.3 percent)		
	NEGSEC (518)	ALL (1816)
Strongly agree	12.4	7.6
Somewhat agree	31.9	22.5
Neutral	6.6	5.9
Somewhat disagree	30.9	34.1
Strongly disagree	18.3	29.8
Truth is absolute, not relative. (+/- 2.3 percent)		
	NEGSEC (519)	ALL (1813)
Strongly agree	59.2	45.4
Somewhat agree	23.9	24.3
Neutral	4.4	8.4
Somewhat disagree	9.4	14.1
Strongly disagree	3.1	7.7
Postmodernism can be compatible with Christianity. (+/- 2.3 percent)		
	NEGSEC (520)	ALL (1808)
Strongly agree	7.1	13.2
Somewhat agree	28.1	29.3
Neutral	13.8	17
Somewhat disagree	22.9	18.8
Strongly disagree	23.1	15.4
Don't know what postmodernism is	5	6.2

Table 4: Responses in percent to questions regarding academic rigor and freedom.

The NoRIGOR group are those who either disagreed or were neutral toward the idea that their college/university is a place of rigorous intellectual activity.

My college/university is a place of rigorous intellectual activity. (+/- 2.3)		
	ALL (1736)	
Strongly agree	19.1	
Somewhat agree	50.7	
Neutral	10.7	
Somewhat disagree	14.9	
Strongly disagree	4.6	
Professors at Christian institutions have more freedom to discuss issues and ask questions than do professors at secular institutions. (+/- 2.3)		
	ALL (1737)	NoRIGOR (487)
Strongly agree	24.1	13.3
Somewhat agree	29.7	28.3
Neutral	19.1	20.1
Somewhat disagree	18.9	20.7
Strongly disagree	8.2	17.5
I am hesitant to address certain important issues in class because I teach at a Christian college/university. (+/- 2.3)		
	ALL (1737)	NoRIGOR (485)
Strongly agree	5.6	13
Somewhat agree	18.7	23.1
Neutral	7.3	7.4
Somewhat disagree	28.1	28.7
Strongly disagree	40.4	27.8

CHAPTER 2

CHRISTIAN SCHOLARSHIP

Opportunities, Realities, and Challenges

SUSAN VAN ZANTEN

The practice of Christian scholarship has been a topic of much discussion during the past three decades, with altar-calls to Christians for a heightened commitment to scholarship and persuasive arguments to the academy that such work should be welcomed. In his landmark *The Scandal of the Evangelical Mind* (1994), Mark Noll lamented that the evangelical community had neglected its responsibility to practice Christian thinking; this "scandal" was followed by George Marsden's promotion of *The Outrageous Idea of Christian Scholarship* (1996), directed toward both a Christian scholarly audience and the broader academy. During this transformative period, much debate has focused on how to define Christian scholarship and the forms such scholarship might take. While some believe that Christian scholarship must be overt, distinctive, and oppositional, Marsden points to a variety of ways in which faith can inform scholarship: as a motivating factor, as an influence on determining applications for the scholarship, as a force in shaping a sub-field or research question, and as a guiding worldview that informs how the scholar sees the field fit into a larger frame of meaning.[1] C. Stephen Evans writes, "Christian scholarship is scholarship that is done to further the kingdom of God. It is scholarship carried out as part of a *calling* by citizens of that kingdom whose character, attitudes, emotions, and convictions reflect their citizenship, and whose work as scholars is shaped by their Christian convictions, emotions, and character."[2] Both Marsden and Evans argue that Christian scholarship can be either implicit or explicit, and that it does not have to be unique or distinctly Christian. Michael Hamilton contends that more Christians should pursue the scholarship of discovery, while Rhonda and Douglas

---

1 George M. Marsden, *The Outrageous Idea of Christian Scholarship* (New York: Oxford University Press, 1994), 64.

2 C. Stephen Evans, "The Calling of the Christian Scholar-Teacher," in *Faithful Learning and the Christian Scholarly Vocation*, ed. Douglas V. Henry and Bob R. Agee (Grand Rapids, Mich.: Eerdmans, 2003), 34.

Jacobson see Christian scholarship as involving "living the questions" as well as searching for answers.[3]

As Christian individuals and institutions began promoting research, scholarship,
and intellectual rigor more deliberately, the declension thesis silently shadowed such
efforts. Growth in academic strength, history shows, has often been accompanied by
a reduction in religious commitment although, as every social scientist knows, correla-
tion does not establish causation. However, as the previous essay demonstrates, CCCU
institutions have resisted secularization, and their faculty continue to articulate a deep
dedication to both the Christian character of their institutions and the vital relationship
of faith and learning. In so doing, they have also pursued a scholarly task. This essay
examines the extent of scholarly activity of Christian college faculty, as well as considers
some of the conditions that inform the production and dissemination of such scholarship. Drawing on the data from the Joeckel/Chesnes survey and other sources, it provides
a brief snapshot of the current CCCU scholarly landscape rather than a widescreen movie
with before-and-after views. That snapshot suggests that scholarship at Christian colleges
needs more affirmation, effort, and support.

The Renaissance of Christian Scholarship

Most observers agree that self-consciously Christian scholarship has undergone a renaissance since the 1980s, with the founding of numerous "faith and learning" professional
societies, a growing number of prominent Christian scholars in the academy, a new willingness across many disciplines to study the impact of religious commitment, and a significant increase in scholarly activity among evangelical Christians. In October 2000, the
cover story of the *Atlantic Monthly* heralded "The Opening of the Evangelical Mind," with
sociologist Alan Wolfe noting "a determined effort by evangelical-Christian institutions
to create a life of the mind . . . . evangelical scholars are writing the books, publishing
the journals, teaching the students, and sustaining the networks necessary to establish a
presence in American academic life."[4] Positively assessing the state of Christian scholarly
activity in 2001, Richard J. Mouw, president of Fuller Seminary, commented that the
evangelical community had moved away from its earlier anti-intellectualism, isolation,
and intra-Christian arguments to engage in ecumenical and academic conversations:
"We have decided to make our Christian voice known, not by way of a critique that is
directed toward the mainstream academy from the intellectual margins, but by forming
coalitions and networks within that mainstream academy."[5]

Similarly, in his 2006 history of CCCU institutions, William C. Ringenberg claims
that "the state of Christian scholarship appears much better than it did in the 1980s
because (1) the Christian academicians are producing more significant works of

---

3   Michael S. Hamilton, "The Elusive Idea of Christian Scholarship," *Christian Scholars Review* 31 (2001): 21;
Douglas and Rhonda Hustedt Jacobsen, *Scholarship and Christian Faith: Enlarging the Conversation* (New York: Oxford
University Press, 2004), 45-48.

4   Alan Wolfe, "The Opening of the Evangelical Mind," *The Atlantic Monthly*, October 2000, 58.

5   Richard J. Mouw, "Assessing Christian Scholarship: Where We've Been and Where We're Going," *Christian
Scholarship . . . for What?* Ed. Susan Felch (Grand Rapids, Mich.: Calvin College, 2003), 58.

scholarship; (2) the Christian academic communities are less isolated, more readily identifying with the contributions of one another . . . and (3) there is a broadening definition
of scholarship that allows the Christian colleges to better realize how well they had been
doing all along in certain aspects of spiritually informed intellectual activity, namely
collegiality and caring, incarnational teaching."[6] In a study of the mounting influence
of evangelicals in various sectors of American society, sociologist D. Michael Lindsay
claims, "As more evangelical scholars have gained a reputation for excellence in fields
such as literary scholarship, psychology, and history, a visible evangelical presence has
emerged in the academy."[7]

The growth in scholarship among evangelical Protestants was fueled, in part, by
new funding opportunities, beginning in the 1990s with a massive program sponsored
by the Pew Charitable Trust. Lindsey comments, "Pew's philanthropy secured academic
responsibility for evangelicals and produced a revolution in evangelical scholarship."[8]
Additional support for Christian scholarship came from the Lilly Endowment Inc., the
Templeton Foundation, the Murdock Foundation, and—on a much smaller scale—the
CCCU Program of Networking Grants for Christian Scholars. Such programs have facilitated networking among Christian scholars both within evangelical circles and across
ecumenical lines, as well as supported scholars forming coalitions within the wider academy and entering the public halls of learning as faithful Christian scholars—publishing
with major university presses and in disciplinary journals; attending, participating, and
taking leadership in professional associations; serving as peer reviewers and academic
accreditation evaluators.

The increase in Christian scholarship has taken place within the broader context
of a significant shift in the American academy. Research, scholarship, and publication
were first adapted as fundamental activities of American higher education in the late
nineteenth century, with the waning of "the old time college"[9] and the foundation of
research universities modeled after the University of Berlin. In *The American Faculty: The
Restructuring of Academic Work and Careers*, Jack H. Schuster and Martin J. Finkelstein
state, "The acknowledgement of scholarship and publishing as centrally important academic values and the consequent reprioritizing of the academic-rewards system led to
the creation of a new academic order. One could plausibly maintain that this transformation in values had settled into place by the early twentieth century, giving rise to a
system of higher education that is still more or less intact a century later."[10] With these
new structures in place and a flood of students entering American higher education after
World War II, the role of a faculty member evolved to include research, scholarship, and

---

6   William C. Ringenberg, *The Christian College: A History of Protestant Higher Education in America*, 2nd ed.
(Grand Rapids, Mich.: Baker, 2006), 217.

7   D. Michael Lindsay, *Faith in the Halls of Power: How Evangelicals Joined the American Elite* (New York: Oxford
University Press, 2007), 101.

8   Ibid., 99.

9   Ringenberg, *The Christian College*, 57-84.

10   Jack H. Schuster, and Martin J. Finkelstein, *The American Faculty: The Restructuring of Academic Work and
Careers* (Baltimore: Johns Hopkins University Press, 2006), xvii.

creative activity. Between 1969 and 1998, faculty increasingly reported self-identifying as scholars as well as teachers, and a "modest increase" was seen in the allocation of time to research and scholarship (although time teaching did not decrease proportionately).[11] Scholarly activity and success, however, are defined differently by institutional type and academic discipline and do not necessarily include publication or even public dissemination. Some institutions define scholarly activity as staying current on recent developments in a field through reading or conference attendance; others require original research, peer-reviewed publications, and conference presentations. For those in the fine arts, scholarly productivity more often takes the form of a performance or production, rather than publication or presentation. But increases in self-identification as a scholar and use of time were accompanied by increased rates of publication, which provides one, albeit limited, measure of scholarly productivity. Schuster and Finkelstein explain,

> Three decades ago the American professoriate was not notably immersed in writing for publication . . . . In 1969 fully half of the faculty reported no publishing—either articles or books—during the previous two years. Since then, however, the act of publication has become much more the norm. Thus by 1998 the proportion of faculty who published had risen sharply from one-half to two in three. And the publication contagion was widespread, plainly affecting faculty at all types of institutions and in most fields of the arts and sciences. Of course, absolute levels of faculty members' publishing continue to be shaped heavily by their institutional environment and disciplinary affiliation: publication activity was highest naturally at research universities and, among fields, in the social and natural sciences.[12]

Scholarly Expectations at Christian Colleges

Within the particular environment of the CCCU, we have limited data about institutional expectations for faculty research and scholarship. In 2006, Harris and Lumsden's analysis found that 86 percent of tenure-granting CCCU schools value research and publishing as somewhat important or extremely important in comparison to 57 percent of non-tenure granting CCCU schools.[13] In making tenure decisions, 64 percent of respondents ranked the number of publications as somewhat important, and 2 percent indicated that it was extremely important. The academic reputation of the presses or journals was not weighed as heavily; only 32 percent found this factor important. Presenting papers was an important factor for granting tenure, according to 84 percent of the respondents, and the authors note that this may be a more typical scholarly activity at CCCU institutions.[14]

---

11   Schuster and Finkelstein, *The American Faculty*, 75-124.

12   Ibid., 99.

13   Scott Harris and D. Barry Lumsden, "Tenure Policies and Practices of American Evangelical Colleges and Universities. Part 2: Institutions Granting Tenure," *Christian Higher Education* 5 (2006): 348.

14   Ibid., 354.

At some Christian colleges, scholarly expectations have become more demanding. A three-year study of CCCU institutions published in 2004 claims, "The standards for research and scholarship are increasing, although teaching loads and committee and community expectations remain the same. For many faculty at these smaller institutions, the new expectations are creating anxiety and fear."[15] Several narrative responses in the Joeckel/Chesnes survey refer to increased expectations without accompanying support. In reply to the question, "What is the most difficult aspect of being a professor at a Christian institution?" one faculty member wrote, "They advocate research and scholarship, but they do not allow adequate time to pursue it." Another said, "Not having sufficient time for research and yet being expected to keep up scholarly pursuit," and a third explained, "I sense very little realistic understanding of what it takes in terms of time and intellectual energy to do rigorous, theologically informed scholarship. The rhetoric does not match what is actually happening in the trenches. We aspire to be taken seriously for our scholarship but are not willing to pay the price."

Although some survey respondents expressed concern about expanding but unsupported institutional expectations for scholarly activity, others spoke of a distinct lack of institutional expectations for or affirmation of research, scholarship, and creative activity. One respondent commented, "I am not encouraged to pursue scholarly activity beyond teaching, nor given time/resources to do so." Another highlighted "a sense of a lack of respect for good scholarship," and a third spoke of "the attitude on the part of some administration that our whole time should be given to school related activities and not allowing enough [time] for research." Similarly, one response stated, "There's no commitment on the part of the administration to make sure faculty have time to think and read and research." The problem is cogently summarized and aptly connected to the teaching mission of CCCU schools in one response: "The lingering heritage of anti-intellectualism combined with underfunding leave little time for scholarship, which undermines real excellence in teaching." The new respect for and renaissance in Christian scholarship has not spread uniformly throughout Christian higher education.

Scholarly Activity at CCCU Institutions

A comparison of data from the 2007-2008 Higher Education Research Institute (HERI) faculty survey with the Joeckel/Chesnes survey reveals that CCCU faculty are not producing as much research and scholarship as undergraduate faculty at other teaching institutions. The HERI data are based upon the responses of 22,562 full-time undergraduate faculty at 372 four-year colleges and universities, which are reported in eight categories—all institutions, public universities, private universities, public four-year colleges, and private four-year colleges (combined and broken down into three sub-groups:

---

15   Kina S. Mallard and Michele W. Atkins, "Changing Academic Cultures and Expanding Expectations: Motivational Factors Influencing Scholarship at Small Christian Colleges and Universities," *Christian Higher Education* 3 (2004): 374.

nonsectarian, Roman Catholic, and other religious).[16] For purposes of comparison, I will use the weighted national norms for four-year publics, all four-year privates, Catholic four-year privates, and other four-year religious privates.[17] Most CCCU institutions are included in the "other religious" category, and, in fact, the Joeckel/Chesnes data and HERI data in this category are fairly similar.

The Joeckel/Chesnes survey provides three lenses for measuring scholarly activity. For literary scholars, historians, and theologians, a book publication represents the academic Holy Grail, but this measure is not as pertinent in the arts or the social, natural, and biological sciences. Slightly over 24 percent of CCCU respondents had published a book during their academic career (FSQ 11). With no measure of the reputation of the press or distinction of university press publications from those issued by evangelical publishers or even vanity presses, this figure must be seen as conservative at best when it comes to measuring academic rigor, although 82 percent of those who had published a book also reported having published "an article in a refereed or peer-reviewed journal" (FSQ 12). In comparison, the HERI survey shows that 33 percent of faculty at four-year public institutions, 30 percent of faculty at all private four-year colleges, and 30 percent of faculty at Catholic colleges had published "a book, manual or monograph." Faculty from a wide range of CCCU institutions report book publications; this activity is not limited to a few colleges: 7 percent of the books reported published came from Calvin, 5 percent from George Fox, and 4.6 percent from Wheaton. Other institutions with over 2 percent of the books reported published include Abilene Christian, Azusa Pacific, Eastern, Palm Beach Atlantic, Seattle Pacific, and Vanguard. The disciplinary areas showing the highest level of book publications were Religion/Theology/BiblicalStudies/Ministry (57 percent), Humanities (36 percent), Communication (25 percent), and Business (21 percent) (Table 1).

A potentially more academically rigorous measure is whether one has written an article published in a refereed or peer-reviewed journal, the standard of excellence in most disciplines. At CCCU institutions, 61 percent of the respondents report having at least one refereed or peer-reviewed journal publication (FSQ 12); HERI data show 80 percent of faculty at four-year public institutions, 72 percent of faculty at all privates, 74 percent of Catholic faculty, and 68 percent of "other religious" faculty having published at least one article in "an academic or professional journal. " At CCCU schools, more faculty in the disciplinary areas of Natural Sciences (74 percent), Religion (72 percent), Humanities (67 percent) and Social Sciences (64 percent) report a peer-reviewed publication than in Communication (60 percent), Business (56 percent), Health Sciences (47 percent), Education (52 percent), and Fine Arts (49 percent).[18] While this result is not unexpected in the explicitly Christian area of Religion (which includes Theology,

16   Linda DeAngelo, et al., *The American College Teacher: National Norms for the 2007-2008 HERI Faculty Survey* (Los Angeles: HERI, 2009).

17   I will not use the university category, for obvious reasons, or the category of "nonsectarian privates," as these tend to be elite liberal-arts schools such as Carleton, Kenyon, and Swarthmore. A few CCCU schools, however, are in this category, such as Taylor and Westmont.

18   Other disciplinary fields had an *n* < 100, and so are not listed.

Biblical Studies, and Christian Ministries), the high percentage of those in the Natural Sciences reporting one peer-reviewed publication is somewhat more surprising (Table 1). The Joeckel/Chesnes survey does not ask about the total number of peer-reviewed articles that a faculty member has published, which means that some of those reporting one publication may not have continued their scholarship after publishing part of their dissertation work, and the HERI data show that "other religious" colleges lag behind in total number of peer-reviewed publications (Table 2). The third measure of scholarly activity in the Joeckel/Chesnes survey asks, "How many essays/papers have you presented at conferences over the past two years?" (FSQ 13). Forty percent of CCCU faculty reported that they had not presented at all; 36 percent had presented 1-2 times; 16 percent had presented 3-4 times; 4 percent had presented 5-6 times; and 5 percent had presented more than 6 times.[19] While there are some active scholars in terms of conference presentations, these figures seem low if we assume that conference presentation is a more likely expectation for CCCU faculty. Limited travel budgets may contribute to these low numbers.

Factors Affecting Scholarly Activity

Kina S. Mallard and Michele W. Atkins found five significant discouragers to producing research among CCCU faculty: 1) lack of time, 2) lack of institutional support, 3) an inability to say no and consequent work overload, 4) constant distractions, and 5) a preference to spend time teaching.[20] The first two factors are institutional; the last three are individual. While no respondents in the CCCU survey spoke of a preference for teaching informing their lack of scholarly and creative activity, the most common account of the challenge of being a Christian college professor speaks of the lack of time, heavy teaching loads combined with additional responsibilities, and difficulties in balancing a complex life.[21] "We wear too many hats," more than one respondent said. As one faculty member wrote, "It's just too much to ask for faculty to teach four classes, mentor, and do research/write (to get promoted)." Another spoke of the difficulties of "juggling the demands of teaching, scholarship, integrating faith and scholarship, serving the college, serving the constituency." Several spoke of the struggles of maintaining a healthy family and church life in the face of professional demands. Many felt that faculty expectations at a Christian teaching college were heavier than those at other teaching institutions, because of the emphasis on mentoring students, participating in chapel, doing community service and short-term mission work, and other co-curricular activities. As one tired but eloquent respondent wrote, "The heightened sense of mission increases obligations, not only institutionally, but in a self-imposed way. We want not only to be good teachers but to impact students spiritually; we want not only to be good researchers but to impact our disciplines in a faith-informed way; we want not only to be competent in

---

19 The HERI survey does not have a comparable category.

20 Mallard and Atkins, "Changing Academic Cultures and Expanding Expectations," 382-83.

21 Low pay was another other frequently mentioned difficulty.

our own discipline, but to gain theological and philosophical competencies necessary to integrate faith with learning in non-facile ways. At its best this project is exhilarating; at its worst it can induce guilt, overload, paralysis, and pretended competence where humility would be more in order."

Comparing teaching at a Christian college to working at a state school, several respondents argued that they faced a greater challenge: "The work load (teaching and service) is higher, so it's harder to maintain professional/personal balance and to make progress on research. Expectations of faculty to be as active professionally as colleagues at state schools combined with the heavier teaching and service emphasis [are unrealistic]. As a department chair, I have a reduced load, but still teach more than colleagues at other institutions. My faculty teach twelve hour loads. The research/service/teaching expectations are not reasonable, and faculty pay for it in damage to their families and their own spiritual lives." Yet several faculty who had taught at both secular and Christian colleges found nothing harder at one than the other. One wrote, "The life of a professor anywhere can be difficult. Balancing the demands can be difficult. I don't believe it is more or less difficult at a Christian university—just different," and another notes the difficulty of "finding time to keep up in my fields of study, but that is due to our being a teaching-focused institution, not a function of being Christian."

The Joeckel/Chesnes survey shows that teaching loads at over half of the CCCU institutions are high: about 52 percent of faculty typically teach four or more courses a semester; 31 percent teach three courses, and 17 percent teach one or two courses.[22] In comparison, at public four-year colleges, 33 percent of full-time faculty were teaching four or more courses when the HERI was administered; at all privates, 35 percent were teaching four or more courses; and at Catholic colleges, 38 percent were teaching four or more courses.[23] A large majority of the CCCU respondents, 67 percent, either strongly or somewhat strongly agreed that they "would welcome a course-load reduction for the express purpose of spending more time doing research" (FSQ 87). Male and female respondents equally welcomed a course-load reduction, with 68 percent of the men strongly or somewhat strongly agreeing, and 65 percent of the women. These attitudes reflect the growth of interest in and devotion to Christian scholarship among faculty, but a desire to spend more time on scholarly activities does not necessarily indicate a lack of interest in or commitment to teaching. Instead, many Christian college faculty identify themselves as "teacher-scholars," with a primary commitment to their students, but with a complementary commitment to scholarship with a recognition that scholarship and teaching are dialogical acts. According to the HERI survey, nearly all faculty at "other religious" colleges (99.1 percent) rate their role as a teacher as personally "very important" or "essential," while 54.7 percent rate research as very important or essential.[24]

---

22   The Joeckel/Chesnes survey was directed toward full-time faculty, but the open-ended responses show that at least some part-time faculty responded.

23   In HERI's category of "other religious" four-year colleges, 42 percent taught four or more courses.

24   DeAngelo, *The American College Teacher*, 27.

As we have seen, many Christian college faculty do conduct research, publish books and peer-reviewed articles, and present at academic conferences, despite a heavy teaching load. Mallard and Atkins found three predictors of scholarly activity among CCCU faculty: 1) research release time, 2) the use of research in teaching preparation, and 3) academic rank.[25] The Joeckel/Chesnes survey data suggest that it is hard to show the relationship between scholarly output and teaching load. Of faculty who have published a book, 11 percent typically teach one or two courses a semester, 36 percent teach three courses, 39 percent teach four courses, and 14 percent teach more than four courses. Fifty-two percent of CCCU faculty typically teach four or more courses a semester, and 49 percent of faculty who have published a peer-reviewed article teach four or more courses a semester. Similarly, 31 percent typically teach three courses a semester, and 35 percent of those who have published a peer-reviewed article teach three courses a semester.[26] Faculty with standard heavy teaching loads may occasionally receive research release time or sabbaticals, allowing them to pursue some limited scholarship. Recent scholarly activity measured by presentations at conferences during the past two years shows more of an impact from a heavy teaching load: 52 percent of respondents (904 of 1731) typically taught four or more courses a semester and approximately 40 percent of them had not presented at a conference during the past two years.

Despite the greater attention to and recognition of Christian scholarship in the post-Marsden era, CCCU faculty still perceive academic hostility to their scholarly work. Twenty percent of respondents strongly agreed that "the secular academy as a whole is dismissive of Christian scholarship," and 48 percent somewhat agreed (FSQ 99). Open-ended responses included comments about the difficulty of "being dismissed by the secular academy," and not "receiving respect and support from colleagues from secular institutions." Personal experience with publication does not have a strong effect on these results: people who had published a peer-reviewed essay were slightly more negative (70 percent) than those who had not (64 percent). Higher percentages of faculty in Business (25 percent), Communication (24 percent), Health Sciences (23 percent), and Social Sciences (23 percent) strongly agreed that the secular academy was dismissive of Christian scholarship, compared to Education (17 percent), Fine Arts (19 percent), Humanities (19 percent), Natural Sciences (18 percent), and Religion (18 percent) (Table 3). Yet in response to the statement "I have had to (or will have to) compromise my faith to some degree in order to succeed in my research/scholarship," 64 percent strongly disagreed, and 21 percent somewhat disagreed. Only about 5 percent of respondents strongly or somewhat agreed (FSQ 100). Once again, there was little difference between those who had a peer-reviewed essay published and those who had not.

---

25   Mallard and Atkins, "Changing Academic Cultures and Expanding Expectations," 380-82.

26   The data on those who teach one or two courses may not be as significant, given the fact that some part-time faculty responded to the survey.

Conclusions and Recommendations

Those CCCU institutions that have increased their scholarly expectations have done so as part of a nation-wide academic movement. Although the public is sometimes suspicious of an emphasis on scholarship at the price of good teaching—a fear that may be exacerbated by lingering elements of anti-intellectualism in parts of the Christian community—Christian scholars have made a compelling case for the importance of Christian thinking and theorizing, the vocational nature of scholarship and research, the broader ways in which scholarship can be defined, and the need for the academy to serve the community and transform culture through scholarship and research. The data reviewed in this essay show that Christian faculty have not achieved the same level of scholarly activity as faculty at other four-year teaching institutions. Without attempting to be university-level researchers or producing sloppy, half-hearted, *pro-forma* scholarship, Christian college faculty should demonstrate a steady scholarly trajectory throughout their professional life within their institutional mission of Christian learning, teaching, and thinking. That trajectory may be slower for some and faster for others. The culture, structure, and support systems of Christian colleges should do more to support appropriate levels of scholarly activity.

In my work in faculty development for over twenty-five years with a wide variety of CCCU institutions, I have found a growing interest on the part of young faculty to pursue scholarly and creative activities, but—with the exception of a few institutions—little affirmation or concrete support for such work. Relatively heavy teaching loads, greater academic and personal advising duties, and limited travel and research budgets are crucial structural detriments. One of the most significant findings from the data is the high percentage of Christian colleges that have a teaching load of four or more courses. Faculty with this kind of load will have little time to devote to research and scholarship during the academic term. Those with three or less courses have more opportunity, although they still may lack the funds to equip a lab, gather national data, or travel to a research site. In order to adequately support scholarship, institutions need to cultivate a campus culture that welcomes, encourages, and rewards scholarly activity; to invest in programs that offer an occasional load reduction and/or sabbatical; and to provide regular funds for travel and research.

The strong belief among faculty that the academy remains hostile to Christian scholarship may have some effect on scholarly production, yet it is difficult to reconcile this belief with the publishing that is done or with the fact that faculty do not think they will need to compromise their faith to succeed in scholarship or research. This may suggest that CCCU faculty are publishing more extensively with Christian presses and journals, rather than university presses and disciplinary journals. The Joeckel/Chesnes data do not report on these kinds of differences, which are important to consider when it comes to having an impact on the academy, discipline, or culture. As one CCCU respondent comments, "Few Christian colleges have the 'publish or perish' attitude. So it is easy for talented faculty to forget that the 'outreach' to the academic world is also very important. It is easy to go off to Christian conferences rather than to the academic professional ones where one needs to be present to 'wave the flag' and build relationships with other good people in the profession."

Those Christian faculty who have published books, written peer-reviewed essays, and presented at disciplinary conferences, despite regular teaching loads of three, four, or even more courses, provide inspirational models. It is possible to conduct a moderately active scholarly life at a teaching-intensive institution without destroying one's personal life.[27] The ability to say no, to successfully juggle competing demands, and to establish regular scholarly habits are necessary individual attributes to be a successful scholar. A comprehensive study of hundreds of novice professors in a variety of types of institutions by Robert Boice identifies the importance of regular scholarly activity. When Boice measured the writing habits and outputs of newly hired professors, he found that one group were "binge-writers," cranking out their scholarship in huge chunks during weekends or vacations, and the other group wrote in brief daily sessions, day in and day out. The regular writers wrote more pages per week, submitted more manuscripts, and had many more manuscripts accepted for publication at the conclusion of the six-year study. Boice recommends that new professors begin with as little as ten-to-fifteen minutes of daily writing, reading, or thinking in order to develop the constant and moderate working habits that facilitate scholarship.[28] Even when one has a heavy teaching load, maintaining a small amount of time for scholarship, difficult as that is, can prove successful. Christian college faculty can also enhance their ability to do scholarship by adjusting their focus from a highly specialized area to one more feasible for their context: from working with a particle accelerator to studying the most effective ways of teaching physics, for example.

Both institutional structures and personal practices can facilitate scholarship. More research needs to be done to identify the amount and type of scholarship that is being produced at CCCU institutions as well as the factors that make such activity possible. Future studies should identify the total number and types of publications, whether they are university presses or peer-reviewed journals; whether the work is in the area of the scholarship of discovery, application, integration, or teaching, in Ernest Boyer's terms[29]; and the degree to which the scholarly work and research informs the faculty member's teaching. Two key factors should be explored: the productivity differences between a three-course load and a four-course load, and the impact of the availability of research funds on scholarly activity. Learning more about what contributes to scholarly productivity would enable CCCU institutions to participate more fully in the renaissance of Christian scholarship.

---

27   Donald E. Hall discusses how to have a scholarly life while teaching a 4-4 load at a state institution in *The Academic Self: An Owner's Manual* (Columbus: Ohio State University Press, 2002); George Slanger discusses reasonable expectations for scholarly productivity with a heavy teaching load in "A Chair's Notes toward a Definition of Scholarship in the Small State University," *ADE Bulletin* 118 (1987): 28-32.

28   Robert Boice, *Advice for New Faculty Members: Nihil Nimus* (Boston: Allyn and Bacon, 2000), 137-56.

29   Ernest Boyer, *Scholarship Reconsidered* (San Francisco: Jossey-Bass, 1990).

Table 1: Percent of faculty who published a book and peer-reviewed article, sorted by discipline. Disciplines with low representation (Library - 22, Engineering - 13, Agriculture - 8, Other - 40) were not included in the analysis.

Discipline	N	Book	Journal
Health Sciences	131	10%	47%
Arts	172	20%	49%
Education	236	17%	52%
Business	159	21%	56%
Communication	73	25%	60%
Social Sciences	237	20%	64%
Humanities	319	36%	67%
Religion/Theology/Bible	185	57%	72%
Natural Sciences	312	13%	74%

Table 2: Percent of faculty publishing articles in academic or professional journals, by number of articles. (Source: 2007-2008 HERI Survey of Full-Time Undergraduate Faculty)

	All	Universities		Four-year Colleges				
	4+yr	Public	Private	Public	All Private	Non-sectarian	Catholic	Other Religious
None	18.8	12.3	13.7	20.1	28.2	26.6	25.6	31.9
1 to 2	17.6	10.9	13.5	21.7	23.2	20.7	24.0	26.4
3 to 4	14.5	12.4	11.5	16.6	15.9	15.5	17.2	15.8
5 to 10	18.4	18.6	16.8	19.9	17.0	18.5	17.0	14.8
11 to 20	12.7	15.7	16.4	11.2	8.8	10.3	8.7	6.6
21 to 50	11.4	17.5	15.8	7.8	5.5	6.7	5.4	3.8
51+	6.7	12.5	12.3	2.6	1.4	1.7	2.1	0.7

Table 3: Faculty who strongly agreed with the statement, "The secular academy as a whole is dismissive of Christian scholarship," sorted by academic discipline.

Discipline	N	Strongly Agree
Education	236	17%
Religion/Theology/Bible	185	18%
Natural Sciences	312	18%
Humanities	319	19%
Arts	172	19%
Social Sciences	237	22%
Health Sciences	131	23%
Communication	73	24%
Business	159	25%

A CODA ON FAITH, LEARNING, AND SCHOLARLY RIGOR

DAVID L. WEEKS AND DONALD G. ISAAK[1]

American evangelicals are often reminiscent of Jeremiah, lamenting one thing after another. With regard to higher education, the woeful tale is about academic apostasy, the abandonment of religious faith—in other words, declension. Indeed, there is a concern among some that evangelical colleges and universities are diverging from their Christian roots. The perceived nemesis is secularization, which celebrates the triumph of scientific rationalism over dogmatic religious belief. However, in their thought-provoking essay, Professors Joeckel and Chesnes argue that empirical evidence from their recent survey provides little support for declension among institutions belonging to the Council for Christian Colleges and Universities (CCCU). We agree, although our assent is nuanced. Underlying questions obscure clear interpretations of the data. There are uncertainties regarding how an evangelical perspective is defined, the extent to which conservative-liberal theological tensions foster notions of incipient declension at CCCU institutions, the impact of homogeneity on academic rigor, and the role of scholarship and classroom faith-integration in promoting academic excellence.

The Perception of Secularization

The Joeckel and Chesnes data confirm that the religious profile of CCCU faculty members, with their unwavering commitment to Christian higher education, is distinctively different from that of faculty members at other colleges and universities. A 2009 study by Neil Gross and Solon Simmons discloses that 23 percent of university professors nationwide describe themselves as either atheist or agnostic (compared to 7 percent in

---

1 We thank our colleagues at Azusa Pacific University, Randy Fall, Jennifer Walsh, and Jim Willis, for carefully reading and commenting on an early draft of this chapter.

the general population).[2] That number rises to 37 percent among faculty members in elite research institutions and to over 60 percent among professors in the natural and social sciences at those elite schools. Religious traditionalists are a small minority at elite doctoral institutions (12 percent), where a mere 1 percent say the designation "born-again Christian" applies "at least slightly." These figures contrast starkly with CCCU institutions where the traditional and "born-again" designations would likely be acceptable to the vast majority of faculty members.

This obvious difference between CCCU institutions and other institutions of higher education, however, does not wholly discount the prospect of declension. First, the declension thesis does not portend a wholesale collapse of Christian higher education; rather it posits steady decay, institution by institution. The data in the Joeckel and Chesnes study are insufficient to make pronouncements about any one institution. Second, there is little consensus on what constitutes declension, or at least a precursor of it. Those most keenly watching for signs of decline are unlikely to compare CCCU professors to their more secular counterparts. They hold CCCU faculty members to a different standard, being wary of those who might espouse secular ideas, adopt secular values, pursue secular agendas, and in the process, undermine the sacred.

Often the perception of secularization is tied to the presence of liberal political and theological points of view that might be indistinguishable from those held by faculty members on wholly secular campuses. In that regard, critics will likely be troubled by some survey findings. For example, the more than 20 percent of CCCU faculty respondents who self-identify as theologically "somewhat liberal" and "strongly liberal" are less likely than their conservative colleagues to believe in biblical inerrancy, less likely to view truth as absolute, less likely to see answers to moral questions in black and white terms, less likely to view the Bible as the only authoritative source of information about God, and are less threatened by evolution, secularism, and postmodernism (Tables 1 and 2). They are more likely to question the Bible, more supportive of women in ministry, and more open to homosexual membership in churches. More likely to identify with the Democratic Party, theological liberals hold more liberal political positions on abortion, climate change, the war in Iraq, embryonic stem-cell research, abstinence-only sex education, and homosexual marriage and civil unions (Tables 1 and 2).

While critics might pounce on such responses, caution is in order for several reasons. First, it is unclear how respondents interpreted particular survey questions. For example, when expressing reservations about the Bible's authority, we do not know whether respondents were thinking about authority in scientific, historical, moral, or doctrinal terms. Second, reliance on the aggregate data about theological liberals disguises the fact that conservatives often agree with their liberal counterparts. For example, 64 percent of conservative respondents believe "it is acceptable to question the Bible"

---

2   The statistics cited in this paragraph are drawn from two studies: Neil Gross and Solon Simmons, "The Religiosity of American College and University Professors," *Sociology of Religion* 70:2 (Summer 2009): 101-129, and Elaine Howard Ecklund and Christopher P. Scheitle, "Religion among Academic Scientists: Distinctions, Disciplines, and Demographics," *Social Problems* 54:2 (2007): 289-307.

and 54 percent believe "the evidence for human-induced climate change is convincing." Third, some self-professed theological liberals express decidedly "conservative" points of view. For example, 33 percent of self-avowed liberal respondents object to homosexual marriage, 21 percent believe in biblical inerrancy, and 34 percent contend "truth is absolute, not relative." The point is that a simplistic reading of the data could mistakenly categorize individuals in ways that undermine efforts to find common ground.

Nonetheless, Joeckel and Chesnes point out that the one-fifth of CCCU faculty members who self-identify as theologically liberal have concerns. The main issue, it appears, are doubts about the willingness to embrace alternative political, theological, and epistemological perspectives. This issue raises difficult questions about how an evangelical perspective is defined and about the latitude that exists within the confines of a common confession of faith.

Because evangelicalism is both a spiritual-renewal movement and a defender of doctrinal orthodoxy, it is not always clear which is preeminent.[3] In practice, the emphasis on a personal relationship with Jesus Christ suggests that sincerity, authenticity, and earnestness may trump doctrine, thus allowing doctrinal flexibility. Those most concerned about declension, however, are unwilling to jettison doctrinal orthodoxy—a vibrant commitment alone does not suffice. It is therefore noteworthy that a substantial majority (76 percent) of theologically liberal respondents are comfortable affirming their institution's faith statement. At the same time, theological liberals are more supportive than their conservative counterparts of greater theological diversity on campus and more inclined to embrace the notion of generic faith statements (Table 3).

Theological diversity and genericism often clash with a popular understanding of worldview thinking. Many assume those who share a worldview not only begin with common assumptions but will infer common conclusions. Experience teaches otherwise. In spite of the umbrella-like nomenclature, shared worldviews, such as a faith statement, fail to produce homogeneity due to the presence of penumbras, things on the periphery that surround the core.[4] The extent of such peripheral regions is uncertain and their relationship to the core is murky. Consequently, institutions struggle to distinguish the penumbral from what lies at the core of their identity. Battle lines get drawn when new political and social issues (e.g. abortion, homosexuality, climate change) or theological formulations (e.g. inerrancy, young-earth creationism, dispensationalism) appear that were not explicitly addressed in traditional definitions of the core, such as the Apostles,' Nicene, and Chalcedonian creeds.

---

3 The best definitions of evangelicalism focus on four hallmarks: 1) respect for the authority, perspicuity, and truthfulness of the Bible; 2) an emphasis on a personal acceptance of the faith, commonly described as conversion or being "born again"; 3) a belief that religious faith should permeate one's life, be shared with others, and be manifested in love for others; and 4) an affirmation of orthodox teachings about Jesus Christ, including his deity, virgin birth, atoning death on the cross, bodily resurrection, and eventual earthly return. The original description along these lines is from David Bebbington, *Evangelicalism in Modern Britain* (London: Unwin Hyman, 1989).

4 There is an interesting parallel in the world of law. In that parallel, social conservatives rail against the very idea of a penumbra because it has, famously, been used to create a "right to privacy," which undergirds abortion rights in the United States. Although such a right is nowhere to be found in the text of the U.S. Constitution, it became a fixture in constitutional jurisprudence when the U.S. Supreme Court found it emanating from the penumbras of the First, Third, Fourth, Fifth, Ninth, and Fourteenth amendments.

The struggle to define boundaries should surprise no one whose worldview takes seriously sin, depravity, and fallibility. Nonetheless, in spite of knowing we see through the glass darkly, we still draw bright lines that divide and destroy the comity that ought to characterize the church. In this regard, evangelicalism is susceptible to one of modernity's great flaws, the ideological temptation. The temptation is to believe we have all the answers and must impose those answers on all community members.

One should not forget that Christians have long differed with one another. Within the CCCU, for example, there are theological differences among the twenty-nine denominational institutions and numerous non-denominational schools as well as political differences within the professoriate on issues such as social welfare, economic policy, even war and peace. Why not disagree without rancor? Christians mirror the strident ideological tone of modern politics when we say, "How can you call yourself a Christian if you do not care for the poor and do not care about climate change?" or "How can you call yourself a Christian if you do not believe in inerrancy or young-earth creationism?"

Perhaps Christian institutions could learn to model civility and charity. Although liberals may shun theological conservatives in secular circles, that is a poor reason to do the same to liberals in CCCU circles. We are, after all, commanded to do unto others as we want them to do unto us, not do unto them what they have done to us. At the same time, theological liberals should know the boundaries at their respective institutions. It is foolish to join an academic community that has clear boundaries only to rail against them, and it is duplicitous to remain at an institution under false pretenses.

This is a good reminder that the one virtue most needed in higher education is the one most frequently absent, namely humility. If humility were the dominant virtue in Christian higher education, then CCCU institutions would indeed be set apart in an arena where pride and arrogance are rampant.

Homogeneity and Academic Rigor

Joeckel and Chesnes conclude their essay fretting about the academic consequences of trying to forestall declension. They contend that homogeneity combined with reticence among some faculty members to raise certain questions impedes academic rigor. Their concern can be viewed differently. Diversity of opinion and breadth of questioning are a part, although a relatively small part, of academic rigor. Rigor is about strictness, exactitude, discipline, challenge. For example, the operational definition of rigor found in the National Survey of Student Engagement (NSSE) relies on measures of time-on-task, high expectations, challenging examinations, the length of writing assignments, the number of assigned readings, and higher order mental activities such as analyzing, synthesizing, evaluating, and applying.[5]

---

5   See George Kuh, "The National Survey of Student Engagement: Conceptual Framework and Overview of Psychometric Properties." http://nsse.iub.edu/2004_annual_report/pdf/2004_Conceptual_Framework.pdf. Also see National Survey of Student Engagement, *Assessment for Improvement: Tracking Student Engagement Over Time—Annual Results 2009* (Bloomington, Ind.: Indiana University Center for Postsecondary Research, 2009).

It is worth recalling that secular institutions have their own challenge with homo-geneity, a challenge rarely described in terms of rigor. For example, the most notable thing about political diversity among faculty members on major college campuses is the relative lack of it. A number of studies show that Democrats outnumber Republicans on college campuses at least four to one.[6] The ratio is seven to one among professors in the social sciences and the humanities.[7] The more prestigious the university, the more politi-cally skewed it is. For instance, a study of voter-registration records discovered there are ten Democrats for every one Republican at UC Berkeley.[8] It seems counterintuitive to say that greater political diversity can be found on CCCU campuses than in the Ivy League, but it is true (Table 4).[9] In addition to a lack of political diversity, there are ques-tions and perspectives that are practically *verboten* on secular campuses. For instance, Christians often feel stifled and are wary about explicitly expressing their point of view. So, given that homogeneity on secular campuses has not led to widespread charges of compromising diversity and impeding intellectual rigor, is it fair to level that charge against the CCCU? Probably not.

Nevertheless, Joeckel and Chesnes remind us of a longstanding pedagogical chal-lenge: how to raise questions and present alternative points of view in a way that benefits students. A viable solution is not readily apparent within the flawed models found in secular higher education. In recent years, the academy has witnessed a clash between a pedagogical approach that emphasizes the disinterested coverage of subject matter and one that stresses advocacy. The disinterested presentation of competing points of view is impractical in many areas of inquiry. Professors are not disinterested inquirers; they have devoted their careers to exploring questions within their disciplines; they have a vested interest in the answers they find most compelling. The advocacy approach is even more troubling with the accompanying politicization of the classroom. Advocacy, in our eyes, is an activity of ideologues, not teachers. From a student perspective, advocacy is often indistinguishable from indoctrination.

---

6   For example, see the "Politics of the American Professoriate" survey, as reported by Neil Gross and Solon Simmons in "The Social and Political Views of American Professors," working paper, September 24, 2007: http://www.wjh.harvard.edu/~ngross/lounsbery_9-25.pdf. Brookings Institution, "National Survey on Government Endeavors" (Princeton Survey Research Associates, November 2001), http://www.brookings.edu/comm/reform-watch/rw04_surveydata.pdf. "North American Academic Study Survey," as reported by Stanley Rothman, S. Robert Lichter, and Neil Nevitte in "Politics and Professional Advancement Among College Faculty," *The Forum* 3:1 (2005): 1-16.

7   See Daniel Klein and Charlotta Stern, "By the Numbers: The Ideological Profile of Professors," *The Politically Correct University: Problems, Scope and Reforms* (Washington, D.C.: American Enterprise Institute, 2009), 15-37.

8   Daniel B. Klein and Andrew Western, "How Many Democrats per Republican at UC-Berkeley and Stanford? Voter Registration Data across 23 Academic Departments," http://swopec.hhs.se/ratioi/abs/ratioi0054.htm.

9   Various scholars have attempted to explain this one-sidedness. One camp, for instance, argues that like-minded faculty hire like-minded applicants. Thus, intentional discrimination has systematically thinned the ranks of political and religious conservatives from college and university faculties. See Daniel Klein and Charlotta Stern, "By the Numbers: The Ideological Profile of Professors." A new argument is that the one-sidedness is due to the fact that higher education careers are more attractive to certain types of people, namely liberals. Professors have been typecast occupationally in much the same way that nurses have been typecast by gender—women go into nursing and liberals go into the professoriate. The latter argument seems a more sophisticated version of the old argument that conserva-tive Christians are anti-intellectual, thus disinterested in the life of the mind. See Neil Gross and Ethan Fosse, "Why Are Professors Liberal?" working paper, January 15, 2010: http://www.soci.ubc.ca/fileadmin/template/main/images/departments/soci/faculty/gross/why_are_professors_liberal.pdf.

For the sake of discussion, we offer a modest idea: promote a teaching philosophy that permits and even encourages advocacy on those matters which everyone explicitly agrees upon (namely, those doctrinal beliefs that historically define Christianity) but expect the fair presentation of opposing points of view on inferences. Not every viewpoint merits consideration, but alternative perspectives should not be disregarded. We do a disservice to students when we caricature minority perspectives or when we fail to remember that supporters of the majority point of view are often ignorant of the arguments for and against it. Both merit consideration. Such a solution is imperfect. Conservatives will be loath to give up advocacy on the hot-button issues on their agenda; liberals will cry that such an approach undermines engaged activism and silences radical critiques of the status quo. On the positive side, such a teaching philosophy would: 1) contribute to academic rigor by requiring students to think about issues rather than rely on the opinions of passionate and persuasive professors; 2) prepare students for graduate school where consideration of alternative points of view and arguments for a particular point of view are important; and 3) grant everyone the freedom to raise almost any question without being viewed as suspect.

Faith Integration

The aforementioned study by Gross and Simmons was not an indictment of religious skepticism; rather it focused on the "surprising" religiosity of the professoriate. They did not expect to find that 52 percent of professors nationwide either believe in God without a doubt or believe in God in spite of some doubts. (Only 20 percent of professors at elite institutions have no doubt about God's existence.[10]) Given that the academy is predominately a secular institution, they opine that the religious beliefs of faculty members must be largely privatized. This is emphatically not the case in the CCCU, where attempts to bring faith to bear in teaching and research are the norm.

The apparent tendency for CCCU faculty members to embrace and to endorse practicing the integration of faith and learning is heartening. Responses to FSQs 18 ("I have a good idea of what is meant by the phrase, 'the integration of faith and learning'") and 19 ("It is not difficult for me to integrate faith and learning in my discipline") are overwhelmingly "strongly agree" or "somewhat agree." Indeed, these survey results from faculty respondents are highlighted by Joeckel and Chesnes, prompting them to conclude, "According to our data, member institutions of the CCCU are places that succeed in cultivating faith and integrating that faith with learning."

The large "strongly agree/somewhat agree" responses to FSQs 18 and 19 certainly bode well for Christian higher education. These results, which are essentially a request for self-evaluation, do not necessarily imply that the integration of faith and learning has a common understanding among CCCU faculty members or is successfully practiced across disciplines. Our conversations with liberal arts professors from diverse disciplines reveal a range of perspectives as to what constitutes the integration of faith and learning.

---

10   Neil Gross and Solon Simmons, "The Religiosity of American College and University Professors," 114.

For some, an important aspect of faith integration is the public display of personal piety, resulting in a proclivity for starting classes with prayers, devotionals, and scriptural passages. Whether the devotional or Scripture passage has direct bearing to the academic topic under consideration is immaterial; the integration is perceived accomplished simply by the proximity of Christian instructors and religious observances to the academic discipline. Others perceive faith integration more in terms of nurturing relationships with students. In this view, an instructor lives out a gentle, humble presence in the classroom, resulting in just, caring treatment of students and eventual spiritual mentoring, both in and out of the classroom.

Yet others might envision faith integration primarily in terms of teaching moral truth to young learners. The survey results provide some evidence for this. Table 5, for example, shows percentages of faculty members who, when making one of the five listed responses to FSQ 39 ("Answers to moral questions are primarily black and white, not shades of gray"), also "strongly agree" they "have a good idea of what is meant by the integration of faith and learning." Table 6 shows percentages of those when making one of the five listed responses to FSQ 39 also "strongly agree" that "it is not difficult to integrate faith and learning in my discipline." Trends in both tables suggest the more certain professors are about moral absolutes, the more likely they are to "strongly agree" about their ability to understand and implement faith and learning in their discipline. Similar trends are obtained when the cross tabulation is done with FSQ 43 ("Truth is absolute, not relative") in place of FSQ 39. A plausible explanation for these tendencies is that some survey respondents who view moral values or truth with no ambiguity, i.e., those who agree with FSQs 39 and 43, see faith integration as imparting similar ambiguity-free values to students. Since little is nuanced, these faculty members would also tend to be more certain as to their understanding of what faith integration is ("strongly agree" with FSQ 18) and their ability to integrate faith and learning ("strongly agree" with FSQ 19).

Finally, there are those who see faith integration more in academic terms where the emphasis is on how the Christian faith enhances our understanding of academic subjects or vice versa. For example, the following from the Azusa Pacific University Institute of Faith Integration indicates how our university intends faculty members to understand faith integration: *Faith integration is understood as theologically informed reflection on integrating faith within the context of academic disciplines, professional programs, and lived practice in order to advance the understanding of Christian higher education and to develop moral leaders who will impact the world.* Statements like this cast the process, if not the purpose, of faith integration outside the realm of personal-faith persuasions. Indeed, the above statement represents an approach to integration of faith with learning that can be pursued by all students, whether or not they have personal-faith convictions.

The perceptions of faith integration outlined above are not comprehensive, nor are they mutually exclusive. However, they illustrate the range of impressions likely present as CCCU faculty members considered survey questions on their personal understanding as to what the integration of faith and learning means and whether they are effective practitioners of faith integration in the classroom.

The fact that CCCU faculty members give very high self-evaluations on both their understanding of the integration of faith and learning and the ease with which they deem they can implement integration in their discipline is intriguing in light of anecdotal evidence, i.e., conversations with a variety of professors at our campus, that indicates otherwise. There is significant consternation among many faculty members on how to define and implement faith integration in academic disciplines outside of theology, philosophy, Christian ministry, and possibly, nursing. During the past several years, our university has designated key faculty persons to serve as faith-integration mentors. A recent observation from one such mentor is that senior faculty members tend to identify faith integration more in the relational terms discussed above, rather than through academic endeavors. Success in implementing integration of faith and learning is seen more in terms of professors nurturing students in their young Christian walk rather than from academic considerations and analyses. This faith-integration mentor went on to point out that since younger faculty members (especially in "non-religious" disciplines) tend to come from research institutions, they often do not have well-formed ideas as to what faith integration in their academic discipline entails. They are sincere, dedicated Christians, but have little, if any, critical exposure of their discipline in the context of Christian faith. Such exposure and analysis were simply not offered in their recently completed graduate programs.

The above observations imply more recent or younger faculty members should be less affirmative than senior faculty members in their responses to FSQs 18 and 19. Tables 7 and 8 show faculty responses to FSQs 18 and 19 according to how many years the respondent has taught at the university or college. Of course, the large majority of all faculty members, irrespective of their length of service, answer affirmative ("strongly agree" or "somewhat agree") to both questions. But, both tables also show newer faculty members are less certain in their affirmative responses. That is, they tend more than do more senior faculty members to "somewhat agree" at the expense of "strongly agree." These trends are especially pronounced in Table 7. Over 76 percent of the most senior colleagues "strongly agree" they have a good idea of the meaning of faith and learning, whereas only 58 percent of the newest faculty members would make that claim. These observations are consistent with the notion that those who recently completed educational-training programs have a greater tendency to recognize their lack of expertise in integrating faith and learning in "non-religious" disciplines. This is not to imply or deny the idea that more senior faculty members have similar lack of expertise but just do not readily recognize it. It may be that more senior faculty members have, over time, developed a clear understanding of faith integration absent any input from graduate-training centers. Alternatively, as suggested by our faith mentor above, more senior faculty members may tend to have a different concept of the scope of faith integration (perceived as more relational), so that understanding of faith integration is assumed irrespective of graduate training in the discipline.

Further comparisons between Tables 7 and 8 reveal that all faculty groups, irrespective of length of service, are somewhat less certain of their ability to implement the integration of faith and learning in their discipline than of their understanding of the term's meaning. The sum of "strongly agree" and "somewhat agree" is high for each length-of-service group in both Tables 7 (93-97 percent) and 8 (83-86 percent). This sum, however, decreases by 10 percentage points or more when comparing each group in Table 8 with its counterpart in Table 7.

Student perceptions of the integration of faith and learning in CCCU institutions are similar to those of faculty members. Students overwhelmingly believe they know what is meant by the integration of faith and learning given that 93 percent agree (including 60 percent "strongly agree") they "have a good idea of what is meant by the phrase, 'the integration of faith and learning'"(SSQ 17). The student response nearly mirrors that of the faculty; the main difference is about 7 percent more faculty "strongly agree" than "somewhat agree" (FSQ 18). In our experience, many students view any Christian activity or discussion in the classroom as pertinent expressions of the integration of faith and learning. Indeed, a recent review at our university by those who oversee student evaluations on how classroom instructors integrate faith with academics is instructive. Virtually any expression of faith in the classroom results in high evaluation marks for an instructor's faith-integration score. It seems that many students have difficulty identifying what the integration of faith with disciplinary learning actually is and recognizing its effective implementation in the classroom, especially when the discipline is not one usually associated with theological endeavors. This should not be surprising given the diversity of faculty member understandings of faith-integration endeavors discussed earlier. So, the strong student agreement with SSQ 17 may result from something other than receiving excellent models of integration of faith with academic disciplines in the classroom.

In summary, we note, as do Joeckel and Chesnes, that CCCU faculty members have a strong sense they understand the meaning of faith integration and can implement it in their academic discipline. It is unlikely, however, survey respondents share a common definition or metric of success in faith integration. Accordingly, one wonders to what extent these positive responses reflect faculty self-perceptions and intentions, in contrast to a clear and unified understanding of faith integration along with effective strategies for implementing it. Newer faculty members tend to be less certain as to what faith integration entails. Faculty members who recently completed graduate programs, where their discipline was addressed in isolation from faith perspectives, are more likely to be refining their understanding of how faith relates to their discipline. More senior faculty members, over time, may have learned how to fuse faith perspectives with their discipline. Or, they may conceptualize the integration of faith and learning more along the lines of faculty-student nurturing instead of in rigorous academic terms. The data do not allow adjudication on this. In any case, it seems that CCCU institutions would benefit from initiatives that provide clear, uniform definitions as to what the integration of faith and learning in various disciplines entails and indicate incipient strategies by which this integration can be accomplished in the classroom. Such initiatives would be especially useful to newer faculty members who teach in "non-religious" disciplines. These initiatives would likely be embraced since newer faculty members not only cite the opportunity to integrate faith and learning more frequently than other reasons for taking a position at a Christian institution, but they do so with greater regularity than do their more senior counterparts (Table 9).

Finally, the Joeckel and Chesnes CCCU survey project provides encouraging evidence that students at CCCU institutions see significant growth in their Christian faith which may be partly due to classroom experiences in which rigorous integration of faith with academic disciplines takes place. Additional insights, however, are needed to determine more precisely how students recognize and respond to appropriate models of classroom faith and learning.

The Scholarly Renaissance

The scholarly renaissance noted in Professor VanZanten's chapter represents one of the most important developments among evangelicals in higher education. Not only have Christian academicians become more active as scholars, but some individuals have risen to national prominence. The work of Alvin Plantinga, Nathan Hatch, Nancey Murphy, Nicholas Wolterstorff, Francis Collins, Michael McConnell, David Lyle Jeffrey, George Marsden, Stephen Carter, Mark Noll, Christian Smith, and several others, is praised in both Christian and secular circles.[11] Regardless, the vexing charge of anti-intellectualism heard throughout the twentieth century will not soon go away.

Evangelicals are known for loving God with their heart and soul and strength, but less so for loving God with their mind. It is as if we fall into the trap of reading Matthew 22:37 and Mark 12:30 as containing multiple commandments, then we highlight the "most important."[12] But the biblical passages do not lend themselves to such an interpretation. We are to love God with *all* our mind, as well as *all* our heart, soul, and strength. Christian colleges are at the forefront of efforts to love God with the mind. Nevertheless, on occasion, students receive conflicting messages on CCCU campuses. Local pastors who speak in chapel, volunteers who lead student Bible studies, organizations that sponsor mission trips around the globe can easily prioritize heart and soul, pitting piety against intellect. These people are not out to disrupt the mission and purpose of Christian higher education; they are simply reiterating the traditional evangelical mission to save souls and serve the needy. In the process, they may inadvertently convey modern canards: reason is at odds with faith, facts are distinct from values, and knowledge is unrelated to conviction.

It is also true that intellectuality in the modern academy has been defined, by and large, by the Enlightenment. The Enlightenment was built upon a new view of the world, one in which human beings through the use of reason, namely the scientific method, could conquer the physical world and remake human nature. Although Christians contributed much to the Enlightenment and were deeply invested in the relief of man's estate, they never fully bought into the whole of modernism. As a result, one historian

---

11   D. Michael Lindsay and Alan Wolfe have done a great service in recognizing a revived life of the mind among evangelicals. See Alan Wolfe, "The Opening of the Evangelical Mind," *Atlantic Monthly* (October 2000): 55-76, and D. Michael Lindsay, *Faith in the Halls of Power: How Evangelicals Joined the American Elite* (New York: Oxford University Press, 2007).

12   "Love the Lord your God with all your heart, and with all your soul, and with all your mind" (Matthew 22:37). "Love the Lord your God with all your heart and with all your soul and with all your mind and with all your strength" (Mark 12:30).

notes, "Americans have in effect been given the hard choice between being intelligent according to the standards prevailing in their intellectual centers, and being religious according to the standards prevailing in their denominations."[13] The choice was obvious for conservative Protestants. Consequently, Alan Wolfe writes, "of all America's religious traditions, evangelical Protestantism, at least in its twentieth-century conservative forms, has long ranked dead last in intellectual stature."[14]

The anti-intellectual charge will never go away as long as self-appointed definers of intellectual integrity exclude faith perspectives and compel the privatization of religious belief. The good news is that this approach was an extension of modernity and shares its fate. The post-modern moment is a brief respite from the era in which modernism discredited Christianity. It is an opportunity.

In the face of these realities, CCCU schools, as VanZanten rightly argues, must be ever more vigilant in providing "affirmation, effort, and support" for the life of the mind. One challenge in this regard is economic. Scholarly activity requires time, lots of it, and time has a price tag associated with it. There is a direct relationship between scholarly productivity and teaching load, size of student body, operating budgets,[15] salary levels, institutional endowments, and percentage of the budget devoted to instruction. Such things profoundly affect the amount of time for scholarship that schools can afford and the extent of institutional research support.

Another challenge is cultural. Many CCCU campuses began as Bible colleges or as liberal arts colleges. As such, their ethos privileged teaching, mentoring, and ministry, not research and writing. To the extent this remains true, and it varies from campus to campus, the establishment of new norms and expectations that prioritize research and writing will take time. As this happens, we cannot forget that publications and presentations are markers of academic success; they should not, however, be mistaken for the whole of it. The real measure of intellectual vitality is not the length of one's C.V., but the extent to which one is a noticed and notable participant in the debates that roil our academic disciplines. To shed the mantle of insignificance, Christians must put forth ideas that peers consider, interact with, and respond to. Otherwise, we languish as mere published (or unpublished) commentators on the ideas of others.

Every generation has people who change the conversation. Recent conversation-changers include Richard Rorty, Edward Saïd, Jean Bethke Elshtain, Václav Havel, Noam Chomsky, Toni Morrison, and Jacques Derrida. Will there be Christian conversation-changers in the decades ahead? Will an evangelical voice be the next Walter Rauschenbusch, Reinhold Niebuhr, Martin Marty, Richard John Neuhaus, or John Courtney Murray? If not, evangelicalism will continue to be seen as an intellectual backwater.

Culture is also shaped, in part, by outsiders. VanZanten points out that 68 percent of survey respondents believe the secular academy is dismissive of Christian scholarship.

---

13 See Sidney E. Mead, "Denominationalism: The Shape of Protestantism in America," *Church History*, 23:4 (December 1954): 291-320.

14 Alan Wolfe, "The Opening of the Evangelical Mind," 56.

15 The average operating budget among CCCU institutions is approximately $40 million.

They have reason to be suspicious. One study, using an American National Election Survey "feeling thermometer," found the most socially acceptable form of blatant prejudice is anti-Christian.[16] Antagonism toward conservative Christians is particularly robust among "seculars," the highly educated, and cultural progressives.[17] This is problematic because cultural, social, and political elites "define for others what is respectable in the realm of belief and permissible in the realm of conduct."[18] One result of the persistent antipathy toward Christians is that they are caricatured with impunity. Calloused insensitivity appears too often, from Michael Weiskopf's *Washington Post* description of evangelicals as "poor, uneducated, and easy to command" to the leading British newspaper's description of evangelicals as "God-fearing rednecks . . . who generally have lost all capacity for rational thought."[19]

In the face of such disdain, cultivating a campus culture that prizes intellectual engagement is hard work. Efforts to do so must be sustained over an extended period of time and must have the full support of boards, presidents, academic administrators, and faculty leaders.

Conclusion

The success of any organization is tied to a clear mission, dutifully followed. With Christ-centered missions at the heart of every CCCU college and university, these schools are at the forefront of evangelical efforts to model and teach what it means to love God with our minds. The Joeckel and Chesnes study reveals much about how students and professors see this mission carried out. In general, it seems virtually everyone is fully committed, and fears of declension across the CCCU are premature. But that is only part of the story. It will be individual institutions that either stand against secularism or fall before its rising tide. Each and every school has a vested interest in ongoing introspection, seeking institutional answers to the questions raised by the Joeckel and Chesnes survey. What lies at the core of an institution's identity? What is the ideal balance between unity and diversity? What does faith integration mean, and how does one best do it in the classroom? What is the role of faculty scholarly activity and how might we foster it? Answers to those questions are central to the success of CCCU colleges and universities. Seeking those answers will require devotion, ingenuity, and goodwill. Institutions can pursue answers in a climate of fear and suspicion or they can model the rallying cry voiced by many Christians since the time of the reformation: "In essentials unity, in non-essentials liberty, in all things charity."

---

16   See Louis Bolce and Gerald De Maio, "Religious Outlook, Culture War Politics, and Antipathy toward Christian Fundamentalists," *Public Opinion Quarterly* 63 (1999): 29-61.

17   The term "seculars" is employed by Bolce and De Maio without definition.

18   Bolce and De Maio cite Gertrude J. Selznick and Stephen Steinberg, *The Tenacity of Prejudice* (New York: Harper and Row, 1969), 187.

19   *Washington Post* (February 1, 1993); *The Times* (October 8, 2005). More accurate representations of evangelicals are found in Andrew Greeley and Michael Hout, *The Truth about Conservative Christians: What They Think and What They Believe* (Chicago, Ill.: University of Chicago Press, 2006);D. MichaelLindsay, *Faith in the Halls of Power: How Evangelicals Joined the American Elite* (New York: Oxford University Press, 2007); and Christian Smith, *Christian America? What Evangelicals Really Want* (Berkeley, Ca.: University of California Press, 2000).

Table 1: Responses (in percent) of self-identified liberal (L) and conservative (C) faculty members who somewhat or strongly disagreed to the following statements.

The Bible is the only authoritative source of information about God.	
L: 70.4%	C: 28.1%
I believe in biblical inerrancy.	
L: 63.5%	C: 16.3%
Answers to moral questions are primarily black and white not shades of gray.	
L: 91.9%	C: 53.8%
Truth is absolute not relative.	
L: 54.6%	C: 11.2%
My college/university has been negatively influenced by secularism.	
L: 70.2%	C: 48.8%
Abortion should be made illegal in the United States.	
L: 73.9%	C: 18.6%
I support abstinence-only sex education.	
L: 69.8%	C: 21.2%
I support the military campaign in Iraq.	
L: 85.9%	C: 35.2%

Table 2: Responses (in percent) of self-identified liberal (L) and conservative (C) faculty members who somewhat or strongly agreed to the following statements.

Postmodernism can be compatible with Christianity.	
L: 68.5%	C: 33.3%
The theory of evolution is compatible with Christianity.	
L: 88.8%	C: 41.4%
It is acceptable to question the Bible.	
L: 88.4%	C: 63.8%
Practicing homosexuals should be allowed membership in a Christian church.	
L: 74%	C: 21.1%
Women should have the right to become pastors.	
L: 96.7%	C: 60.8%
The evidence for human-induced climate change is convincing.	
L: 93.6%	C: 54%
Federal government agencies should provide funding for embryonic stem cell research.	
L: 72%	C: 18.6%
Homosexuals should be given the right to marry.	
L: 45.6%	C: 4.1%
Homosexuals should be given the right to form civil unions.	
L: 79.4%	C: 30.7%

Table 3: Responses (in percent) of self-identified liberal (L) and conservative (C) faculty members who somewhat or strongly agreed to the following statements.

I am comfortable affirming my college's/university's faith statement.	
L: 75.6%	C: 85.9%
Diversity of theological opinions among faculty and students is healthy for a Christian college/university.	
L: 98.4%	C: 83.5%
I wish my college's/university's statement of faith were more generic and more broadly defined Christianity.	
L: 46.9%	C: 16.6%

Table 4: Political Affiliation of College/University Faculty Members

	North American[1] Academic Study Survey	Princeton[2] Research Associates	Politics of[3] the American Professoriate	Joeckel/ Chesnes Survey
	(1999)	(2001)	(2006)	(2007)
Democrat	50%	55%	50%	22%
Republican	11%	6%	14%	46%
Independent	33%	37%	35%	25%
Other	5%	1%	n.a.	8%

Table 5: Percent of faculty members with indicated response to "answers to moral questions are primarily black and white, not shades of gray" who also strongly agree they "have a good idea of what is meant by the integration of faith and learning."

Strongly agree	74.6%
Somewhat agree	71.9%
Neutral	68.5%
Somewhat disagree	64.9%
Strongly disagree	66.9%

1   North American Academic Study Survey. See Stanley Rothman and S. Robert Lichter, "The Vanishing Conservative—Is There a Glass Ceiling," in *The Politically Correct University: Problems, Scope and Reforms* (Washington, D.C.: American Enterprise Institute, 2009), 60-75.

2   Brookings Institution. "National Survey on Government Endeavors" (Princeton Survey Research Associates, November 2001).http://www.brookings.edu/comm/reformwatch/rw04_surveydata.pdf .

3   Politics of the American Professoriate survey. See Neil Gross and Solon Simmons, "The Social and Political Views of American Professors," Working Paper, Sept. 24, 2007: http://www.wjh.harvard.edu/~ngross/lounsbery_9-25.pdf.

Table 6: Percent of faculty members with indicated response to "answers to moral questions are primarily black and white, not shades of gray" who also strongly agree "it is not difficult for me to integrate faith and learning in my discipline."

Strongly agree	69.6%
Somewhat agree	58.3%
Neutral	53.7%
Somewhat disagree	54.9%
Strongly disagree	56.2%

Table 7: Faculty member responses to "I have a good idea of what is meant by the phrase, 'the integration of faith and learning'" according to years taught.

How many years have you taught at your college/university?			
0-5	6-10	11-15	16 or more
Strongly agree	58.3%	67.7%	70.1%	76.3%
Somewhat agree	34.6%	26.7%	24.4%	20.6%
Neutral/Disagree	7.1%	5.6%	5.5%	3.1%

Table 8: Faculty member responses to "It is not difficult for me to integrate faith and learning in my discipline" according to years taught.

How many years have you taught at your college/university?			
0-5	6-10	11-15	16 or more
Strongly agree	53.9%	55.6%	59.8%	60.0%
Somewhat agree	28.7%	27.5%	24.4%	25.5%
Neutral/Disagree	17.4%	17.0%	15.8%	14.5%

Table 9: Faculty member responses to "Why did you take a job at a Christian college/university?" according to years taught.

How many years have you taught at your college/university?				
	0-5	6-10	11-15	16 or more
Commitment to Christian higher education	35.2%	41.7%	45.3%	56.5%
Opportunity for me to integrate faith and learning	37.0%	31.4%	25.2%	21.6%
Frustration with secular schools	2.7%	1.9%	3.0%	1.9%
Only job I could get	6.9%	4.9%	8.1%	3.7%
Other	18.2%	20.0%	18.4%	16.3%

Bibliography: Part One

Benne, Robert. *Quality with Soul: How Six Premier Colleges and Universities Keep Faith with Their Religious Traditions*. Grand Rapids, Mich.: Eerdmans, 2001.

Boice, Robert. *Advice for New Faculty Members: Nihil Nimus*. Boston: Allyn and Bacon, 2002.

Campolo, Anthony. "The Challenge of Radical Christianity for the Christian College." In *Faithful Learning and the Christian Scholarly Vocation*, 139-157. Edited by Douglas V. Henry and Bob R. Agee. Grand Rapids, Mich.: Eerdmans, 2003.

DeAngelo, Linda, et al. *The American College Teacher: National Norms for the 2007-2008 HERI Faculty Survey*. Los Angeles: HERI, 2009.

Evans, C. Stephen. "The Calling of the Christian Scholar-Teacher." In *Faithful Learning and the Christian Scholarly Vocation*, 30-45. Edited by Douglas V. Henry and Bob R. Agee. Grand Rapids, Mich.: Eerdmans, 2003.

Hall, Donald E. *The Academic Self: An Owner's Manual*. Columbus: Ohio State University Press, 2002.

Hamilton, Michael S. "The Elusive Idea of Christian Scholarship." *Christian Scholar's Review* 31 (2001): 21.

"A Higher Education." *Christianity Today*, June 2005, 31.

Harris, Scott and D. Barry Lumsden. "Tenure Policies and Practices of American Evangelical Colleges and Universities. Part 2: Institutions Granting Tenure." *Christian Higher Education* 5 (2006): 348.

Heie, Harold. "Integration and Conversation." In *The University Through the Eyes of Faith*, 61-74. Edited by Steve Moore. Indianapolis, Ind.: Light and Life Communications, 1998.

Holmes, Arthur. *The Idea of a Christian College*. Grand Rapids, Mich.: Eerdmans, 1975.

Jacobsen, Douglas and Rhonda Hustedt Jacobsen, eds. *Scholarship and Christian Faith: Enlarging the Conversation*. New York: Oxford University Press, 2004.

Lindsay, D. Michael. *Faith in the Halls of Power: How Evangelicals Joined the American Elite*. New York: Oxford University Press, 2007.

Lyon, Larry and Michael Beaty. "Integration, Secularization, and the Two-Spheres View at Religious Colleges: Comparing Baylor University with the University of Notre Dame and Georgetown College." *Christian Scholar's Review* 29:1 (1999): 99.

Mallard, Kina S. and Michele W. Atkins. "Changing Academic Cultures and Expanding Expectations: Motivational Factors Influencing Scholarship at Small Christian Colleges and Universities." *Christian Higher Education* 3 (2004): 374.

Marsden, George. *The Outrageous Idea of Christian Scholarship*. New York: Oxford University Press, 1994.

――――, *The Soul of the American University: From Protestant Establishment to Established Nonbelief*. Oxford: Oxford University Press, 1994.

McMurtrie, Beth. "Do Professors Lose Academic Freedom by Signing Statements of Faith?" *Academe*, May 24, 2002, A12.

Mouw, Richard J. "Assessing Christian Scholarship: Where We've Been and Where We're Going." In *Christian Scholarship . . . for What?*, edited by Susan Felch. Grand Rapids, Mich.: Calvin College, 2003.

Noll, Mark A. "The Future of the Religious College." In *The Future of Religious Colleges: The Proceedings of the Harvard Conference on the Future of Religious Colleges*, 73-94. Edited by Paul J. Dovre. Grand Rapids, Mich.: Eerdmans, 2002.

Roberts, Jon H., and James Turner. *The Sacred and the Secular University*. Princeton: Princeton University Press, 2000.

Schuster, Jack and Martin J. Finkelstein. *The American Faculty: The Restructuring of Academic Work and Careers*. Baltimore: Johns Hopkins University Press, 2006.

Sloan, Robert B. "Preserving Distinctively Christian Higher Education." In *The Future of Christian Higher Education*, 25-36. Edited by David S. Dockery and David P. Gushee. Nashville, Tenn.: Broadman & Holman, 1999.

Palmer, Parker J. *To Know as We Are Known: Education as Spiritual Journey*. San Francisco, Ca.: Harper San Francisco, 1993.

Patterson, James. *Shining Lights: A History of the Council for Christian Colleges & Universities*. Grand Rapids, Mich.: Baker Academic, 2001.

Reisberg, Leo. "Enrollments Surge at Christian Colleges." *Chronicle of Higher Education*, March 5, 1999, A44.

Ringenberg, William C. *The Christian College: A History of Protestant Higher Education*. 2d. ed. Grand Rapids, Mich.: Baker, 2006.

Sawatsky, Rodney J. "Prologue: The Virtue of Scholarly Hope." In *Scholarship and Christian Faith: Enlarging the Conversation, 3-14*. Ed. Douglas Jacobsen and Rhonda Hustedt Jacobsen. Oxford: Oxford University Press, 2004.

Wolfe, Alan. "The Opening of the Evangelical Mind." *Atlantic Monthly*, October 2000, 58.

Wolterstorff, Nicholas. "The Mission of the Christian College at the End of the Twentieth Century." In *Educating for Shalom: Essays on Christian Higher Education, 27-35*. Edited by Clarence W. Joldersma and Gloria Goris Stronks. Grand Rapids, Mich.: Eerdmans, 2004.

———, *Reason within the Bounds of Religion*. Grand Rapids, Mich.: Eerdmans, 1984.

PART TWO

FAITH AND
CAMPUS CULTURE

CHAPTER 4

THICK ECUMENISM

The Possibility of Enlarging Our Circles at Christian Colleges and Universities

PHILIP IRVING MITCHELL

"In a world where the Church is no longer one, where markets proliferate and the Church is made invisible amid the welter of these choices, the uniformity of truth will emerge perhaps in a peculiar way, simply as the *subjection to form* itself, the vehicle for time's renewal, each fractured church's historical weight and worry. Unity will be freed as we carry division upon our bent backs. . ." —**Ephraim Radner**

"Creatures thus image God *by following him, by entering into the very way of God as he himself has revealed that way in history.*" —**David L. Schindle**r

The mark of a significant study is not always a surprising finding, but it helps. When its results are counter-intuitive it offers an opportunity for new questions and second looks. In some areas, the Joeckel/Chesnes survey confirms what we long suspected. For example, CCCU faculty, in large part, value the Christian beliefs and confessions of faith of their institutions,[1] and over half the faculty surveyed (56.9 percent; FSQ 23) disagreed that their university statements of faith should be more generic. None of this is unexpected for those who teach at a CCCU institution. We, by and large, want to work at Christian colleges and universities, places that are committed to a holistic immersion of their academic cultures in the waters of baptism. However, the Joeckel/Chesnes survey also tells us things that should make us stop and think. It finds, for example, that a large majority of our primarily evangelical faculty either strongly disagreed or somewhat disagreed (70.3 percent; FSQ 29) that Roman Catholic faculty should not be allowed to teach

---

1 The survey's findings: the majority value the Christian belief and confessions of faith of their institutions (65.8 percent strongly agree, 24.4. percent somewhat agree; FSQ 22) and only 0.8 percent disagreed that their institutions should maintain their Christian identity (FSQ 25).

at CCCU institutions. At first blush, this finding contradicts our comfort-level with our particular faith statements. A number of potential reasons explains why this is the case, including the remarkable change of relations between evangelical and Roman Catholics in the United States in the last twenty-five years.[2] This sea change in attitudes suggests a general larger evangelical openness to other Christian traditions, at least within institutions of higher education, and perhaps merits asking if our sense has changed of what those faith statements imply.

Rather than argue the why of this felicitous moment in history, however, in this essay I want to explore how CCCU institutions might take this possibility seriously. More precisely, I want to argue that Alasdair MacIntyre's model of tradition offers a framework in which CCCU colleges and faculties might go about expanding their hiring and campus participation to a broader circle of faith; I am as curious about our Protestant schools hiring other qualified Protestants as I am about our schools hiring Roman Catholics and the Eastern Orthodox. What I will contend below is that this is not a process of mere pragmatism, or even "mere Christianity," but one of "thick ecumenism"[3]; that is, this process requires a deep engagement with the history and beliefs that make up our faith traditions and a widening of our faculties that nonetheless keeps faith with those traditions. It also requires consistent listening and truthful hospitality from our campus cultures.

We should begin by acknowledging that this is not an institutional question for all Christian colleges. Robert Benne's *Quality with Soul* observes four ways that church-related colleges in the United States incorporate faith: orthodox, critical mass, intentionally pluralist, and accidentally pluralist. While the pluralist campuses have either an intentional or token presence from their sponsoring religious traditions, they adopt primarily secular paradigms as their organizational visions. Orthodox and critical-mass schools, like those in the CCCU, orient themselves around more explicitly Christian visions. What makes the critical-mass campus different from the orthodox one is its attempts to be more inclusive of voices outside its tradition while continuing to privilege that tradition.[4] Historians George Marsden and James Tunstead Burtchaell have both narrated the ways in which colleges historically associated with Christianity grew increasingly secular in the United States, and their findings are troubling to be sure for many on CCCU campuses. We clearly want to remain both faithful to what we believe and open to our Christian brothers and sisters. The question for us, then, can be put this way: Can an orthodox school stay orthodox while including some aspects of the critical-mass institution? Or if it becomes a critical-mass institution, will it only be a matter of time before it goes the way of first intentional and then accidental pluralism?

2 Cf. Mark A. Noll and Carolyn Nystrom, *Is the Reformation Over? An Evangelical Assessment of Contemporary Roman Catholicism* (Grand Rapids, Mich.: Baker Academic, 2008).

3 This term is taken from Steven R. Harmon's *Towards a Baptist Catholicity: Essays on Tradition and the Baptist Vision* (Eugene, Ore.: Wipf & Stock, 2006), 16-17. He is obviously playing off Clifford Geertz's "thick description" in Geertz, *The Interpretation of Cultures* (New York: Basic Books, 1977).

4 Robert Benne, *Quality with Soul: How Six Premier Colleges and Universities Keep Faith with Their Religious Traditions* (Grand Rapids, Mich.: Eerdmans, 2001), 48-53.

If, as Joeckel and Chesnes argue in Part One, Chapter One of this volume, the slippery-slope model is overdone and the dangers are not that rampant, then should conservative Protestant Christian colleges make way for a wider circle of consent and dissent within their faculties and administrative staffs? After all, while the secularization thesis certainly has historical merit to it, it does not follow that it is an inevitable one. At the very least, the global resistance to Western secularism should give one pause when assuming that Christian colleges in the United States must inevitably weaken their faith commitments as their academic standards are strengthened. At the same time, if nothing else, Marsden and Burtchaell help us identify potential pitfalls, and some of these are worth considering if we seek to expand the circle. As Marsden points out, the liberal vision of personal and academic freedom in the United States, ensconced in the American Academy of University Professors (AAUP) and in the disciplines themselves,[5] made the community freedom of faith-based institutions increasingly suspect, even irrational.[6] Freedom in this vision encourages, then demands, a privatization of religious practices and worldviews. In turn, Burtchaell also warns of a pattern of deferral to an academy that rendered Christian colleges "helpless to prevent their sense of religious self-identity from degrading into one of morals, then piety, then manners, then class or ethnicity or nationalism."[7] As such institutions allowed first their faculties, then their governance, to be motivated by academic and cultural respectability, they found themselves having to appeal to a lowest common denominator of belief. Most CCCU faculty members acknowledge that this pressure continues in some form or other.[8] If we are to expand our circles, in short, we cannot play by the rules of liberal secularism.

How might that enlarging proceed in a way that does not threaten our faith traditions? Admittedly, the process I am considering here requires not just faculty openness, but administrative and trustee support, staff awareness, and student responsiveness. It is impossible to consider all these factors here, but given willing trustees and a university president who ask the right questions for hiring, how might faculty at CCCU schools prepare the way for opening their circles? I would begin by suggesting that we need conscious and concentrated reflection on what Robert Bellah and associates, in their 1985 classic *Habits of the Heart,* call "communities of memory." A community of memory

---

5   In particular, the American Academy of University Professors' 1915 *Declaration of Principles,* its 1940 *Statement of Principles on Academic Freedom and Tenure* (with its 1970 Interpretative Comments and 1988 and 1996 Reviews) the 1967 *Joint Statement on Rights and Freedoms of Students,* as well as the deeply ideological 1986 *Observations on Ideology,* all attempt to balance conflicting goods in higher education, but at a cost to religious colleges. Phrased as questions, their concerns include: what responsibility do professors have to their professional disciplines, to their students, to their institutions, to the general public, and to the truth? And what kinds of freedom from government or administrative interference should they be afforded as a result? Moreover, what kinds of freedoms do students have, and are these freedoms extensions of the disciplinary freedoms? Equally of concern to colleges and universities with a religious purpose, should any protections be guaranteed to institutions, along with their faculties and student bodies, on the basis of faith confession?

6   George Marsden, *The Soul of the American University: From Protestant Establishment to Established Nonbelief* (Oxford: Oxford University Press, 1996), 397, 423, 433-440.

7   James Tunstead Burtchaell, *The Dying of the Light: The Disengagement of Colleges and Universities from Their Christian Churches* (Grand Rapids, Mich.: Eerdmans, 1998), 836.

8   Thus, at least half of survey respondents (54 percent; FSQ 97) believe that they have more freedom in their institutions than do their counterparts at secular institutions, and in large part (67.6 percent; FSQ 99) hold that the secular academy is dismissive of Christian scholarship.

ties together narratives of its history with preparation of its members for the future. It passes on its history to each generation by retelling its story, especially through and by accounts of exemplary persons. Such narratives focus on their virtues or vices, successes or failures, heroism and/or suffering, and by doing so, they should also give the community a sense of its possible future. Learning such stories inculcates faithful practices that strengthen the community.[9] For a Christian college, the community of memory is not just its immediate institutional one, but the collective memory of its larger Christian tradition, as well as the intertwining history it has with its sister traditions. This suggests that enlarging the circle of Christian confession in our schools will be in part a deeply historical project, one that focuses on exemplary Christian lives across our various pasts, including those of Roman Catholic and Eastern Orthodox origin. Serious attempts to include such stories in our chapel worship, in our faculty workshops, and in our curriculum can begin to cultivate the theological and ethical imaginations of our universities. In part we need this to inculcate a sense of loyalty to the larger Christian story, but we also need in many institutions to encourage faculty to identify with their institutions and not just their disciplinary profession.

However, the community of memory alone is not enough. A community can appear to keep faith with its memory even as it morphs in radical ways. For example, too often Christian colleges give lip service to an Enlightenment narrative of diversity and tolerance without asking to what end these values are given. As Wendy Brown, A. J. Conyers, and Susan Mendus have shown from differing perspectives, the rhetoric of tolerance has often served to engender the nation-state while limiting and even eliminating local communities of gender, ethnicity, and faith.[10] Nonetheless, even if we acknowledge that the "communitarian individual," to borrow Jean Bethke Elshtain's term,[11] is formed and informed by a number of other persons and social groupings, for the Christian not just any individual freedom will do, nor just any community freedom. What *Habits of the Heart* overlooks is how to judge whether a community is staying faithful to its past. Not every new narrative or new practice that arises, even with the past in mind, can be said to stay true to its formative beginnings.

While CCCU faculties should recognize that we are part of communities of memory, we also need to be reflective on the nature of healthy traditions. Alasdair MacIntyre's *After Virtue* continues to offer a thoughtful definition of a tradition as a growing, intentional, and directional social practice. He defines a tradition thusly: "Any coherent and complex form of socially established cooperative human activity through which goods internal to that form of activity are realized in the course of trying to achieve those

---

9 Robert Bellah, et al., *Habits of the Heart: Individualism and Commitment in American Life,* updated ed. (Berkeley: University of California Press, 1996), 153-154.

10 Wendy Brown, *Regulating Aversion: Tolerance in the Age of Identity and Empire* (Princeton: Princeton University Press, 2006); A. J. Conyers, *The Long Truce: How Toleration Made the World Safe for Power and Profit* (Dallas: Spence, 2001); and Susan Mendus, *The Politics of Toleration in Modern Life* (Durham, N.C.: Duke University Press, 2000).

11 Jean Bethke Elshtain, "The Communitarian Individual," in *New Communitarian Thinking: Persons, Virtues, Institutions, and Communities,* ed. Amitai Etzioni (Charlottesville: University Press of Virginia, 1995), 99-109.

standards of excellence which are appropriate to, and partially definitive of, that form of activity, with the result that human powers to achieve excellence, and the human conceptions of the ends and good involved, are systematically extended."[12] Much like learning to play a musical instrument or a sport, traditions have at their heart certain pursuits and goods that are shared by their practitioners, and as its goods are lived out, the tradition further refines the meaning of those goals. If we accept that the end of Christian cultural practices is the love of God and neighbor, the increase of shalom, and/or "to glorify God and enjoy him forever," then such ends orient the academic virtues that we seek to inculcate in students. While diversity, for example, is a great good within our confessional traditions, its purpose is not an unquestioning acceptance of the post-modern consensus but rather the promotion of the charity and harmony of God's peace. What MacIntyre reminds us is that tradition does not imply that a Christian college need never change its approaches or structure. There may be (indeed often are) new ways to pursue agreed-upon goals. It is possible for a tradition to be adaptive, yet failing or succeeding insofar as it continues to refine and clarify its search for particular goods with an overarching "hypergood" in mind (to use Charles Taylor's term).[13] If the true *telos* of the tradition is lost, the tradition ceases to be faithful to its beginnings. The pursuit of tolerance can be judged to have failed at a Christian institution if it results in an increasing distrust of theological discourse or New Testament ethics, intermediate practices that have as their end the truth about God's word and God's world.

How might, then, a CCCU college faculty, with MacIntyre's formulation in mind, expand the circle of confession while avoiding a weakening of its doctrinal and ethical commitments? How might we continue to pursue our chief faith ends in an academic manner even as we adapt in other ways? We should begin with a deep engagement with our doctrinal and denominational pasts. CCCU schools need to engage more fully our histories, not just in pursuit of positive examples, but also with a deep study of their beliefs and formative events. We need a closer study of the contexts that formed us and more detailed discussions of how these do or can undergird our current academic pursuits. In our often post-denominational situation, Christian schools are faced with the double-sided challenge of relearning the narratives of their own denominational and interdenominational past as well as the global narrative of historic Christianity. Yet a clear sense of denominational history and of its doctrine, its liturgy, and its hermeneutic is essential to our institutions if we are to continue in an orthodox, recognizable form into the future.

We can gain facility with our histories by an intentional practice of academic dialogue with other positions and communities. Of course, we already do this to some extent. Most of our institutions study a broad variety of perspectives, Christian and non-Christian, and to a greater or lesser degree engage persons outside our faith traditions as guest speakers, interviewees, and so on. However, if we are ever to hire Christians outside

---

12   Alasdair MacIntyre, *After Virtue*, 2nd ed. (Notre Dame, Ind.: University of Notre Dame Press, 1984), 187.

13   Charles Taylor, *Sources of the Self: The Making of Modern Identity* (Cambridge, Mass.: Harvard University Press, 1989), 63-73.

our immediate circles, we will need to further clarify the differences between evangelistic engagement, interreligious dialogue, cooperative collaboration, and thick ecumenism. The latter is important because, in hiring someone as a member of our faculties, we are inviting him or her into a deeper formative engagement with the life of the school and its academic future. What would a practice of thick ecumenism look like, and how should it be guided by the kind of teleological practice that MacIntyre outlines? I would argue for the following six characteristics as a bare minimum:

- It must of necessity be more than "mere Christianity": a simple consensus is not enough.
- It must be historical in its descriptions, for we are not mere individuals cut off from our communities across space and time.
- It must be truly thick in its descriptions, something at which our academic cultures are particularly good, given the chance.
- It must be true in its descriptions, avoiding distortions of others and their communities.
- It must be eschatological in its impulses, seeking to hold past and future together.
- It must recognize the historical stability of the traditions within the conversation, yet work against the hardening of these traditions.

Part of what I am assuming here is that working towards the healing of the division of Christianity is a good thing, something which is at the heart of Jesus' prayer in John 17 "that we all may be one." Thick ecumenism can certainly begin with a thin consensus of common confession, but it cannot stay there because the central doctrines of the faith intersect and branch out in their numerous implications for all of life. Even C. S. Lewis, who employed the term "mere Christianity," acknowledged that one eventually had to leave the hallway of mere consensus for the rooms where faith traditions actually live and abide.[14] What we believe about the nature of salvation, for example, has implications as to what we believe about the Church, the last things, confession and forgiveness, the language of prayer, ethical decision-making, our relation to other belief systems, and so forth. Ecumenism at its best promotes a hospitable conversation among Christian traditions, searching for points of commonality and difference. It is not a simple exercise in comparative theology, liturgy, or spirituality. Unfortunately, the ecumenical project in the mainline has often been co-opted by either mere consensus or by agendas alien to orthodox Christianity.[15] Instead, our hope should be that this conversation will mutually illuminate all involved and that this illumination will offer a continued course correction

---

14   C. S. Lewis, *Mere Christianity* (New York: Collier Books, 1952), 12.

15   I do acknowledge that throughout this essay I am assuming that CCCU schools would primarily be interested in hiring other Christians who can confess the fundamentals of the faith as found in the Apostles and Nicene Creeds. I do, however, understand that the question of what actually constitutes orthodoxy is itself a point of debate.

in doctrinal development and polity. The true "mere Christianity" is, in one sense, still waiting for us in the *eschaton*.

Here, then, is where a vision of thick ecumenism can help us. If and when we invite members of a different denominational tradition to be part of our faculties, we should be inviting them to assist in the pursuit of our orienting hyper-goods. They agree to enter our conversation and practice, not on the basis of mere consensus or by way of a secularist or pluralist practice of privatization, but thickly engaged with how their own tradition has interacted and should interact with ours. Admittedly, mapping out ahead of time how this will proceed is difficult to predict since the truth is in the details, but I do think we can gain a general sense of what would be needed. The guiding distinctives of our traditions obviously have much to say about the academic enterprise. The Orthodox stress on lived theology and *theosis*; the Wesleyan quadrilateral of reason, Scripture, tradition, and experience; the Roman Catholic balance of nature and grace, faith and reason; the Reformed stress on Christ as transformer of cultures; the Mennonite stress on peace and justice; the Baptist conversation surrounding soul competency and congregational discipline, just to name a few, are each going to offer a different tone to our academics due to variations in our histories and emphases, and thus these distinctives will guide their professors differently. (I mean the term "professor" here in both its confessional and academic senses.) A Baptist school hiring a Mennonite will begin the conversation around different matters than a Reformed school hiring a Methodist or a pan-evangelical institution hiring an Eastern Orthodox. And hopefully, after hiring, this conversation would only deepen over time and careers.

What we should not do, however, is begin the conversation at the point of deepest tension. We need to begin with the broad consensus that we do share and practice hearing each other when our vocabularies of choice are slightly different. Take, for instance, David Bebbington's famous quadrilateral of evangelicalism. Bebbington finds the following always present in evangelicalism: "*conversionism*, the belief that lives need to be changed; *activism*, the expression of the gospel in effort; *biblicism*, a particular regard for the Bible; *crucicentrism*, a stress on the sacrifice of Christ on the cross."[16] Southern Baptists and United Pentecostals would share much—similar senses of the need for a decision to follow Jesus; a history of cultural engagement often despite a rhetoric of embattlement; a high place for Scripture in the life of Christian practice; and often very similar views of the atonement and hymnology. Yet obviously there would also be important differences in their history and stress—most Baptists being distrustful of a doctrine of second blessing, tepid about the manifestation of the miraculous, and often surprised by differences in hermeneutical tones and shades. Some might find these differences on the surface less important in, say, the teaching of biology or sociology versus philosophy or theology, but even in the former these beliefs have some level of impact upon faculty

---

16   David W. Bebbington, *Evangelicalism in Modern Britain: A History from the 1730s to the 1980s* (London: Routledge, 1989), 3. I confess to a bit of a subversive impulse here because I do recognize that neither all Baptists nor all Pentecostals would consider themselves evangelical, to begin with. Nonetheless, I think Bebbington's categories are shared by these two groups and would make a useful place to start.

and students in conversation, on role models, mentorships, choices of churches, and ministries with which to partner.

There ought to be a clear sense of the overall goals of the institution when it hires faculty from the other traditions. This ought to include a conversation about the nature of belief and Scripture. CCCU faculty overall tend to have fairly stable beliefs about the Bible, though they recognize that their beliefs can change over time,[17] and while they have diverse feelings about a belief in biblical inerrancy (FSQ 36), they overall regard the Scriptures as authoritative (FSQ 33). At the same time, this high biblicism does not prevent over half of faculty from accepting other authorities to some degree as having truths to teach about God (FSQ 32) or from allowing others to question the Bible (FSQ 34). How might these committed yet flexible attitudes manifest themselves in including our theological counterparts?

In 2006, Alan Jacobs of Wheaton College examined in *First Things* the case of Joshua Hochschild, then assistant professor of philosophy at Wheaton, whose contract was not renewed when he converted to Roman Catholicism. Hochschild believed that he could as a self-identified "evangelical Catholic" profess and agree with Wheaton's statement of faith, while the college's president, Duane Litfin, held that what Hochschild could affirm was not the entire intent of Wheaton's Protestant evangelical founders. Jacobs believes that Wheaton ultimately lost something in not extending Hochschild's contract, but even he acknowledges that the scenario of a Catholic faculty member who believes in the Immaculate Conception of Mary would not be an easy and seamless transition for a school such as Wheaton: "I am sure President Litfin has thought more than a few times of how he might handle the first phone call from a Baptist or Presbyterian parent irate because his daughter, under the influence of a charismatic Catholic professor, has just expressed (while nervously clicking the beads of her rosary) her desire to be received into Mother Church."[18] Of course, such conversions are happening anyway, as many CCCU faculty will attest, even without hiring RCC faculty members. Jacobs concludes that history may not be on Wheaton's side much longer, and that the future will force us, Orthodox, Catholic, and Protestant, to work and teach side-by-side. His scenario points to an important aspect of just how and under what conditions of practice professors of one Christian tradition might go about teaching and mentoring students of another: Do we possess the character to be orthodox yet inclusive?

The findings of the Joeckel/Chesnes survey should give us hope in these matters. Most faculty (87.4 percent; FSQ 35) believe that theological diversity is good for a Christian university, and in large part (83.5 percent; FSQ 79) most find that "a spirit of humility and charity" among faculty exists in their institutions and to a less, but still substantial, extent between administration and faculty (59.9 percent; FSQ 81). What we cannot forget here, I would argue, is that our differences are not to be checked at the door, but neither are they simply to be ignored as irrelevant; rather, we are to find within our

---

17   60.6 percent noted that their interpretation of Scripture had not changed in the previous year (FSQ 30), but 58.6 percent recognized that it could in the future (FSQ 31).

18   Alan Jacobs, "To Be a Christian College," *First Things* (April 2006), 19.

traditions the rationale for assisting each other in a thickly ecumenical manner. What, then, are the virtues necessary for this to happen in a deeply Christian way? As Parker Palmer explains, "If truth is personal and communal, then our search for the truth—and truth's search for us—will neither actively suppress nor passively concede our differences, but will invite them to interact in faithful relationship."[19] Personalism at its best challenges us to recognize that the narratives of our lives are integral to such a project, that our Christian faith is tied to these journeys, including our academic journeys, and somehow they must be incorporated into a thick ecumenism. Our individual freedom as morally aware beings with openness to the future is tied to our place in community, "our rootedness," as Simone Weil was wont to stress.[20] Parker Palmer argues that the community in obedience to the truth is neither a civic community nor a therapeutic one. The civic community is a "relation of strangers . . . who must learn to hang together lest they hang separately," while the therapeutic community too easily equates emotional intimacy with community. Academic rigor, instead, requires "an ethos of trust and acceptance."[21] The experience of the Christian university, especially, should challenge the notion that we are citizen strangers existing in a weary social compact of tolerance for mere survival. An ecumenism that is truly deep and interlaced can do better than this.

Theologian Elizabeth Newman has written on several occasions about the nature of Christian hospitality and its epistemological and ethical benefits. She wryly observes, "The Christian conviction that our final end is the love and service of God interrupts rational liberal discourse and therefore seems out of place," or as Richard Rorty sums it up: "They [theists] are crazy because the limits of sanity are set by what *we* [the heirs of the Enlightenment] can take seriously."[22] Since this issue has been dealt with ably in other places, I do not see the need here to mount an extensive critique of the Enlightenment claim to objectivity or of neo-pragmatic visions like that of Rorty. Nor am I denying that a willingness to test the various traditions that form one's own (or a student's) self-understanding is a necessary part of higher education. Nonetheless, there is a sense in which we need to understand that even our disagreements must derive from and be oriented toward something other than radical individualism. As Newman observes, "What the world of Rorty and [John] Rawls cannot allow is that saints like Ignatius of Loyola do not simply choose their final end out of a number of possibilities . . . . Ignatius did not choose to love and serve God but rather was *given* the grace and power to do so in a way so compelling he could not do otherwise. He thus lived out a very different political vision from the one embraced by Rorty and Rawls."[23] Newman's point is that the

19   Parker Palmer, *To Know as We Are Known: Education as a Spiritual Journey* (San Francisco: HarperOne, 1993), 66.

20   Simone Weil, *The Need for Roots*, trans. Arthur Willis (London: Routledge, 2002), 43-44.

21   Palmer, *To Known as We Are Known*, xiii, xvii. Of course, Palmer is addressing a far larger academic scope than the one I have in mind here, but his basic insight is one that resonates with orthodox Christian ontology and epistemology.

22   Quoted in Elizabeth Newman, *Untamed Hospitality: Welcoming God and Other Strangers* (Grand Rapids, Mich.: Brazos, 2007), 124.

23   Newman, *Untamed Hospitality*, 124. Also cf. Elizabeth Newman, "The Politics of Higher Education: How the Love of Hospitality Offers An Alternative," in *The Scholarly Vocation and the Baptist Academy*, eds. Roger Ward and

way we go about dialogue and inclusion is markedly different than that of the secular, liberal vision. As Christians we are formed by being the Body of Christ; we share the possibility of searching for a common good that arises out of our sharing in faith, hope, and love; we partake of the Triune fellowship of God and thus can know a measure of friendship that arises out of a commitment to speaking the truth in love. Of course, it is one thing to give assent to this in theory, quite another in practice. Yet, if this becomes the *telos* that orients our enlarging of the circle, then we may just find that our reasons for ecumenical inclusion are different from the mainline academy, as are our choices for how we go about it.

Talking in these terms does not excuse us from the hard work of crafting policies and practices that enshrine these ideals. Factors include not only intentional conversations about church history, theology, and spiritual practice, but also the daily practice of embodied living, teaching, and research. We will need to address the specifics of contract renewal, tenure (when applicable), committee service, faculty development, and departmental specifics. (For example, some Christian universities might find the hiring of a faculty member outside the confessional circle more acceptable in Business as opposed to Theology.) We will have to think long and hard about valuing each faculty member as a person made in God's image even as we also maintain the community's freedom to continue to keep faith with its past. We will also need specific academic and spiritual practices that shape us ecumenically in pursuit of our chief ends as Christian schools. If we hold to a belief that the marriage supper of the Lamb is what awaits us in the eschaton, then the dominant metaphor of our engagement is not that of negotiation and compromise, but of feasting and fellowship.

In light of this hope, instead of Lewis's metaphor of separate rooms, Kevin J. Vanhoozer employs the image of table fellowship in which the varying interpretative traditions and practices come with their noisy conversation to sup together, not just for a rowdy table-pounding boasting match, nor for a polite "no-offense-intended" high tea, but for a true family meal. Vanhoozer points out that this family diversity has its very legitimacy in the "Pentecostal plurality" of Scripture's own canonical diversity. We sup together that we might become stronger together. We are about more than sampling each other's dishes in smorgasbord gluttony; we are learning to "taste" better by cultivating together a culinary delight in all that is true and beautiful.[24] Such a gourmet practice should be the mark of the Christian university. We risk distorting Christianity, as well as other Christians, when with narrow blinders we see our own beliefs, churches, or denominations as the sole keeper of the faith. Our judgments of history are what make ethical constants and ecumenical Christianity possible. While we wait for the marriage supper, we now gather around the Lord's Table with our partial traditions on our bent backs. Even noisy table fellowship has certain rules of conduct, and the ones who are hosting the meal have a certain precedent as to what fare is offered and in what order

---

David P. Gushee (Macon, Ga.: Mercer University Press, 2008), 166-196.

24   Kevin J. Vanhoozer, *The Drama of Doctrine: A Canonical Linguistic Approach to Christian Theology* (Louisville: Westminster John Knox, 2005), 272-278.

the courses come. To follow the metaphor through to the end, the question that remains for CCCU schools is how to invite new cooks to join in meal preparation in such a way that the fundamental character of the cuisine does not change but rather discovers its own innate possibilities. Table fellowship has many a story worth telling, but then, so does cooking in the kitchen.

CHAPTER 5

FAITH AND CAMPUS CULTURE

Are Faculty and Students
on the Same Page?

CAROL WOODFIN

Faculty and students share a common faith experience on campus, yet diverge in some surprising ways. My main conclusion from the Joeckel/Chesnes survey is that students in Council for Christian Colleges and Universities (CCCU) schools are more open-minded and willing to question their faith and deal with controversial issues than faculty perceive. Secondly, students, while remaining theologically conservative, are in some instances *less* conservative than faculty. Finally, the Christian "atmosphere" on campus—chapel, the numerous opportunities for Bible studies, mission trips, or other ministries—often touted as attractive by faculty, students, parents, administrators, student development officers, and outside constituencies has a surprisingly *negative* effect on the faith development of many students.

Theologically, 68.8 percent of faculty identified themselves as conservative, yet one-fifth (20.8 percent) called themselves theological liberals (FSQ 5). Of the faculty, 31.6 percent did *not* identify themselves as being conservative. Students identifying themselves in the theologically conservative ranks amounted to 59.8 percent of survey respondents (SSQ 10), nine percentage points *fewer* than faculty. As with faculty, the strongest percentage of student answers was "somewhat conservative" (44.9 percent, close to the faculty's 46.4 percent). Significantly fewer students than faculty, however, were strongly conservative theologically with 14.9 percent (compared to 22.4 percent of faculty). Students in the liberal camp comprised 17.8 percent of respondents, only slightly less than that of faculty, with both at about 20 percent. Adding in those students who were not Christians at 1.2 percent (not an option for CCCU faculty) and those who answered neutral (21.1 percent) means 41.1 percent of students did not identify themselves as theological conservatives, compared to 31.6 percent of faculty. Thus, our students are not identifying themselves as theologically conservative as frequently as are faculty, an interesting result and something that should encourage hesitant or fearful faculty to become more comfortable addressing controversial issues. On some specific issues, however, students were more often in the "conservative" camp than faculty.

Faculty showed variety on whether the Bible is "the only authoritative source of information about God": 56.2 percent agreed, but 38.5 percent disagreed (FSQ 32). Student responses to the same question showed 70.8 percent agreed; 11.1 percent were neutral; and 19.1 percent disagreed (SSQ 23). On the claim of biblical authority as the only source of authoritative information about God, therefore, students more strongly affirmed it than did faculty.

Faculty admitting to having doubts over the Bible's authority in the past year were rare (FSQ 33), with only 12.7 percent agreeing they *had* had doubts, compared to 79.0 percent who claimed *not* to have had doubts. Though few faculty admitted their own doubts, 70.2 percent agreed "It is acceptable to question the Bible," while 17.6 percent did not (FSQ 34) and 87.4 percent agreed that "diversity of theological opinions among faculty and students is healthy for a Christian college/university" (FSQ 35), while only 6.8 percent strongly or somewhat disagreed. Most (70.3 percent) believed Roman Catholics should be able to teach at traditionally Protestant universities (FSQ 29). No survey questions dealt with other non-Protestant Christians, or whether someone of a different Protestant denomination from the school's sponsoring body would be welcomed. Nor was there a student question referring to more religious diversity among the faculty. Philip Irving Mitchell's essay in this volume explores the significance of having a more denominationally diverse faculty, making compelling points about the ways in which more diversity would allow not only representation of more viewpoints, but also a currently missed opportunity for faculty at single denominational schools to grow in their faith and appreciate their own traditions more deeply through their encounter and debates with those from other Christian traditions.

Few students had doubts about the Bible's authority over the past year: 69.7 percent had *not* had doubts, but 20.8 percent *did* have doubts (SSQ 24). More students admitted to having doubts about biblical authority than did faculty, and fewer had *not* had doubts. While faculty should hope such doubts will lead to spiritual growth, they are an indicator that students are less secure in or confident of their views on the Bible than faculty. Most students agreed, though, it was "acceptable to question the Bible" (61.2 percent), while 23.0 percent did not (SSQ 25), less than the faculty numbers.

Among faculty, 58.1 percent agreed on biblical inerrancy, while 28 percent did not (FSQ 36). Student belief in biblical inerrancy was strong (49.1 percent) but about one-fourth (24.6 percent) admitted they did not know what it was, and 10.0 percent stated they did not believe in it. Students agreeing with biblical inerrancy were thus fewer in number than the faculty, though fewer strongly stated they did *not* believe in inerrancy (SSQ 27).

A flashpoint along the "conservative" and "liberal" spectrum is the question of whether women have the right to become pastors. Among students, 38.7 percent, the highest sector, strongly agreed, and 18.1 percent somewhat agreed, for a total of 56.8 percent generally in favor of women pastors; 29.7 percent strongly or somewhat disagreed (SSQ

49). Faculty on this issue were more "liberal," with 54.5 percent strongly agreeing with a women's right to pastor; 16.5 percent somewhat agreeing—i.e., a total of 71.0 percent agreeing, 14.2 percentage points higher than the students. Fewer faculty than students somewhat or strongly agreed women should *not* have the right to become pastors: 21.3 percent (FSQ 70). This information is interesting in that most faculty respondents were men, while most student respondents were women (FSQ 2, SSQ 1), though it would be incorrect to assume that all women are pushing for female pastors or women's rights in general.

Faculty reported very solid church attendance with 93.3 percent attending at least once a week (FSQ 8). Even the "slackers" make it at least twice a month, while less than 2 percent admitted to attending only every six months or less. Solid church attendance is thus the norm among survey respondents. A similar question would have been interesting for students, especially in light of their comments on being surrounded by a Christian community on campus, which will be discussed below.

There is a solid picture of spiritual growth among faculty and students. The broad question (FSQ 17 and SSQ 16)—"As a result of the time I've spent at my college/university, my faith has . . ."—shows the faith of 79.8 percent of faculty has grown ("much stronger": 31.1 percent; "somewhat stronger": 48.7 percent). A fairly high number of faculty, 16.5 percent, said their faith had "stayed the same" while only 3.7 percent believed their faith became weaker as a result of their time at the university. Students also asserted their faith had become stronger as a result of the time at their institution (SSQ 16), with 34.6 percent saying it became much stronger and 44.0 percent somewhat stronger, for a total of 78.6 percent claiming growth in their faith, about the same as for faculty. The "stayed about the same" response was 17.3 percent for students (a high percentage, as with the faculty, which is difficult to assess and could be either positive or negative). Those whose faith became weaker was 4.8 percent, slightly higher than the faculty answer. The answers on growth in faith are positive; however, in both the student and faculty cases this growth may not be directly attributable to the fact of being at the university itself, but rather may have to do with church involvement or personal efforts at growth.

Of faculty respondents, 60.6 percent disagreed with the following statement: "My interpretation of the Bible has changed sometime within the past year" (FSQ 30). However, 58.6 percent agreed it was possible their interpretations might change in the future (FSQ 31). A large number, 72.7 percent, reported having few doubts about their faith in the past year, but 20 percent did (FSQ 37). There was not a question on whether students had doubts about their faith in general, as there was for the faculty.

Questions asked of students regarding biblical interpretation reveal that 61.8 percent agreed that their interpretation of the Bible had changed in the past year (SSQ 21), about the same as the faculty responses. Most students allowed for possible changes in interpretations in the future (SSQ 22) with 71.9 percent agreeing, 13.3 percentage points higher than the faculty. These responses suggest an openness that we as faculty may not adequately recognize in our students.

On the three main factors for spiritual growth on campus identified by the Joeckel/Chesnes survey—chapel attendance, classes, and faculty—the results show that faculty and students are growing in their faith due to the Christian campus culture. Faculty answers to "My college/university is a place of vibrant spiritual activity" show 81.6 percent affirming. Only 7.3 percent felt the campus was not such a place (FSQ 91). There was not a similar general question on the student survey. Other possible sources of growth, such as on-campus Bible studies, mission trips, or fellowship among students, have not been dealt with in the quantitative-data questions, but will be explored in the section on open-ended student answers, as will factors that inhibit student spiritual growth.

A slightly higher percentage of students (56.6 percent) agreed that chapel enhanced their faith than did faculty (49.4 percent). The neutral answers in both cases were very high (faculty: 27.3 percent; students: 20.9 percent). Fewer students than faculty felt chapel *did not* enhance their faith (16.9 percent of students, 20.9 percent of faculty; SSQ 13, FSQ 14).

Whether classes they have taken enhanced faith (SSQ 14), 77.8 percent of students agreed, higher than the positive response for chapel; 7.2 percent disagreed, another stronger indicator that classes more strongly enhanced faith than chapel. (Meanwhile, 81.7 percent of faculty agreed the classes they had taught had enhanced their faith [FSQ 15].) Exactly how a faculty member's faith was enhanced by the classes he or she taught remains unanswered. From my own experience, the ways would include research and preparation of the material, relationships developed with students in class due to discussions, particularly if there were faith issues involved, and establishing a rapport with students that then might lead to a good relationship outside of class where we could discuss important life issues. I am rarely inspired to grow spiritually by my own lectures. Some open-ended student comments reveal ways they have experienced faith in their classes.

Faculty responses to "Other faculty at this college/university have enhanced my faith" (FSQ 16) reveal that many faculty are talking with and learning from their colleagues, and growing spiritually as a result of this rapport. Students likewise experience most faith enhancement from their professors (SSQ 15). Of chapel, classes, and faculty, faculty comes out as the strongest factor in faith enhancement for both faculty and students (85.9 percent and 82.0 percent respectively), with classes second (81.7 percent for faculty; 77.8 percent for students), and chapel in third place (49.4 percent for faculty; 56.6 percent for students). In the cases of classes and faculty enhancing students' faith, the percentages were lower than those among faculty, while the percentage of students whose faith was enhanced by chapel was higher than that of the faculty.

Faculty were less than enthusiastic about chapel being or becoming mandatory for faculty (FSQ 26), with 57 percent disagreeing, while 27.3 percent agreed with mandatory chapel for faculty. The strongest percentage group were those who "strongly disagreed," with 35.3 percent. Views on mandatory chapel services for students were mixed as well (SSQ 35), with 41.5 percent in favor. A higher percentage disagreed that there should be mandatory chapel: 47.2 percent. The strongest percentage number, 29.8 percent, *strongly* disagreed about having mandatory chapel, not quite as high as the faculty.

Faculty and student concerns about chapel were that it was not culturally diverse enough or did not draw on enough worship traditions, such as the liturgical tradition

(FSQ 106, SSQ 56). One student of Irish, Scottish, and Cherokee background noted the lack of cultural diversity in chapel: "It's almost like going to a foreign country twice a week. Chapel is also way too loud—they try to make it into a hard rock concert" (SSQ 56). One respondent complained she did not like the contemporary worship style: "I have come to strongly hate worship music" (SSQ 55). Still another loathed the "awful contemporary Christian music, which no one else seems to notice is horrendous" (SSQ 56). One said the most difficult thing about being a student at a Christian university was "bad chapels" (SSQ 56). Another student said he enjoyed chapel services, but did not like the time it took up in a hectic day. One characterized some of her fellow students as "pop Christian" students, and disliked going to chapel where she had to "listen to the rock concert they call worship" (SSQ 56); another did not like the music, "but since that is the cool way to worship, the feeling is that I have to enjoy it or there's something wrong with me" (SSQ 56). One student tied mandatory chapel into a larger principle, claiming it was "equivalent to making religion mandatory within a nation, which defeats the entire purpose and destroys the sanctity of religion" (SSQ 56).

It was interesting that in neither the faculty nor the student open-ended responses that I explored were there any *specific* descriptions of wonderful chapel services. These views on chapel attendance from faculty and students deserve more research. Both the numerical and qualitative data of this survey do not point to many rebellious or resentful students (or faculty for that matter). We should reconsider the role of chapel on our campuses. Dismissing chapel requirements is considered one of the first steps down the "slippery slope" to secularism. We may not wish to eliminate chapel, but those in charge of this aspect of campus life should be interested in this part of the survey data. What ways other than *requiring* chapel could create a time and space for collective worship that truly draws from a variety of traditions, denominational customs, and musical styles? Such times of worship could be one way of promoting the kind of ecumenical interchange on campus that Mitchell called for in his essay in this volume. Colleges generally focus on the chapel *speaker* for the day or week (a very Protestant approach!). Instead, we could reduce the time and focus spent on preaching and speaking, and learn new ways to share a Christian "life together."[1] I have seen this attempted in morning prayers and Newman Club masses. We could also explore something similar to the Anglican Evensong. Bringing good preachers and speakers to campus is often a good encounter for faculty and students with other perspectives. But we must be more creative in enriching campus worship at more levels than music and preaching.

In the answers to the question on whether faculty believed Christian universities were superior to secular ones, one of the constant comments was that Christian higher education provided a holistic education, with faculty concerned not only about academics, but about the character and spiritual lives of their students (FSQ 104). Students "can express themselves as fully faithful beings." There was "freedom to express the reality of Christ." "We love our students and pray for them, and our office doors are open." A

1   See Dietrich Bonhoeffer, *Life Together* (San Francisco:HarperSanFrancisco, 1978).

Christian education better prepares students "to deal with the issues that are faced in real life" and provides "more exposure to a full range of ideas." Faculty care about students "as if the students are our own flesh and blood." These advantages were attributed to small classes, low student-to-faculty ratios, and institution size, as well as the sense of calling professors had to their profession that pushed them to care and to seek excellence.

Students offered similar answers as faculty when asked whether the education at a Christian university is superior to that at a secular school (SSQ 55). Though less likely to use the term "holistic," student comments indicated an appreciation for the emphasis in their educations on more than academics. Education at Christian colleges has "Christian under and overtones," wrote one student. Another cited "unparalleled bonds with class-mates and professors." "Classes seem warmer to me"; "Professors are motivated by more than just money and status, they actually care about you and your relationship with Christ," which makes students want to learn; "I have a reason and hope for learning. I am worshipping God through my learning"; "Christian schools cause students to think about their education as an opportunity rather than a means to an end. A Christian education opens students' eyes to the spiritual and moral questions of the world, asks them to search for meaning, gives them a longing for a purpose higher than themselves and their career goals." Students appreciated the fact that faith was not "compartmen-talized as irrelevant." They appreciated the sense of community, which they noted their friends did not have at state schools. Others wrote, "I love the Christian passion behind my professors' lessons"; "I am learning to live the life of the redeemed human being, not just the proud, wise, materialistic one"; the "Christian aspect" was not forced on students, but "we look at the truly hard 'problems/questions' and not everyone stays true in their faith once they have wrestled through them"; "All questions are fair game and we are very willing to listen to disagreeing viewpoints."

For purposes of my focus on faith and campus culture, heavy faculty course loads (FSQ 86) are relevant in that many faculty members indicated it interfered with their abil-ity to spend time with students, be a role model, and take a holistic interest in students outside the classroom. The highest percentage of faculty (38.3 percent) teaches four courses per semester or trimester (FSQ 86).[2] Added to course load is usually administra-tive work, committees, or sponsorship of student groups.

Faculty expressed concern that time constraints interfered with "trying to care about students beyond academics" (FSQ 106). Another found "balancing the parent-pastor-professor role" difficult (FSQ 106). Faculty with heavy workloads faced "the expectation that we are to be spiritual as well as academic mentors to individual students when our teaching is heavy and when our opportunities for research in our field are limited" (FSQ 106). Another found it difficult to balance demands of time "that flow from the holistic educational philosophy that leads to members of the faculty being involved in the spiritual, moral, social and physical development and well-being of our students, in

---

2   A fortunate 17.0 percent teach one to two courses, 30.8 percent teach three, and an unenviable 13.9 percent teach more than four.

addition to their intellectual development" (FSQ 105). Time was limited to "be a minister to students as well as stay active in my field" (FSQ 106). Others were concerned with modeling the life of a Christian to students and a fear that if they failed students could gain a negative impression of Christianity (FSQ 106).

These comments reveal that faculty take very seriously the role of mentoring and modeling the lives of Christians to their students, to the point of worrying about whether they were up to the task, and lamenting that there was not more time to invest in students and their spiritual development. There is significant frustration that faculty are not able to do more of it and do a better job.

Though academic freedom and academic rigor will be addressed by other authors in this volume as they relate to other matters, where they apply to faith and spiritual growth of students and faculty, they are worth briefly noting here as well. Most faculty believe they have academic freedom (86.7 percent, FSQ 96), but 9.7 percent did *not*. Most faculty (68.5 percent) did not feel restricted from dealing with "certain important issues in class because I teach at a Christian college/university" (FSQ 98); yet almost one-fourth (24.2 percent) *did* feel restricted. Some responses to FSQ 106 on the difficulties of being a professor at a Christian college do in fact reveal that hesitation and fear do exist on our campuses.

One respondent said she self-censored on certain topics. Some faculty feared expressing opinions on Christianity that were different from those of the administration. Too much "uniformity of thought" was another concern (FSQ 106). One wrote that students were only interested in "God stuff" and there was too much nurturing of their spiritual lives and not enough focus on academics (FSQ 106). "Student expectation of grace and mercy for their repeated sloth and shoddy work," and "being merciful and understanding without being an enabler of poor student habits" may ring too true to many of us (FSQ 106).

Expressing the issue of faculty hesitation to address some issues in the classroom in a more sanguine manner was one professor who faced "the delicate and high stakes balance of helping [students] maintain/preserve their faith while simultaneously helping them open their worldview up to new ideas and ways of thinking as educated persons" (FSQ 106). The lack of diversity among students leads them to assume they are right, so they are not open to explore issues, complained another professor. "Dissent of any sort, or questioning of some sorts, is viewed as very dangerous" (FSQ 106).

As the next section will show, students describing their difficulties as students at Christian universities face some of the same hesitations and fears—perhaps even more— as faculty if what they thought and believed were outside the general faith climate on campus. The students' comments are strong and eloquent, and should stir faculty to reassess concerns about students' willingness to be challenged in their faith.

I found the open-ended answers to the question "What is the most difficult thing about being a student at a Christian college/university?" (SSQ56) to contain the most interesting data. Because this question asked about difficulties, the answers show students' problems. This should not give the impression that students are unhappy with their decision to attend a Christian university.[3] Over 90 percent of students agreed that their decision to attend a Christian institution was a good one (SSQ 11).

After reading faculty comments about narrow-minded and sheltered students, I expected to find numerous student complaints that their professors were too "liberal" or were negatively challenging their faith. I thought I would encounter evidence of student resistance to being challenged to think more critically about their faith and difficult questions. The opposite was true. Only about twenty students complained about faculty not being Christians, not being good Christians, teaching them things different from what they believed, or failing to integrate Christianity into their classes enough or at all (SSQ 56).

Most students believed their lives were sheltered or somewhat sheltered at their college or university (62.9 percent; SSQ 34). In addition, 27.1 percent of faculty said students are sheltered; 21.1 percent said they are not; and 51.8 percent said somewhat sheltered (FSQ 50). Most, if not all, students were—sometimes almost desperately— *longing* for more questioning and challenges, even to their faith. Though some were glad to be in a sheltered environment where they could explore issues without ridicule, others were disappointed they were not more frequently challenged or in contact with more religious diversity among students and faculty. Said one student, "I feel sometimes that an all Christian university hurts students by not showing them the true mosaic of humanity" (SSQ 56). The most common student complaint was that they felt as if they were living in a "bubble." The word "bubble," in fact, appears 134 times in student responses to SSQ 55 and SSQ 56.

A very common lament, and one that surprised me, was that being in a sheltered, Christian environment was actually causing many students to become complacent in their faith, or even hurting their faith. Since most students, based on the quantitative data, fall into the theologically conservative range, these responses were too common to be coming only from "liberal" or disgruntled or rebellious students.

Many students complained that both faculty and students assume all students think alike, that there is a closed-mindedness on campus, or that they were *stereotyped* as being closed minded. One, interestingly, said religion was not even discussed that much on campus because everyone (falsely) believed others thought the same on religious issues. Many looked askance at other students for being narrow minded or "naïve and conservative" (SSQ 56). Some said it was wrong for Christian universities not to challenge such views but instead further shelter them: "I love my professors, but the student body is very sheltered and ignorant" (SSQ 56). One complained, "95 percent of our students are cookie cutter images of their parents. They don't have their own identity, belief system, core values, and they are the most judgmental of all. Plus, more than half of the students don't practice what they preach" (SSQ 56). One expressed his irritation at the "'I was saved when I was three' students" (SSQ 56).

---

3   91.8 percent of students claimed they were pleased with their decision to attend a Christian university, with only 3.2 percent unhappy with their decision (SQ11).

"Schools do a poor job of exposing new perspectives on Christ," said one student who did not like teaching that came across as the final authority on faith (SSQ 56). Others complained about the "narrow-mindedness of the faculty and students" and the "one-sided opinions being presented as fact" (SSQ 56). One said the most difficult thing was "having Christianity forced upon you . . . [with] little room to refute God, to argue with him and find your own way." Another wrote she was always being told what the Bible means, when there were multiple ways to interpret things (SSQ 55). Another said "diverse opinions are not appreciated" as they should be in higher education, though admitting most professors did let students grow and find themselves (SSQ 56).

One who *was* being challenged in his faith wrote that it was difficult, but good for him (SSQ 56). Still another realized she was "being challenged to take my faith to the next level," though she was experiencing some self-doubt, even depression, but trusting in God nevertheless (SSQ 56). Another admitted to struggling with her faith, but realized this was not a bad thing: "I have realized my faith is very much not my own, and am in the process of re-examining what my relationship with God means to me." She was, however, getting some flak from other students for not being a "cookie-cutter Christian" like the majority at the school. This student concluded, "The pressure to be the 'right' kind of Christian is overwhelming" (SSQ 56).

Some students' comments on professors' efforts to integrate faith and learning or on how faith was frequently brought into the classroom were negative: "I do not like that God is referenced in my classes. I am in college to learn about my major not to study Christianity" (SSQ56), and "I get frustrated when my professors preach more than they teach" (SSQ 56). One said the most difficult thing for him was "Dealing with professors who quote from the Bible while being lazy and failing to be diligent in their job" (SSQ 56). "[T]he professors tend to let religion interfere with the science of what needs to be taught. Religion should not affect how a professor teaches certain subjects" (SSQ 56). One criticized professors' prayers before class as "phony," commenting, "One even read his prayer from a 'cheat sheet,'" though the student had to admit she peeked in order to gain this knowledge (SSQ 56).

Several students complained that the lack of diversity limited their growth, because they did not have to defend their faith or learn from those of other faiths. "I miss being on the 'front line' and being around a diverse group of people" (SSQ 56). One whose friends in high school were non-Christians, including Hindus, Buddhists, and Satanists, found it hard to be around Christians all the time. He felt being only around Christians was making him *less* tolerant and open to diversity (SSQ 56). Another said she was "not surrounded with other opinions and views which results in me not knowing how to respond to people of other faiths or no faith" (SSQ 56). Others noted the lack of evangelistic opportunities on an all-Christian campus.

On the issue of student hypocrisy, 36.4 percent of faculty agreed with the statement, "Religious hypocrisy among students is a problem at my college/university"; 38.8 percent disagreed, while 24.8 percent remained neutral on this question, a higher neutral response than for most questions (FSQ 93). Since the student data reveal great concern about hypocrisy, these responses could indicate that faculty do not know their students very well, or since they see students' public images more than how they act outside of class, levels of student hypocrisy may be unknown to the faculty. There was not a quantitative question asking *students* to assess student or faculty hypocrisy.

Many students did, however, complain of hypocrisy among students, those who judged others, those who were superficial in their faith, or those who did not challenge them as fellow Christians to develop. One wrote: "It was hard to find Christians willing to be 'real' who would help them sharpen their faith" (SSQ 56). One said he was "always watching [his] back" because of judgmental people (SSQ 56). One even said there was "shunning" on campus (SSQ 56). One student put the problem vividly when she complained of those on campus who were judgmental and "think because they are Christians they can throw the Bible at you. Right and wrong are right and wrong, but even Jesus didn't throw the Bible at people" (SSQ 56).

Some students were irritated by pressure from other students to become involved in an overabundance of Christian activities. Another said people expected your life always to be "peachy keen" (SSQ 56), so it was hard to face struggles and not be judged, or to find a good listening ear. In a poignant expression of concern, one noted, "All of the people living in quiet desperation is tough. There is a lot of hiding here, a lot of deception" and lying to keep rules which are "little more than Bible camp dos and don'ts" (SSQ 56).

Many students felt they and others were just going through the motions of Christianity. They felt they would be more pro-active about their faith if they were at secular universities, perhaps actively seeking out Christian fellowship or Bible study groups or going to a local church more frequently (SSQ 56). One said he had grown up in a Christian family and that Christianity had become "too run of the mill for me" (SSQ 56).

Many felt students were not living out their faith since it was "easy to get lazy and make excuses that you were going to chapel and getting the Christian teaching, praying, etc. all the time. It is hard to remain consistent with your personal devotions and not just faking with the actions [*sic*] in the setting you are in" (SSQ 56). The prevalence of a Christian atmosphere on campus gave some a false sense of security in their faith, a lukewarmness, or spiritual apathy. "It becomes really easy to flow with the 'I'm religious' crowd" (SSQ 56). Some admitted they "don't put effort into their walk with Christ because they feel as though they'll grow through being in the 'Christian' environment" (SSQ 56). One lamented something she called "faith floating"—that is, not being challenged to think about faith so "you just float" (SSQ 56). Another wrote of experiencing a "God overload" (SSQ 56), while another said, "Everything is churched out of me here . . . jammed into me everywhere. I get so sick of it" (SSQ 56).

One student went so far as to claim, "I really strongly believe that being at a Christian university is the most dangerous place for a Christian to be. It is so easy to become stagnant in one's faith and just 'go with the flow.' It is so easy to fall into the temptation of just going through the motions and doing what a 'good Christian' should do. I find it hard to go to chapel and other events simply because I feel led to; it is always because I feel like I should or that people will judge me if I don't" (SSQ 56).

Conclusion

One of the great strengths faculty respondents to the survey noted about Christian higher education was that it is "holistic." Faculty at Christian schools are concerned not only about academics, but also about the student as a human being. Yet, according to answers to the question about difficulties of being a professor at a Christian institution, numerous factors may limit a professor's ability to become involved in students' lives, such as time constraints, course load, and committee demands. The fact that many professors seem to fear being honest and open with their students also inhibits offering a holistic education to our students. If professors were more aware of the student responses of the Joeckel/Chesnes survey, things could be very different. Students seem to be longing for more honesty and openness among their peers. The recurrence of the term "bubble" by students to describe their Christian campuses suggests a negative side of the Christian college experience for students that needs to be taken into account as faculty are trying to integrate faith and learning, and as student-life and campus-ministries directors plan Christian opportunities for students on campus. Students complained about the ease of becoming "complacent" or "lazy" in their faith since they were constantly surrounded by Christians and Christian activity. Faculty at CCCU institutions should take a long, hard look at whether some of what they are trying to do on Christian campuses has become, or may become, counterproductive.

I offer the proposition that we should consider scaling back some of the "Christianness" of our campuses. By this, I mean the outward image of a very vocal and energetic type of Christian experience and an overabundance of on-campus ministry options. What can be detrimental to spiritual growth is when there is a presumption among students, faculty, or administrators that a certain type of "God talk" means one is better spiritually, or that Christian commitment can be assessed by how active students are in campus Bible studies, worship teams, and mission trips. I do not advocate doing away with ministry and discipleship activities for students. Nor am I saying that a particular expression of the evangelical faith is not valid. But, as many students observed, they were getting an overload. Local churches, community ministries, and students themselves could all benefit from more encouragement to step out of or even to pop the "bubble" of being around campus Christians almost all the time. I have been wrong in the past to conclude that a Christian environment on campus was always conducive to Christian growth. Students expressed concern about the constant exposure to Christians and Christian thinking. These students are not just those who self-describe as more "liberal" than other students or those who are non-Christians. Students want more diversity in thought and experience.

I came away from my data analysis with a renewed commitment to challenge my students to think more deeply and to lighten up on my concerns about dealing with controversial issues.

My plea to other faculty, based on my interpretation of the survey data, is to become more "real," as the students put it, less hesitant about presenting a diversity of ideas to students, even on controversial faith issues, even challenging them to think more deeply about their faith and life's questions in ways they have never done. They can take it. There is no need for faculty to show contempt for students' current beliefs, nor reason to be aggressive in our challenges. Nor should we desire immediate change or conclude that *our* faith is the most valid and true. But challenge students we must. Probably few faculty would disagree that challenging students to think is a major goal of our teaching. Perhaps the results of this study can help us face the task with renewed confidence that many of our students will join us in the quest and lead us to become stronger in our teaching—and in our faith.

FAITH AND CAMPUS CULTURE

Living and Learning in the Questions

WAYNE BARNARD

CHAPTER 6

"Faith is being sure of what we hope for and certain of what we do not see." **—Hebrews 11:1**

"The only appropriate attitude for man to have about the big questions is not the arrogant certitude that is the hallmark of religion, but doubt." **—Bill Maher**

Having worked with adolescents and university students for more than thirty years, and now having been away from campus leadership for more than two years, I approach the Joeckel and Chesnes data with an informed and experienced, but also fresh, perspective. I now interact across the United States with university students from varied campus cultures—secular and faith-based, public and private—expanding my perspective of the Christian college phenomenon, especially as it relates to faith and campus culture. The intentional integration of faith and learning throughout the four-year undergraduate Christian higher education curriculum is clearly absent for students on secular campuses. Even students who are actively involved in Christian campus ministries—Campus Crusade for Christ, InterVarsity Christian Fellowship, Coalition for Christian Outreach, Reformed University Fellowship, Kai Alpha, and many others—do not have the same opportunities for the comprehensive integration of faith and learning that can and does happen with faith-based institutions.

The present volume provides yet another opportunity to test the claim that the "Christian university seeks to provide an overarching framework that gives a sense of purpose and unity for everything from English Literature to chapel to intramural soccer."[1] Campus culture is both created and sustained by the realities of the classroom, residence hall, sports arena, boardroom, alumni gatherings, and chapel. Both policies and practices reflexively instruct and construct the culture that exists on the campuses of faith-based institutions of higher education. Philip Irvin Mitchell's argument for "thick ecumenism" within the faculty at CCCU institutions and Carol Woodfin's analysis of the beliefs and behaviors of faculty and students from these institutions lay an important foundation for discussing, as articulated by Ostrander, what is perhaps the singular goal of Christian higher education: "The purpose of a Christian college isn't simply to hand you a complete Christian worldview on a platter; rather, it's to start you on the process of developing a comprehensive, coherent, yet dynamic Christian worldview."[2] The challenge for those of us further along in our development is to value this purpose for what it truly is—a launching pad from which students are able to question often and deeply. As Mark Batterson, pastor of the National Community Church in Washington, DC, a church comprised primarily of recent college graduates and young DC professionals, suggests, "Most academic programs revolve around force-feeding knowledge rather than unleashing curiosity. The result? We learn some things. But we lose what is most important: the love of learning. Curiosity dies a slow death. And we forget most of what we learned in the first place anyway. Holy curiosity asks the tough questions, the honest questions, the questions everyone is afraid to ask. God isn't threatened by those questions. He loves them."[3]

My major professor in my masters program at St. Mary's University in San Antonio, Texas, first opened my mind to the world of such tough, honest questions. A Christian clinical psychologist and a Marianist sister, Dr. Grace Luther looked across the room during a one-on-one case review session and said, "Wayne, people with all the *right* answers never ask the *important* questions." As a recent graduate from a CCCU university courageously pursuing graduate studies at a Catholic university, I was initially perplexed by my new mentor's statement. Soon, however, I discovered the brilliance of her instruction—I had somehow come to believe that my undergraduate Christian education had prepared me to answer every question one could ask, perhaps even before it was asked. My own Christian worldview had been carefully and systematically constructed exactly like that of a graduate from another CCCU institution, Rachel Held Evans, author of *Evolving in Monkey Town: How a Girl Who Knew All the Answers Learned to Ask the Questions*, who acknowledges that she "used to think that the measure of true faith is certainty. Doubt, ambiguity, nuance, uncertainty—these represented a lack of conviction, a dangerous weakness in the armor of the Christian soldier who should 'always be ready with an answer.'"[4]

Christian higher education, though certainly not perfect in form or function, provides a rich environment both inside and outside the classroom for students, faculty,

---

1   Rick Ostrander, *Why College Matters to God: Faithful Learning and Christian Higher Education* (Abilene, Tex.: Abilene Christian University Press, 2009), 19.

2   Ibid., 22.

3   Mark Batterson, *Primal: A Quest for the Lost Soul of Christianity* (Colorado Springs: Multnomah Books, 2009), 96.

4   Rachel H. Evans, *Evolving in Monkey Town: How a Girl Who Knew All the Answers Learned to Ask the Questions* (Grand Rapids, Mich.: Zondervan, 2010), 218.

and other educators to deeply engage dynamic faith in the midst of life's greatest social, political, and theological questions. The permission to live and learn in these questions can be genuinely advanced by campus cultures imagined and created with an appropriate balance of challenge and support, allowing students to develop in heart, soul, and mind as they relate their emerging identities within their expanding social structures.

The purpose of this essay is to expand imaginations to the intersections of faith and campus culture at our institutions; to recall what was, to challenge what is, and to open a dialogue for what could be; and to highlight the strengths of Christian higher education as articulated by this study and other essayists that can aid us in preparing our students as critical thinkers, capable of engaging and making culture with Christian conviction while still remaining civil and hospitable in conversations potentially ladened with controversy and disagreement. Finally, examples of current praxis among many of our institutions will further awaken our imaginations toward new possibilities.

The contributions of Philip Irvin Mitchell and Carol Woodfin have set the stage well for my own thinking and discussion. Mitchell has ably articulated both the need for and the possibility of expanding our faculty circles to invite in Christian educators from other denominations, including Roman Catholic and Orthodox traditions. His analysis of the data suggests that faculty are open to such a move, that not all CCCU institutions need make this shift, and that those institutions that do move in this direction need not be destined toward the slippery slope to secularization. In fact, Mitchell artfully incorporates images from C. S. Lewis and Kevin J. Vanhoozer, making a clear case for moving us from "separate rooms"[5] to "table fellowship,"[6] a campus culture enlivened by family fellowship—agreeing and disagreeing, challenging and being challenged, exploring and finding, but never losing sight of family, the family historically and traditionally rooted in loving God with heart, soul, and mind, and neighbors as ourselves. Mitchell makes it clear that "thick ecumenism" is indeed at work, but calls for courageous creativity in realizing the unity for which Jesus prayed and ultimately died.

Woodfin's analysis of the Joeckel and Chesnes data indicates that students and faculty, though similar in some instances, vary in their openness to controversy and willingness to ask difficult questions, perhaps more so than faculty realize; that students and faculty are theologically conservative, though students to a lesser degree; and that many of the components of Christian culture on our campuses—chapel, mission, and service trips, Bible studies and other student ministry opportunities—may have an adverse effect on the spiritual nurture and development of some students. I find that such variances are not too surprising, as students are young in both experience and development. It is notable, however, that a general sense of openness among students and faculty exists, such that we have the opportunity within supportive environments to challenge our students with disparate viewpoints, allowing them to think critically

---

5   C. S. Lewis, *Mere Christianity* (New York: Collier Books, 1952), 12.

6   Kevin J. Vanhoozer, *The Drama of Doctrine: A Canonical Linguistic Approach to Christian Theology* (Louisville: Westminster John Knox, 2005), 272-278.

concerning important questions so that they begin to find their own voices and to form their own beliefs.

The Intersection of Faith and Campus Culture

The essential parts exist at our CCCU institutions for fully developed, faith-filled campus cultures, but the whole is always greater than the sum of its parts. My experience in Christ-centered higher education is that we are easily lulled into believing that because all of the right ingredients exist, Christian faith will always inform, form, and transform our campus cultures. This is Woodfin's finding regarding what is often considered the Christian "atmosphere" on our campuses. This osmotic understanding of culture-making is not only mistaken; it is dangerous. For too long Christian higher education has depended on rules, policies, and church-like practices to promote a "form of godliness but denying its power."[7] Gratefully, we are awakening to the understanding so masterfully articulated by Dallas Willard in *The Divine Conspiracy*.

> One of the greatest weaknesses in our teaching and leadership today is that we spend so much time trying to get people to do good things without changing what they believe. It doesn't succeed very well, and that is the open secret of church life [or Christian university life]. We frankly need to do much less of this managing of action, and especially with young people. We need to concentrate on changing the minds of those we would reach and serve. What they do will certainly follow, as Jesus well understood and taught.[8]

Too many of our strategic initiatives relative to faith and campus culture are focused on what students do, or do not do, more so than with what students believe, or do not believe. To the extent that we focus on behavior to the exclusion of belief, we seek to control by rules and regulations—curfews, dress codes, mandatory chapel, policies on sex, alcohol, etc. Campus culture thus becomes what we make of it, an environment of constraint and restriction that ultimately foils our best chances for working together as students, staff, and faculty to create the ethos for which we long. This ethos is one of freedom—to think, to question, to challenge, to explore—the freedom Andy Crouch posits in *Culture Making: Recovering our Creative Calling*, when he writes, "Culture is the realm of human freedom—its constraints and impossibilities are the boundaries within which we can create and innovate."[9]

Kenda Creasy Dean, in *Almost Christian*, describes the faith of today's adolescents as lukewarm. In an interview with *Youth Worker Journal*, Dean suggests "the faith that teens have looks very much like the faith of their parents. It's not shaking up their lives in any

---

7 2 Timothy 3:5 (NIV)

8 Dallas Willard, *The Divine Conspiracy: Rediscovering our Hidden Life in God* (San Francisco: Harper Collins, 1998), 307-308.

9 Andy Crouch, *Culture Making: Recovering our Creative Calling* (Downers Grove, Ill.: InterVarsity Press, 2008), 35.

discernable way."[10] She suggests that "consequential faith makes a difference in the way you live and orient yourself. It's the integrating identity of our lives."[11] On our Christian campuses we want the faith we teach and integrate within our holistic curriculum, both inside and outside the classroom, to be consequential faith—faith that is taught, not caught like a common cold or the flu. Catholic theologian and educator Thomas Groome, quoting portions of the General Directory of Catechesis[12], defines this faith as

> a way of believing, a way of worshipping, and a way of living; it is cognitive, affective, and behavioral; it engages people's minds, emotions, and wills; it is to permeate how we make meaning out of life, the quality of all our relationships, and the ethic by which we live. In consequence, catechesis [Christian education] is to promote a lived, living, and life-giving faith; it is to inform, form, and ever transform people as faithful apprentices "in communion and intimacy with Jesus." It is simply not possible to be a disciple of Jesus within one's head alone; one must be formed to "walk the walk" as well as to "talk the talk."[13]

So what does this have to do with teaching and learning in Christian higher education? I believe it is the very core of our vision and purpose. Students commit four years of their lives to our campuses because at some level they, or their parents, believe that a Christian liberal arts education is the best preparation for the rest of their lives—church, work, graduate studies, family, career. Though they may not fully understand why this is true, for the majority, this is their foundational belief. We as Christian educators, on the other hand, know full well why this is true. As Groome further articulates,

> That education is a spiritual affair is not a new notion. Indeed, this is the better understanding that has endured throughout the history of Western civilization. Some 2500 years ago, Plato described the function of the teacher as "to turn the soul" of students toward the true, the good, and the beautiful. Augustine, writing circa 400 C.E., said that the teacher's function is to engage "the teacher within" each person, and he meant the divine presence at the core of people—their very soul.[14]

The ethos for which we long is a campus culture that values the freedom for teachers "to turn the soul" and for students to connect with "the teacher within." Only then will lasting transformation begin: "Do not conform any longer to the pattern of this world, but be transformed by the renewing of your mind. Then you will be able to test and approve what God's will is—his good, pleasing and perfect will."[15]

10 Jennifer Bradbury, "Called but Not Committed," *Youth Worker Journal* (July/August, 2010): 22.

11 Ibid., 22.

12 http://www.vatican.va/roman_curia/congregations/cclergy/documents/rc_con_ccatheduc_doc_17041998_directory-for-catechesis_en.html

13 Thomas Groome and Michael J. Corso, eds., *Empowering Catechetical Leaders* (Washington, DC: National Catholic Educational Association, 1999), 239.

14 Thomas Groome, "Religious Knowing: Still Looking for that Tree," *Religious Education* 92:2 (1997): 204-226.

15 Romans 12: 2 (NIV)

What Was, What Is, and What Could Be

Mitchell opened the dialogue about communities of memory by "tying together narratives of its history with preparation of its members for the future."[16] I agree that it is necessary for us to consider from whence we have come regarding faith and campus culture. Though our CCCU institutions are not all alike, we share similar histories with respect to our campus cultures, especially as related to being guardians of Christ-centered higher education. "In the 19th century it was believed that the most effective way to deepen a person's spiritual life was to increase her knowledge about God. People behaved—and still behave—as though the spiritual part of a person is a separate component that can be worked on and developed in isolation from the rest of a person. This approach has been refined with great fervor over the last 100 years and in some ways has just recently hit its stride."[17] Though specifically addressing the church context, Doug Pagitt, pastor of Solomon's Porch in Minneapolis, Minnesota, further articulates that he has "become convinced that our misguided belief that life change can come through proper knowledge acquired through education has failed to produce the kind of radical commitment to life in harmony with God in the way of Jesus that we are called to. When the realities of life crash into our knowledge of God, faith is often the prime casualty."[18] We want the lived faith of our students to withstand the realities of life, and such faith does not come all at once as some type of cosmic force field granted with a diploma at our commencement exercises. Instead, the faith integrated in the learning on our campuses needs to be a faith that is discovered and is sustained as life unfolds, as realities of famine, genocide, oil spills, bank failures, home foreclosures, cancer, and terrorist attacks strike our collective human experience.

Each new experience should cause our graduates to ask new questions, the answers to which lead them to explore and to discover what it means to live their faith in each new day, one day at a time. Such exploration and discovery are the results of deliberate engagement with faculty and undergraduates whereby students are encouraged to wrestle with doubts and fears, uncertainty and questions. Because we teach them to think, to question, to challenge, they dig deep within themselves and within their faith communities to find places where they are free to call upon the Lord with reckless abandon and to find faith in the very midst of doubt, hope in the presence of darkness. Such resolve is no accident; it is the intentional, ongoing process of integrating who they are in the Lord with who they are in their relationships—with family, friends, co-workers, and neighbors. Pagitt further articulates the changes we hope are evident on our campuses when he writes: "It seems to me that our post-industrial times require us to ask new questions, questions that people 100 years ago would have never thought needed asking. Could it be that our answers will move us to reimagine the way of Christianity

---

16   Philip Irving Mitchell, "Thick Ecumenism: The Possibility of Enlarging Our Circles at Christian Colleges and Universities," 80.

17   Doug Pagitt, *Reimagining Spiritual Formation: A Week in the Life of an Experimental Church* (Grand Rapids, Mich.: Zondervan, 2003), 22.

18   Ibid, 23.

in our world? Perhaps we as Christians today are not only to consider what it means to be a 21st century church, but also—and perhaps more importantly—what it means to have a 21st century faith."[19]

Pagitt's challenge is especially relevant when we consider the view of religious faith depicted in the controversial documentary entitled *Religulous*. In this film, Bill Maher states that "faith means making a virtue out of not thinking . . . allowing human beings who don't have all the answers to think that they do."[20] In a world of big questions, "the only appropriate attitude for man to have . . . is not the arrogant certitude that is the hallmark of religion, but doubt." In Maher's way of thinking, "doubt is humble, and that is what man needs to be, considering that human history is a litany of getting [everything] dead wrong."[21] Though replete with satire seemingly intended to strike a painful, if not deadly blow to Christianity and other world religions, *Religulous* exposes what Kenda Creasy Dean describes as "the church as [many] come to know it," not the "church as it's called into being by Christ."[22]

A more serious "outsiders" view was researched by The Barna Group and presented to the Christian community by David Kinnaman and Gabe Lyons in *unChristian: What a New Generation Really Thinks About Christianity . . . and Why It Matters*. Kinnaman and Lyons reflect from this research that "one of the generational differences is a growing tide of hostility and resentment toward Christianity . . . . The image of the Christian faith has suffered a major setback. Our most recent data show that young outsiders have lost much of their respect for the Christian faith."[23] Perhaps the more disturbing discovery is "outsiders direct their skepticism toward all things Christian; the faith itself, the people who profess it, the Bible, and Jesus Christ."[24] Like it or not, this is the cultural context of our students and graduates, one that is both post-modern and post-Christian. The way we teach, mentor, and do life with our students is critical in preparing them "to be defined by [their] service and sacrifice, by lives that exude humility and grace."[25] These are the actions and attitudes that will change the world, and our Christian campuses are well positioned to integrate living, learning, and faith with such intention that students are both prepared for life and taught how to live it. The claims of our mission statements "to change the world" must begin and end with leading our students into a life of being transformed—personally and collectively as the body of Christ. The true witness of Christ in culture is not an institution; it is the living, faithful expression of Jesus Christ in transformed persons.

---

19 Ibid, 22.

20 Larry Charles and Bill Maher, *Religulous*, DVD (Santa Monica: Lionsgate, 2009).

21 Ibid.

22 Bradbury, *Called but Not Committed*, 24.

23 David Kinnaman and Gabe Lyons, *unChristian: What a New Generation Really Thinks About Christianity . . . And Why It Matters* (Grand Rapids, Mich.: Baker Books, 2007), 24.

24 Ibid.

25 Ibid, 206.

Strengths of Christian Higher Education

The primary strength of Christian higher education lies in the firm belief that all truth is God's truth, that nothing exists that cannot be fully engaged in the pursuit of integrating faith and learning. In his famous lectures on John Calvin, Abraham Kuyper stated, "There is not one square inch of the entire creation about which Jesus Christ does not cry out, 'This is mine! This belongs to me'!"[26] In 1970, Dr. John C. Stevens, eighth president of Abilene Christian University, made a similar statement in his inaugural address:

> There are no subjects on this earth, or in outer space, or in the metaphysical realm, which we cannot study on the campus of a Christian institution of higher learning. Everybody can know our basic commitment, but I hope that people will also realize there are no closed minds and no off-limits subjects on this campus so long as in our teaching and practice we operate within the framework of our historic commitment. We can study— and I hope with a fair and reasonable approach—even those viewpoints which might not be in agreement with our basic presuppositions. In this way we can see to it that students and faculty are aware of the currents and crosscurrents of our age and that the education to be pursued at a Christian college is highly relevant.[27]

Great women and men of faith in the histories of our institutions have laid foundations upon which we can boldly stand as we embrace the most challenging questions of our day with the resolve to unabashedly pursue truth in all its forms—socially, politically, ethically, and morally. I believe the twenty-first century invites, challenges, even compels us to move beyond a fear-filled, insular past, beyond the status quo of the present, and into the open, expansive potential of the future. Our students hunger, just as the women and men of Jesus' day, to hear truth resound in the midst of disparate viewpoints, converging cultures, and difficult times in ways that create amazement—more than an emotional response, the deep and meaningful response of one's inner soul to the pure and powerful truth of Creator God as his Kingdom breaks forth on earth, just as it is in heaven. Our students long to know, to see, and to experience Jesus in the flesh—through individual Christians and through collective bodies of Christ—loving those who are not often loved, understanding those who are not easily understood, and living among those whose lives are not lived in ways that meet our predetermined checklist of what is acceptable. This is the Jesus our students encounter in Scripture, but whom they sometimes do not see in our churches and schools. Our challenge is to remember that unless our institutions are comprised and led by women and men who are continually being transformed by the renewing of their minds, our students will likely not learn also to submit their minds to renewal in Jesus Christ, renewal that leads to transformational living in a world in desperate need of nation-changers.

Such an opportunity knocked on the door of my campus on March 27, 2006, when thirty-two young people forming the 2006 Soul Force Equality Ride arrived for a two-day

---

26   Abraham Kuyper, *Lectures on Calvinism* (Grand Rapids, Mich.: Eerdmans, 1931), 99.

27   See Abilene Christian University, http://www.acu.edu/aboutacu/administration/stevens/inaugural.html

campus conversation to explore with our students, staff, and faculty their purpose as a group of lesbian/gay/bisexual/transgender/queer (LGBTQ) activists. The Soul Force website stated the purpose of the 2006 Equality Ride as follows:

> The Equality Ride is a traveling forum that gives young adults the chance to deconstruct injustice and the rhetoric that sustains it. It allows emerging young leaders to unite in the struggle for common equality. The idea is this. We get on a bus and journey to various institutions of higher learning. Through informal conversation and educational programming we explore concepts of diversity, comparing the effects of inclusive and exclusive viewpoints. More practically, we share and gain insights about how our beliefs influence policy and culture, thereby impacting society. Our goal is to carefully and collectively examine the intersection wherein faith meets gender and sexuality. Such discourse, especially when it affirms the beauty of our differences, plays an essential role in creating a safe learning and living environment for everyone.[28]

Did Kuyper and Stevens have this scenario in mind when they each made bold statements of conviction with respect to the range of creation that could be openly discussed and explored on our Christian college campuses? I dare say they did. In fact, I believe campus conversations and learning experiences such as occurred in the spring of 2006 on the campus of Abilene Christian University and other CCCU campuses are exactly what Christian higher education is all about. After weeks of preparing our students, staff, faculty, and alumni for this important two-day event, we were pleased to welcome our guests, first at the hotel where we provided their lodging, and then on our campus for a welcome meal with students and faculty. I'll never forget ushering our guests into dinner and inviting them to complete and affix a name tag to facilitate learning one another's names when one of the young female riders looked into my eyes and tentatively said, "You mean, you want to know our names?" My heart broke as I reflected upon the many and cruel ways these young people had been treated on other campuses—spat upon, mocked, cursed, arrested. At that very moment I was so thankful that the collective wisdom of our university agreed that we should welcome the Equality Riders with the love and compassion of Jesus. Later that Sunday evening during the nine o'clock student communion service I had started years before as campus minister, another of the young female riders, a self-proclaimed wiccan, turned to me with tears in her eyes and said, "Had I known years ago that Christianity could be like this, I'd have given it another chance."

Two days later, after all the conversations, worshipping together in chapel, eating together at table, providing free medical care in our campus clinic, laughing together and crying together, agreeing and disagreeing (often with firm conviction from both parties), we all hugged one another as new friends and said our goodbyes. I still keep in touch with several students from the 2006 Equality Ride. Though I suspect neither of us has changed our foundational beliefs surrounding our two-day conversation, I believe we

---

28   See Soul Force: http://www.soulforce.org/article/1625

can all say with complete assurance that we are better human beings for having engaged each other in honest, open dialogue, maintaining civility and practicing hospitality, and in so doing, we are both changed.

What are the current topics that run the risk of being labeled "off limits"? Will our hearts and minds remain open "so long as in our teaching and practice we operate within the framework of our historic commitment"? The 2010 CCCU International Forum provided us with a remarkable opportunity to initiate an open study and dialogue about science and faith pertaining to new-world-versus-old-world creationism, race, gender, prejudice, and other social-justice concerns. These and other topics do and will confront our students and graduates for the foreseeable future. The disciplines they study bring to bear perspectives of science, history, society, theology, politics, and philosophy, and the faith they are developing further informs their thinking as they question God, their world, their experience, and their future. This is the stuff from which Christian higher education is able to cultivate meaningful relationships among students and faculty—relationships of trust and admiration, respect, and value.

As Christian institutions of higher education, we would do well to consider other campus conversations that would allow us to engage with one another in thoughtful and intentional dialogue concerning the global issues facing twenty-first century humankind. Such engagement could be broader and deeper with the "thick ecumenism" suggested by Mitchell. Beyond mere pragmatism or mere Christianity, broadening the circle of faith through our hiring practices would include important voices of Christian history and tradition, thereby giving our students the expanded Christian worldview necessary to interact with culture in the work of making meaning of current and future challenges. Mitchell posits that "committed yet flexible attitudes" with respect to biblical inerrancy (FSQ 36), Scripture as authoritative (FSQ 33), the acceptance of other authorities regarding truths to teach about God (FSQ 32), and allowing others to question the Bible (FSQ 34) open the dialogue for creating inclusive hiring practices. He offers further hope by citing the Joeckel and Chesnes data related to the importance of theological diversity within the Christian university (FSQ 35) and the "spirit of humility and charity" present among faculty and among administration and faculty (FSQ 81). These findings neither prescribe nor proscribe Mitchell's challenge of "thick ecumenism," but they certainly suggest that faculty, as essential parts of Christian higher education, provide influential voices in leading the holistic change in Christ-centered education that will likely occur in the near future, or as he summarizes from Alan Jacobs's conclusion in his article "To Be a Christian College," "the future will force us, Orthodox, Catholic, and Protestant, to work and teach side-by-side."[29]

After considering Woodfin's analysis of the Joeckel and Chesnes data, as well as my own comprehensive analysis, I am again struck by students' perception of a protective "bubble" and "sheltered" life on our campuses. My own perspective as a former chief student development officer is that our students do not live within a "bubble" when it comes to the many and varied issues they and their peers confront on a daily basis, and that any sense of living

---

29 Alan Jacobs, "To Be a Christian College," *First Things*, April 2006, http://www.firstthings.com/article/2007/01/to-be-a-christian-college--1.

a "sheltered" life on our campuses has more to do with students' perceptions formed from reading many of our codes of conduct as well as from the rhetoric used to communicate these behavioral expectations. Considerable attention should be given among our student-development and campus-ministry staff to the culture we make on our campuses through our written and spoken communication regarding our student handbooks and codes of conduct. Our students long for safe environments in which to acknowledge their struggles and mistakes and find restorative solutions and loving, forgiving attitudes. To the extent that our "rules and regulations" create barriers between our students and us, we are hindered in our ability to meet them where they live. As faculty and staff work to build essential and important bridges, students will connect at deep and significant levels, and we must be readied with appropriate training and with sanctioned and approved time and availability to receive students within safe and supportive environments. In my experience, most concerns noted in Woodfin's analysis of the data can be addressed with these positive changes in campus culture: allowing students, staff, and faculty the time and space openly to engage one another in relevant conversation; seeking points of connection in areas of life of most interest and importance among students; and providing necessary processes for relating the big questions of life with the faith, hope, and love that are the core of our Christian faith.

Conclusion: Practice to Praxis

The "declension thesis," "slippery slope to secularization," and "loss of Christian identity" reservations discussed in Part One, Essay One have validity as indicators of critical thinking, but should our mission become moribund, interrupting and sidetracking the personal and institutional transformation necessary for unified and transformational relevancy in the twenty-first century, we will have allowed fear to rule the day. Rather, our hope should lie in a present that is always and at every time deeply rooted in the coming of Jesus Christ, from his first coming to his promised return.

My own sense is that with a clear historical understanding from whence we have come, we are being pulled into the future by our loving Father who desires that we become transformed more and more into his image as we live incarnate lives in our ever-changing world. It has been popularly stated that transformed persons transform persons. I believe this conception is more essential today than ever before. "Change" has been the hallmark of mission statements and political campaigns, but what does it really mean? Is it a matter of growing weary of status quo, looking to ride the wave of the next best thing, or change for change's sake? Or, is it the intention derived from deep human understanding that all is not right.

In my work with International Justice Mission, I encounter a new generation of faith, hope, and love—students who know and understand from the depths of who they are in Christ Jesus that to live rightly relative to God and in relationship to everyone and everything surrounding them, and to make right in their world what is not right, is the purpose for which they have been called by God. These students are making decisions about life—meaning, purpose, and vision—based on their deep sense that God is calling them as agents of change—locally and globally—to seek justice, to love mercy, and to walk humbly with God. These students confront us with a curiosity and enthusiasm for engaging complex issues in a multifarious world, and as educators and Christian institutions of higher education, we need to model for them what it looks like to be nation-changers. In *Transformations at the Edge of the World*, Cynthia Toms Smedley challenges us to engage this convergence of our students and their learning—both on our campuses and abroad. Toms Smedley frames this curiosity and enthusiasm as "restlessness" and suggests, "The restlessness of youth is not easily silenced. Questions of personal identity collide with the big questions of life: 'Who am I? What do I believe? How can my small earthly life make an eternal difference?' Restless notions are not quenched with superficial words or Sunday school answers. In fact, spiritual hunger leads many young adults to press the boundaries of knowledge, to bump against authority, and to challenge the status quo."[30] As students engage their learning on our campuses and in our programs, we have the responsibility to partner with them, integrating their living and learning with a consequential faith.

Our great hope is that fear will not paralyze our faith in God's work of unifying understandings of truth so that his work of bringing all things together under Christ might be more fully realized within our time. It is clear that Christian higher education is changing. Many and varied examples of forward-thinking practices are present on our campuses—the "thick ecumenism" realized in hiring practices and student organizations at Messiah College such as the Newman Club,[31] the SST program (service-learning) at Goshen College,[32] the Masters of Arts in Transformational Urban Leadership (MATUL) at Azusa Pacific University, [33] the San Francisco Urban Program of Westmont College,[34] Gordon in Lynn (living and learning program) at Gordon College,[35] LEGS at Letourneau University,[36] Best Semester at the CCCU,[37] Sankofa at Bethel University,[38] and the John Perkins Center at Seattle Pacific University.[39] These and many other initiatives have been imagined and implemented so that faith and campus culture at our schools might open to God's leading in the twenty-first century and deeply impact important and necessary changes in our attitudes and established practices for the praxis of integrating faith and learning. "Today's students bring new challenges to universities wishing to encourage moral and spiritual development. Modern students are open in ways that may facilitate encounters with diverse people and ideas, stimulating crises of faith that can nurture spiritual maturation."[40]

---

30   Cynthia Toms Smedley, "The Journey Inward," *Transformations at the Edge of the World* (Abilene, Tex.: Abilene Christian University Press, 2010), 31.

31   See Messiah College. http://www.messiah.edu/org/

32   See Goshen College. http://www.goshen.edu/sst/

33   See Azusa Pacific University. http://www.apu.edu/clas/globalstudies/urbanleadership/about/

34   See Westmont College. http://www.westmont.edu/_offices/urban/

35   See Gordon College, http://www.gordon.edu/gordoninlynn

36   See Letourneau University. http://www.legsresearch.org/

37   See CCCU Best Semester. http://www.bestsemester.com/

38   See Bethel University. http://cas.bethel.edu/campus-ministries/outreach/sankofa/

39   See Seattle Pacific University. http://www.spu.edu/depts/perkins/

40   Charles E. Stokes and Mark D. Regnerus, "The CCCU and the Moral and Spiritual Development of Their Students: A Review of Research," *CCCU Research Series* (Washington DC: CCCU, 2010), 13.

Bibliography: Part Two: Faith and Campus Culture

Abilene Christian University. http://www.acu.edu/aboutacu/administration/stevens/inaugural.html

Azusa Pacific University. http://www.apu.edu/clas/globalstudies/urbanleadership/about/

Batterson, Mark. *Primal: A Quest for the Lost Soul of Christianity*. Colorado Springs: Multnomah Books, 2009.

Bebbington, David. W. *Evangelicalism in Modern Britain: A History from the 1730s to the 1980s*. London: Routledge, 1989.

Bellah, Robert, et al. *Habits of the Heart: Individualism and Commitment in American Life*. Updated ed. Berkeley: University of California Press, 1996.

Benne, Robert. *Quality with Soul: How Six Premier Colleges and Universities Keep Faith with Their Religious Traditions*. Grand Rapids, Mich.: Eerdmans, 2001.

Bethel University. http://cas.bethel.edu/campus-ministries/outreach/sankofa/

Bradbury, Jennifer. "Called but Not Committed." *Youth Worker Journal*, July/August, 2010, 22.

Brown, Wendy. *Regulating Aversion: Tolerance in the Age of Identity and Empire*. Princeton, N.J.: Princeton University Press, 2006.

Burtchaell, James Tunstead. *The Dying of the Light: The Disengagement of Colleges and Universities from Their Christian Churches*. Grand Rapids, Mich.: Eerdmans, 1998.

Conyers, A. J. *The Long Truce: How Toleration Made the World Safe for Power and Profit*. Dallas: Spence, 2001.

Council for Christian Colleges and Universities. http://www.bestsemester.com/

Crouch, Andy. *Culture Making: Recovering Our Creative Calling*. Downers Grove, Ill.: InterVarsity Press, 2008.

Elshtain, Jean Bethke. "The Communitarian Individual." In *New Communitarian Thinking: Persons, Virtues, Institutions, and Communities*, 99-109. Edited by Amitai Etzioni. Charlottesville: University Press of Virginia, 1995.

Evans, Rachel H. *Evolving in Monkey Town: How a Girl Who Knew All the Answers Learned to Ask the Questions*. Grand Rapids, Mich.: Zondervan, 2010.

Geertz, Clifford. *The Interpretation of Cultures*. New York: Basic Books, 1977.

General Director of Catechesis. http://www.vatican.va/roman_curia/congregations/cclergy/documents/rc_con_ccatheduc_doc_17041998_directory-for-catechesis_en.html

Gordon College. http://www.gordon.edu/gordoninlynn

Goshen College. http://www.goshen.edu/sst/

Groome, Thomas. "Religious Knowing: Still Looking for that Tree." *Religious Education* 92:2 (1997): 204-226.

Groome, Thomas and Michael J. Corso, Eds. *Empowering Catechetical Leaders* (Washington, DC: National Catholic Educational Association, 1999).

Harmon, Steven R. *Towards Baptist Catholicity: Essays on Tradition and the Baptist Vision*. Eugene, Ore.: Wipf & Stock, 2006.

Holcomb, Gay L. and Arthur J. Nonneman. "Faithful Change: Exploring and Assessing Faith Development in Christian Liberal Arts Undergraduates." *Directions for Institutional Research* 29:1 (2004): 103.

Jacobs, Alan. "To Be a Christian College." *First Things* (April 2006), http://www.firstthings.com/article/2007/01/to-be-a-christian-college--1

The John Jay Institute. http://www.johnjayinstitute.org

Kinnaman, David and Gabe Lyons. *unChristian: What a New Generation Really Thinks About Christianity*. Grand Rapids, Mich.: Baker Books, 2007.

Kuyper, Abraham. *Lectures on Calvinism*. Grand Rapids, Mich.: Eerdmans, 1931.

Letourneau University. http://www.legsresearch.org/

Lewis, C. S. *Mere Christianity*. New York: Collier Books, 1952.

MacIntyre, Alasdair. *After Virtue*. 2nd ed. Notre Dame, Ind.: University of Notre Dame Press, 1984.

Marsden, George. *The Soul of the American University: From Protestant Establishment to Established Nonbelief*. Oxford: Oxford University Press, 1996.

Mendus, Susan. *The Politics of Toleration in Modern Life*. Durham, N.C.: Duke University Press, 2000.

Messiah College. http://www.messiah.edu/org/

Newman, Elizabeth. *Untamed Hospitality: Welcoming God and Other Strangers*. Grand Rapids, Mich.: Brazos, 2007.

_____. "The Politics of Higher Education: How the Love of Hospitality Offers An Alternative." In *The Scholarly Vocation and the Baptist Academy,* 166-196. Edited by Roger Ward and David P. Gushee. Macon, Georgia: Mercer University Press, 2008.

Noll, Mark A. and Carolyn Nystrom. *Is the Reformation Over? An Evangelical Assessment of Contemporary Roman Catholicism*. Grand Rapids, Mich.: BakerAcademic, 2008.

Ostrander, Rick. *Why College Matters to God: Faithful Learning and Christian Higher Education*. Abilene, Tex.: Abilene Christian University Press, 2009.

Palmer, Parker. *To Know as We Are Known: Education as a Spiritual Journey*. San Francisco: HarperOne, 1993.

Pagitt, Doug. *Reimagining Spiritual Formation: A Week in the Life of an Experimental Church*. Grand Rapids, Mich.: Zondervan, 2003.

Radner, Ephraim. *Hope among the Fragments: The Broken Church and Its Engagements of Scripture*. Grand Rapids, Mich.: Brazos, 2004.

Schindler, David L. *Heart of the World, Center of the Church: Communio Ecclesiology, Liberalism, and Liberation*. Grand Rapids, Mich.: Eerdmans, 1996.

Seattle Pacific University. http://www.spu.edu/depts/perkins/

Service-Learning. http://www.servicelearning.org

Soul Force. http://www.soulforce.org/article/1625

Taylor, Charles. *Sources of the Self: The Making of Modern Identity*. Cambridge, Mass.: Harvard University Press, 1989.

The Trinity Fellows Program. http://fellows.trinitycville.com/

The Trinity Forum Academy. http://www.ttf.org/academy

Weil, Simone. *The Need for Roots*. Translated by Arthur Willis. London: Routledge, 2002.

Vanhoozer, Kevin J. *The Drama of Doctrine: A Canonical Linguistic Approach to Christian Theology*. Louisville: Westminster John Knox, 2005.

Westmont College. http://www.westmont.edu/_offices/urban/

Willard, Dallas. *The Divine Conspiracy: Rediscovering Our Hidden Life in God*. San Francisco: Harper Collins, 1998.

PART THREE

ASSESSING THE *IN-LOCO-PARENTIS* MODEL

IN LOCO PARENTIS

Strengths, Weaknesses, and Future Directions

CHAPTER 7

C. ERIC JONES AND APRIL L. CUNION

"**W**e get it," Jennifer thought to herself. "How many times do we really need to be told always to swipe our cards and sign in when visiting a dorm? How often must we be reminded that no alcohol is allowed, that we must attend fifteen chapels each semester, and that we are not allowed to wear anything skimpy on campus?" Jennifer's initial enthusiasm about being away from home and "living on her own" was dissipating as each hour of freshmen orientation seemed to be another block stacked upon a wall separating her from what once seemed would be life lived as she wished. Her consolation: "at least I can eat and sleep when I want to, sort of." Jennifer's experience is common for those entering a Christian university, and it exemplifies the realization by many students that they still lack complete control over how they live despite leaving their parents' home. The foundation for these behavioral requirements also reflects how institutions play roles in and bear serious responsibilities for moral development in Christian higher education.

As demonstrated in this mock scenario, many universities which are members of the Council for Christian Colleges and Universities (CCCU), in addition to providing academic instruction, attempt to provide a structure for the moral development of students through adoption of an *in-loco-parentis* model. This model, literally translated as "in the place of a parent," might differ from institution to institution through the distinct rules and behavioral codes implemented, although as a whole, the CCCU universities share the goal of developing moral character in their students as a result of these policies.

This chapter will present existing research and theory related to parenting, identity formation, and agency as a context in which to interpret results from the Joeckel/Chesnes survey. It should be noted up-front that one limitation of our data is that we primarily assessed academic institutions with moderate behavioral regulations, which might decrease the variability of the data, thereby limiting our ability to detect conceptually meaningful differences among types of "institutional parenting." In other words, sur-veying schools with behavioral regulations higher in control of students (e.g., Bob Jones University) and schools higher in autonomy of students (e.g., a majority of state schools) than the colleges and universities we sampled would likely provide comparisons useful in detecting optimal levels of institutional behavioral regulation. Keeping that in mind, let us now turn our attention to the data.

Evaluation of the Data: Perceptions of the In-Loco-Parentis Model

In the Joeckel/Chesnes survey, the majority of faculty and student respondents indicated that their school maintains rules regarding alcohol consumption (99 percent of faculty and student respondents; FSQ 46, SSQ 30) and premarital sex (98 percent of faculty and student respondents; FSQ 47, SSQ 31), and to a lesser degree, regulations regard-ing curfew (84 percent of faculty respondents, 70 percent of student respondents; FSQ 48, SSQ 32) and dress code (77 percent of faculty respondents, 73 percent of student respondents; FSQ 49, SSQ 33). When asked about their agreement with these rules and codes of conduct, most faculty members supported the reasonableness and fairness of these policies within their institutions. Likewise, the majority of students reported that they had not broken rules related to codes of conduct at their institutions.

Although the majority of faculty and students reported complete compliance, there is also a noted trend in both faculty and student surveys toward emphasizing the importance of rules and student participation in policies considered to be more significant, those that enforce regulations against alcohol consumption and premarital sex, than rules relating to curfew and dress code. This distinction leads to a demarcation between "essential" areas for *in-loco-parentis* policies (i.e., policies enforcing abstinence from alcohol and premarital sex) and "less important" issues (such as dress code and curfew). The importance of the essential policies reflects current research trends supporting an increase in rates of binge drinking[1] and casual sex[2] among undergraduate college students.

With respect to the minority who reported breaking rules related to conduct poli-cies, breaking one of the "essential" rules led to correlated reports of breaking rules related to all other policies. For example, significant correlations emerged between stu-dents reporting alcohol use and engaging in premarital sex ($r = 41$, $p < .001$), breaking curfew ($r = .37$, $p < .001$), and breaking dress code ($r = .20$, $p < .001$). When assessing individual universities as separate samples, the same correlational patterns emerged. Different observations could be drawn from these data. Specifically, we immediately see that breaking one area of the conduct code "opens the door" for a student to break additional components of conduct policies. This may be an effect of self-reporting in the data. That is, perhaps more students are breaking codes of conduct and not admitting

---

1   Lloyd D. Johnston, Patrick M. O'Malley, and Jerald G. Bachman, *Monitoring the Future National Survey Results on Drug Use, 1975-2002. Volume II: College Students and Adults* (Bethesda, Md.: National Institute on Drug Abuse, 2003).

2   Shirley S. Feldman, Rebecca A. Turner, and Katy Araujo, "Interpersonal Context as an Influence on Sexual Timetables of Youths: Gender and Ethnic Effects," *Journal of Research on Adolescence* 9 (1999).

these discrepancies, whereas students who were willing to admit their violations of conduct were also more willing to report multiple violations. Nevertheless, according to the data, students who reported breaking essential rules of conduct were more likely to report breaking other rules of conduct when compared to students who did not report breaking one of the essential rules.

Overall, the data suggest that codes of conduct are effective in limiting potentially destructive behavior and can be considered a strength in the evaluation of CCCU institutions. However, it is appropriate for the Christian community to further assess the developing student in the midst of the *in-loco-parentis* model and to articulate the ideal level of oversight necessary for jointly building moral character and developing autonomy in the life of the student.

Relationship to Parenting Models

Indeed, one might consider that all universities assume a parental role in the life of the developing student, whether that role is more consistent with an authoritarian style (i.e., one who is high in control and low in autonomy-granting), an authoritative style (i.e., one who is moderate in control and moderate in autonomy-granting), or a laissez-faire or permissive style (i.e., one who is low in control and high in autonomy-granting).[3] From this perspective, perhaps the most important question for institutions concerns balance: how do we best develop an appropriate balance between exerting control and granting autonomy in the lives of our students?

Research suggests that the authoritative parenting style best prepares the developing child and adolescent for enhanced self-control, high self-esteem, and social and moral maturity.[4] In relationship to the *in-loco-parentis* model, this style of parenting would continue to make reasonable demands of the young adult (exhibiting control), but would also offer up appropriate autonomy for making choices commensurate with the young adult's level of moral development. By striking the appropriate balance between provided autonomy and expected self-control, the institution is more likely to avoid the extreme negative behavior associated with being overly permissive and the stunted moral growth associated with being overly controlling.

Some reflections on the need for increasing autonomy for CCCU students might be solicited from respondent views on whether or not students are sheltered. The majority of faculty members (51.8 percent; FSQ 50) indicated that students were "somewhat" sheltered, whereas students were less decisive, with 37.7 percent indicating feeling "somewhat" sheltered and 37.4 percent reporting not feeling sheltered (SSQ 34). Although these results do not call for significant changes to the current *in-loco-parentis*

---

3 Diana Baumrind, "Current Patterns of Parental Authority," *Developmental Psychology* 4 (1971).

4 Paul R. Amato and Frieda Fowler, "Parenting Practices, Child Adjustment, and Family Diversity," *Journal of Marriage and Family* 64 (2002). See also Kathleen Mackey, Mary Louise Arnold, and Michael W. Pratt, "Adolescents' Stories of Decision Making in More and Less Authoritative Families: Representing the Voices of Parents in Narrative," *Journal of Adolescent Research* 16 (2001). In addition, see Laurence Steinberg, Nancy E. Darling, and Anne C. Fletcher, "Authoritative Parenting and Adolescent Development: An Ecological Journey," in *Examining Lives in Context*, ed. Phyllis Moen, Glen H Elder, Jr., and Kurt Lusher (Washington, D.C.: APA, 1995).

model of most CCCU universities, they do suggest that we may be limiting the autonomy of students for making decisions regarding their moral development and creating a separatist effect where university culture and life experiences differ from the demands and temptations experienced outside of the university.

Students commonly reflected this drawback of feeling sheltered in their open-ended responses to the question: "What is the most difficult part about being a student at a Christian college/university?" Representative examples include the following responses:

- "Sometimes I feel like I live a sheltered life and that it will hurt me in the future when I get out in the 'real world.'"
- "I feel sheltered from what the rest of the world thinks and the way in which they act. I feel that some people who attend this school try to shut themselves off from the rest of the world because of all the sin in it. We are somewhat secluded from the 'outside' world."
- "The most difficult part of being a student at a Christian university is finding chances to make my moral decisions because they are my own, and not simply because it is what the community expects. Leaving the bubble of a Christian campus can be shocking for some people because they are no longer able to lazily form their beliefs, but instead need to actively take a stand in their own convictions."

With respect to the rules on campus in connection with autonomy, some students also mentioned difficulties with the conduct rules in their responses to the same open-ended question. Some sample responses included the following:

- "I don't like all the rules. For example, I think that a Christian above the age of 21 should be allowed to drink in moderation. I don't think a Christian college/university should try to regulate that—it is a personal choice."
- "Having to agree with and abide by a set of rules which you had no part in making."
- "The most difficult part about being a student at a Christian college is feeling that we are 'parented' and 'babied' by the University. We are adults and should be treated as such—the rules and boundaries at college are more strict than I ever had while living at home (and my parents are very protective of me!)."

In observation of these responses, one important need surfaces. In their open-ended responses, students who reported knowing more about the rationale behind the development of the rules were more likely to be satisfied in the conduct policies of the university. It seems imperative from these data that academic institutions need to be more forthcoming with students regarding the rationale for conduct policies and the importance of these policies for their growth and development. In parallel with the authoritative parenting style, explanation of the rules connects the parental-authority figure with the developing child and allows for conversation about why the rules or policies are enforced, as well as noting the reinforcements or punishments that will be provided for engaging or defying these policies. If students are not aware of the rationale behind the conduct policies, they are less likely to perceive the importance of these rules for developing their moral lives and therefore less likely to appreciate the rules.

One Caveat: Spiritual Development

Interestingly, one area of divergence from support of the *in-loco-parentis* model was observed in response to spiritual growth and development. In the Joeckel/Chesnes survey, faculty members were asked whether or not chapel should be mandatory for faculty. Likewise, students were asked if chapel should be mandatory for students. In both groups, the modal response was to "strongly disagree" with mandatory chapel attendance (35.3 percent of faculty respondents; 29.8 percent of student respondents; FSQ 26, SSQ 35). This difference suggests that faculty and students view spiritual development as more of an internalized process, whereas other forms of moral development, related to alcohol and sex, are appropriately monitored externally.

Certain trends in the data also suggest developmental shifts with respect to mandatory chapel requirements from students. Specifically, as undergraduate students aged, they were more likely to "strongly disagree" with mandatory-chapel rules (34 percent of seniors compared to 25 percent of freshmen). Additionally, longer commitments to the Christian faith were related to less desire for mandatory chapel attendance (48 percent of students identifying as being a Christian for eleven years or more disagreeing or strongly disagreeing to mandatory chapel versus 44 percent of students identifying as being a Christian for less than five years disagreeing or strongly disagreeing).

Some students reflected a feeling of constriction in their spiritual development with rules relating to spiritual growth in their open-ended responses to the question, "What is the most difficult part about being a student at a Christian college/university?" Some examples include the following responses:

- "Sometimes just keeping your faith real is hard. It is easy to get lazy and make excuses that you are going to chapel and getting the Christian teachings, praying, etc., all the time. It is hard to remain consistent with your personal devotions and not just faking it with the actions in the setting you are in."
- "It is very easy to become very comfortable and stagnant in your faith because you do not have to defend your faith every day and it seems very easy to be surrounded by Christian activities. You are not forced to seek out small groups and churches that will help you grow in your faith."
- "Being intentional about my faith. I feel like its 'good enough' to just be at a Christian university. Sometimes my faith feels like homework, which is a horrible thing that I struggle with daily."

These developmental shifts toward desiring more control over spiritual development highlight differences originally postulated by Allport[5] separating extrinsically oriented expressions of religiosity from intrinsic orientations. Allport found evidence of spiritual maturity in those employing an intrinsic religious orientation. Elaborating on the effects of religious orientations on adjustment, Ryan, Rigby, and King[6] further subdivided intrinsic religious orientations. They termed an internalized expression of religion that was associated with conflict and pressure *introjection*, while internalized expressions of religion related to volitional choices were termed *identification*. Those endorsing an identification perspective were more likely to promote adaptive psychological adjustment and development. In connection with parenting styles, identification would follow an authoritative style, suggesting that students need to have the opportunity to express their spirituality out of a volitional choice (rather than feeling pressured to complete spiritual activities) for optimal development. Data from the Joeckel/Chesnes survey suggest that spiritual development is a needed area of divergence from the *in-loco-parentis* model within CCCU schools.

In conclusion, the agreed-upon strengths of the *in-loco-parentis* model relate to controlling negative, physical behaviors (i.e., drinking alcohol and engaging in premarital sex) that can be monitored by the university and *decrease* the extent of negative behaviors in the life of the student. The weaknesses of the *in-loco-parentis* model relate to facilitating positive, internal growth (i.e., spiritual growth) that cannot be monitored externally and are intended to *increase* positive behaviors in the life of the student.

Relationship of In loco parentis to Identity Development

Decisions made in response to the most appropriate "parenting style" of the university also relate to implications for the development of student identity. Specifically, the dimensions of autonomy and control relate to various forms of identity expression for adolescents and young adults who are formulating the ways in which they perceive themselves. Marcia[7] postulates four alternative paths for identity development for the rising adolescent:

- identity diffusion (the individual who has not met an identity crisis and has not made a commitment to an identity; the individual shows little interest in formulating a personal identity)
- identity foreclosure (no identity crisis occurs as the individual has accepted an identity without questioning the validity of this identity; an example would be following a family tradition in vocational selection without questioning one's interest in that vocation)

---

5   Gordon W. Allport, *The Individual and His Religion* (New York: McMillan, 1950).

6   Richard M. Ryan, Scott Rigby, and Kristi King, "Two Types of Religious Internalization and Their Relations to Religious Orientations and Mental Health," *Journal of Personality and Social Psychology 65* (1993).

7   James E. Marcia, "Development and Validation of Ego-Identity Status," *Journal of Personality and Social Psychology 3* (1966).

- identity moratorium (the individual is in the midst of an identity crisis in this stage, but has not made a decision regarding future vocational selection)
- identity achievement (the individual has gone through an identity crisis and has made a commitment to his or her identity and related vocation)

Research suggests that those in the stage of identity achievement have a better sense of their own strengths, weaknesses, and individuality. In essence, those who have addressed an identity crisis and made a subsequent commitment to their identity and vocational path are more likely to have a formed identity. A clear concern of the *in-loco-parentis* authoritarian model (where control is high and autonomy is low) is that students would not have an opportunity to engage in an identity crisis that would allow them to reach the achievement stage of identity formation. Rather, students would be more likely to be limited to the stage of identity foreclosure. Relating back to the differences between extrinsic and intrinsic identity development,[8] lack of volitional choice in decisions related to one's future identity leads to psychological maladjustment.

More clarification regarding the role of the university in relationship to identity development is needed. It would seem logical that the authoritative style would be best related to identity development in students, but even within an authoritative model, a student would need to be given enough freedom to successfully move into a state of identity crisis in order to reach identity achievement. The overarching question is whether we are providing students with enough freedom to engage in these stages of identity development, which again highlights the importance of balance between control and autonomy within the university.

Limitations

As noted above, one limitation of the current findings is that the Joeckel/Chesnes survey primarily assessed academic institutions with moderate behavioral regulations. This finding is adaptive in support of an authoritative parenting role (in difference from more authoritarian or permissive parenting styles) for the universities represented, but also limits the variability of our data. If we had data from institutions more representative of other parenting styles, then we may see greater contrast among student perceptions and outcomes.

Additionally, a limitation for the implications of the study lies in the challenges of predicting one "parenting approach" for the entire university. The data suggest that a particular set of rules does not meet the needs of all students of the university. Instead, students at different stages of physical development, moral development, social development, and spiritual development enter the university and progress toward maturity in these areas at differing rates. Although separate parenting models (specifically in relationship to level of control and autonomy) might be adaptive for different students, by

---

8   Christopher P. Niemiec, Richard M. Ryan, and Edward L. Deci, "The Path Taken: Consequences of Attaining Intrinsic and Extrinsic Aspirations in Post-College Life," *Journal of Research in Personality* 43 (2009).

necessity, the universities adopt one universal policy. Therefore, we recognize that one *in-loco-parentis* style does not fit all, but we support the adoption of unified policy for ease.

Future Directions

Assisting students in perceiving the rationale of the constraints. From our evaluation of the *in-loco-parentis* model, we observe three separate options that a university might choose to take for optimizing moral development and improving student compliance with codes of conduct. One path would be to retain the current code of conduct with a better explanation of the rationale for the rules. As noted above, when students reported knowing more about the rationale behind the development of the rules of conduct at their universities, they were more likely to be satisfied with the conduct policies. It seems imperative from these data that academic institutions need to be more forthcoming with students regarding the rationale for conduct policies and the importance of these policies for their growth and development. Aligning with the authoritative parenting style, an explanation of the rules allows for conversation about why the rules or policies are enforced, as well as noting the reinforcements or punishments that will be provided for engaging or defying these policies. Our conclusion is that institutions should be more active in relating this rationale to students throughout their tenure at the university and at their different levels of development.

Providing developmentally consistent behavioral regulation. A second path toward increased moral development would be to loosen rules developmentally by allowing students to have more freedoms as they demonstrate maturity with age. Data suggest seniors desire, and may need, less guidance concerning moral behavior than do freshmen. Assuming these desires reflect actual, significant personal changes from one's freshman to senior years, it is likely the institutional structure designed to facilitate moral development adaptively fits with only a small portion of one's educational experience. Yet institutional rules do not typically vary with the developmental changes of students. Better institutional parenting might be achieved by increasing the flexibility of rules to better match students' level of moral development. As mentioned in the limitations section, this pathway would necessarily be more difficult to monitor for the university, although this would likely best meet the needs of achieving an authoritative parenting role.

Increasing student ownership of behavioral regulation. A third path would be to increase overall "ownership" of the codes of conduct by having older students explain behavioral codes and the rationale for these policies to underclassmen. Research has shown people tend to exhibit attitudes and behaviors highly consistent with a position once they publicly commit to that position.[9] Through this process of identification with the policies, students will likely endorse greater support for and belief in the codes of conduct. Additionally, explaining the rules to others will better reinforce the students' personal understanding of the rules.

---

9   Arthur A. Stukas, Mark Snyder, and E. Gil Clary, "The Effects of 'Mandatory Volunteerism' on Intentions to Volunteer," *Psychological Science 10* (1999). See also Jonathan C. Younger, Lucy Walker, and A. John Arrowood, "Postdecision Dissonance at the Fair," *Personality and Social Psychology Bulletin* 3 (1977).

In review, the data from the Joeckel/Chesnes survey demonstrate support for the *in-loco-parentis* model for *decreasing* negative behaviors in the life of the student, although support was not garnered for rules related to internal growth intended to *increase* positive behaviors in the life of the student. The options for future directions described above are only three of many potential ways that a university might foster identity development. As we further address the *in-loco-parentis* model, the question of identity development will be the key area of investigation.

IN LOCO PARENTIS

An Evolving Concept

EDEE M. SCHULZE AND PAUL BLEZIEN

Introduction

Conduct codes and the complexities involved in determining and enforcing them are familiar topics of conversation for student-life administrators. These conduct codes (policies, rules, and expectations that guide the behavior of members of the community) are determined by mission statements, moral principles, legal developments, and the traditions of the institution. We learn much about the shaping of student behavior from history, from our experiences, and from the perspectives of faculty and students. To say that developing a conduct code that effectively shapes character is a difficult task would be a vast understatement. Likewise, to assume that student-life educators could shape the moral decisions of students simply through conduct codes—separate from the experience of community or from the classroom experience—would be preposterous. Because conduct codes are such a common characteristic of colleges and universities, faith-based and otherwise, and because character development is such an important issue in higher education today, a discussion about conduct codes in the context of an exploration of the Christian college phenomenon is entirely appropriate and relevant. But this discussion must be framed in a larger context: enabling the growth of young men and women to maturity must be a "whole-person" task.

Consequently, to do justice to history and the professional work of student affairs (also referred to as student life, student development, or student personnel), this essay must challenge the premises on which the Joeckel/Chesnes survey questions were formed as well as the questions themselves. While we acknowledge and applaud their efforts, a different approach to the topic is required. This essay attempts to launch an educational conversation among academic-affairs faculty, student-life educators, and students at Christian institutions regarding conduct codes and the underlying assumptions on which they are built.

To frame an appropriate conversation about conduct-code effectiveness, this essay will first address the survey and the shortcomings in its development. We will trace the history and dissolution of *in loco parentis* (meaning "in the place of parents") as an operating concept within higher education, specifically within Christian colleges and universities. Next, we will briefly explore the distinctive task of Christian institutions, namely shaping the moral lives of students. At CCCU member institutions, this responsibility, which lies with faculty *and student-life professionals*, is especially relevant to our discussion given the survey results. Then, three stances regarding student-behavior codes as delineated by David Hoekema will be explained. Finally, we will present the model offered by several authors for the development of a type of community that morally shapes students, an end that many of our campuses are already striving to achieve. These thoughts become the foundation for our recommendations.

The Survey

In the Joeckel/Chesnes survey, questions were asked of 1,900 faculty members from ninety-five institutions and 2,300 students from twenty CCCU institutions. These questions, some of which related to student conduct, were inherently flawed or the methods by which they were asked were flawed. For example, student-life administrators were not included in the survey, although students' co-curricular experiences may account for 90 percent of a student's life on campus. In addition, questions to the faculty and students were not parallel, with one exception. Faculty were asked about their perceptions of the frequency of student incidents of binge drinking and the percentage of students who have had premarital intercourse, as well as for their opinions on whether or not their institution's rules for students on alcohol, sex, curfew, and dress code were fair and reasonable (FSQs 30, 31, 32, and 33). On the other hand, questions to the students related to their own behavior and if they had broken their school's regulations pertaining to alcohol, sex, curfew, and dress code. The students were not asked about the frequency with which they had broken the rules nor were they asked their perceptions regarding the frequency of incidents for these kinds of behaviors within the student body. In a more parallel manner, both faculty and students were asked their views on whether or not students live sheltered lives. There was a statistically significant difference in the responses of faculty and students to this question. Students were more inclined to *disagree* that they lived sheltered lives at their schools (Table 1).

There are four problems with the questions pertaining to conduct codes and student behavior. In designing their survey, Joeckel and Chesnes intended these questions to gather data to evaluate the *in-loco-parentis* model on Christian campuses. First, and most fundamentally, the topic assumes that campuses are operating on the principles of *in loco parentis*. As this essay will explain, *in loco parentis* as an operating philosophy is outdated, irrelevant, and, in any type of universal institutional application, does not have the support of the legal system. A developmental and community-based approach has replaced *in loco parentis* legally, philosophically, and pragmatically across the spectrum of Christian colleges.

Second, the formulation and wording of the questions indicate a lack of essential understanding of the philosophical, theological, and missional premises that underlie conduct codes and developmental processes employed to manage student behavior and help students grow holistically. In essence, the survey questions were based on the wrong assumptions.

Third, the questions asked are perspectival in nature. If the purpose of the survey was to determine the effectiveness of conduct codes in changing student behavior, inquiries about faculty and student perspectives do not provide that information. The survey asked the wrong questions of the wrong audience.

Fourth, the questions asked of students were different from the questions asked of faculty. The structure of the surveys limits sophisticated inferential comparisons. It would have been interesting, perhaps even helpful, to ask both faculty and students the same questions regarding their perceptions of the percentage of the student body who break the rules at their schools regarding alcohol, sex, curfew, or dress code. But this was not the case. Therefore, unfortunately, the survey questions regarding conduct codes do not address effectiveness. The methodology of the survey on this topic is ineffective.

In loco parentis

Through the end of the 1950s, secular and church-related colleges and universities in the United States operated under the principles of *in loco parentis* by exercising authority over and taking responsibility for students' personal lives and conduct as well as their academic pursuits.[1] David Hoekema describes *in loco parentis* as a legal doctrine that educational authorities used as a foundation for a broad range of regulations over student conduct.[2] He summarizes four related but distinct powers or immunities: "First, the institution had the *authority to direct the behavior* of students . . . . Second, as a consequence, the institution had the *authority to punish* rule violations . . . . Third, the institution's position *in loco parentis* carried with it a special *responsibility of care* for students . . . . Fourth, the college or university also enjoyed, to a certain degree, an *exemption from limits on searches* carried out in conjunction with the enforcement of school rules."[3]

With the cultural upheaval of the 1960s, however, secular schools quickly abandoned this overarching responsibility and role in students' lives and many mainline church colleges and universities quickly followed suit. In recent decades, the notion that an institution holds parental duties and privileges has come increasingly under attack. Significant court cases and mounting emphasis on individual student rights brought the entire concept of *in loco parentis* into question, further contributing to the erosion of

---

1   Robert Benne, *Quality with Soul: How Six Premier Colleges and Universities Keep Faith with Their Religious Traditions* (Grand Rapids, Mich.: Eerdmans, 2001), 15.

2   David Hoekema, *Campus Rules and Moral Community: In Place of in loco parentis* (Lanham, Md.: Rowman & Littlefield Publishers, 1994), 21.

3   Ibid., 27-28.

a college's formerly strong parental role. The plausibility of the *in-loco-parentis* model eroded each time students successfully challenged it, either individually or in groups. Hoekema indicates that the college's authority to set and enforce rules that are, in its judgment, necessary to maintain good order and an appropriate atmosphere for educational purposes and to direct student behavior in a broad range of areas is the element of *in loco parentis* that has been supported and reaffirmed by the courts on many occasions at every level.[4] However, as an overall operating model at most institutions, including Christian institutions, *in loco parentis* is no longer used.

It is important to note that at the same time institutions were withdrawing from *in loco parentis* to guide their work, the profession of student affairs was emerging as a more powerful influence. The vacuum left when faculty and staff abandoned the *in-loco-parentis* philosophy and moral formation responsibilities was filled by professional administrators trained in psychology, sociology, educational theory, theology, administration, and leadership. The special relationship once recognized both legally and socially under the broad heading of *in loco parentis* no longer determined the privileges and responsibilities of colleges with respect to control of student behavior. Instead, a new professionalism and a new profession with different philosophies and guiding principles replaced it, as will be described further in this essay.

The Role of the Traditions of an Institution

Over time, the ethos of a campus forms at the intersection of its mission, tradition, and, if faith-based, its theology. Hoekema writes that the result of these intersections places institutions somewhere along a continuum from restrictive to directive to permissive. One school may have restrictive codes to manage certain behaviors known to be problematic on campus and in the lives of its students, whereas another school may be more permissive, depending upon its intersection with its tradition, mission, and theology.

Hoekema calls the first position on the continuum a "restrictive stance," meaning that an institution takes a more limiting approach to behaviors and implements strict behavior codes. Hoekema names this stance *in loco avi*, or "in the place of grandparents." The institution provides a set of identifiable values for the students. But perhaps more important than the set of values is how the institution responds to students when they make choices outside the boundaries. If an institution uses a developmental approach in a "restrictive" environment, it will likely be based on efforts to refine students' character for their long-term well-being.

Hoekema describes another stance on the other end of the continuum, the "permissive stance." Institutions in this category believe that both the legal status of students and the lack of clear moral authority on the part of the institution regarding traditional mores militate against controlling objectionable student behaviors (e.g., alcohol use, visiting hours, and sexual activity). These institutions have redirected their efforts

---

4 Ibid., 34.

toward managing behaviors based primarily on legal parameters and have adapted what Hoekema sums up as a philosophy of *non sum mater tua* ("I'm not your mother").

Hoekema's third alternative is the "directive stance," which would be placed on the continuum between "restrictive" and the "permissive." This one he calls the *in-loco-avunculi* ("in-the-place-of-the-uncle") philosophy. From this stance, an institution seeks neither to control behavior directly nor to leave it wholly to student discretion. Behavior is influenced by means other than disciplinary sanctions and rules, such as incorporating units related to drug and alcohol education in all freshman orientation classes or placing high expectations on faculty and staff behavior to ensure that they model strong moral character.

In all likelihood, most institutions exhibit characteristics of each of these approaches. A Christian college campus may exhibit some indications that it falls primarily into one category and some indications that it falls into one or both of the other categories as well, depending on the particular behavior in question or the situation. It would not be unusual to find that on some topics the institution functions "restrictively," when in other areas it may be more "directive" or even "permissive." Again, the conduct code is only the beginning of the process. Students' lives are shaped by what happens after a behavior or attitude is identified as problematic for them or for the community. Ideally, at this point the conversation begins between a student-life educator and the student regarding the moral implications of choices, current and future, with the goal of leading the student to greater levels of growth, development, and maturity.

Moral Formation in the Co-Curricular Realm

Foundational to CCCU membership is that schools must meet two criteria: a Christ-centered mission and an employment policy in which only those who profess faith in Jesus Christ can be hired as full-time faculty members and administrators (non-hourly). The unifying task and mission are the shaping of all elements of students' lives, including the shaping of the moral elements of them as persons. In fact, Christian institutions often promote their commitment to ethical development in a student as a significant distinguishing benefit of a faith-based campus. However, rather than expressing the concepts of moral formation under the heading of *in loco parentis*, these days it is most often expressed in the idea of holistic development, including character development. Emphasizing the community nature of this responsibility, Arthur Holmes says that at their best these communities function single-mindedly with a sharp focus on their mission of integration of faith with life, learning, and serving.[5]

So it follows that a student-life mission statement and other guiding policies and procedures at a CCCU school, including the policies and conduct statements, must align with, flow from, and be rooted in the institution's Christ-centered mission and its history in the Christian faith. Just as a professor at a Christian institution seeks to integrate faith

5 Arthur Holmes, *The Idea of a Christian College*, revised edition (Grand Rapids, Mich.: Eerdmans, 1991), 45 and 80.

with classroom learning, so too the student-life educator seeks to integrate biblical and theological perspectives into his or her developmental work with students.

While all campus members have a responsibility for the development and enhancement of a holistic community, student-life personnel have a particular responsibility for establishing developmental philosophies that shape students' co-curricular experiences (outside the classroom) where students spend a significant amount of time each week. This includes the formation of educational programs, policies, and procedures in areas such as residence life, leadership development, student activities, counseling services, athletics, career services, spiritual formation, and service activities. All these are designed to support, challenge, nurture, and protect individual community members and the community as a whole.

The Integration of Faith with Conduct Codes

Student-life offices, which typically have responsibility for conduct codes, policies, and procedures that are necessary for orderly and effective operation of an institution, are an integral part of the overall mission. The individual development of the student, the formation of campus community, and the establishment of an ethos consistent with the biblical mission and the tradition of the institution are primary objectives for student life. Rules safeguard individuals and the community, but they are also the touch point for many students in their formation. Every disciplinary encounter is a teaching moment to inquire about the student's behavior, his or her thinking that contributed to current behavior choices, and the relationship of character formation to future decisions. Relationships with students are the context for this developmental work, while justice and mercy serve as the biblical principles that shape disciplinary outcomes. These disciplinary situations are also times when students learn that decisions have consequences— for themselves and for the community—and that maturity means taking responsibility for their actions. Most importantly, the disciplinary encounter is redemptive, which sometimes means that grace is given. Other times, the most redemptive response is to hold students accountable for their decisions, depending on a variety of variables within the situation. Approaching conduct codes and behavior violations this way is evidence that integration of faith has occurred in the co-curricular realm.

In *The Idea of a Christian College*, Holmes describes the integration of faith with learning and living according to an ethical and a worldview approach. Both of these are helpful to the discussion of conduct codes on Christian college campuses.

As students interact on and off campus, they experience the intersection of values with daily lives. Components of conduct codes may be related to widely accepted ethical principles (e.g., intolerance for hate speech) or to behavior standards about which there are different perspectives within a community (e.g., smoking). But whatever the rule violation is, a moral element is introduced because an individual's integrity and respect for the community and its standards are at stake. Some rules are historically in place at institutions in order to create an atmosphere most conducive to the accomplishment of mission and to protect the environment, and students are asked to contribute to community enhancement by abiding by the conduct code. When students encounter and respond to life situations, including rules that govern campus life, Holmes says they deal with what ethicists call "middle-level concepts," which means they relate the factual circumstances of a situation to the ethical questions that surround or underlie them. In taking the ethical approach to moral development, Holmes describes three types of questions that prompt the integration of faith with the discussion of a situation. These are 1) "What are the facts in the case, including contributing causes and possible consequences?" 2) "What middle-level concepts are involved? What are the purposes God intended for this area of human activity?" and 3) "What policy or action is called for in this kind of case or situation? How can we pursue proper purposes with justice and with love for all those involved?"[6]

These middle-concept questions are very similar to the typical questions a student-life professional might ask in a conduct-code violation situation. For example, the first questions a dean would ask a student are fact based: "What happened?" "What did you do?" "What are the causes of this situation and what have been the outcomes so far?" The second set of questions to a student are often motivational or integrative, such as "Why did you do what you did?" "Where is God in all this?" "How does this relate to other things you are seeing in your life or learning in your classes?" "How does it connect to the kind of person that you desire to be?" This is where a student-affairs educator can see the interchange between a student's choices and actions and his or her thinking and theology about the situation. Finally, a dean would seek to discern "next steps" by asking, "Where do we go from here? What needs to happen now to make this right . . . for you and for the community?"

Holmes also describes a worldview approach to moral formation that is all-encompassing and has full integration as its goal. Its primary purpose is not to insulate and protect students, but rather to educate them as responsible citizens, as fully devoted Christ-followers, and as those who will make a positive impact on the campus community and beyond. It is our charge as moral educators to develop responsible agents, but prerequisite to responsible action are reflection and valuing, both of which are the intent and content of corrective conversations when students break rules. As an individual's worldview solidifies, he or she sees all things, including motivations for and consequences of behavior choices, in relationship to God as Creator, Redeemer, and Lord. When student-life educators respond to violations of conduct expectations in a holistic and developmental manner as described here, they are seeking to accomplish the primary purpose for education at every Christian college or university: the formation of a Christ-centered and whole person who can think about all of life from a Christian worldview.

Conduct Codes within Community

So what is the context for the development of morals and ethics? Is it the rules or conduct code? Certainly conduct codes contribute, but they are static or "dead" as mere rules or

---

6　Ibid., 51-52.

"laws." In western society, moral choices are viewed as fundamentally individual deci-sions. This ideology, says Hoekema (1994), has been vital in establishing a broad range of personal and political liberties, yet it has been grossly inadequate as an account of our moral life and action. Further, it falls far short of what we are called to as believers in Christ and members of the kingdom of God. An individualized mindset does not fully account for all elements in social decision-making. All people make their choices in the context of community, but believers are commanded to do this with intentionality, humility, kindness, and love (Phil. 2:2-4, Rom. 12:3, 10). The creation, preservation, and nurture of such a community on a Christian college campus is not only a worthwhile goal; it is imperative.

The most powerful tool in the development of moral character is a moral com-munity. Holmes envisions a community where faith is integrated with learning and living, and that is rich in the relationships that shape the morals and ethics of students. Within these communities conduct codes exist, but they exist primarily for the purpose of shaping character and because of the kind of community to which we are called. A community like this can far more profoundly shape the moral character of students because moral communities:

1. Are based upon a commitment to Jesus Christ and his Lordship, thereby creating an atmosphere that encourages spiritual growth;
2. Are committed to the development of whole and holy persons who are prepared for effective service as God has equipped and called them;
3. Have integrity as a foundational value;
4. Provide significant growth-producing relationships for students with their peers, faculty, staff members, student-life professionals, family members, the Christian community in general, and non-Christians;
5. Provide meaningful educational activities that help prepare students to engage in sound moral thinking and living in congruence with what they know to be right;
6. Encourage collaboration between faculty and student-life educators as co-workers committed to the common task of educating students to integrate their faith, learning, and living;
7. Promote relationships within the community that are essentially active, influential, and sometimes necessarily reactive and restorative. Developmental interventions are tailored to individuals or groups in order to be most effective at reaching developmental and transforma-tive goals;
8. Foster the practice of responsible Christian freedom; and
9. Teach members to hold one another accountable, confronting one another in love as they work together to live in faithfulness both to God's Word and to our own word.

These principles are not only the goal for a campus community, but are also a powerful rationale for the proper use of conduct codes on Christian campuses. Conduct codes can be improperly used when they are administered as a means for compliance rather than as an avenue for transformation (more punitive and less redemptive). Therefore, student-life policies regarding conduct and violation responses should be built on and grounded in the principles of a moral community. The result should be the development of morally sensitive citizens concerned about their own well-being, the well-being of others, and the well-being of the community.

Recommendations

In their first recommendation in the previous essay, Jones and Cunion suggest assisting students in perceiving the rationale of constraints. They are correct in stating that students would be better served if they understood the conduct codes and the philosophy behind them. We recommend that efforts be made on the part of student-life personnel to educate faculty on the rationale and principles that undergird conduct codes and redemptive discipline. Student-life personnel should be intentional and conscientious about this educational role they play within the community and provide active leadership in this area. As a result, student-life educators and faculty could perhaps better understand each other and collaborate in the moral-formation task with students for which they both have responsibility, though in different roles.

Second, Jones and Cunion recommend developmentally consistent behavior regulation and increasing ownership of behavior regulation by students. On many campuses, this is already happening as students have increasing freedom in their living environments as they progress through their college years and older students are involved in behavior code and rationale explanations to younger students. On those campuses for which this is not the case, those strategies should be considered and, if possible, pursued.

We offer two recommendations as a result of interacting with this survey and the data. First, we recommend that campuses engage in their own process of assessing the effectiveness of their campus codes. This is a complex assessment exercise, admittedly. However, there are qualitative and quantitative means by which to explore the question. The process would necessarily involve identifying what learning outcomes the campus seeks from its conduct codes and from the resulting conversations with students who are in violation of its standards. This alone would be a highly beneficial activity for most campuses. Assessment measures would need to include moral-formation questions and could include interviews with or surveys of those who have been involved in conduct-code conversations—near the time of the occurrence, a year later, and a few years after they graduate. The formation of residence-director and dean focus groups, sharing their observations and perceptions of trends within the student culture specific to moral formation and the effectiveness of conduct codes, would be very valuable. Faculty focus groups or surveys regarding their experiences and observations about the effectiveness of behavior codes in behavior and attitude change would provide another critical perspective and data set. Surveys of the student body in general about their campus experience with the campus-conduct code and what they are experiencing among their peers would also be necessary. This kind of data, gathered over several years, would provide objective information and indicators to campus administrators about how effective the institution's conduct code is in developing whole persons.

Second, we recommend that faculty, student-life, and spiritual-formation educators on Christian college campuses engage in regular in-depth dialogue about the character formation responsibility we all carry. These groups must agree about the centrality of moral formation on our campuses. Mutual understanding of roles in accomplishing this task with students is necessary, and mutual support of colleagues as each fulfills his or her respective role is imperative. In the Joeckel/Chesnes survey, 89.9 percent of faculty "strongly agree" and another 8 percent "somewhat agree" that their institution should maintain its Christian identity (FSQ 25). We suspect if student-life personnel were surveyed they, too, would indicate a strong commitment to the same goal. Most faculty and student-life educators would agree that conduct codes are a substantial expression of an institution's identity. However, the dialogue between faculty and student-life personnel on how we are doing on this seems sparse, if it exists at all.

Conclusion

Conduct codes must necessarily address student behavior, but it is critical to remember that behavior is not the sole or even the primary focus. With the rise of developmental and community-focused models for responding to students' behavior, institutional philosophy has shifted from outward compliance to internal transformation. Particularly for Christian colleges, this is congruent with the mission of the institution, which includes the character formation of students. Moral development and spiritual transformation in the heart of the student for the sake of current and future life development are paramount.

Table 1: Perceptions by faculty and students of whether students live sheltered lives at CCCU campuses. Differences in responses were statistically significant ($p < 0.05$, chi-square goodness of fit test).

	Faculty	Students
Yes	27.1	25.2
No	21.1	37.4
Somewhat	51.8	37.7

CHAPTER 9

IN LOCO PARENTIS

From a Student and Faculty Perspective

ALLISON SANDERS AND SAMUEL JOECKEL

We enthusiastically embrace Edee M. Schulze and Paul Blezien's call to "launch an educational conversation" among student-life administrators, faculty, and students. Indeed, intra-campus dialogue is critical within CCCU institutions that seek to cultivate what Schulze and Blezien refer to as the "holistic" development of students.[1] Both faculty and staff—from the university president to the residence-life director to the assistant professor—play important roles in this task. Students' perspectives are similarly invaluable, as the authorship of this very essay attests. We also recognize that student-life administrators face a particularly challenging job. Don Gehring, the first president of the Association for Student Judicial Affairs, refers to student-affairs administrators as a "besieged clan"; they face pressure and criticism from all sides: presidents, faculty, parents, and students.[2] We believe that Schulze and Blezien pinpoint the method for ameliorating this difficult situation: mutual understanding. As they write, ". . . student-life educators and faculty could perhaps better understand each other and collaborate in the moral formation task with students for which they both have responsibility, though in different roles."[3]

Mutual understanding, however, need not downplay differences of opinion. In fact, articulating differences lays the groundwork not only for healthy dialogue but for fruitful steps forward in policy making, finding common ground within our differences as we proclaim with conviction what we believe to be best for our Christian institutions. We continue the dialogue in this spirit as we marshal the following two arguments. First, the

---

1   Edee M. Schulze and Paul Blezien, "*In Loco Parentis:* An Evolving Concept," 127, 132.

2   Quoted in Brent Paterson and Bill Kibler, Foreword, *The Administration of Campus Discipline: Student, Organizational and Community Issues*, eds. Brent Paterson and William Kibler (Asheville, N.C.: College Administration Publication, Inc. 1998), xi.

3   Schulze and Blezien, "*In Loco Parentis*: An Evolving Concept," 135..

in-loco-parentis model has hardly fallen into disuse within the CCCU; it is, with some minor qualifications, still operational within Christian higher education. Second, we argue that the *in-loco-parentis* model has implications that stretch beyond the personal morality of students, influencing not only their moral and spiritual lives but their intellectual lives as well. We conclude by standing together in agreement with Schulze and Blezien in endorsing a community-wide approach to the holistic development of students.

Is *In Loco Parentis* Dead?

Schulze and Blezien claim that *in loco parentis* is "outdated" and "irrelevant" within Christian higher education and that it "is no longer used."[4] While it is true that the *in-loco-parentis* model has been abandoned by state and secular schools, it is simply untenable to claim that the model has experienced the same fate within CCCU institutions. In their narrative tracing the rise and fall of *in loco parentis,* Schulze and Blezien draw from Robert Benne's *Quality with Soul*, which avers that *in loco parentis* has fallen into desuetude. They neglect, however, Benne's later schematization of colleges and universities into various types, one of which Benne refers to as "orthodox schools," which "want to assure that the Christian account of life and reality is publicly and comprehensively relevant to the life of the school by requiring that all adult members of the ongoing community subscribe to a statement of belief."[5] Benne's description clearly aligns CCCU institutions with the orthodox-school model. Benne continues, "Christian personal moral ideals [at orthodox schools] are articulated and rehearsed repeatedly. These schools *are willing to take the in loco parentis role* with regard to the formation of their students."[6]

Schulze and Blezien also draw from Arthur Holmes, who, as they rightly attest, notes the communal nature of moral formation within the context of Christian higher education. But Holmes also makes it clear that this emphasis on community has not divorced Christian colleges and universities from the *in-loco-parentis* model. He writes, "*In loco parentis* meant that American colleges accepted responsibility for all sides of student life. The Christian college *has not abandoned that notion*, but nowadays it is more often expressed in the idea of a college community."[7]

Schulze and Blezien rely most heavily, however, on David Hoekema's *Campus Rules and Moral Community*, which offers tongue-in-cheek alternatives to the displaced *in-loco-parentis* model, alternatives with names like *in loco avi, in loco avunculi,* and *non sum mater tua.* We call attention to the significant fact that Hoekema wrote *Campus Rules and Moral Community* before he joined the faculty at Calvin College. His book focuses on a diverse array of mostly secular colleges and universities, a focus evident in the fact that of the many institutions to which Hoekema sent questionnaires (from which he gleaned

---

4   Edee M. Schulze and Paul Blezien, "*In Loco Parentis*: An Evolving Concept," 128 and 130..

5   Robert Benne, *Quality with Soul: How Six Premier Colleges and Universities Keep Faith with Their Religious Traditions* (Grand Rapids, Mich.: Eerdmans, 2001), 50.

6   Ibid., 61, emphasis added.

7   Arthur Holmes, *The Idea of a Christian College* (Grand Rapids, Mich.: Eerdmans, 1975), 77, emphasis added.

the data for his book) only one—Calvin College—was a member of the Consortium of Christian Colleges and Universities, now the CCCU. Consequently, while Hoekema has written a valuable book on campus rules within secular schools, it does not specifically address, again because of his data set and focus, the unique character of distinctly Christian education.

As Schulze and Blezien observe, Hoekema does flesh out an orientation toward codes of conduct that he calls the "restrictive stance," a stance that entails clear rules on such issues of personal morality as sexual ethics and alcohol use. Hoekema describes it thusly: "In these areas [of personal morality], even universities and colleges that have explicitly renounced their former status *in loco parentis* still act in the way that was mandated by that model."[8] Of the restrictive, directive, and permissive stance, we find the restrictive stance to be most relevant to CCCU institutions.

Schulze and Blezien's objections to the Joeckel/Chesnes survey notwithstanding, we find that the data from the survey corroborate this claim. Of the more than two-thousand students from twenty different CCCU institutions who took the survey, only 0.4 percent stated that there are no rules regarding alcohol at their institution (SSQ 30); only 1.7 percent said there were no rules regarding sex (SSQ 32); a minority of 30 percent stated there were no rules regarding curfew (SSQ 32); and a similar minority of 28 percent said there were no rules regarding dress (SSQ 33). Considering these data, we find it hard to believe that *in loco parentis* no longer operates at CCCU institutions. Of course, the model has been relaxed in some ways. For instance, we imagine dancing is no longer forbidden at any CCCU institutions; and chaperones probably do not monitor all social events on campuses. But the rules cited above (among others) amount to a student-behavior model that is hard not to identify as *in loco parentis*. At the very least, these rules necessitate or imply that the institutions that enforce them have the "authority to direct the behavior of students"; have the "authority to punish rule violations"; and assume a "special responsibility of care for students."[9] These three powers, outlined by Hoekema, characterize the *in-loco-parentis* doctrine that is clearly in effect among CCCU institutions.

The Dangers of the Restrictive Stance

In order to fruitfully "launch an educational conversation" on moral development in higher education, there must first be an honest acknowledgment of the situation at hand. The *in-loco-parentis* model that is in fact in place among CCCU institutions too often exhibits a stark disparity between its motivations and outcomes, a disparity that poses potentially serious threats to students' personal growth and development. When students comply with restrictive moral rules, they may expose themselves to an impersonal religiosity, unquestioned ideas of morality, and an inauthentic faith . The seventeenth-century poet and polemicist John Milton specifically addressed these particular dangers in his *Areopagitica* (1644), explaining that a cloistered virtue is no virtue at all, as virtue

---

8   David A. Hoekema, *Campus Rules and Moral Community: In Place of* In loco parentis (Lanham, Md.: Rowman & Littlefield Publishers, Inc., 1994), 139.

9   Ibid., 27-28.

must be tested to prove itself and flourish. His enduring assessment of virtue pertains strikingly to the *in-loco-parentis* model.

When students are subjected to numerous restrictions and when administrations defend moral codes for students in a theocratic manner, students respond. They may, for instance, be provoked into a rebellion they might have never acted upon at a university with less restrictive policies. As Benne writes, "[orthodox colleges] are so public and enthused about their religious and moral vision that they often stimulate pockets of rebellion among students who consider their atmosphere oppressive or hypocritical or both."[10]

One may glimpse evidence of these pockets of rebellion in the Joeckel/Chesnes survey through the difference between freshmen's and seniors' infringements of moral-code policies regarding curfew, sex, and alcohol. Of all freshmen surveyed, 13 percent have broken rules on curfew, whereas 24 percent of seniors have done so. Although this is a significant but not overwhelming discrepancy, that may be because curfew rules generally become more relaxed for upperclassmen; therefore, there are not as many rules for them to break. And while 7 percent of freshmen have broken rules on sex, a significantly higher 18 percent of seniors have done so. Eight percent of freshmen have broken rules on alcohol, whereas a dramatically higher percentage of seniors (over five times more than freshmen) have broken alcohol rules: 42 percent (Table 1). The trend is for more students to break rules throughout their entire college career, a trend that logically follows from (among other causes) a waning respect for the *in-loco-parentis* model and increasing antagonism with student-life administration. C. S. Lewis aptly describes this reaction: "widespread drunkenness is the father of Prohibition and Prohibition of widespread drunkenness. Nature, outraged by one extreme, avenges herself by flying to the other."[11]

What Is a "Sheltered" Student?

The integration of faith and learning is a crucial distinction within CCCU institutions, a distinction that allows students to consider spirituality in an intellectual environment that can stimulate them to deeper exploration of their faith. This distinction is not only an indispensable characteristic of CCCU institutions; it also has the potential to enhance dramatically the cultures of campuses where it is applied well. When Christian distinctives are not applied well, however, they undermine both the faith and the learning of students. Some students may experience an aversion to Christianity, and others may take on an untested, "cloistered virtue" that Milton criticizes as "a blank virtue, *not* a pure."[12] The latter students are essentially sheltered students who exhibit an attitude too easily encouraged by *in loco parentis*, an attitude that stifles academic intellect. This outcome is distressingly antithetical to the formation of what Daniel Taylor calls "reflective

---

    10   Benne, 61-62.

    11   C.S. Lewis, Afterword to the third edition of *The Pilgrim's Regress* (Grand Rapids, Mich.: Eerdmans, 1992), 207.

    12   John Milton, *Areopagitica* and *Of Education* (Wheeling, Ill.: Harlan Davidson, 1951), 18.

Christians," those "who have brought their God-given intelligence and imagination to bear on the society in which they have lived."[13]

Evidence from the Joeckel/Chesnes survey suggests that those faculty who believe their students are sheltered connect that sheltered condition to campus rules for students. For instance, consider the divergent responses to questions regarding campus rules between faculty who do not believe their students live sheltered lives (abbreviated hereafter as NSL—not sheltered life—faculty) and faculty who do believe their students live sheltered lives (abbreviated hereafter as SL—sheltered life—faculty). Eighty-eight percent of NSL faculty agree with alcohol rules for students on their campuses, versus 72 percent of SL faculty. The discrepancy widens dramatically when considering those who "strongly agree": while 61 percent of NSL faculty *strongly agree* with the rules, only 38 percent of SL faculty strongly agree. Rules regarding sex follow a similar pattern: 69 percent of NSL faculty strongly agree with these rules, while 51 percent of SL faculty strongly agree. A majority of 68 percent of NSL faculty agree with the policies related to curfew, whereas a minority (albeit it a large minority) of 49 percent of SL faculty agree. Finally, 43 percent of NSL faculty strongly agree with dress-code rules while only 27 percent of SL faculty strongly agree. SL faculty thus seem to make a connection between sheltered students and moral rules on campus (Table 2).

Further analysis of NSL and SL faculty reveals disturbing trends. SL faculty are less likely than NSL faculty to identify their institutions as places of robust scholarly activity. While 77 percent of NSL faculty agree that their college is a "place of rigorous intellectual activity," 57 percent of SL faculty agree. A majority of 59 percent of NSL faculty strongly believe they possess academic freedom versus a minority of 33 percent of SL faculty. A similar majority of 67 percent of NSL faculty believe they "have more freedom to discuss issues and ask questions than do professors at secular institutions"; only 43 percent of SL faculty agreed to this proposition. Finally, while 15 percent of NSL faculty agreed that they were "hesitant to address certain important issues in class because they teach at a Christian college/university," SL faculty were more than twice as likely to admit hesitance: 36 percent (Table 3).

We note further disturbing trends in the divergent responses between these two groups with respect to alterity on campus, by which we mean charity and openness to minority and/or marginalized groups. For instance, only 35 percent of NSL faculty strongly agree that "diversity of theological opinions among faculty and students is healthy for a Christian college/university," whereas 59 percent of SL faculty strongly agree to this statement. Similarly, while a minority of 34 percent of NSL faculty strongly disagreed with the proposition that "Roman Catholics should not instruct at a Christian college/university that has Protestant origins," a majority of 56 percent of SL faculty strongly disagreed. SL faculty were more than three times as likely to disagree that female faculty at their institution "are treated equally to male faculty": 36 percent versus 11

13   Daniel Taylor, *The Myth of Certainty: The Reflective Christian and the Risk of Commitment* (Downers Grove, Ill.: InterVarsity Press, 1992), 15.

percent. Moreover, while 21 percent of SL faculty disagreed that female students "are treated equally to male students," only 6 percent of NSL faculty disagreed. Finally, SL faculty were more than twice as likely as NSL faculty to disagree that the student body at their institution "is racially diverse": 73 percent versus 36 percent (Table 4).

The consistent trends between faculty who believe their students are sheltered and who disagree with campus rules for students establish an important connection: while, not surprisingly, the term "sheltered student" is related to the moral code for students on campuses, the term "sheltered student" is also relevant to intellectual life and attitudes toward alterity on campus. The idea of a "sheltered student" may then very well overlap with the idea of a "sheltered scholar," therefore, or even a "sheltered human." As the restrictive nature of *in loco parentis* prohibits students from making independent decisions about their own behavior, this passivity—or shelteredness from independent decision-making—extends to their academic acumen and openness to unpopular and even unfamiliar ideas.

A cloistered intellect and perspective that do not encourage academic rigor or inquiry follow from the cloistered virtue that *in loco parentis* produces among well-behaved students. The principle of *in loco parentis* therefore too easily militates against the very educational core of CCCU institutions, largely for the sake of promoting a restrictive atmosphere to express a distinctively Christian element within higher education. But since the Christian distinctive produced is that of a cloistered virtue, the restrictive model is counter-productive.

Standing and Working Together on Points of Agreement

Schulze and Blezien clearly want to distance the CCCU from the *in-loco-parentis* model, despite the abundant evidence that the model's principles clearly operate on Christian campuses. Nevertheless, we stand together with Schulze and Blezien in promoting a community-wide approach to student development, thereby endeavoring what they believe is already accomplished: the disintegration of the *in-loco-parentis* model.

This task might begin by de-emphasizing rules. In fact, explaining "how values are transmitted," Holmes shows that a less restrictive code of conduct seems most compatible with an academic environment: "Young people assimilate [values] more from example than precept, more from their peers than from their elders, and more by being involved than by being spectators. Values can be caught from the contagious example of a community at work, in this case a community of enthusiastic and well-equipped scholars who infect their students with a love for learning and involve them in disciplined work. As teachers inspire students and students infect other students, a climate of learning emerges."[14] Hoekema perfectly explains the relative importance of rules when he writes, "The maxim of classical conservatism in government seems to apply in this context: The discipline system is best, we might say, that disciplines the least."[15] The rules of

---

14   Holmes, 62.

15   Hoekema, 144.

in loco parentis are obviously not in this vein, but a more holistic conception of conduct certainly fits Hoekema's explanation that "on the whole, the more successful a code of student conduct is in achieving its aims, the less it is needed and the less frequently its procedures are called into use. A system of rules that adequately protects the rights of all and also enjoys broad student support may become invisible in its influence on student conduct."[16] Hoekema describes a system that fits—rather than threatens—the spiritual and intellectual integrity of its students.

Again, like Schulze and Blezien, we believe moral formation occurs within a community. Consequently, dialoguing on the matter could only help. In fact, more dialogue seems to be the straightforward solution to many issues. For example, if student-life administration justifies moral-code policies with biblical support as many campus administrators aim to do, a dialogue can be organized between the student-life administrators and the biblical-studies professors to discuss the biblical support for certain policies. After all, students display more respect for the rules whose rationale they understand. As Jones and Cunion observe, "When students reported knowing more about the rationale behind the development of the rules of conduct at their universities, they were more likely to be satisfied in the conduct policies."[17] The dialogue between student-life administrators and biblical-studies professors would undoubtedly better explain many of the rules, as well as create an opportunity for the two separate branches of the college/university to become better involved with one another. In our experience, student-life personnel are often more willing to bridge the conversation gap between academic faculty and student-life administration. Professors need to show more willingness to cooperate with student-life departments in helping students cultivate their moral identity.

A holistic view of students' education thus logically entails the involvement of all campus bodies, including those members whose job is undeniably pedagogical—the faculty. According to Derek Bok, "It is not the place of faculty members to prescribe what undergraduates ought to consider virtuous. But surely faculties should do whatever they can to prepare their students to arrive at thoughtful judgments of their own."[18] Indeed, evidence from the Joeckel/Chesnes survey suggests that faculty are in a position to wield tremendous influence on the personal beliefs of students: while 57 percent of students agree that attending chapel at their institution has enhanced their faith, 82 percent agree that faculty has enhanced their faith (SSQs 13 and 15). Endorsing a policy that makes the student acquisition of virtue co-curricular, Shawn Floyd argues "that an analysis of virtue itself suggests its cultivation must occur within a pedagogical context." Floyd concludes that if this academic consideration of virtue is indeed important, "then it is only natural to make moral formation a central aim of our educative practices."[19] Faculty possess the invaluable potential to unify an academic understanding of values with their

---

16 Ibid.

17 C. Eric Jones and April L. Cunion, "*In Loco Parentis*: Strengths, Weaknesses, and Future Directions," 120..

18 Derek Bok, *Our Underachieving Colleges: A Candid Look at How Much Students Learn and Why They Should Be Learning More* (Princeton: Princeton University Press, 2006), 150.

19 Shawn Floyd, "Morally Serious Pedagogy," *Christian Scholar's Review* 36.3 (2007): 245.

students' actual lives—a potential that can come to fruition with cooperating campus bodies. Faculty certainly cannot replace student-life personnel and the important work they do; but faculty should at least be able to assist them.

In order for student-life administration, faculty, students, and other campus members to achieve this goal of holistic education, they should employ similar modes of discourse. That is, if diverse bodies on campus unite to encourage the cultivation of ethics in students, then they should speak a similar language so as to avoid transmitting mixed messages. Chapel speakers, for instance, should be wary of the sort of populist, reductive discourse that oversimplifies complex issues for the sake of widespread appeal to the student body. When speakers employ such discourse, students may too often experience educational vertigo as they exit chapel and walk across campus to their philosophy class on ethics or their biblical-hermeneutics class. [20]

This problem can be compounded when chapel is mandatory for students and, in some cases, for faculty. As a mandatory activity and a unified, collective source of moral and theological instruction for the entire campus community, chapel contextualizes ethical and faith commitments within a framework of compulsion. (Most student participants in the Joeckel/Chesnes survey disagreed that attending chapel should remain or become mandatory for students [SSQ 35]; most faculty disagreed when responding to the same proposition for faculty [FSQ 26].)

The sort of discourse employed on campus when engaging the important issues of faith, learning, and virtue—whether in the classroom, chapel, or student-life venue— should be characterized by the two foundational elements of Christian higher education: faith commitment *and* intellectual rigor. Contrasting discourses produce confused students who might negotiate this dilemma by compartmentalizing their faith and their intellect. This may breed, on the one hand, mistrust in those who lean more toward the faith side of this false dilemma, creating a suspicion of their professors and, on the other hand, cynicism in those on the intellectual-rigor side, predisposing them to ridicule student-life administration. Neither response is helpful for the ultimate goal of cultivating Christian virtue in students.

If the *in-loco-parentis* model is indeed abandoned and moral formation involves the whole campus community, many negative ramifications of the restrictive stance would be eliminated. The students of CCCU institutions should have the opportunity, depending on whether their respective colleges/universities were to choose to implement some sort of forum, to become involved with the policies that directly affect their lives. Faculty should likewise assist student-life professionals in the important work they do. All efforts should be directed by campus-wide conversations, rooted in community faith commitments and traditions. If a college or university realizes the organic nature of effective policy-making, then a truly educational setting may emerge from what may otherwise be considered mere fundamentalism.

---

20 Of course, since we have issued in this essay a call for greater diversity in education, we do not imply that populist discourse should be censored on campus. It should be explored, studied, and, when necessary, critiqued.

Table 1: Percent of students who have reported breaking university conduct rules, sorted by class.

Have broken rules regarding:

	Freshman (621)	Sophomore (517)	Junior (544)	Senior (578)
alcohol	8.4	18.3	24.9	42.2
sex	6.5	8.1	11.5	18.1
curfew	13.2	25.1	28.2	24
dress-code	8	8.6	10	8.3

Table 2: Responses in percent of faculty who perceive students not living sheltered lives (NSL) compared to those who do perceive students living sheltered lives (SL) in regards to questions about university rules.

My institution's rules for students regarding alcohol are fair and reasonable:		
	NSL (379)	SL (488)
Strongly agree	60.9	37.5
Somewhat agree	26.9	34.2
My institution's rules for students regarding sex are fair and reasonable:		
	NSL (375)	SL (485)
Strongly agree	68.5	50.7
Somewhat agree	21.3	25.6
My institution's rules for students regarding curfew are fair and reasonable:		
	NSL (375)	SL (484)
Strongly agree	43.7	22.1
Somewhat agree	24	26.7
My institution's rules for students regarding dress code are fair and reasonable:		
	NSL (376)	SL (483)
Strongly agree	42.8	27.1
Somewhat agree	22.6	26.5

Table 3: Responses in percent of faculty who perceive students not living sheltered lives (NSL) compared to those who do perceive students living sheltered lives (SL) in regards to questions about university academic climate.

My institution is a place of rigorous intellectual activity:		
	NSL (367)	SL (467)
Strongly agree	26.2	13.9
Somewhat agree	51.2	42.6
I possess academic freedom at my institution:		
	NSL (367)	SL (468)
Strongly agree	59.4	33.3
Somewhat agree	31.9	44.2
Professors at Christian institutions have more freedom to discuss issues and ask questions than do professors at secular institutions:		
	NSL (366)	SL (469)
Strongly agree	35.5	14.9
Somewhat agree	31.1	28.1
I am hesitant to address certain important issues in class because I teach at a Christian university:		
	NSL (365)	SL (470)
Strongly agree	3.0	12.3
Somewhat agree	12.3	24

Table 4: Responses in percent of faculty who perceive students not living sheltered lives (NSL) compared to those who do perceive students living sheltered lives (SL) in regards to questions about "alterity" on campus.

Diversity of theological opinions among faculty and students is healthy for Christian college/university:		
	NSL (378)	SL (489)
Strongly agree	34.7	58.7
Somewhat agree	33.1	45.5
Roman Catholics should not instruct at a Christian college/university that has Protestant origins:		
	NSL (381)	SL (490)
Strongly disagree	34.4	56.1
Somewhat disagree	25.5	25.1
Female faculty at my institution are treated equally to male faculty:		
	NSL (367)	SL (469)
Strongly disagree	3.3	10.7
Somewhat disagree	7.9	25.4
Female students at my institution are treated equally to male students:		
	NSL (365)	SL (471)
Strongly disagree	1.1	6.6
Somewhat disagree	4.9	14.2

The student body at my institution is racially diverse:		
	NSL (365)	SL (470)
Strongly disagree	26	38.1
Somewhat disagree	9.6	34.5

Bibliography: Part Three

Allport, Gordon W. *The Individual and His Religion*. New York: McMillan, 1950.

Amato, Paul R., and Freida Fowler. "Parenting Practices, Child Adjustment, and Family Diversity." *Journal of Marriage and the Family* 64 (2002): 703-716.

Baumrind, Diana. "Current Patterns of Parental Authority." *Developmental Psychology* 4 (1971): 1–103.

Benne, Robert. *Quality with Soul: How Six Premier Colleges and Universities Keep Faith with Their Religious Traditions*. Grand Rapids, Mich.: Eerdmans, 2001.

Feldman, Shirley S., Turner, Rebecca A., and Araujo, Katy. "Interpersonal Context as an Influence on Sexual Timetables of Youths: Gender and Ethnic Effects." *Journal of Research on Adolescence* 9 (1999): 25-52.

Hoekema, David A. *Campus Rules and Moral Community: In Place of in loco parentis*. Lanham, Md.: Rowman & Littlefield Publishers, 1994.

Holmes, Arthur F., *The Idea of a Christian College*. Revised edition. Grand Rapids, Mich.: Eerdmans, 1991.

Johnston, Lloyd D., Patrick M. O'Malley,, and Jerald G. Bachman. *Monitoring the Future: National Survey Results on Drug Use, 1975-2002. Volume II: College Students and Adults*. Bethesda, Md.: National Institute on Drug Abuse, 2003.

Mackey, Kathleen, Mary Louise Arnold, and Michael W. Pratt. "Adolescents' Stories of Decision Making in More and Less Authoritative Families: Representing the Voices of Parents in Narrative." *Journal of Adolescent Research* 16 (2001): 243-268.

Marcia, James E. "Development and Validation of Ego-Identity Status." *Journal of Personality and Social Psychology* 3 (1966): 551-558.

Niemiec, Christopher P., Richard M. Ryan, andEdward L. Deci. "The Path Taken: The Consequences of Attaining Intrinsic and Extrinsic Aspirations in Post-College life." *Journal of Research in Personality* 43 (2009): 291-306.

Richard M. Ryan, Scott Rigby, and Kristi King. "Two Types of Religious Internalization and Their Relations to Religious Orientations and Mental Health." *Journal of Personality and Social Psychology* 65 (1993): 586-596.

Steinberg, Laurence D., Nancy E. Darling, and Anne C. Fletcher. "Authoritative Parenting and Adolescent Development: An Ecological Journey." In *Examining Lives in Context*, 423-465. Edited by Phyllis Moen, Glen H. Elder, Jr., and Kurt Lusher. Washington, D.C.: American Psychological Association, 1995.

Stukas, Arthur A., Mark Snyder, and Gil Clary. "The Effects of 'Mandatory Volunteerism' on Intentions to Volunteer." *Psychological Science* 10 (1999): 59-64.

Younger, Jonathan C., Lucy Walker, and John A. Arrowood. "Postdecision Dissonance at the Fair." *Personality and Social Psychology Bulletin* 3 (1977): 284-287.

PART FOUR

ACADEMIC FREEDOM

CHAPTER 10

THE HESITANTS AMONG US

The Tightrope Act of Christian Scholarship

JOE RICKE

I. Preliminary Semi-Scientific Snapshot

As a self-identified campus malcontent (for the greater good of the community, of course), I found the results of the Joeckel/Chesnes survey surprising and hopeful in regard to academic freedom.[1] Almost half of those surveyed strongly agreed with the statement that "I possess academic freedom at my college/university" (FSQ 96). Another 40 percent somewhat agreed. In fact, over half believe that "Professors at Christian institutions have *more freedom* to discuss issues and ask questions than do professors at secular institutions" (FSQ 97).[2] Further, I was pleased to discover that over two-thirds could disagree with the statement, "I am hesitant to address certain important issues in class because I teach at a Christian college/university" (FSQ 98). Critics of Christian higher education, especially those committed *a priori* to the idea that faith statements and theological commitments undercut the possibility of legitimate academic activity, should take note.[3] Those engaged in Christian higher education (inside "the bubble" as one respondent called it) might be

---

1　I use "Academic Freedom" to mean the actual legal protection of research and teaching as provided for by the traditions of university education, overseen by groups such as the AAUP, and guaranteed (with specific limits) by Christian college and university handbooks. I use "academic freedom" to refer to the more general notion that faculty and students should have the freedom necessary to pursue their studies (and teaching) without coercion, constraint, or fear of reprisal. One might say that we have a great many academic-freedom "issues" in our colleges and universities, for a variety of reasons, but that very few of these actually become Academic-Freedom cases.

2　This particular article of faith (not sure yet if it's part of "the Christian worldview") is part of what I call "the Marsden Effect." Recently, under its influence, Azusa Pacific University has rewritten its statement on academic freedom to replace the language of "limits" with "opportunities" and the somewhat disingenuous concomitant that faith commitments provide a more expansive definition of academic freedom than those found in the secular university. See Elizabeth Redden, "Academic Freedom, Christian Context," *Inside Higher Ed. Com*. March 2, 2009, http://www.inside-highered.com/news/2009/03/02/azusa.

3　Marsden demonstrates the ubiquity of this attitude in the modern university. The ultimate version is that held by philosopher Simon Critchley that to be a scholar is necessarily to be an atheist. See his *Very Little . . . Almost Nothing: Death, Philosophy, Literature* (New York: Routledge, 1997), 3.

forgiven if they take a moment to rejoice that most of our faculty feel comfortable living out—in classrooms, laboratories, stages, lecture halls, and chat rooms—the dictum that "All truth is God's truth." Listen carefully and we might even hear a few "I told you so's" directed at the secular academy, which rejects what Newman called "the queen of the sciences" (theology)[4] and "as a whole is dismissive of Christian scholarship" (or so almost 70 percent of respondents believe; FSQ 99).[5]

Before taking a closer look and, frankly, before turning a more critical eye on this apparent success story, we should find joy and hope (if not comfort and self-satisfaction) in these data. Given the high level of importance traditionally attached to academic freedom in higher education and especially in light of the historic tension between faith and reason (or "Jerusalem and Athens") which Christian scholars have inherited (the significance of which some of our detractors and perhaps even our supporters do not understand), "doing" academic freedom at all is commendable. This relationship between the knowledge of faith and the knowledge obtained by reason has always been a kind of dangerous high-wire act for would-be Christian scholars. Acknowledging that historical reality, we should just be grateful that the tight-rope walkers yet wobble. And maybe even flourish in (and add new flourishes to) their dangerous, necessary vocation.

II. The Shadows

What, though, are we to make of the negative evidence? If academic freedom is, arguably, the *sine qua non* of the academic project, how do we interpret the data that one-tenth of our colleagues disagreed with the statement that they have academic freedom? Other responses also must give us pause. Less than one-fifth strongly agree that "my college/university is a place of rigorous intellectual activity" (FSQ 94). Further, and perhaps most troubling, almost one-fourth of those surveyed agreed that "I am hesitant to address certain important issues in class because I teach at a Christian college/university" (FSQ 98). At the extreme perhaps, one respondent claimed that the most difficult thing about being a professor at a Christian college is "the feeling that I cannot address some very 'real world' problems/topics in the classroom for fear of losing my job." While we celebrate that most are *not* hesitant, we should ask what hinders so many from doing something so foundational as "addressing important issues" in the classroom.

Further, we all know what just one Academic Freedom case (like those which eventually come to involve the AAUP) can do to the life of an institution, the reputations of the people and schools involved, and, beyond that, to the reputation of the Christian academy

---

4 See George Marsden, "Theology and the University: Newman's Idea and Current Realities," in *The Idea of the University*, ed. Frank M. Turner (New Haven: Yale University Press, 1996), 302-317.

5 Marsden's uber-thesis, so to speak. Critics, of course, contend that the "dismissal of Christian scholarship" is due more to the narrow focus of most of that scholarship and the narrowing effect of our reactionary attitudes towards the larger scholarly community. Alan Wolfe claims "It is because so many evangelicals heeded Marsden's warning that their scholarship, rather than storming the gates of elite academia . . . has taken its place as its own subculture, complete with journals, conferences, and publishing houses. Even in their best work evangelical scholars cite one another far too often. Their conclusions win more applause among fellow believers than among the unconvinced." See Alan Wolfe, "The Opening of the Evangelical Mind," *Atlantic Monthly*, October 2000, 76. It sometimes appears, on our own campuses, that publication by a Christian press or on a "Christian topic" (as such) often trumps quality scholarship which does not specifically reference such topics and/or is published in "secular" journals.

(and even the Christian community) at large. In light of the trauma of such cases, whether or not they end up with the school on the AAUP censured list, most of us would agree that even one is one too many. Further, we recognize the degree to which other academic-freedom conflicts—which, for whatever reasons, never rise to the level of an "Academic-Freedom case"—set off unsettling reverberations in the life of a university. In this context, then, we should consider the possible implications of a good number of those working in our institutions who believe that they do not possess academic freedom and/or those who claim to be hesitant about addressing certain important issues in our classrooms.[6]

With the help of the Joeckel/Chesnes survey, we can isolate certain segments of our population (specifically those who disagree that they possess academic freedom and those who agree that they are hesitant to address important issues) and compare them to the total group of respondents. In doing so, I hope to identify some specific concerns reflected in their critical responses and, finally, to provide some tentative interpretation. Why, though, attend to these critics' voices at all? What hath Jerusalem to do with surveys anyway? After all, we all are familiar with the stereotypical disgruntled faculty member, always ready with an opinion critical of the administration, the admissions staff, even the football mascot. (In fact, one works in my office and looks in my mirror when shaving.) The problem with the professor-who-cried-wolf dismissal of such critics, however, is that it predisposes us to ignorance. It is possible (possible, I say) that I may have complained once too often about the mind-numbing over-reliance on PowerPoint on my campus, but that doesn't discount my criticism today of the fact that my office building smells like sewage. It does. I permit myself this little digression because, as the survey makes clear, the respondents who believe that they *do not* possess academic freedom are, in general, characterized by a more critical attitude towards their institutions on almost every issue. The answer, of course, to the question of why we should consider the concerns of a critical minority relates to our desire for the truth and our realization that divergent voices (see Jesus, Socrates, and the police chief in *Jaws*) make a highly significant contribution to a community of truth-seekers (if not comfort-seekers).

III. Preliminary Profile of "Academic Freedom" Group

What, then, are some of the characteristics of the group who disagreed with the statement, "I possess academic freedom at my college/university"? Interestingly, they differ only slightly from the total group of respondents in several areas we might expect to find difference, such as gender, ethnicity, education, years as a Christian, publication history, and other questions (Table 1). Differences begin to appear especially relating to political/social/theological issues which, for want of better terms, we might identify as *conservative/*

---

6 Although this particular question identifies an important concern, both the terms "hesitant" and "important" are ambiguous and, therefore, the responses are somewhat ambiguous. For example, some teachers who identify themselves as "hesitant" may still overcome that hesitancy and address the issues. To others, "hesitant" might signify "do not address at all." Others might define "important" much differently than I would. For some, what is "most important" may be that which will lead to community, good relationships, and an absence of conflict, On a campus like mine, which prides itself on its "community ethos," scholars need to be extra vigilant against polite forms of "Prior Restraint and Censorship." For an excellent discussion of this point, see Anthony Diekema, *Academic Freedom and Christian Scholarship* (Grand Rapids, Mich.: Eerdmans, 2000), 27-28.

liberal (Table 2). The academic-freedom group (AF) tends to be more liberal, sometimes significantly so, when compared with the total group (T) and even with other isolated groups which we might also expect to lean left. Only 30 percent of the AF group identify their political affiliation as Republican (compared with 46 percent of the total group). They are significantly more likely to agree that "the theory of evolution is compatible with Christianity," that "the evidence for human-induced climate change is convincing," that the government "should provide funding for embryonic stem cell research," and that "homosexuals should be given the right to marry." In similar ratios, they were more likely to disagree with "the military campaign in Iraq" and that "abortion should be made illegal in the United States." Further, they tend to be "epistemological liberals."[7] They are twice as likely to strongly agree that "Postmodernism can be compatible with Christianity." They are much less likely to strongly agree that "truth is absolute, not relative" and twice as likely to "strongly disagree" with that proposition. In terms of biblical/theological assumptions, less than half identify themselves as theological conservatives, compared with 69 percent of the total group. They were much more likely to "have had doubts over the past year" about the Bible and about their own faith, to believe that "it is acceptable to question the Bible," to agree that "my interpretation of the Bible [may] change," and to believe that "diversity of theological opinions among faculty and students is healthy for a Christian college/university." They were less likely to agree that "the Bible is the only authoritative source of information about God" and to believe in biblical inerrancy.[8]

Interestingly, those "hesitant to address certain important issues" (H) tend to be not only more "liberal" than the total group but even more "liberal" than the AF group. In other words, those who identify themselves as "hesitant" to bring up certain important issues are, ideologically, more likely to question political, theological, and biblical hegemonies, whether in the classroom or not. That they may or may not define that as an issue of "academic freedom" speaks to the rather fluid use of the term.[9] An even greater distinction between the H group and T group may be observed in response to the statement, "Professors at Christian institutions have more freedom to discuss issues and ask questions than do professors at secular institutions" (FSQ 97). Less than 7 percent of the H group strongly agreed with this statement (compared to 24 percent of T) and 24 percent strongly disagreed (compared with 8 percent of T). The smaller academic-freedom group, perhaps attending to the use of the word "freedom" in the question, was even more critical. Only 20 percent of them agreed at all that Christian universities are characterized by "more freedom to discuss issues and ask questions," whereas 69 percent specifically disagreed (Table 3).[10] Despite slight differences, the basic similarity of the AF group to the H group

---

7 See Joeckel and Chesnes, "A Slippery Slope to Secularization?"

8 Interestingly, Bible and Theology faculty were also less likely to identify themselves as inerrantists than the total group, perhaps because they are the only faculty who really know what "inerrancy" means.

9 Although the H group tended to agree that they possessed academic freedom at their schools, yet still only 21 percent of them strongly agreed compared to 47 percent in the total group.

10 This is an issue with strong opinions on both sides. A great many faculty responded to the open-ended question about whether Christian universities were superior to secular ones with a strong statement about the high level of academic freedom (in its looser usage) at Christian schools and the almost complete absence of the same at secular

on this question will help make distinctions as significant differences arise in response to other questions. On the other hand, we do not want simply to "use" the "hesitants among us" as a "control group." Although their concerns may not always be specifically expressed in statements containing the phrase "academic freedom," that this rather large minority among us registers such discomfort with open discussion of serious issues on our campuses should be of concern to readers of this book.

That faculty in our institutions who identify themselves as being further left than most of their peers (and the survey clearly highlights the conservative leanings of Christian college faculty) express concern about academic freedom should, perhaps, be no surprise. Neither should the reality that some faculty feel that their freedom is "limited." Of course, almost everyone agrees that academic freedom has some limits. The exact definition, interpretation, and implementation of those limits become problems of defining and "doing" academic freedom and Academic Freedom in the CCCU. In his *Idea of a Christian College*, Arthur Holmes defines academic freedom "as freedom to explore the truth in a responsible fashion." He qualifies "responsible" by claiming that academic freedom must be practiced in "concern for the common good of the community," with attitudes of "humility and awe," and within a commitment to the "framework of belief confessed by [the professor's] college." Indeed, academic freedom, for Holmes, involves "working loyally . . . rather than acting like iconoclasts or teaching subversion."[11] Clearly, in Holmes' view, academic freedom has strong limits (although many of them would be difficult to determine and would seem to provide faculty with little defense in cases of, say, inadequate "humility and awe"). More recently, Anthony Diekema has argued, relying heavily on Marsden's critique of the secularized university, for "worldview" as the Christian scholar's major "limit" or "freedom."[12] Many faculty, however, might want to qualify their commitment to such an idea, depending upon just who has a say in formulating and promulgating that worldview, how that worldview is interpreted and applied, and how much freedom faculty have to be part of the dialogue of interpretation and application.[13]

The problem of limits, therefore, is always more than the simple fact of the limits. Instead, major issues arise especially when those limits are not clearly stated and/or consistently applied. If they are ambiguous or if they seem malleable or open to quick revision (especially under pressure from certain "constituencies"), they all too easily become not so much limits on academic freedom as sleight-of-hand tricks, with faculty

---

universities. This may, of course, reflect reality accurately and these faculty members may, in fact, be deeply engaged in dialogue with the secular academy. It may, to some degree and/or in some cases, reflect the Marsden Effect.

11   Arthur Holmes, *The Idea of a Christian College* (Grand Rapids, Mich.: Eerdmans, 1975), 85.

12   See Diekema, *Academic Freedom*, especially 44-81. Diekema offers a wealth of examples and discussions of policies and mission statements, not to mention his personal experiences at Calvin, especially in the case of science professor Howard Van Till. Eugene Habecker argues for "mission statements" as limits in "Academic Freedom in the Context of Mission," *Christian Scholar's Review* 21 (1991): 175-181.

13   "Worldview" language has had favored status in Christian colleges at least since Holmes. For a lengthy recent defense of worldview thinking, see David Naugle, *Worldview: The History of a Concept* (Grand Rapids, Mich.: Eerdmans, 2002). For a witty but serious critique of the dominance of the "worldview" paradigm, especially the degree to which it has been co-opted by the Christian Right and the Christian education establishment, see Jack Heller's two essays in the online journal, *The New Pantagruel* 1.3 (Summer 2004) and 1.4 (Fall 2004), http://www.newpantagruel.com/issues/1.3/christian_college_professor_fl.php.

as victims.[14] Nicholas Wolterstorff, although agreeing that "all educational institutions attach qualifications to academic freedom," warns that conflicts occur in religious universities "when religious qualifications are applied unjustly, that is, when they are never fully stated, or not stated clearly in advance, when their application is arbitrary and irregular, or when there's no recourse available to the victim."[15]

In the looser sense of the term, however, respondents repeatedly used academic freedom as a marker for something more (or less) than suggested by these academic-freedom crises and Academic-Freedom cases. They often invoke it to describe a campus atmosphere open to dialogue and the free exchange of ideas, even when those ideas might challenge received orthodoxies and/or long-standing assumptions. Clearly, in that light, some of our more "liberal" faculty believe that their orientation makes them suspect on campus and, at least in some cases, whether they finally do or do not "address certain important issues in class," they see this as an obstacle to academic freedom (or a reason for "hesitation"). Many of the following qualitative responses to the open-ended question, "What is the most difficult thing about being a professor at a Christian university?" bear this out.

For example: "Being somewhat liberal . . . . The fear of saying something or revealing a belief that will not be considered acceptable." "I am less conservative in my beliefs than many of my students, and do not always feel comfortable in discussions about social and moral issues." "While I am free to discuss anything in the classroom, I am not free to take a strong position on several politically related issues. We have freedom to discuss, but not freedom to voice dissenting opinions." "Witnessing the chilling effects of authoritarian conservatism." "Always having to hide any beliefs that are a little more liberal than the official policy at the institution." "[Absence of] academic freedom. Being subject to a conservative board of trustees."

IV. Closer Look: Correlation with Religiosity and Administration Concerns

As shown, those who disagree that they possess academic freedom (AF) may be identified as "more liberal" than the total group of respondents. However, somewhat surprisingly, other even "more liberal" groups—notably those who "hesitate to address certain important issues" (H)—are yet significantly more likely to affirm that they possess such freedom (although still less likely to do so than the total group). How, then, can we identify other concerns which animate the AF group? In fact, the survey provides two clusters of questions which help provide even clearer distinctions between the AF group and the T group. I call these the Religiosity cluster (REL) and the Administrative Concerns cluster

14   In the John Sanders case with Huntington College, the decision not to renew Sanders' contract was based on powerful denominational figures who found his open theism "very troubling." Clearly, however, it was the fact that he was a Bible professor (rather than, say, a business professor), as well as a popular and controversial author that led to his dismissal. The president admitted that "there is no requirement for professors on this issue" and that "we have some other faculty who are open theists, but they're not teaching theology or Bible." In this case, the rather slippery limits on academic freedom came down to a freedom to believe in but not gain a hearing for one's ideas. I doubt this is what Huntington's president had in mind when he added to *Christianity Today*: "For all Christian colleges, academic freedom is bounded in some way." See Stan Guthrie, "Open or Closed Case?" *Christianity Today*, December (Web-only) 2004, http://www.christianitytoday.com/ct/2004/decemberweb-only/12-20-32.0.html.

15   Wolterstorff quoted in "Conference Looks at Religion and Academic Freedom," *Acadame Online*, July-August 2000, http://www.aaup.org/AAUP/pubsres/academe/2000/JA/AW/relconf.htm.

(ADMN). The AF responses to the REL questions are especially instructive, once again, when viewed in conjunction with the H group. Both H and AF, as earlier established, are more liberal than the total group (H much more so). Similarly, when it comes to Religiosity on campus, the survey indicates that both groups tend to be far more critical than the total group. Interestingly, though, the H group is much closer to the total group (T) than to AF on every Religiosity question. (In other words, AF is significantly more critical of religiosity than the more liberal H group.) Further, on religiosity issues, the difference between AF and T is more pronounced than on the liberal/conservative questions we analyzed previously.

For example, the AF group is much less likely to agree (and even less likely to strongly agree) that "attending chapel," "teaching classes," or "relationships with other faculty" "have enhanced their faith." Only 11 percent say their faith has become "much stronger" as a result of being at their institution, contrasting with 31 percent of T but also sharply contrasting with 23 percent of H. Perhaps even more surprising, only 35 percent of AF strongly agree that "I am comfortable affirming my college's/university's faith statement" (compared with 66 percent of T).[16] Over half strongly disagree that chapel should remain or become mandatory. In regards to whether their campus was characterized by "vibrant spirituality," only 13 percent of the AF group strongly agreed, compared with 31 percent of T (Table 4). Although no specific questions in the survey connect disaffection with campus religiosity to academic freedom, the co-related data above as well as the qualitative data provided in the open-ended questions do suggest just such a connection. Here is a sample of relevant responses to the question, "What is the most difficult thing about being a professor at a Christian university?"

"Balancing the rational with the spiritual in ways that don't upset the constituency." "Always being careful not to offend students by telling them what is going on outside the bubble of Christianity." "The pervasiveness of oversimplified ideas that become faith tests and a faith discourse deeply implicated in the national politics of the so-called "'Christian right.'" "A few students, staff and faculty are 'doctrine-spies' whose primary preoccupation is whether or not one believes the right things, in their view." "Encouraging a critical engagement with matters of religion among students, faculty, and administration is difficult when reinforcement of existing belief is more highly valued." "Limitations of openness of thought and expression of ideas that do not conform to doctrine." "After having taught in a secular institution, I found the students at a Christian university to be amazingly unchristian in their attitudes and behaviors . . . . Unforgiving, entitled, arrogant." "Dealing with arrogance among faculty that seems to say that because we are a Christian college we are RIGHT." "Working within a sheltered community of faith."

---

16   This is especially significant in light of arguments by Diekema and others that the voluntary nature of faith-bounded "limits" guarantees academic freedom. See his unconvincing argument in Diekema, *Academic Freedom*, 70. Critics, even relatively friendly ones like Alan Wolfe, see faith statements as the greatest hindrance to academic freedom in Christian colleges. I disagree in principle, but some of his observations about the naiveté of the "purely voluntary act" theory seem accurate and even prophetic, especially after the Joshua Hochschild incident at Wheaton in 2005. See Wolfe, "Opening of the Evangelical Mind," 74.

Perhaps the co-related survey data, taken in light of the open-ended comments, reflect a problem that some faculty have with the overall "weight" of religiosity on our campuses. Given the huge emphasis on the Bible, theological formulations, and religious activities of all sorts, those who approach these differently from the majority or feel out of step (in terms of philosophy or praxis or both) may interpret this as a kind of limit on their academic freedom. Such limits may not always be part of "official" university policies or practices but more part of the inherited and/or affirmed campus culture. In this way, the critical concern with faith statements ("doctrine," "existing belief") may be the tip of a larger iceberg of wariness about "interpretive communities" and commitments and expectations, some acknowledged and some not, on our campuses. Especially if faculty experience these "norms" as anti-intellectual or even unfair, they might lean toward interpreting this as an academic-freedom issue.

The survey identifies a further and even more distinct marker, however, of the AF group by means of the cluster of questions I have labeled ADMN. Again, the AF group is significantly more critical in its responses than the T group (Table 5). What's more, in this case, the H (hesitant) group, although always more critical than T, is actually closer to T than AF.

In other words, as with the religiosity issue, the survey demonstrates an obvious concern other than and more important than the liberal/conservative issues provoking the dissatisfaction of those who identify a lack of academic freedom. The responses from the AF group to these questions tend to strongly disagree with any positive statements about the administration. For example, 73 percent disagree (41 percent strongly) that "conflict between faculty and administration at my college/university is charitably resolved" (compared with 27 percent of T). Only 1.8 percent of those who lack academic freedom strongly agree to the statement! Similarly, 73 percent disagree (42 percent strongly) that "a spirit of humility and charity between faculty and administration exists at my college/university" (compared with 25 percent of T). Comparing the one question (FSQ 84) that combines ADMN concerns with REL concerns—"The administration at my college/university performs its work in a Christ-like manner"—yields an inverse ratio. Only 5 percent of the AF group strongly agree (compared to 34 percent of T). Almost 30 percent strongly disagree (compared with 5 percent of T). Not surprisingly, the AF group is ten times less likely to strongly agree that "morale among faculty at my college/university is good" (2 percent to 21 percent). Clearly, then, although those whom we have identified as the AF group tend to be significantly more critical of their institutions than the overall group of faculty respondents on every possible topic, they diverge most emphatically in their attitudes towards religiosity and administrative issues. Although they tend to be more "liberal" on political and theological matters, their perspectives on critical attitudes towards campus religiosity and administrative issues distinguish them from the even more "liberal" H group. What remains for us to determine is the degree to which their attitudes are the result of their observation of particularly problematic circumstances on their campuses (such as perceived unfair treatment of a colleague or themselves), some generally negative predisposition towards their school's mission and community ethos, or something else completely.

V. Conclusions

The Joeckel/Chesnes survey gives us much to chew on now and work on going forward. The good news is that the majority of CCCU faculty agree that they possess academic freedom. Although we should be concerned that so many are "hesitant to address certain important issues in the classroom," we must view this in light of a history which is fraught with tension over just how the relationship between church and the academy should be fleshed out. That, of course, is no excuse for us to be hesitant about addressing our own important issue. I hope this information provokes us to thoughtful reflection and careful action and keeps us from the kind of triumphant attitude about academic freedom in the Christian academy which has become an unintended byproduct of the Marsden Effect. Faith statements, worldviews, mission statements, and confessions do, indeed, make our task what it is—worthwhile, yes, but also very challenging. Such a load of *a priori* pressures on scholarship can, but perhaps need not, influence us to ignore or even silence voices and perspectives to which we should attend. Such "big ideas" may indeed motivate us to seek all of God's truth, wherever we might find it. Yet they may also, without the appropriate counter-pressures of freedom, diversity, and faculty governance, effectively short-circuit the laborious task of scholarship, substituting apologetics for discovery.[17] One indicator of those concerned about their academic freedom is a more "liberal" or at least divergent stance (politically and/or theologically). If we are serious about modeling the rich variety of both God's creation and God's church, as well as demonstrating credibly our "openness" to other perspectives (not just complaining that others are not open to ours), we should continue our efforts to make welcome a diverse community of scholars. This, of course, needs to occur within the limits of our faith and mission statements, but that "limit" should not be a one-way street. Indeed, faculty should be involved in shaping, reviewing, and revising those statements for as long as we affirm that our truth-seeking project is ongoing. Further, the fact remains that those who claim not to possess academic freedom, admittedly a minority on our campuses, are specifically characterized by a negative stance towards campus religiosity and administration. It seems clear that the typical non-denominational "faith-and-practice" atmosphere of many CCCU schools does not necessarily translate into an all-inclusive religious environment. Perhaps, as suggested earlier, there is some negative connection between a sense of the overwhelming influence on our campuses of certain community religious beliefs and behaviors (and the interpretive constructs which under-gird them) and intellectual freedom. It is also likely that those who identify the campus

---

17   See Norman Klassen and Jens Zimmerman, *The Passionate Intellect: Incarnational Humanism and the Future of University Education* (Grand Rapids, Mich.: Baker Academic, 2006), for their excellent discussion of the potential for limiting full-hearted and open-minded academic excellence by excessive attention to "worldview." "One of the ways Christians foster the impression of arrogance and shy away from the rich complexity of common grace is their insistence on reframing the terms of intellectual discussion. Worldview thinking can itself encourage an attitude of detachment" (182).

religious culture with the administration may find those very practices toxic simply by connection to a leadership they identify as un-Christlike, uncharitable, and proud.

Three concluding post-scientific unscripts. First, given the key role played by faith statements and mission statements in Christian colleges and universities, and given the possibility for disaffection we have noted from those who do not feel totally "on-board," Christian colleges and universities should pay close attention to the way those statements are composed, adapted, revised, and promulgated. A "top-down" approach may seem efficient in the short run, but in an academic institution, thoughtful faculty will not be comfortable, in the long run, working within limits and under a weight that they don't really "own." Second, in relation to religiosity and academic freedom, it would be interesting to know more about how these seemingly unrelated topics coalesce in faculty dissatisfaction. I have suggested that there may be a general sense, among some, that religious/spiritual concerns trump academics on their campuses, and that the robust discussion of material that might be seen as antagonistic to those concerns is discouraged.

Finally, we should come to terms with the Marsden Effect. George Marsden's powerful critique of the secularized modern American university has clearly taken on a second life in the CCCU. The fear of "the slippery slope to secularization" (and related concerns) has come to motivate not only much of our theorizing but also our new faculty orientation, faculty development, and self-definitions (in catalogs, promotional materials, mission statements, and, now, even academic-freedom statements). There is something noble in making sure that we keep the soul in the university. There is something misleading, however, in the article of faith that Christian colleges have more freedom, for example, than secular universities. We generally have more freedom to discuss some ("Christian") things and to discuss everything in some ("Christian") ways. Even then, those freedoms are limited (not all "Christianities" are equal on our campuses). And everything else we do is limited by those "freedoms" (like having a discussion about homosexuality without theological/biblical guidelines). Often very limited. This may be a good thing, but let's not rush to an illogical "moral-equivalence" theory of limits. Because all academic freedom is limited, all limits are not equal. Faith statements, mission statements, pressures from churches, community traditions, complaints from parents (and administrators who pay too much attention to them), financial concerns—all of these and others as well make it likely that Christian scholars have less freedom, in many cases, than those working in the secular university. That is a choice we make, a choice we embrace, perhaps. But we must continue to work hard to define and guard academic freedom as we move forward, especially as we attempt to speak to and "go into" all the world, our greatest "constituency." To redefine our limits as freedoms (and the secular university's freedoms as limits) may play well in Peoria, but it's the kind of religiosity that involves a dumbing down of the Christian academic project when we are in most need of the unique gifts of a new generation of faithful and fearless scholars.[18]

---

18   Deep thanks to Nate Antiel, my former student and now a graduate student at Trinity College Dublin, for his helpful research and lively discussion on this topic. May he be faithful, fearless, and fully employed.

Table 1: Comparative responses of faculty in percent to various background questions.
T—Total group of faculty respondents (N = 1907)
AF—Those who disagreed that they possessed academic freedom (N = 168)

Years teaching at present school		
	T	AF
0-5	31.7	33.9
6-10	25.1	31.5
11-15	12.5	11.3
16 or more	30.7	23.2
Gender	T	AF
Male	62.3	63.1
Female	37.7	36.9
Ethnicity	T	AF
Caucasian	94.3	94
Black	1.5	1.8
Asian	1.3	2.4
Hispanic	1.2	0.6
Other	2	1.8
Highest degree earned		
	T	AF
PhD	61.4	63.7
EdD	9.2	9.5
MFA	1.9	5.4
MA/MS	19.5	13.1
MBA	1.8	1.8
MDiv	0.9	0.6
Other	6.8	6
How long one has been a Christian		
	T	AF
Less than 1 year	0.2	0.6
1 – 5 years	0.3	0
6 – 10 years	1.0	1.2
11 – 15 years	2.0	3
16 – 20 years	4.6	4.8
More than 20 years	92	90.5
Has written a published book		
	T	AF
Yes	24.1	23.8
No	75.9	76.2

Table 2: Comparative responses in percent to "Liberal/Conservative" questions

T—Total group of faculty respondents (N = 1907)
AF—Those who disagreed that they possessed academic freedom (N = 168)
H—Those who agreed that they were "hesitant to address certain important issues" (N = 420)

What is your political affiliation?			
	T	AF	H
Democrat	21.6	27.4	34.3
Republican	46.1	30.4	30.2
Independent	24.8	32.1	27.4
Other	7.7	10.7	8.3
The theory of evolution is compatible with Christianity			
	T	AF	H
Strongly agree	25.5	34.7	37.4
Somewhat agree	28.4	29.3	28.8
Neutral	11.1	11.4	9.4
Somewhat disagree	16.5	12	12.2
Strongly disagree	18.6	12.6	12.2
The evidence for human-induced climate change is convincing.			
	T	AF	H
Strongly agree	36.2	44.6	47.6
Somewhat agree	28.6	25	27.9
Neutral	13.9	14.3	11.4
Somewhat disagree	12.5	9.5	9.3
Strongly disagree	8.8	6.5	3.8
Federal government agencies should provide funding for embryonic stem cell research.			
	T	AF	H
Strongly agree	13.6	20.4	23.6
Somewhat agree	18	20.4	21.5
Neutral	18.6	24	22.4
Somewhat disagree	13.9	10.8	11
Strongly disagree	35.9	24.6	21.5
Homosexuals should be given the right to marry.			
	T	AF	H
Strongly agree	6.4	11.4	12.7
Somewhat agree	7.8	9	10.6
Neutral	10.8	12.7	16.3
Somewhat disagree	14.4	19.3	19.9
Strongly disagree	60.7	54.8	40.5
I support the military campaign in Iraq.			
	T	AF	H
Strongly agree	15.7	9.6	11.3

Somewhat agree	24.2	15	16.8
Neutral	11.1	8.4	8.4
Somewhat disagree	13.9	14.4	15.3
Strongly disagree	35.1	52.7	48.2

Abortion should be made illegal in the United States.

	T	AF	H
Strongly agree	35	24.4	22.4
Somewhat agree	22.3	19	20
Neutral	9.8	13.1	10
Somewhat disagree	15.5	16.7	19.1
Strongly disagree	17.4	26.8	28.4

Postmodernism can be compatible with Christianity

	T	AF	H
Strongly agree	13.2	26.8	22.2
Somewhat agree	29.3	25.6	31.6
Neutral	17	14.3	16.3
Somewhat disagree	18.8	15.5	15.1
Strongly disagree	15.4	11.9	7.7
Do not know what "Postmodernism" is	6.3	6	7.2

Truth is absolute, not relative.

	T	AF	H
Strongly agree	45.4	29.9	32.1
Somewhat agree	24.3	26.1	22.5
Neutral	8.4	13.8	11
Somewhat disagree	14.1	15	19.1
Strongly disagree	7.7	14.4	15.3

Would you consider yourself to be theologically conservative or liberal?

	T	AF	H
Strongly conservative	22.4	14.3	10.2
Somewhat conservative	46.4	34.5	38.1
Neutral	10.8	20.2	15.2
Somewhat liberal	17.1	22	29
Strongly liberal	3.7	8.9	7.9

I have had doubts over the past year about the Bible's authority.

	T	AF	H
Strongly agree	3.2	8.4	5.7
Somewhat agree	9.5	12.6	13.1
Neutral	8.2	13.8	13.4
Somewhat disagree	15.2	10.8	20.3
Strongly disagree	63.8	54.5	47.5

It is acceptable to question the Bible.			
	T	AF	H
Strongly agree	35.5	45.2	46.8
Somewhat agree	34.7	29.2	30.3
Neutral	12.2	12.5	11.2
Somewhat disagree	9.2	7.1	7.2
Strongly disagree	8.4	6	4.5
It is possible that my interpretation of the Bible will change sometime in the future.			
	T	AF	H
Strongly agree	14.4	22.6	16.9
Somewhat agree	44.2	41.1	44.9
Neutral	14	14.9	14.3
Somewhat disagree	14.5	8.9	11.9
Strongly disagree	12.8	12.5	11.9
Diversity of theological opinions among faculty and students is healthy for a Christian college/university.			
	T	AF	H
Strongly agree	46.5	68.3	62.3
Somewhat agree	40.9	25.6	28.8
Neutral	5.7	2.4	4.6
Somewhat disagree	5.7	2.4	3.8
Strongly disagree	1.1	1.2	0.5
The Bible is the only authoritative source of information about God.			
	T	AF	H
Strongly agree	38	28	23.9
Somewhat agree	18.2	16.1	17.2
Neutral	5.2	7.7	6.2
Somewhat disagree	21.8	25.6	27.2
Strongly disagree	16.7	22.6	25.5

Table 3: Comparative responses of faculty in percent to FSQ 97.

T—Total group of faculty respondents (N = 1907)
AF—Those who disagreed that they possessed academic freedom (N = 168)
H—Those who agreed that they were "hesitant to address certain important issues" (N = 420)

Professors at Christian institutions have more freedom to discuss issues and ask questions than do professors at secular institutions.			
	T	AF	H
Strongly agree	24.2	3.6	6.7
Somewhat agree	29.8	16.8	20.3
Neutral	19	10.8	16.2
Somewhat disagree	18.9	30.6	32.9
Strongly disagree	8.1	38.3	23.9

Table 4: Comparative responses in percent to "Religiosity" questions

T—Total group of faculty respondents (N = 1907)
AF—Those who disagreed that they possessed academic freedom (N = 168)
H—Those who agreed that they were "hesitant to address certain important issues" (N = 420)

Attending chapel at my college/university has enhanced my faith.		
	T	AF	H
Strongly agree	13.3	4.8	9.8
Somewhat agree	36.1	21.4	30.1
Neutral	29.7	31.5	25.3
Somewhat disagree	12.5	19.6	18.6
Strongly disagree	8.4	22.6	16.2

The classes I've taught at this college/university have enhanced my faith.		
	T	AF	H
Strongly agree	38.9	23.8	31.4
Somewhat agree	42.8	40.5	45
Neutral	14.8	26.8	16.9
Somewhat disagree	2.6	8.3	5.2
Strongly disagree	0.9	0.6	1.4

Other faculty at this college/university have enhanced my faith.		
	T	AF	H
Strongly agree	44.9	23.2	36.7
Somewhat agree	41	39.3	42.1
Neutral	9.7	19	12.1
Somewhat disagree	3.2	13.1	6.2
Strongly disagree	1.2	5.4	2.9

As a result of the time I've spent at my college/university my faith has		
	T	AF	H
Become much stronger	31.1	11.4	23.4
Become somewhat stronger	48.7	43.4	48.6
Stayed the same	16.5	28.9	19.9
Become somewhat weaker	3.1	12	6.2
Become much weaker	0.6	4.2	1.9

I am comfortable affirming my college's/university's faith statement.		
	T	AF	H
Strongly agree	65.8	34.7	45.7
Somewhat agree	24.4	36.5	33
Neutral	4.7	12	9.8
Somewhat disagree	4	12	9.1
Strongly disagree	1.1	4.8	2.4

Attending chapel should remain (or if applicable become) mandatory for faculty at my college/university.			
	T	AF	H
Strongly agree	10.2	4.8	6
Somewhat agree	17.1	13.7	13.9
Neutral	15.7	11.9	11.3
Somewhat disagree	21.7	18.5	21.1
Strongly disagree	35.3	51.2	47.7
My college/university is a place of vibrant spiritual activity.			
	T	AF	H
Strongly agree	30.9	12.5	21.8
Somewhat agree	50.7	42.9	51.7
Neutral	11.1	22	16
Somewhat disagree	6.1	15.5	7.7
Strongly disagree	1.2	7.1	2.9

Table 5: Comparative responses in percent to "Administration" questions

T—Total group of faculty respondents (N = 1907)
AF—Those who disagreed that they possessed academic freedom (N = 168)
H—Those who agreed that they were "hesitant to address certain important issues" (N = 420)

Conflict between faculty and administration at my college/university is charitably resolved.			
	T	AF	H
Strongly agree	14.4	1.8	10
Somewhat agree	45.5	15.5	36.8
Neutral	13.6	10.1	15
Somewhat disagree	17.4	32.1	22.9
Strongly disagree	9.1	40.5	15.3
A spirit of humility and charity between faculty and administration exists at my college/university.			
	T	AF	H
Strongly agree	19.4	3.6	14
Somewhat agree	45.9	17.3	39.5
Neutral	9.3	6.5	9.3
Somewhat disagree	15.9	31	21.7
Strongly disagree	9.5	41.7	15.5
The administration at my college/university performs its work in a Christ-like manner.			
	T	AF	H
Strongly agree	34.3	4.8	22.4
Somewhat agree	37.3	17.3	34.8
Neutral	12	18.5	17.2
Somewhat disagree	11.1	29.8	15
Strongly disagree	5.2	29.8	10.5

Morale among faculty at my college/university is good.			
	T	AF	H
Strongly agree	20.5	2.4	12.2
Somewhat agree	43.2	18	38.9
Neutral	10.9	12.6	14.1
Somewhat disagree	17.1	34.1	19.6
Strongly disagree	8.2	32.9	15.3

CHAPTER 11

FEAR NOT

Security, Risk, and Academic Freedom

DAN RUSS

Recently, my colleagues and I were hosting one of our annual dessert parties for new students. Faculty invite ten to fifteen students to our homes on the final night of orientation, before the serious work of registration and new classes begin. After a bowl of ice cream and some cookies and coffee, we all introduced ourselves and enjoyed a few minutes of discussion. On this particular evening we invited students to raise any questions about Gordon College and the academic experience. To my surprise, one student asked: "Now that I have chosen Gordon, why is this the right choice?" While one of my colleagues from the Philosophy Department waxed eloquent in response, I half listened while wondering how I should answer such a question. When my colleague finished, I simply added, "You made the right choice to come to Gordon because we can tell the whole truth." I went on to explain that most secular institutions of higher learning deny, ignore, or are indifferent to any truth claims grounded in religious faith, biblical texts, and church tradition, and some insist that holding to religious truths precludes the exercise of academic freedom. I went on to qualify my claim for Christian higher education by confessing that while Christian professors in a Christian college can tell the whole truth, we often do not for fear, individually or institutionally, that we will offend or anger some constituents: the administration, the board, our students, their parents, or some of our colleagues.

In light of such apprehensions, it makes sense that the first words in Samuel Joeckel and Thomas Chesnes' essay are "a fear variously named among those committed to Christian higher education . . . ."[1] Based on the responses to their survey of over 1900 faculty members of most of the institutions belonging to the CCCU, Joeckel and Chesnes focus on the fear of secularization's impact on Christian higher education and how it

---

1 Joeckel and Chesnes, "A Slippery Slope to Secularization?," 29.

controls and diminishes the possibility of academic freedom. They assert, and I agree, that the threat of secularization that produces what our colleague Joe Ricke terms "the Marsden Effect" is highly exaggerated, if we take seriously the empirical data revealed in the survey.[2] Those data show that most of the faculty members surveyed affirm the Christian character of their institutions and do not want them to conform to the model of secular institutions, and that most of them take their personal faith and calling as teacher/scholars very seriously. This causes Joeckel and Chesnes to conclude that "the formation of a university so vigilant against secularization . . . stifles the spirit of open inquiry and underestimates the value of the diversity of thought."[3]

While I, too, find objectionable the siege mentality that many Christian institutions foster, I think that the data reveal a more complex and perhaps deeper reason for the ethos of fear found in Christian institutions, particularly as it speaks to this issue of academic freedom. In reviewing the answers among faculty who represent a broad range of Christian perspectives theologically, politically, and epistemologically, I was struck not by their many and strong differences about controversial issues, but by the strong consensus that they possess academic freedom at their respective institutions. I would have expected that the mostly theologically conservative respondents, who represent 69 percent of all survey participants (FSQ 5), would agree with the statement, "I possess academic freedom at my college/university" (FSQ 96). In fact, almost 87 percent somewhat or strongly agree that they have academic freedom. So, this implies that over half of the approximately 30 percent who self-identify as liberal or neutral about the theologically conservative/liberal question assert that they possess academic freedom. However, when the statement is posed that "I am hesitant to address certain important issues in class because I teach at a Christian college/university" (FSQ 98), almost 70 percent disagree, which appears to return to the liberal/conservative divide. In other words, the 18% of those who affirmed their academic freedom seem to back off on how free their academic freedom truly is, if they hesitate "to address certain important issues" because they teach at a Christian college. Admittedly some of this 18% could be self-identified conservatives, which makes the question even more problematic. In short, I want to understand why faculty members who are on opposite sides of a number of crucial theological, political, and epistemological issues should so entirely agree with one another about possessing freedom at their institutions. Additionally, I want to explore other findings that reveal profound restrictions on academic freedom at Christian institutions despite the self-perception of the 87 percent mentioned above.

Before exploring this question, I think it is important to remember that this ethos of fear is not peculiar to Christian institutions. Colleagues in secular universities often fear that they will not receive tenure if they risk a scholarly perspective that does not conform to the school of thought or ideology of the tenured faculty in their department, if they speak out at a faculty meeting in disagreement with the prevailing perspective of their

---

2 Joe Ricke, "The Hesitants among Us," 153 and 162.

3 Joeckel and Chesnes, "A Slippery Slope to Secularization?," 39.

colleagues, if they challenge the status quo in a committee, or if they in any way offend the department chair, the academic dean, or the provost. These fears do not automatically subside after tenure, since these same people influence future promotions. We must also keep in mind that academic freedom, as has often been said, is not academic license to say what one pleases in any way one wishes. As Eugene H. Bramhall and Ronald Z. Ahrens explain, secular academic institutions limit academic freedom in at least three ways: professors are free "to teach and research in certain areas" in which they have expertise and for which they were hired because they are not experts on everything; they cannot use "speech that is offensive, harassing, or hateful," including forcing their political opinions on their students and colleagues; and finally, "the secular academy imposes restrictions on academic freedom by limiting religious speech."[4] The last point calls to mind C. S. Lewis offending his Oxford colleagues, because he, a literary scholar, wrote books about the Christian faith. Of course, it might also be argued that because he was not a biblical scholar or theologian, he spoke outside his field, which is not protected by the rules of academic freedom. As former Harvard President Lawrence Summers discovered, asserting an opinion not strictly in one's field can result in being dishonorably discharged from even the most prestigious administrative position in the country. I suspect that if we surveyed over 1900 professors from secular institutions and asked them to agree or disagree with the statement "I possess academic freedom," a significant percentage would strongly or somewhat disagree.

The complex realities that restrict academic freedom in Christian institutions of higher education are rooted in much more than a fear of secularization. The restrictions grow out of a deep distrust between a significant percentage of faculty and their administrations as well as distrust among their fellow faculty members in the minds of one quarter to one third of the faculty surveyed. The restriction on academic freedom also arises, in the minds of over half of those surveyed, from a teaching load that precludes a serious commitment to original scholarship and creative pedagogy. A third inhibition to academic freedom is evident in the majority of faculty who believe that the secular academy is "dismissive" of Christian scholarship. Finally, academic freedom is inhibited by the profound differences about core values among the faculty. Consider with me each of these and how they converge to threaten or deny academic freedom at Christian institutions.

First, authentic academic freedom can only exist and flourish in a community that trusts each other. When about 40 percent of the survey respondents are neutral or disagree that "conflict between faculty and administration is charitably resolved" (FSQ 82), why should a faculty member risk teaching or writing something controversial? In addition to the larger fear of being denied tenure or promotion, how many faculty members want to suffer through being dressed down by the department chair or dean? And over 30 percent are neutral or disagree that the administration is doing a good job (FSQ 83).

---

4   Eugene H. Bramhall and Ronald Z. Ahrens, *The Future of Religious Colleges* (Grand Rapids, Mich.: Eerdmans, 2002), 316-317.

Moreover, the distrust is almost as strong among the faculty (over 25 percent) who do not agree that they resolve conflicts charitably among themselves (FSQ 80). So not only do a significant minority have an antagonistic relationship with the administration, but over a quarter are not confident that many of their colleagues "have their backs." Just as it matters little what the law says if you do not trust lawyers and judges, the academic-freedom policies in the faculty handbook are only as good as the trustworthiness of those who implement them. Unless CCCU institutions take seriously this crisis in trust, academic freedom is an empty ideal for a significant minority of faculty.

In addition to this relational threat to academic freedom, there are institutional factors that transcend any particular set of personalities that come and go. Simply stated, the presumption of academic freedom is that teachers/scholars will take time to reshape their classes in light of their ongoing research and writing as well as contribute fresh findings to their guilds. But when just over half of the respondents say that they teach four or more courses per term (FSQ 86), and over two-thirds indicate that they "would welcome a course-load reduction for the express purpose of spending more time doing research" (FSQ 87), it is evident that most CCCU faculty are too busy to give much thought, time, and energy to researching their fields and re-visioning their courses. They are consumed in the serious business of teaching and the advising and committee work that attend it. They do not have time for the classic Christian ideal of school as *schola*, which once meant the leisure work to look back into history and to be initiated into the great conversation, to be inducted into one's discipline, to participate in authentic collegiality, to research and write, and to contemplate and imagine what it means to be fully human.[5] Instead, professors teaching four or more courses to students taking five or six courses must work relentlessly to prepare, teach, and grade so that students can get courses "out of the way" and earn as many credits as quickly as possible. Too often, the demands of such a teaching load cause professors to repeat to each new cohort of students the once-fresh ideas they generated early in their careers. No wonder under a quarter of those surveyed report having written a published book (FSQ 11) and less than two-thirds have published an article in a peer-reviewed or juried journal (FSQ 12). Just as we are told that hungry children cannot learn much unless they are first fed, so faculty members who are overwhelmed with their basic duties are starved for time and energy to exercise their academic freedom. The institutions that demand such a workload from their faculty send a clear message that academic freedom is, at best, an ideal that the faculty must accomplish despite lacking the support of the institutions' practices. Or to borrow, if not abuse, the line from "Me and Bobby McGee," [academic] "freedom's just another word for nothing left to lose."

These institutional impediments to the practical exercise of academic freedom in the Christian academy are reinforced in the minds of many Christian faculty members by the attitude toward Christian scholarship in the larger academy. Only 18 percent of those surveyed disagree that "The secular academy as a whole is dismissive of Christian

---

5   Josef Pieper, *Leisure: The Basis of a Culture* (New York: Random House, 1963), 20.

scholarship" (FSQ 99). What impact does this dismissive attitude among secular colleagues have on Christian scholars who have reason to believe that they are not taken seriously if they either are identified as faculty members of faith-based institutions or they incorporate explicitly Christian scholarship into their research and writing? We know how difficult it is for all scholars, especially young scholars, to be published in juried journals or by top university presses. How discouraging must it be to believe that one ought to hide any Christian perspective and/or hide one's affiliation to the Christian academy? While I agree with Ricke that Marsden's work has helped create an overreaction among Christian institutions about the threat of secularization—and a majority of those surveyed would apparently agree (FSQ 20)—when it comes to the disdain with which Christian scholarship is held in the secular academy, an 80 percent consensus cannot be explained or explained away by the "Marsden Effect." In short, no matter how much authentic academic freedom Christian faculty are permitted by policy, by trusted relationships with administrators and faculty, and by virtue of a balanced workload and such benefits as regular sabbaticals, the anti-Christian bias in the larger academy cannot but have an influence on the sense of academic freedom within the Christian academy.

Finally, the survey gives evidence to administrators and faculty who hold to the conservative theological, political, and epistemological convictions that founded most Christian institutions and are held to by most of their constituents that there is a significant minority of faculty who disagree with these convictions. In other words, the majority of the faculty surveyed and the administration and board who hold in trust the institutions, their histories, and their traditions have reason to fear what a significant number of their faculty might teach and publish in the name of academic freedom. This disparity begins, perhaps, from the fact that less than half say they took a job at a Christian institution because of a commitment to Christian higher education (FSQ 20). This does not mean that the others cannot be outstanding Christian scholars and teachers, but it does say that the majority only had a vague sense of the ideals and ethos of a Christian institution of higher learning. Almost 90 percent said that they received a good education at a secular college or university (FSQ 101), from which we may infer that the secular academy, which most believe to be "dismissive of Christian scholarship," has shaped the intellectual perspectives of most CCCU faculty members. It should not surprise us, therefore, that almost 10 percent are neutral or disagree about being "comfortable" signing the faith statements of their respective institutions (FSQ 22). When given the statement, "If I no longer agreed with my college's/university's faith statement, I would leave," 12.5 percent ranged from strongly disagreeing to somewhat disagreeing and 17.4% were neutral about what appears to me to be a clear question of personal integrity (FSQ 24). While we all understand that many faculty sign a faith statement that they might not interpret as strictly as some of their colleagues would, this statement is about knowing you disagree and staying anyway. In other words, this is a matter of integrity versus holding on to one's job. Add to this that about one-fifth entertained doubts about their faith (FSQ 37) and about the authority of Scripture (FSQ 33) in the past year, and we have to say that whether or not secularization of the Christian academy is a primary cause, a significant percentage of Christian faculty are deeply ambivalent about the deepest values of the communities they serve. How can either they or their colleagues exercise academic freedom that might involve revealing such profound and fundamental doubts?

If these restrictions to academic freedom, whether internal to our respective institutions or external in the larger academic culture, are to be overcome, we in CCCU institutions—faculty and administrators—must be clear about what we must hold in common, about how we can differ, and about how to move from where we are to what we can become. First, we must clearly understand among our colleagues what we mean by academic freedom. Obviously, we cannot mean exactly what the American Association of University Professors (AAUP) means, because it denies that academic freedom can exist if faculty members are required to subscribe to any religious or dogmatic beliefs. This largely twentieth-century perspective of academic freedom categorically opposes those truths that ground the Christian tradition. So while there is much overlap between the AAUP and CCCU institutions concerning academic freedom, we in the Christian academy start from a different place: what Gordon College calls "freedom within a framework of faith."

Let's not deceive ourselves; all academic freedom is within a framework of something. Donald Cowan reminds us not to confuse learning, that "internal action of individuals," with education, that "communal process, institutionalized by society for its own benefit: to preserve the ideals and memories it considers valuable, but also to produce competent workers and tranquil citizens for the status quo."[6] The most elite institutions of higher learning are bound by this social contract, whether the great state universities funded by and accountable to state legislatures or the great private institutions, sponsored by and serving the values of their donors. All academic institutions live in this tension between the search for truth as understood by individual professors and serving the constituents that make it possible to enjoy this pursuit. It is a dance, and every institution must dance it. We do not need to apologize that Christian institutions are Christ-centered and Scripture-bound, as have been most of the great universities from the Middle Ages through much of the nineteenth century. Indeed, not without tensions, modernity, including enlightened political ideals and modern science, was birthed by free-thinking scholars most of whom operated within a framework of faith. Our academic freedom functions within this covenant with the Christians we serve and the Christian traditions that bind us to the past and guide us to the future.

So here we are: Christian colleges and universities who must wrestle with academic freedom in a larger academy and culture that is committed, often dogmatically, to secular creeds. These are the times in which we live. These are the challenges we face. This is our story, and as Aristotle tells us, all stories begin *in medias res*. We did not ask to live in a postmodern or secular culture. We were not consulted by the Germans who gave rise

---

6   Donald Cowan, *Unbinding Prometheus: Education for the Coming Age* (Dallas: Dallas Institute Publications, 1988), 15.

to the modern research university and its scientific model of academic freedom: what Donald Cowan calls "the myth of fact."[7] Cowan explains that myth is "a large overarching metaphor that gives philosophical meaning to the experience of everyday life." He adds: "It is difficult to see the myth one lives in; like the air, it is necessary but invisible."[8] The myth of fact emerged in the Renaissance and by the late nineteenth and early twentieth centuries had become the academic air we breathe: measurement, research, data, hard numbers, statistics, polls, and so forth. As a physicist, Cowan is not disparaging the brilliance and importance of modern science, but he is critiquing its blindness to its own limits and how, in its obsession to demythologize all arenas of rational study, it forgets that it too sees through a myth darkly. CCCU institutions must navigate between the Scylla of our secular peer institutions that would conform us to their values through regional and other accrediting associations and the Charybdis of churches trying to conform us to their misunderstanding of Christian higher education, confusing the role of the church and the academy. Moreover, we have politicians and businessmen trying to turn us into vocational training institutions to fill their immediate need for a "work force." This pressure to fulfill immediate needs conflicts with the primary contribution that higher learning can offer a society: teaching the young to learn the wisdom of the past so that they can imagine a future twenty or thirty years out, when they will become society's leaders—affording them and the societies they serve the freedom not to be trapped in the trends and illusions of their own times.[9]

Back to the question: what can we do to transform this ethos of fear that limits the academic freedom in too many of our Christian colleges and universities? First, we can do little about the dismissive attitude of the secular academy. Alan Wolfe praised many evangelical scholars and institutions in his much-quoted 2000 *Atlantic Monthly* article, "The Opening of the Evangelical Mind," but he chides evangelical scholars for not "storming the gates of elite academia" and he criticizes evangelical institutions for requiring faculty to hold to the institutional faith statements.[10] However, when he spoke at our own institution a few years ago, praising and chiding us, he later confessed that he probably could not carry on the kind of philosophical scholarship that he does were he not serving in a Catholic institution. In other words, a secular scholar of Wolfe's quality and character enjoys a kind of freedom in a framework of a historic Catholic faith that he might not enjoy as a sociologist working in an institution committed to the myth of fact. Building on Wolfe's ambivalent confession, I encourage more Christian scholars to storm the gates of "elite academia," if that is their calling, but also encourage those of us called to serve in Christian academe to research and write excellent work that furthers the pursuit of truth in our various guilds, not fearing in our postmodern milieu that our Christian convictions are less valued than other "faith perspectives" of the secular academy. Likewise, we should not fear bringing the Alan Wolfes to our own campuses, to

---

7   Ibid., 4.

8   Ibid.

9   Ibid., 132-134.

10   Alan Wolfe, "The Opening of the Evangelical Mind," *Atlantic Monthly*, October 2000, 55-76.

challenge our faculty and students to learn from them and, when necessary, to disagree with them. Our students' education is deepened and broadened when they witness their professors engaging leading secular thinkers in robust and respectful dialogue. As Harold Heie has rightly pointed out, "We Christians do not have a stellar record of knowing how to talk with each other respectfully and charitably about our disagreements." He goes on to say that such conversation is an act of obedience to the truth that "Jesus Christ calls all Christians to love others."[11] But to do so, our institutions—their administrations, boards, and faculty—must risk being criticized by those who want our educational institutions to be, in Arthur Holmes' words, "an indoctrination center or political tool."[12] On the other hand, if the larger secular academy expressed no qualms about Christian colleges and universities, we should be equally worried that we have been co-opted by the culture. As H. Richard Niebuhr observed in his landmark work *Christ and Culture,* there are a number of ways the church has dealt with the tensions between the Christian faith and the dominant culture, but it must remain a tension, and one in which we fear God so that we are free not to fear the considerable power of a culture that would conform us to its values.[13]

While we have little control over the dominant culture, we have a great deal of control over the cultures of our various CCCU institutions. This being so, we need to find ways to reestablish trust between faculty and administration as well as among faculty, if we truly want an ethos of freedom. At the risk of sounding pious, we should take our lead from St. Paul, who helped create and worked to resolve the contentious cultural clashes of the early church. As the apostle to the Gentiles, Paul was bold in confronting the ethnic and religious biases of the early Jewish Christians, a confrontation which created countless tensions among his contemporaries as they wrestled with how Jewish the Christian faith must be and how goyish non-Jewish Christians can be and still be Christians. But as much as Paul is rightly seen as the great diversifier of the early church, he was also one who spoke and acted boldly to keep the unity of the faith. In Ephesians he admonishes his readers about the virtues that enable a church of diverse peoples with diverse gifts to be unified: "Then we will no longer be infants, tossed back and forth by the waves, and blown here and there by every wind of teaching and by the cunning and craftiness of men in their deceitful scheming. Instead, speaking the truth in love, we will in all things grow up into him who is the Head, that is Christ" (4:14-15 NIV). The crucial principle and practice Paul describes is expressed in his phrase "speaking the truth in love." Too much of the ethos of the academy, including the Christian academy, is about cunning, craftiness, and deceitful scheming. How many graduate students have been the victims of their dissertation committee members using them as a battleground to engage in skirmishes with a colleague whose perspective they hold in contempt? How often do we hold debates and engage in polemics when we invite speakers or hold conferences rather than

---

11 Harold Heie, *Learning to Listen, Ready to Talk* (New York: iUniverse, 2007), xxii.
12 Arthur Holmes, *The Idea of a Christian College* (Grand Rapids, Mich.: Eerdmans, 1987), 62.
13 H. Richard Niebuhr, *Christ and Culture* (New York: Harper Colophon Books, 1975).

gather thinkers who profoundly disagree but are concerned about seeking and speaking the truth in love, not demeaning the opponent to win the debate? If Christian colleges and universities are to be places where those of different perspectives can freely speak, there must be lavish and loving communication between administrators and faculty, faculty and faculty, and faculty and students. I hasten to add that the goal is truth, and truth is not the same as honesty. Indeed, honesty without truth and love is usually a weapon that teachers can use to intimidate and bully their students, that faculty can use to abuse their colleagues, and that administrators can use to cower the faculty. In other words, an ethos of academic freedom is not characterized by members of the community saying anything they please to anyone at anytime. Administrators must risk vulnerability with faculty and students, while not violating ethical and legal boundaries. Faculty must risk researching, writing, and teaching controversial ideas but with due respect for the appropriate audiences and with due humility about their own fallibility. And we must honor each other's gifts and roles. Even in the most harmonious academic community, how freedom is experienced by students, teachers, and administrators will always be different, not to mention the diverse perspectives among disciplines and among those who lead the academic enterprise, those whose primary work is institutional stability.

Let me suggest three practical ways of building trust over time. First, individuals must take seriously the biblical mandate to go to those with whom there is an offense. Otherwise anger and fear fester and scheming naturally follows, whether in the ignorance and resentment of our own minds or with co-conspirators who sympathize with us. Second, the administration and faculty must meet regularly and be fearless to address issues proactively as they arise, whether in private appointments, departmental and divisional meetings, or full faculty meetings. And finally, institutional life must be characterized by events, places, and times where we talk, break bread, laugh, argue, and worship with each other. The least such experiences do is to help us to know our colleagues as sisters and brothers in Christ, as mothers and dads, as mortgage holders and citizens, and as kayakers and knitters. The academy's great strength is its intellectual focus and its ability to mind the culture and the church, but the implicit problem with this strength is that we live in our heads and reduce our colleagues and ourselves to that one dimension of life. If an institution in which distrust has been fostered over years of poor communication and political scheming undertakes to transform the community into an ethos of trust, everyone must realize that it will take time. Peter Drucker has suggested that it takes five years from the initial commitment to such an undertaking to the point that it is simply the way we relate to each other.[14]

Transforming a faculty from scheming to trust is daunting, but it is possible for almost any institution that dares to take a Christ-like approach to how its members relate to one another. More daunting for many Christian institutions is how to address the overload that characterizes more than half of the CCCU institutions. For no matter how lavish and loving the communication becomes, an overworked faculty can exercise

---

14   Peter Drucker, *Managing the Non-Profit Organization* (New York: Harper Collins, 1990), 83.

little by way of freedom to think, research, write, and teach. Most of our institutions are tuition driven and the overwhelming "overhead" to maintain them is compensation for the faculty and staff. Boards and administrations of such institutions fear that if they reduce the course loads of their faculty and grant traditional sabbaticals, they simply will "price themselves out of the market" or begin an initiative that cannot be sustained. Added to these fears is the reality that many donors, including some board members and administrators, do not consider researching and publishing as important. As Mark Noll has pointed out, beginning with the publication of *The Scandal of the Evangelical Mind*, the genius of evangelicalism is our belief that a person can come to faith in Christ *now*, that the hungry should be fed *now*, that God speaks to us *now*, and that Jesus may return at any time. But one does not do authentic scholarship now. It is a laborious and inter-generational enterprise.

However, if a Christian college or university wants truly to free its faculty or at least part of its faculty to pursue scholarship, it is possible but risky. First, one can set out, as has been done at some of the leading Christian colleges, to increase tuition and giving to enable faculty to carry a normal teaching load of no more than three courses per term, with the understanding that they are expected to pursue scholarship and publications. Inseparably bound to this initiative is the need for all faculty to be able to apply for and, if qualified, receive a sabbatical for one semester at least every seven years. My own institution does so every five years and has been able to do so because only one course of the normal three courses is covered by an adjunct that must be paid a stipend. The other two are covered by colleagues, helping to make it financially sustainable. Instead of a course reduction for everyone or in addition to this, some institutions have two tracks for faculty: those who are primarily teachers and carry a heavier teaching load and those who are teacher/scholars, who carry a reduced teaching load. In many cases, faculty members self-select based on what they consider to be their own strengths and professional goals. Not only does this approach free the teacher/scholar to invest more time and energy into scholarship, but it frees those who have a passion for teaching from the burden of scholarly pretense. Also, many colleges invite donors to fund an endowed chair that frees up a proven scholar from most, sometimes all, of his or her teaching duties in order to flourish in scholarship and to be an ambassador at large for the institution. Of course, the practice of open and lavish communication needs to accompany such changes, if we want to avoid hurt feelings and professional jealousies, especially as we move toward dual tracks and endowed chairs. Finally, the administration needs to constantly review those responsibilities placed on faculty outside teaching and scholarship. It is easy to steal our colleagues' *schola* in the busyness of running the institution through countless committees and meetings. The administration's primary responsibility to the students and faculty is to guard the sacredness and excellence of the classroom and of the faculty's availability to their students.

We would like to think that faculty signing a faith statement and being committed to the integration of faith and learning along with a robust chapel program and a solid biblical/theological core for all students would distinguish as Christian an institution of higher learning. However, without an authentic commitment to academic freedom within a framework of Christian faith, Christian colleges and universities easily become either sanctified versions of secular institutions or oppressive and contentious organizations that drive honest questions and discussion underground and produce a scheming and polarized faculty and administration. Speaking the truth in love is the only way I know to live in the tension that we call freedom. If we believe that truth sets us free and that perfect love casts out fear, then we need to have the courage to encourage one another, individually and institutionally, to risk living, studying, teaching, and writing as truthfully and lovingly as we know how. It is risky. That is the nature of freedom, whether political or academic. If our ultimate goal is to secure our jobs or to secure our institution financially, academic freedom is not possible.

Finally, Christian colleges and universities must be transparent with their faculty and other constituents about how free individual faculty members are to interpret faith statements and institutional mission. The guiding principle here is freedom based on love: of Christ, of Scripture, of our institutional traditions, and, of course, of one another. But such freedom is not boundless. Even the AAUP recognizes that academic freedom is about teaching the truth as we see it in our disciplines. This does not include all of our personal opinions and hobby horses being foisted upon our students and colleagues, especially if these opinions are expressed in disrespectful and intimidating ways. Therefore, Christian institutions that require their faculty to sign faith statements and to subscribe to codes of behavior that serve the missions of their institutions must make clear those core values from the beginning and keep the dialogue open with faculty as they move through their respective careers. This should include a mutual responsibility between faculty and administration to encourage each other to uphold those values but to understand that words are said and that decisions are made that could cause us to doubt one another. When this happens, the offended party should seek understanding and reconciliation in the spirit of grace, acknowledging that we do not always know what we think we know and that each of us struggles and falters in our respective journeys. We also need to have the personal integrity, as administrators or professors, to walk away with grace from an institution with which we have come to fundamentally disagree. This is the right and loving action.

"It is for freedom [including academic freedom] that Christ has set us free," declared St. Paul (Gal. 5:1). But freedom is not freedom without risk, whether for faculty members who must be willing to risk their secure positions, for administrators who must be willing to risk their institution's reputation and their own positions, or students who must be willing to risk searching for the truth that sets us free. If we will not risk, we are not free.

WHAT IS FREEDOM FOR?

Rhetoric and Reality at Christian Colleges

CHAPTER 12

DAVID A. HOEKEMA

To be appointed to a special committee entrusted with the formulation of a new mission statement is a high honor, a sign that a faculty member has earned the trust of administrators and colleagues and that her experience and wisdom have won broad respect. Such honors, of course, do not come without costs. It is not just the hours devoted to committee meetings—that is only the beginning. Later comes the challenge of listening patiently and making careful notes when colleagues critique draft versions of the statement, no matter how ill-informed or idiosyncratic their comments may be. Many rounds of revision, careful preparation and packaging for board discussion, and still more revisions are likely to follow. But at the end of it all, one hopes, will come a sense of deep satisfaction. A revised statement of mission can aid in institutional renewal and guide campus leaders in building from present to future strengths. It can reaffirm for insiders, and explain to outsiders, the compelling vision and the unique environment for scholarship and learning that characterize the life of one's campus.

But mission statements embody lofty ideals, while daily life on campus is more a matter of practicality, compromise, and limited resources. No doubt there are days in between meetings of the drafting committee when its members wonder whether they are teaching in the same institution that their new statement describes. On Tuesday afternoon, they reflect, we proclaimed our core identity as a community of faithful Christian scholars who love the Lord, care for their students, foster wide-ranging intellectual inquiry for faculty and students alike, and seek renewal and transformation in society. But on Wednesday morning, they find themselves still living among whining colleagues, grade-grubbing students, and unresponsive administrators.

Recent years have witnessed the publication of many studies exploring the status and prospects of Christian higher education. The very proliferation of these books—an entire shelf full of them—reminds us of the persistent anxieties that motivate their writing: Can Christian liberal arts education survive the challenges of an increasingly secular academy, a faltering economy, and a generation of churchgoers with a diminishing sense of loyalty to either their childhood denomination or their alma mater? What strategic adaptations to changing circumstances help an institution grow and flourish? What new directions that appear so promising today will prove to be dead ends, exacerbating rather than resolving current problems? Questions such as these are on the mind of every college president, dean, development officer, and faculty member on campuses that hold fast to their religious roots.

In addressing these perplexing questions, most of the books on the Christian higher education shelf base their diagnoses on mission statements, catalogs, and interviews with administrators and faculty. Few have even attempted to supplement these sources by doing what Samuel Joeckel and Thomas Chesnes have done in their study: surveying individual faculty members concerning their assessment of the intellectual, spiritual, and collegial atmosphere on their campuses. Joeckel and Chesnes have in effect set mission statements aside and bracketed out all the rest of the official rhetoric in order to zero in on the daily life of the men and women who constitute the faculty ranks at member institutions of the Council for Christian Colleges and Universities. Nearly 1900 of them, at 95 institutions, took the time to answer more than a hundred Likert-scaled questions about what their campus does well or does poorly, whether it measures up to its ideals in matters of collegial relations and spiritual integrity, and whether academic freedom is a reality on their campuses or only a distant aspiration.

Let me say candidly that I have some misgivings about these data and the method by which they were gathered. Joeckel and Chesnes gathered faculty email addresses wherever they could, without notifying or requesting assistance from the institution, and then sent their survey instrument directly to individuals. They flew under the radar in this way—so I have been told—in order to ensure honesty in the responses and allay any worry that a critical comment about the president would find its way to the president's inbox. No doubt this did elicit more candor, but it also communicated a certain degree of mistrust.[1]

The same purposes might have been achieved just as effectively, without any appearance of concealment or impropriety, by building an information firewall between the administration of the survey and the submission of completed questionnaires, as is the practice when many of our campuses cooperate with national surveys by the Higher Education Research Institute (HERI) of the University of California at Los Angeles. Administrators are asked to provide email addresses and given an opportunity to review the survey instrument, but responses are reported to them only in an aggregated and anonymous form. I do not want to press this point too hard, however. It may well be that the campuses where faculty morale is lowest are also campuses whose administrators would have refused to cooperate in any sort of independent assessment.

---

1   Administrators were fully involved in the second round of surveys distributed to students, but the response rate was far lower than in the faculty survey. Perhaps this was in part because of misgivings over assisting in stage two of a survey when stage one had been conducted in a clandestine way.

In any case, by fair means or foul, a wealth of information has been gathered and laid out for our study and interpretation. There is no sign that the unusual data-collection process elicited flip answers or invited angry venting. Indeed, the written comments to open-ended questions show that most respondents took the survey seriously and gave carefully considered answers (even if some also complained about the inordinate burden of being the subject of surveys). Let us look more closely, then, at what we can learn from the survey results about the state of Christian higher education, as perceived by its faculty participants, in the first decade of the twenty-first century.

Each section of the present collection focuses on one broad area of college life and institutional mission. Some of these are of equal importance at small colleges and large universities, Bible schools and medical schools, religious and secular: How can we attain racial and ethnic diversity, for example, and ensure gender equity? What is the right balance between promoting teaching and encouraging scholarship? Others have special relevance to Christian higher education: How should faith shape scholarship and learning, in science and in other areas? What elements of campus ethos contribute to faith formation? Are parietal rules, drinking bans, and dress codes important in building a strong Christian community, or are they sustained only by nostalgia and desire for control? On the first set of issues, there can be fruitful conversation and mutual learning among Christian colleges, nonreligious liberal arts colleges, and state universities. Asked about the second set of areas, however, administrators and faculty at religiously unaffiliated institutions would respond: these are matters of personal choice, and they are none of our business as an institution.

Our focus in this set of essays is on issues of academic freedom, issues that do not fall neatly into either of the above areas. Goals and expectations are in some ways the same, in other ways entirely different, at different kinds of institutions. Moreover, a great deal depends on just how we phrase our questions—abstractly or concretely, in a vacuum or in a particular cultural and social context.

At the most abstract level, first of all, academic freedom is a core value on every campus. At colleges and universities in Manhattan and in Middletown, with student bodies of 500 or 50,000, at Cozy Corner Christian College and at Gigantic State University—at every institution today every faculty member and nearly every president, dean, and board member would readily affirm the importance of wide-ranging inquiry and vigorous debate, within the institution and within the professional disciplinary guilds. Whether Baptist or agnostic, Catholic or Jewish, Wesleyan or Wiccan, all of us who inhabit the academy today have come to affirm John Stuart Mill's doctrine that the best remedy for falsehood is not suppression and punishment but open confrontation, in the marketplace of public and private debate, with the truth.

But our unanimity begins to unravel when we descend from the high-altitude view and try to negotiate the treacherous terrain that lies beneath us. We can still agree on some specific applications, to be sure. Does academic freedom protect a European historian who insists that the Nazis were right about superior and inferior races? Of course not. But on other questions our paths will part. Does academic freedom protect a philosophy professor who embraces Simon Critchley's view that philosophy in the modern era must begin with atheism?[2] If the class is at Gigantic State, the answer is clearly yes—this is just what academic freedom is supposed to protect. If it's at Cozy Corner, on the other hand, the answer is no. Academic freedom cannot be invoked in defense of such a frontal assault on the institution's core commitments.

Nowhere is academic freedom a matter of boundless license, after all. There are things that can't be said or written even in the most tolerant secular universities, because they transgress the bounds of reasonable and respectful academic discourse. But in that context religion is considered a matter of individual choice, and neither theism nor atheism is out of bounds. At many Christian colleges, on the other hand, academic freedom protects debate and discussion within the boundaries of common commitments to Christian belief and practice. It allows room—or at least it should allow room—for challenges to prevailing interpretations of the college's or the sponsoring denomination's central commitments, scriptural and theological. There is no room, however, for direct attack on those commitments. Faculty who find they can no longer endorse their institution's confessional requirements need to look for a new employer. This is not a denial of academic freedom. Rather, it is a consequence of the underlying purpose of academic freedom, which is the continued health and vigor of an academic community. Freedom is not a grant of immunity for anything one may say or do. Rather, it enables and facilitates the flourishing of intellectual life for particular individuals in particular communities.

Above I gave two sharply contrasting examples—defending racial hierarchy and promoting atheism. The real issues that become test cases for academic freedom at CCCU campuses usually fall somewhere in between. Is "Open Theism" a defensible position regarding divine foreknowledge and human freedom? Is the "JEPD" hypothesis concerning authorship of the Pentateuch compatible with a high view of scriptural inspiration? Should we look for unique patterns of neurological activity during prayer and meditation, and if we find them will they have theological import? Your dean and president might disagree sharply with my dean and president, even if we serve at sister institutions in the same theological or denominational family.

Suppose a colleague publishes an article that pushes the boundaries on a sensitive issue and draws the attention of administrators and board members. What will be the institutional response? At your college it might be a news release and a leg up on internal research funding. At mine, it might be a stern warning and a classroom reassignment to protect impressionable first-year students. Is your campus, then, committed to academic freedom, while mine has opted instead for indoctrination? Or has your campus fallen for the pernicious delusion that freedom means license to say anything, while mine strives to remain a genuine community of learning and scholarship in which we are mutually accountable in matters of intellectual and spiritual integrity? We could argue for a long time without being able to agree on the answers.

---

2   Simon Critchley, *Very Little . . . Almost Nothing: Death, Philosophy, Literature* (New York: Routledge, 1997).

Here is where the picture provided by the present study is so valuable—and so rare. Joeckel and Chesnes have slipped under the perimeter fences that surround Christian college campuses in order to poll individual faculty on the campus environment as they experience it. Writing a mission statement and a preface to the faculty handbook that uphold academic freedom is easy. Translating such statements into a level of confidence and trust that facilitates free and open debate, however, is far more difficult. The present study helps us see the extent to which reality matches rhetoric.

Note first some background information relevant to the assessment of academic freedom. One of the most striking findings of the entire survey is the astonishing unanimity of 1900 faculty members on the importance of maintaining their institutions' Christian mission. Fully 98 percent either agreed or agreed strongly on this (FSQ 25).[3] On what else can you imagine getting 98 percent of your colleagues to agree? "Is the Pope Catholic?" was not one of the questions on the survey, but if it had been I suspect there would have been considerably less unanimity in the responses.

This is a very encouraging witness to CCCU faculty commitment to their institutions, as is the high level of agreement with the institutional faith statement (90 percent; FSQ 22). An overwhelming majority also affirm that "it is not difficult for me to integrate faith and learning in my discipline" (84 percent; FSQ 19). Two more results corroborate the finding that, by and large, the enterprise of Christian higher education is achieving its core purposes with regard to enhancing faculty commitment: 86 percent report that interactions with other faculty have strengthened their faith (FSQ 16), and 80 percent affirm the same concerning the overall effect of serving on the faculty (FSQ 17).

It would be interesting to have comparative data for institutions outside the CCCU where strong religious roots have produced a different sort of institutional profile, such as Catholic and Lutheran colleges and universities. We would find much lower percentages in all four of these categories, I am certain—not because these institutions are less Christian, or less intentional about their religious mission, but because their emphasis has shifted from common doctrinal affirmation to shared participation in a religiously grounded mode of liberal education that accommodates faculty and students from many traditions. My own first academic employer, St. Olaf College in Minnesota, was then and remains today an institution profoundly influenced by its Lutheran heritage, and it is still under a form of church governance. I have no doubt that a large majority of its faculty would affirm their support for its mission statement, which is forthrightly Christian.[4] But many faculty members are not Lutheran; a few are Jewish or Moslem; and probably no more than half would highlight "integration of faith and learning" as a central goal of their professional lives. Religious life on campus is vibrant and varied; faculty and students speak freely and

---

3   Here and below, for simplicity, I will cite figures that combine those who "strongly agree" with those who "agree," and similarly for the other end of the Likert scale, unless something unusual about the subcategories calls for comment.

4   Here is its first paragraph: "St. Olaf, a four-year college of the Evangelical Lutheran Church in America, provides an education committed to the liberal arts, rooted in the Christian Gospel, and incorporating a global perspective. In the conviction that life is more than a livelihood, it focuses on what is ultimately worthwhile and fosters the development of the whole person in mind, body, and spirit." See http://www.stolaf.edu/church/identity/introduction.html

frequently about matters of faith in the classroom; and yet there is far greater religious diversity among both faculty and students than at Bethel University or Northwestern College, two CCCU members located nearby in the Twin Cities.

The data that we have provide clear evidence that faculty at CCCU schools continue to embrace a confessional model of Christian higher education. They do not see the more pluralistic model coming to the fore on their campuses, nor would they prefer it. Fewer than one-third (29 percent) believe secularism has had a negative impact on their campuses (FSQ 20). Even fewer (24 percent) would favor a broader and "more generic" statement of Christian mission (FSQ 23). Granted, over half (57 percent; FSQ 26) favor voluntary rather than compulsory chapel services, and slightly more than half (51 percent; FSQ 14) report that chapel attendance has not enhanced their faith or are neutral or undecided on this question. These responses suggest some dissatisfaction with the religious atmosphere on campus. But on other measures, such as whether classroom teaching and interaction with colleagues have made a positive contribution to faith development, large majorities answer affirmatively (82 percent and 86 percent; FSQs 15 and 16). And in any case a wholly voluntary chapel program can be a vital part of campus life in many different contexts. When I gave a chapel talk at St. Olaf last year I was surprised to find student attendance to be somewhat higher, and faculty and staff attendance far higher, than on a typical day at Calvin, my home institution.

A few survey responses seem to suggest excessive rather than deficient commitment to a faith tradition. To put it bluntly, some faculty members seem altogether too certain of their own convictions. Who are the 503 respondents, for example, 27 percent of the total, who regard it as impossible that their interpretation of the Bible will ever change? (FSQ 31) Do they take great care when reading recent biblical scholarship to ignore anything that challenges their preconceptions? One wants to remind these colleagues that we are all fallible humans seeking the truth, not infallible divinities.[5] But let's be charitable and attribute this bizarre claim of personal rather than scriptural inerrancy to careless reading of the question rather than to simple pig-headedness.

The common ground revealed in some of the survey responses concerning institutional mission puts into sharper relief the more divided responses that were given to survey questions regarding academic freedom. These have already been discussed in a careful and illuminating way by my co-contributors Joe Ricke and Dan Russ. Let me offer some comments on their findings.

The insights Ricke draws from the survey data arise from a close examination of the responses from certain subgroups of respondents. He observes, for example, that among respondents who do not believe they enjoy academic freedom, the percentage of those who hesitate to address certain important issues in class is much higher than in the entire group. The percentage who find "a spirit of humility and charity" obtaining between

---

5 I would also like to have a talk with the 39 percent of Christian college faculty who do not always separate recyclable items from garbage! At least half of them, judging by the following question, also piously affirm that Christians should care for the environment. The picture comes to mind of a happy Christian family singing "This Is My Father's World" while tossing candy wrappers and soft drink cans out their car window (FSQs 60 and 61).

administration and faculty is only one-third as high in this subgroup, while only one-tenth as many strongly agree that morale among faculty on the campus is good. These data point to a high degree of alienation and exclusion among some faculty. Ricke further observes that this is strongly correlated with a questioning attitude on theological matters and with a tilt toward what is conventionally labeled the liberal end of the political spectrum.

These conclusions need to be tempered by two cautions. First, the number of respondents in this subgroup of CCCU faculty who do not believe their academic freedom is protected is small, fewer than 10 percent of all respondents. It is risky to draw conclusions from statistical comparisons between a subgroup of only 168 respondents and the rest of a sample set of nearly 1900. Second, as Ricke acknowledges, it is likely that many, if not most, of these responses come from individuals who have been caught up in particular disputes involving their own work or that of close colleagues. Statistical summaries cannot separate thoughtful responses based on broad experience and reflection from responses expressing frustration and anger over a particular case—perhaps one that, although initially mishandled, will eventually come to a fair resolution.

Indeed, it is tempting to turn Ricke's conclusion concerning the existence of an alienated and discontented minority on its head. In light of the numerous occasions when Christian college presidents, deans, and boards have put faculty in the crosshairs of theological and political attack in recent decades, the number of survey respondents who report that they do indeed enjoy academic freedom is remarkably high. If we were to ask a random sample of faculty at Gigantic State U the same question about their own circumstances, we might well get a comparable positive response of 90 percent. But if we asked the Gigantic State faculty whether their colleagues over at Cozy Corner Christian enjoy academic freedom, I suspect no more than 10 percent would say yes. And yet, across nearly a hundred Christian campuses, 90 percent of the faculty said yes. On balance this is very good news about the vitality of our institutions.

But perhaps we are being too hasty. Consider the second subgroup at which Ricke looks more closely: the 24 percent who report that they "hesitate to address certain issues in class because I teach at a Christian college/university" (FSQ 98). The wording of the question is somewhat ambiguous: one could respond positively either because of fear of punishment or simply because one judges some topics are too difficult for one's students to study and process. After all, of the 420 respondents who said that they felt uncomfortable dealing with some issues in class, about two-thirds report that their academic freedom is protected.[6] Still, Ricke is probably right to perceive in this response a sign of dissatisfaction with the campus atmosphere. His additional analysis bears this out: those who hesitate to bring controversial topics into their classes have less confidence in their administrators, are substantially more hospitable to gay partnership and to evolutionary theory, and are twice as likely to label themselves theologically liberal (37 percent of the subgroup, 21 percent of all respondents).

---

6 This is a simple calculation: only 168 respondents said that they lacked academic freedom, so approximately 250 reported that they do have the freedom to address difficult issues and yet hesitate to do so.

No wonder these colleagues hesitate to speak candidly in the classroom on some issues: they know that some of their views would be challenged, if not dismissed, by many colleagues and administrators. And yet, by a two-to-one ratio, they believe they do enjoy academic freedom. A more complex picture suggests itself than Ricke's account of an alienated and frustrated minority. What if the survey instrument had asked for a response to a somewhat different statement: "I hesitate to address certain important issues, although I know I am free to do so and my colleagues and administrators would probably back me up"? A positive response to this statement would indicate that self-censorship is more influential than peer or institutional pressure in inhibiting open discussion in the classroom.

An additional survey response not specifically highlighted in Ricke's essay strikes me as one of the most troubling: slightly fewer than two-thirds of all respondents (64 percent) are willing to affirm that faculty morale on their campuses is good (FSQ 85). Several other questions expand on this judgment: approximately two-thirds credit the administration with doing its work well (70 percent; FSQ 83), with behaving in a Christ-like manner (71 percent; FSQ 84), and with maintaining "a spirit of humility and charity between faculty and administration" (65 percent; FSQ 81). Another key to morale problems comes in the last section of the survey, when only slightly more than two-thirds of respondents (71 percent) report observing "rigorous intellectual activity" on their campuses (FSQ 94). These are surely essential characteristics of a healthy community of learning—good morale, capable administrators, and a lively intellectual life. If the institutions were living up to the rhetoric of their mission statements, all of these numbers would surely be in the nineties, not the sixties and low seventies. With this in mind Ricke's concerns over alienated faculty subgroups no longer seem overstated.

It is a commonplace of American political polling that the average citizen hates Congress as an institution but thinks well of his own congressional representative. Here we seem to find the reverse: CCCU faculty members overwhelmingly affirm the central values and mission of their institutions, but a significant minority lack confidence in the individuals entrusted with implementing them. Once again some of these responses are doubtless shaped by recent personal experiences, with some of the rawness of wounds not yet healed. But we are looking here at responses from the entire population surveyed, not just from a small subset, and the lessons they suggest need to be taken very seriously. Faculty may affirm that they enjoy academic freedom, but if that freedom is not enjoyed in a community of learning characterized by trust, mutual respect, and intellectual challenge, its value is limited.

In the narrative responses to some survey questions one finds eloquent expressions of frustration over the lack of support from colleagues as well as administrators for rigorous critical inquiry. Asked whether students receive a superior education at Christian institutions, for example (FSQ 104), respondents offered these comments:

> It can be better in certain disciplines . . . and in some ways it promotes a more integrated approach to life (integrating faith and work) after graduation,

but I do not believe that overtly Christian education is necessarily or consistently better than secular education in any purely academic sense. In fact, it is often inferior—not just because of the possibility of bias and censorship, but because the pervasive, prideful assumption of superiority often makes for a lazy approach to both scholarship and teaching, what one of my colleagues calls being "lazy for Jesus."

Evangelical colleges tend to focus more on projecting the image of vibrant intellectual activity than they do on the vigorous pursuit of academic endeavors . . . . There is a tendency for students to be attracted to these institutions as a means of protecting themselves from "dangerous" intellectual ideas or to isolate themselves from diverse others.

No, I would not say superior. Theologically, it may of course be better. However, intellectually it may be weaker. I find that students here are exposed to less diversity, less controversy, have professors who publish less and attend conferences less, and are less likely to have doctoral degrees.

The survey did not ask respondents to indicate whether they have ever been faculty members at a nonreligious college or university, but it is evident in the narrative comments that confidence in the superiority of Christian institutions is negatively correlated with experience in any other setting. One faculty member bemoans the "politically correct thinking at secular institutions" that is "shaped by a Marxist critique of justice and radical feminism"; another asserts that "many secular colleges and universities . . . are without collaborative training for the student," and that they do not produce graduates "capable of independent thinking and analysis." Such wild claims appear to be based not on experience and observation but on stereotypes advanced by a few of the ideologically motivated critics of higher education. Teaching for a year or two at a secular liberal arts college or state university campus, or even spending a few days there, would quickly reveal their absurdity as generalizations. If CCCU schools do indeed offer students a superior education—as in many instances they do—it is not because every secular university is a Maoist camp engaged in indoctrination and mind control.

Dan Russ's wide-ranging reflections on the survey supplement some of the concerns already raised by Joe Ricke with several additional matters. First, he notes that workload issues cannot be divorced from issues of morale, scholarly achievement, or institutional mission. Let me underscore the importance of this observation in the context of the recent history of the academy. In recent decades the life of a faculty member has become far more busy and complex. There has been some relief from once-burdensome tasks (I am just old enough to remember how hard it is to correct a minor typo on a green mimeograph stencil, how faint was the image, and how smelly the paper of an early-generation photostatic copy), but this has been more than counterbalanced by ever-expanding responsibilities outside the classroom: answering students' and colleagues' emails, telephoning prospective applicants, meeting heightened expectations for research and scholarship, submitting numerous internal and external reports, and—yes, we may as well say it—completing questionnaires about Christian higher education that arrive unannounced in one's inbox.

The survey touches only lightly on these gradual encroachments into daily life in its questions about teaching workload and desire for more released time. Moreover, these data were gathered early in 2007, before the US economy was devastated by bankers' and investors' greed and regulators' inattention. The economic pressures on private higher education have only become more intense in the intervening three years. More than half of survey respondents reported teaching four courses each term, and this number has surely not diminished (FSQ 86). What has diminished on many campuses, unfortunately, is the availability of travel and research support, even while institutional expectations for publications and other professional activity continue to ratchet upward.

Russ is right to point to these economic factors as important contributors to faculty dissatisfaction. It should be noted, however, that they affect other private institutions in just the same way as Christian colleges and that the pressures and demands on faculty members at state universities are no less intense. Many of us teaching at Christian colleges have worked for several years now with no annual salary raise or cost-of-living adjustment, but few have opened a pay envelope to find our salaries abruptly reduced by 9 percent, as did faculty at California state institutions in 2009. The rain falls on, and the drought afflicts, the just and the unjust alike.

Both Russ and Ricke warn us against seeing a so-called "Marsden Effect" of creeping secularization in every adaptation to new circumstances, and rightly so. Secularization is not an aggressive cancer metastasizing across the academy. On the contrary, it is a stance that some institutions have chosen, in place of their earlier religious identity, for complex reasons specific to their histories and the opportunities that they faced. Sometimes the new identity has been deliberately and consciously chosen, and sometimes it has arrived as the sum of many small changes.[7] But there is no unavoidable slippery slope in the vicinity, but rather a fork in the road. Many first-rate colleges have chosen the path of secularization, while others have chosen to hold to their religious roots. CCCU members are in the second group, having adapted and revised their religious commitments without renouncing them.

Take note, in this regard, of the inconsistency between the responses to two survey questions: more than two-thirds (67 percent) believe "the secular academy as a whole is dismissive of Christian scholarship" (FSQ 99), and yet respondents are nearly unanimous (89 percent, or 94 percent if we remove those who have attended only Christian institutions) in their positive assessment of their own advanced study at secular universities (FSQ 101). Moreover, only one in twenty (5 percent) has found it necessary to "compromise my faith to some degree in order to succeed in my research/scholarship" (FSQ 100). If the guerrilla cadres of secularism have really driven religion out of the nation's

---

7   I have argued in a review of Marsden's work that there is no such general effect, but that secularization has usually resulted from unanticipated consequences of actions intended to strengthen rather than dilute an institution's distinctive mission. See "Dangerous Curves"[a review of George Marsden, *The Soul of the American University*], *Perspectives* 9:9 (November 1994): 19-20. See also "Keeping Faith in the Christian College, Past and Present" [a review essay on Robert Benne, *Quality with Soul*, and Arthur Holmes, *Building the Christian Academy*], *Perspectives* 18:1 (January 2003): 15-20.

universities, why are Christians (and others) still receiving such good training there, and why do so few experience a secular bias in their scholarly work?

These responses lead us to another survey item that both Ricke and Russ discuss: more than half the respondents believe there is "more freedom to discuss issues and ask questions" at Christian institutions than elsewhere (FSQ 97). Twenty-four percent strongly agree with this statement, 30 percent agree somewhat, and an unusually high 19 percent neither agree nor disagree. One of the narrative responses puts the point baldly: "The phrase 'secular university' is an oxymoron; they do not tolerate ideas outside of their value system; they do not truly allow academic freedom" (FSQ 104).

"There is something misleading" here, notes Ricke: if we are honest we will all recognize that Christian college faculty have more freedom in some areas, less in others. Moreover, when freedom is curtailed at some Christian colleges, the limits are often drawn very firmly by an edict from the president's office. Those who transgress these limits are sometimes gently persuaded to come back to the fold, but more often they must dodge shotgun pellets fired from the institutional equivalent of prison watchtowers. The affirmation that there is less freedom at a nonreligious college or state university—Ricke calls it an "illogical 'moral-equivalence' theory of limits"—is an article of faith among Christian college faculty, not a reasonable conclusion drawn from the available evidence.

Equally disturbing, the smugness with which Christian colleges claim a higher degree of academic freedom is often accompanied by uninformed and misguided criticism of the professional organizations that serve as guardians of faculty rights in the United States. I am sorry to find that Russ has fallen into this trap.

In this regard I can write from personal experience. In 2009 I served on an investigative committee for the American Association of University Professors, the organization to which Russ attributes "a largely twentieth-century perspective of academic freedom" that "categorically opposes those truths that ground the Christian tradition." The AAUP, Russ charges, "denies that academic freedom can exist if faculty members are required to subscribe to any religious or dogmatic beliefs." In fact, when the national office of the AAUP decided to launch an investigation into allegations by a Bible instructor at a Christian university that his tenure had been terminated without due process, the office's communications with the administration repeatedly emphasized that its goal was to protect faculty members' procedural rights, not to meddle in matters of religious mission or faculty requirements. When I was asked to serve on the investigative committee, the staff emphasized that they wanted to include someone with an insider's understanding of how academic freedom can best be articulated and upheld in an evangelical Protestant institution.

I will not delve into any of the details or name the institution in question here. Our report, which was adopted by the AAUP national council and eventually led to a formal motion of censure, is a public document available on the AAUP website and published in its journal, *Academe.* The investigation was lengthy and laborious—each of us contributed hundreds of hours of uncompensated time—and our hopes that the university would respond to AAUP concerns by working out a mutually acceptable compromise were repeatedly dashed. But let me emphasize this: not for a moment did any member

The Christian College Phenomenon

of the AAUP staff or council suggest that religious affirmation inherently undermines academic freedom, nor do any of the documents promulgated by AAUP make such an assertion.[8] The violations that the university was found to have committed included breaches of minimum standards of procedural fairness, such as notice of charges and opportunity to rebut them, and arbitrary departures from its own stated procedures. Removing confessional requirements for faculty would have accomplished nothing to allay AAUP concerns. Keeping them in place but adopting policies to assure that they would be fairly and consistently applied, on the other hand, would have brought the investigative process to a quick halt and avoided the eventual motion of censure. Russ's characterization of AAUP and its expectations is simply incorrect. It is a valuable ally, not an adversary, of those who seek to ensure the preservation of academic freedom at CCCU institutions.

I wish it were possible to regard situations such as this as rare exceptions to an atmosphere of free inquiry and mutual respect within clearly stated confessional bounds. But all of us who work in Christian higher education know too many similar stories. They demonstrate the naiveté of the notion that faculty at Christian colleges generally enjoy greater academic freedom than their colleagues elsewhere. Sometimes this is true: matters of faith and personal conviction arise frequently and naturally in a Christian academic community, in ways that are less frequent and can be more problematic at a state university. Yet too often the very same convictions that should facilitate an atmosphere of openness and honesty are employed as bludgeons against critics.

Let me give the survey's respondents the last word, drawing on the thoughtful answers to a question about the most difficult challenges they face (FSQ 106). The complaints of narrow-mindedness expressed here, significantly, are more often directed against intolerant and inflexible student attitudes than toward explicit institutional restrictions. Here and there we find complaints about "lack of commitment by the administration to academic excellence" and the necessity of "playing games with administrators," which probably does not refer to lunch-hour basketball. Others refer to a general atmosphere inhospitable to critical inquiry, a degree of "closed-mindedness by students, faculty, administration and staff." Among the comments on this dimension of faculty life are these three:

> . . . I cannot address some very "real" world problems [as] topics in the classroom for fear of losing my job. Image is everything on our campus.
>
> While I am free to discuss anything in the classroom I am not free to take a strong position on several politically related issues. We have freedom to discuss, but not freedom to voice dissenting opinion.

---

8 The 1940 *Statement of Principles Regarding Academic Freedom and Tenure*, still a key part of AAUP policy, rnandates that "limitations of academic freedom because of religious or other aims of the institution should be clearly stated in writing at the time of the appointment." The language used here is negative in tone, a carryover from the early days of AAUP when its founding leaders were eloquent apologists for secularization. But in practice, for the past half-century at least, the AAUP has recognized the legitimacy of religious requirements and demanded only that they be clearly communicated and fairly administered. This document and others related to academic freedom can be found at http://www.aaup.org/AAUP/pubsres/policydocs/contents/

The most difficult part of working at a Christian university is working with other Christians. So doing is alternately depressing, infuriating, and occasionally inspiring.

These are only a few voices out of nearly 2000, but they surely speak for many others. Yet the picture we gain from all these responses is by no means uniformly bleak. "I have not found a difficult part yet," writes one respondent, and another observes, "I am in my 38th year here and have found no great difficulty during all of those years." Money and workload worries figure prominently, as do students who demand high grades for shoddy work. And then there is this poignant protest against the inherent tensions of a teacher-student relationship that involves both encouragement and evaluation: the hardest thing about my job, wrote one faculty member, is "giving an F to a saint and an A to a sinner."

We are all saints, of course, in this enterprise of Christian higher education; and we are all sinners, too. Well, perhaps not all: nearly a third of us, the survey discloses, are such moral exemplars that in the past year we have committed no moral lapses causing us twinges of guilt (30 percent, plus another 10 percent who aren't sure or can't remember; FSQ 75). If only the apostle Paul had been given access to this survey he would have revised the third chapter of his letter to the Romans: "all have sinned and fall short of the glory of God, except for one-third of Christian college professors." I am certain that no one at Calvin College gave this answer. "Total depravity" is not just a Calvinist doctrine; it is a way of life.

Saints or sinners, the responses that we on the faculty of Christian colleges and universities gave to the survey show that we stand firmly behind our institutions' resolve to uphold their Christian mission, even while we can't escape nagging worries about whether our institutions stand behind us in our work of preparing young men and women to be critically and constructively engaged in church and society. Let us hope that broad dissemination of the present study and wide-ranging discussion of what it tells will hasten the day when the only games that faculty members have to play with administrators are on the basketball court.

Bibliography: Part Four

Cowan, Donald. *Unbinding Prometheus: Education for the Coming Age*. Dallas: Dallas Institute Publications, 1988.

Critchley, Simon. *Very Little . . . Almost Nothing: Death, Philosophy, Literature*. New York: Routledge, 1997.

Diekema, Anthony. *Academic Freedom and Christian Scholarship*. Grand Rapids, Mich.: Eerdmans, 2000.

Dovre, Paul J., ed. *The Future of Religious Colleges*. Grand Rapids, Mich.: Eerdmans , 2002.

Drucker, Peter. *Mangaging the Non-Profit Organization: Principles and Practices*. New York: Harper Collins Publishers, 1990.

Habecker, Eugene. "Academic Freedom in the Context of Mission." *Christian Scholar's Review* 21 (1991): 175-181.

Guthrie, Stan. "Open or Closed Case?" *Christianity Today*, December 2004.

Heie, Harold. *Learning to Listen, Learning to Talk: A Pilgrimage Toward Peacemaking*. New York: iUniverse, 2007.

Heller, Jack. "Christian College Professor Flunks Christian Worldview Tests." *The New Pantagruel* 1.3 (Summer 2004).

Hoekema, David. "Dangerous Curves" [a review of George Marsden's *The Soul of the American University*]. *Perspectives* 9:9 (November 1994), 19-20.

_____ , "Keeping Faith in the Christian College, Past and Present" [a review essay on Robert Benne's *Quality with Soul* and Arthur Holmes's *Building the Christian Academy*]. *Perspectives* 18:1 (January 2003): 15-20.

Holmes, Arthur. *The Idea of a Christian College*. Grand Rapids, Mich.: Eerdmans, 1975.

Klassen, Norman and Jens Zimmerman. *The Passionate Intellect: Incarnational Humanism and the Future of University Education*. Grand Rapids, Mich.: Baker Academic, 2006.

Marsden, George. "Theology and the University: Newman's Idea and Current Realities." In *The Idea of the University*, 302-317. Edited by Frank M. Turner. New Haven, Conn.: Yale University Press, 1996.

Naugle, David. *Worldview: The History of a Concept*. Grand Rapids, Mich.: Eerdmans, 2002.

Niebuhr, H. Richard. *Christ and Culture*. New York: Harper Colophon Books, 1975.

Redden, Elizabeth. "Academic Freedom, Christian Context." *Inside Higher Ed. Com.* March 2, 2009.

Wolfe, Alan. "The Opening of the Evangelical Mind." *Atlantic Monthly*, October 2000, 76.

PART FIVE

RACIAL/ETHNIC DIVERSITY

RACE AND ETHNICITY IN CCCU SCHOOLS

Rhetoric and Reality

ALVARO NIEVES

CHAPTER 13

That diversity remains an important issue in the academy seems evident in a pull-out section of the *Chronicle of Higher Education* for October 18, 2009, entitled *Diversity in Academe*.[1] Topics included issues of diversity relating to race, ethnicity, foreign students, gender, class, sexual orientation, and disability. On the first page, California State University Chancellor Charles B. Reed is shown speaking at a Los Angeles church: "He says the system will be 'stepping up outreach' to minority students, including working with black churches."[2] In addition to this lead article, the issue contains nearly a dozen articles as well as data on the race and ethnicity of faculty members at over 1,400 colleges.[3]

I am now approaching three decades of teaching in an evangelical Christian college. During that time I have had opportunities to interact with colleagues at my own college as well as others in Christian and secular schools. I have seen the challenges, the successes, and the disappointments with regard to issues of diversity. I have discovered that there are well-meaning people at all levels who sincerely recognize the need for greater diversity for spiritual, ethical, and practical reasons. There are others who still simply "don't get it" or are sincerely opposed to any proposed solutions that resemble what they see as affirmative action or "reverse discrimination."

In the Introduction to this book the editors reference a 1991 volume[4] that presented the problem of race and ethnicity in schools of the Council for Christian Colleges and Universities (CCCU, then the Christian College Coalition). They further state that "in

---

1 *Diversity in Academe, Chronicle of Higher Education,* Section B, October 18, 2009.

2 Ben Cose, "Diversity Takes a Hit During Hard Times," *Chronicle of Higher Education,* October 18, 2009, B1.

3 *Chronicle of Higher Education,* October 18, 2009, B42-B54.

4 D. John Lee, Alvaro L. Nieves, and Henry L. Allen, eds., *Ethnic-Minorities and Evangelical Christian Colleges* (New York: University Press of America, 1991).

the years since . . . the CCCU has taken steps to redress this problem."[5] The editors accurately relate that the Coalition formed the Minority Concerns Project in 1991, "which created networks for minority faculty and students and also co-sponsored conferences and workshops."[6] I was privileged to be the plenary speaker at one of the first of these conferences and workshops held in Washington, D. C. This project originated under the leadership of then President Myron Augsburger. Concerning what was seen as a quite successful project by faculty and staff of color (who were also included) the editors state, "In 1994, however, this venture fizzled and died." It must be noted that among those of us who had seen it as an important breakthrough which had the potential to change the way the Coalition was viewed by faculty, staff, and students of color, it didn't fizzle; rather it was killed because of objections coming from some constituents of the Coalition. Whether this is true or only the perception of minority participants is open to discussion. The difference in perception may be an indication, however, that there is potentially still a critical difference between dominant and subordinate group members involved in our mutual enterprise. We must also remember the Thomas Theorem, which states, "If men define situations as real, they are real in their consequences."[7] These consequences are still evident among numbers of non-white faculty who remain skeptical of what has often been seen as the CCCU's rhetoric of diversity.

The Purpose and Plan of the Chapter

Clear differences in perception and opinion between majority and minority people can often hamper progress that members of both groups sincerely desire. In this chapter I will attempt to assess the progress that has been made in increasing diversity in CCCU institutions. I will first look at the percentages of minority faculty and students at several points in time. Second, I will examine differences in attitudes by race in an attempt to discern whether there is sufficient evidence to support the "Two Nation Hypothesis" suggested by Andrew Hacker[8] or the Kerner Commission's report.[9] This might lead us to conclude that there is still a significant difference in perceptions between dominant and subordinate groups. Third, I will explore the responses to open-ended questions in the Joeckel/Chesnes survey in an attempt to ascertain whether any differences that may appear in the more quantitative analysis are corroborated in these statements.

Describing Diversity

The importance of the presence of faculty of color in determining whether or not a campus is perceived as racially and ethnically diverse seems apparent. In addition, the

---

5   Samuel Joeckel and Thomas Chesnes, Introduction, 19.

6   Ibid..

7   W. I. Thomas and D. S. Thomas, *The Child in America: Behavior Problems and Programs* (New York: Knopf, 1928), 571-572).

8   Andrew Hacker, *Two Nations: Black and White, Separate, Hostile, Unequal* (New York: Scribner, 2003).

9   United States Kerner Commission, Report of the National Commission on Civil Disorders (Washington, D. C. Government Printing Office, 1968).

substantive nature of the contribution of diverse faculty in presenting alternative perspectives to their students in the classroom seems a reasonable inference. One indicator of improvement in the diversity of CCCU member schools would be growth in the percentage of faculty of color in those institutions. An examination of data over the last twenty years seems to suggest that such improvement may actually have occurred. Because of the paucity of data available by year and the lack of precise comparability[10] it is not possible to determine whether or not the growth is statistically significant. Table 1 provides the average percentages for non-white faculty by year for the five years for which data were available. The percentages appear to rise steadily. The one slight dip in 2007 is due to the fact that these numbers are computed from the sample survey used for this book. The most accurate numbers for faculty are likely those reported in the 2009 *Chronicle of Higher Education* for the 2007-2008 academic year and the aggregate percentage provided by the CCCU and taken from the IPEDS data base.

An additional indicator of increasing campus diversity in the CCCU member institutions is the percentage of students of color enrolled in each school. Table 2 provides the average percentage for selected years between 1983 and 2003. CCCU colleges saw minority enrollments increase, on average, from 7.24 percent in 1983 to 13.27 percent in 2003 and 13.32 percent in 2007.

Assessing Diversity among Faculty

The presence of a diverse population of faculty and students, defined in terms of race and ethnicity, does not alone guarantee diversity in other dimensions. As suggested previously, the assumption is that perceptions driven by race and ethnicity provide important variety, but too often, minority scholars have experienced pressures to conform to majority viewpoints. Cain Hope Felder, writing about the experience of African American scholars, states: ". . . blacks report dissonance between what they know and what they were taught, and they tell of a kind of profound liberation when they finally are able to challenge substantially some of the conventions . . . ."[11]

The presence of minority faculty is thus important to the presence and the empowerment of minority students and minority colleagues. As Felder explains it, most minority scholars have come through an educational system themselves that largely represents a white, male, Eurocentric hegemony. If this is the case, we will not be surprised to discover differences in the experiences and the attitudes of faculty who are dominant and subordinate group members.

In this section I examine some of those differences by looking at faculty responses to particular questions asked in the Joeckel/Chesnes survey, beginning with a description of the survey sample as it relates to this chapter. Subsequent to the description I will

---

10   The percentages for 1989 and 2007 are from surveys whose representativeness cannot be guaranteed. The percentages for 1998 and 2003 come from aggregate data provided by the CCCU originating in the IPEDS data base. The 2009 data is from the *Chronicle of Higher Education* which is the only data set providing faculty numbers for each institution.

11   Cain Hope Felder, ed., *Stony the Road We Trod: African American Biblical Interpretation* (Minneapolis, Minn.: Augsburg Fortress, 1991), 5.

explore relationships among key variables that may assist in discovering whether or not differences exist between identifiable groups of interest.

Of the 1,907 who responded to the faculty survey, the overwhelming majority self-identified as white or Caucasian (94.13%; FSQ 3). Each of the other categories represented 2 percent of the sample or less. The complete breakdown by race and ethnicity is provided in FSQ 3. The largest of the non-white categories is "other" which makes any generalizations about minority faculty from the present data problematic. Nevertheless I will attempt to convey an understanding of the data that have been collected. However, conclusions drawn from these data must be seen as strictly exploratory in nature. At best they may provide suggestions for further research which will be addressed at the end of the chapter along with possible policy recommendations.

Assessing Diversity among Faculty

Drawing on data from the survey with an attempt to determine differences requires some modification of the data, due largely to the small number of non-white respondents. As shown previously, non-white faculty represented less than 6 percent of the total number of faculty responding. In order to be able to do more than simply present percentages in various response categories, it was useful to collapse or compress response categories for most questions. For many of the questions, for example, respondents were provided a statement for which the possible responses were "strongly agree," "somewhat agree," "neutral," "somewhat disagree," and "strongly disagree." To use the existing five categories of race and ethnicity along with five responses of agreement would create a five-by-five table almost guaranteeing empty cells. To avoid this problem I made two adjustments by collapsing variables from five response categories to two. The race and ethnic variable is thus divided into white and non-white. The five-point Likert-type scale items were similarly broken down into two categories. "Strongly agree" and "somewhat agree" were grouped together as were "strongly disagree" and "somewhat disagree." Since it is impossible to know whether a neutral response is truly neutral or leans in one direction or another, I simply recoded it as a missing response and did not incorporate neutral responses into the analysis.

The survey was divided into areas of discourse that focused on objective information such as gender, ethnicity, length of service, whether or not faculty considered themselves theologically conservative or liberal, and how long they have been a Christian. In addition, there were questions regarding faculty attitudes. If diversity is to be more than the superficial aspect of skin color, it can be informative to identify whether race and ethnicity relate to differences in objective characteristics or attitudes. In testing differences between white and non-white faculty, a number of techniques was used, including analysis of variance and cross tabulation (using Pearson chi square or Fisher's Exact Test). Generally speaking I will employ a p-value approach which will allow the reader to see the computed level of significance. In the social sciences, a p-value less than .01 is usually considered highly significant; between .01 and .05 is considered significant and between .05 and .10, mildly significant. Above .10 results are considered non-significant.

Although many would prefer values lower than .05, others are willing to accept significance less than .10, especially for exploratory research.[12]

To begin with, it is reasonable to expect that on average white faculty will have greater longevity than will non-white faculty. The original question allowed for four possible responses: 1. "0-5 years"; 2. "6-10 years"; 3. "11-15 years"; and 4. "16 or more." In order to get a more realistic picture of the number of years, I imputed a new value based on the mid-point of each of the first three categories such that 0-5 became 2.5, 6-10 became 7.5 and 11-15 became 12.5. Since the fourth category (16 and above) was open-ended I, conservatively and arbitrarily, imputed a value of 20. The null hypothesis to be tested is that there is no difference between white and non-white faculty in terms of average years served. The alternative hypothesis is that mean longevity for white faculty is greater than the mean longevity for non-white faculty. The imputed mean for white faculty was 10.6365 and for non-white faculty 6.4509. A one-way analysis of variance resulted in an F statistic of 37.050 with 1 degree of freedom, significant at $<.001$. The null hypothesis is rejected and the alternative hypothesis, that white faculty have greater longevity than non-white faculty, is supported.

One section of the Joeckel/Chesnes survey addresses a broad theme of "campus climate." Responses to a number of statements were tested to determine whether or not there were significant differences in how white and non-white faculty perceived campus climate. For many, there were no significant differences. Among these statements were the following[13]: "Morale among faculty at my college/university is good" (FSQ 85, .278); "I possess academic freedom at my college/university" (FSQ 96, .316); "The student body at my college/university is racially diverse" (FSQ 88, .20); "The administration at my college/university performs its work in a Christ-like manner" (FSQ 84, .290); "Conflict between faculty and administration at my college/university is charitably resolved" (FSQ 82, .471). In all of these statements the majority of both white and non-white faculty responded "Strongly or somewhat agree."

In a number of additional items, however, there are some differences in the way white and non-white faculty perceive aspects of the campus climate. Results indicate a number of significant or mildly significant differences. On the basis of these findings it appears that, although a majority of white and non-white faculty agree, non-white faculty are more likely to disagree that "conflict among faculty is charitably resolved" (FSQ 80, .016). Similarly and consistently, non-white faculty are more likely than white faculty to disagree that a "spirit of humility and charity exists among faculty . . ." (FSQ 79, .080). Whether because of the issues represented in these questions or because of fewer years of longevity and less experience, 33.7 percent of non-white faculty compared to 25.7 percent of white faculty agree with the statement, "I am hesitant to address certain issues in class" (FSQ 98, .060).

---

12   James K. Skipper, Jr., Anthony L. Guenther, and Gilbert Nass, "The Sacredness of .05: A Note Concerning the Uses of Statistical Levels of Significance in Social Science," *American Sociologist* 2 (1967): 16-18.

13   The question number and the p-value for the Fisher's Exact Test are given in parentheses. Note that Fisher's Exact Test is a test of significance to test for association in a 2 X 2 contingency table.

Another section of the survey bore the heading "Faith and the Christian College" and dealt with both belief and practice. The former included statements on biblical inerrancy and biblical authority, while the latter addressed items such as chapel attendance and biblical interpretation. Race and ethnicity were not significantly associated with belief in inerrancy, with approximately two thirds of whites and non-whites agreeing with the statement, "I believe in Biblical inerrancy" (FSQ 36, .50). Neither was it associated with biblical authority. Approximately 60 percent of both white and non-white faculty agreed that the "Bible is the only authoritative source of information about God" (FSQ 32, .339).

In spite of what appears to be an overall biblical orthodoxy, 68.9 percent of whites and 56.2 percent of non-whites agree that "it is possible that my interpretation of the Bible will change in the next year" (Q. 31). Because it is unclear how race/ethnicity influences the choices on biblical orthodoxy, a two-tailed test was employed. The white and non-white differences in responses to this statement appear when respondents disagree. Here, 31 percent of whites and nearly 44 percent of non-whites disagree with the statement. The Fisher's Exact test was significant at .014 two tailed. Assessing agreement with the statement "It is acceptable to question the Bible" (FSQ 34) revealed that a higher percentage of whites (80.5) than non-whites (70.5) agreed, while a higher percentage of non-whites (29.5) than whites (19.5) disagreed (p-value = .028 two-tailed).

These results seem to suggest greater orthodoxy among non-whites, although more work is called for to confirm this possibility. Yet, when asked, "Would you consider yourself to be theologically conservative or liberal?" roughly three-fourths of both whites and non-whites self-identified as strongly or somewhat conservative. The remaining one-fourth of both groups self-identified as strongly or somewhat liberal (FSQ 5, .337), indicating no association between race/ethnicity and conservatism/liberalism.

On the behavioral side, one question seemed particularly interesting. The statement, "Attending chapel should remain (or become) mandatory for faculty" (FSQ 26), would appear to reflect a kind of conservative behavioral expectation. Nevertheless when examined for a race/ethnicity association none was found (p-value = .437, non-significant). Perhaps more interesting is that over two thirds of faculty disagreed with the statement regardless of race or ethnicity.

Assessing Diversity among Students

For the survey of students, the percentage of students who self-identified as other than Caucasian or white is larger than was the case among faculty and arguably much more useful for analysis. SSQ 4 provides the race and ethnicity numbers and percentage breakdown for the student sample. There is greater diversity in the student data set than for faculty in that just over 13 percent of students were non-white compared to fewer than 6 percent of faculty.

Member schools of the CCCU are often perceived to be overwhelmingly racially white, economically well off, and politically Republican. As we have seen above, faculty are, at over 94 percent, overwhelmingly white. Student enrollments are less white, at roughly 87 percent. While we do not have data to assess economic variability, we can test the hypothesis that race and political affiliation are associated. As can be seen in Table 3, non-white students are nearly three times more likely to identify as Democrat (28 percent non-white, 10 percent white). They are also more likely than white students to identify as independent or other. White students, on the other hand, are more likely to identify as Republican (66.3 percent white, 39.5 percent non-white). The chi-square statistic supports the hypothesis that race and political affiliation are significantly associated (Chi-square = 94.82, 3 df, p-value < .0001).

The type of high school that students attend is often seen as an indicator of how well prepared a student is likely to be for college. In some ways this can also be seen as a surrogate measure for family income because students from wealthier families are more likely to be able to afford private schools. Wealthier families are also more likely to be able to choose home schooling. The hypothesis to be tested here is that race and high school type are significantly associated. Because of the limited non-white sample size, I have collapsed the private Christian high school and private non-Christian high school responses into a single private high school category. As may be seen in Table 4, the data reveal that non-white students are significantly more likely to attend public high schools and less likely to attend private high schools or be home schooled (chi-square = 7.77, 2 df, p-value = .020).

In general, minority males are less likely to enroll in and remain in college than are minority females. Here I test the hypothesis that non-white students enrolled in CCCU institutions are less likely to be male and more likely to be female. This hypothesis is supported by the data (see Table 5), which show that 21.8 percent of non-white students are males compared with 28.5 percent of white students. Similarly, 78.2 percent of non-white students are female compared to 71.5 percent of white students (Fishers Exact is significant at .013).

Quantitative Differences Evidenced in Faculty and Students

Consideration of the above results suggests that there are both similarities and differences among white and non-white faculty. From the outset it was quite logical to expect that white faculty would have greater longevity considering the history of race relations during the period of institutional growth in terms of enrollments and in an increasing acceptance of the need for diversity. At the same time, concerns are sometimes expressed that differences in attitudes and behaviors might negatively affect the institutional character.

For example, there is some fear that faculty of color may be qualitatively different kinds of Christians than the majority and as a result may be seen as a threat to long existing traditions. The results of this study indicate that there is little cause for concern since there is little difference in theology between white and non-white faculty or white and non-white students.

Faculty and Student Responses to the Open-Ended Question on Diversity

One of the open-ended questions asked, "What is the most difficult part about being a student (professor) at a Christian university?" For both students and faculty of color who responded to this free-response question there were indications that minority status played a significant part in their institutional experience, since race was not an explicit part of the question. Of the 261 non-white students who responded to this question, there were just over twenty-five statements relating to racial or ethnic diversity. This compared with five statements from 112 faculty of color who responded to the survey. Responses from minority students were relatively simple, general statements relating to diversity, such as the following: "not very diverse," "lack of diversity," and "feeling like the minority." Some students also responded in greater detail, indicating that they have experienced the strain of being part of the non-white minority in majority white institutions. One student wrote, ". . . that it is predominantly White and the feeling that sometimes I don't feel like I belong." Another demonstrates that there is a clear self-awareness of their status by writing, "I am a minority and I am seen that way." Several other students wrote, "Feeling like the minority," "Being a minority, even in my style of worship." Elaborating, one student wrote: "I have double jeopardy. I am a minority and a female and I feel those two groups are discriminated against." The difficulty of being in the minority is expressed by one student: "There are not a lot of us students (of color) for one" and "it is a little harder than I expected." That minority students stand out on our campuses may be what one student is expressing when she responds, "More is expected from you! And everybody watches your every move." Another student sums up the campus racial-climate issue, recognizing the consequences of limited minority enrollment by writing, "The low amount of racial diversity can make it feel lonely in some ways. Other students who are not accustomed to being in a multi-racial environment, whether Christian or not, will treat me differently or be intimidated by me." Several students of color summed up the problem with one word: hypocrisy. It was interesting to note that several faculty also indicated they had difficulty dealing with what they perceived as hypocrisy, especially as relates to race and ethnicity.

Of the 2,070 white students who responded, approximately thirteen commented on the lack of diversity, usually in a short or even incomplete sentence, such as: "Little to no diversity," "Lack of diversity," and "Not being exposed to any diversity." Another student explained in a little more detail that ". . . there isn't very much diversity. And because of that, a lot of people have stereotypes and a misconception of minorities. That is a frustration." Still another student remarked, "I don't know whether or not other Christian institutions are very racially diverse but I know that is one of [our school's] downfalls."

Responses to this free-response question from faculty of color were generally slightly longer than student responses. Addressing the issue of campus racial climate, one faculty member wrote succinctly that "Christian schools tend to be way behind on issues of ethnic and cultural diversity." Supporting this contention, another faculty member wrote, "Being a minority from a 'third world country' I believe that the missionary discourse constructs a false and negative image of other countries on campus. My students' papers contain stereotypes that I never saw at secular universities." This respondent concluded by indicating how very troubling this was.

One faculty member communicates the difficulty as "Being African-American in institutions that profess Christianity and don't recognize that their racism is not biblical." Another writes: "Being Asian-American and not neo-conservative are two strikes against me." This faculty member broadens the climate issue from race and ethnicity to possible political differences when writing, "Trying to extricate a student's faith from socio-political assumptions makes life difficult for all." That this is a repetitive theme seems to be indicated by another respondent who identifies the difficulty of "Working to fight against common cultural Christian beliefs among white, evangelical Americans."

This section has presented comments mainly from non-white faculty. It should be noted that this may be because white faculty do not generally address issues or concerns related to race, ethnicity, or diversity. Of 112 non-white faculty members responding, there were a dozen responses to the above open-ended question that involved the issues of concern. Among the 1,795 white faculty responding only one did so. This faculty member wrote: "I don't think it is difficult at all. I welcome the diversity of thought and racial makeup of my college. It makes the classroom a wonderful slice of society and opens opportunity to discuss difficult issues." This difference between white and non-white faculty is consistent with the tendency of majority group members not having to face such issues on a regular basis. Many, if not most, minority faculty are aware of facing these issues on a daily basis.

Summary and Conclusions

It is clear that some progress is being made in the area of racial and ethnic diversity in member institutions of the CCCU. At the same time, however, it is also clear that problems still exist. White and non-white faculty and students agree that racism still exists and members of both groups recognize problems within their campus communities. It is important that a commitment to diversity be communicated at all levels. The CCCU could, perhaps, take more of a leadership role in altering how the Council is perceived among white and non-white faculty, students, and staff in member institutions.

It is equally important that a commitment be developed and communicated within each institution. This will call for leadership and cooperation between faculty, administration, and boards of trustees if diversity is truly valued. Faculties and boards could consider adopting and publishing the commitment to diversity, which includes valuing racial, ethnic, and gender diversity. They could also commit to actively recruit people from groups underrepresented on their campus. In addition, they might consider ways in which the college or university can become a more welcoming place for the underrepresented among them.

The implementation of such a policy must occur at different levels of organization and activity. The first and perhaps the most important of these would be in the area of recruitment, which tends to impact both hiring and student enrollment. One area of particular importance involves a conscious attempt to make the interview process culturally sensitive. This is clearly necessary for hiring faculty, administrators, and staff. It is also important where interviews are required of prospective students. It is absolutely essential, for example, to recognize that people from minority groups often have orthodox views that are expressed in what appear to be non-orthodox ways. In many Black and Latino traditions, for example, there is a greater likelihood for views that appear to Whites as socially and politically liberal but actually maintain a theologically conservative view of faith and lifestyle. If this is not understood it may make it less possible to diversify.

If recruiting is successful, it is then necessary to consider issues of retention and advancement. For faculty and staff this will be enhanced if mentors are available to non-whites who are often without the networks more naturally available to whites. It's also necessary to recognize, acknowledge, and honor those minority and women faculty who are likely to have heavier advising loads because they are often among the few to whom minority students can comfortably relate. It is equally important for leaders in academic and administrative departments to maintain open communication with minority faculty and be able to listen to concerns without an attitude that the minority individuals are simply being "oversensitive."

Another area of concern involves curricular matters. If departmental curricula neglect works by minorities and women, we are not preparing students for living in a diverse and complex world. Neither are we going to be attractive to faculty who are at the cutting edge in their disciplines. Curriculum review is important to the success of the academic enterprise and doubly important to whether or not we are perceived as comprehensively committed to diversity.

Perhaps one of the more important areas involves departments of campus or student life. In this area it is important that our student-development leadership be sensitive to the problems and concerns of minority students for whom they are responsible. An extremely important responsibility involves dealing quickly, honestly, and straightforwardly with incipient racism on campus in the dorms, classrooms, and anywhere students interact. It may also be necessary to establish good relationships with local police departments. Minority students on campuses that are located in predominantly white areas may be at particular risk when walking or driving through otherwise white neighborhoods. These students must feel supported.

We have generally been quite good at emphasizing personal responsibility at a very individualistic level. We must grow in our ability to function as a community that promotes relational justice. If we are successful, it is likely that we will become institutions that more adequately reflect the kingdom of God.

Table 1: Percent Non-White Faculty by Year in CCCU Institutions

Year	Percent Non White Faculty
1989	2.11
1998	3.60
2003	6.52
2007	5.90
2009	7.02

Table 2: Percent Non-White Students by Year in CCCU Institutions

Year	Percent Non Whitestudents
1983	7.24
1989	8.63
1995	8.94
1998	11.13
2003	13.27

Table 3: Student Political Affiliation by Race/Ethnicity

			Race/Ethnicity		
			White	Non-White	Total
	Democrat	Count	210	73	283
		% within Race/Ethnicity	10.1%	28.0%	12.1%
	Republican	Count	1373	103	1476
		% within Race/Ethnicity	66.3%	39.5%	63.3%
	Independent	Count	245	42	287
		% within Race/Ethnicity	11.8%	16.1%	12.3%
	Other	Count	242	43	285
		% within Race/Ethnicity	11.7%	16.5%	12.2%
Total		Count	2070	261	2331
		% within Race/Ethnicity	100%	100.0%	100.0%

Pearson Chi-Square = 94.820, 3 df, P-value <.001

Table 4: High School Type by Race/Ethnicity
Pearson Chi-Square = 7.777, 2 df, p-value = .020

			Race/Ethnicity	Total	
			White	Non-White	White
What kind of high school did you attend?	Public High School	Count	1434	200	1634
		% within Race/Ethnicity	69.3%	76.6%	70.1%
	Private High School	Count	489	52	541
		% within Race/Ethnicity	23.6%	19.9%	23.2%
	Home School	Count	147	9	156
		% within Race/Ethnicity	7.1%	3.4%	6.7%
	Total	Count	2070	261	2331
		% within Race/Ethnicity	100.0%	100.0%	100.0%

Table 5: Gender by Race/Ethnicity

		Race/Ethnicity		Total
		White	Non-White	White
Male	Count	589	57	646
	% within Race/Ethnicity	28.5%	21.8%	27.7%
Female	Count	1481	204	1685
	% within Race/Ethnicity	71.5%	78.2%	72.3%
Total	Count	2070	261	2331
	% within Race/Ethnicity	100.0%	100.0%	100.0%

Fisher's Exact Test significant at 0.013

UNDERSTANDING CCCU FACULTY OF COLOR

CHAPTER

14

JENELL WILLIAMS PARIS AND MICHELLE KNIGHTS

Diversity, along many dimensions including race, ethnicity, religion, disability, sexual orientation and gender, is important in the academy—in campus arenas such as faculty recruitment, advancement and retention, student recruitment and retention, administrative leadership, staff, curriculum, co-curriculum, campus climate, and more. Accordingly, many Christian colleges and universities highlight the importance of racial and ethnic diversity across campus and the curriculum. Alvaro Nieves documents the growth of students and faculty of color at Council for Christian Colleges and Universities (CCCU) member institutions. He asserts the importance of not only increasing numbers, but also understanding differences in perception and opinion between people of various groups. He recommends renewed attention to many areas of campus life, including recruitment, retention, advancement, curricular life, co-curricular life, and communication of the institution's commitment to diversity.

Building on Nieves's chapter, we argue that the Joeckel/Chesnes data mostly agree with previous studies about faculty of color at predominantly white colleges and universities, and previous studies of CCCU faculty as well. We urge CCCU administrators and faculty to act on the knowledge we already have, which highlights both the value of faculty of color to CCCU colleges and universities and the inequities in their work experiences. First, we review the literature regarding the experiences of faculty of color at predominantly white colleges and universities, including CCCU member institutions. In analyzing the Joeckel/Chesnes data set, we focus on faculty of color and their views on campus climate, intellectual life, and salary. The Joeckel/Chesnes survey asked respondents to report their ethnicity, with choices including Caucasian, Black, Asian, Hispanic and Other. We will discuss our findings with language congruent with the literature, referring to those who self-defined as Black, Asian, Hispanic or Other as "faculty of color," and referring to Caucasian as "white" or "majority."

Faculty of Color at Predominantly White Colleges and Universities

In her literature review regarding faculty of color teaching in predominantly white colleges and universities, Christine Stanley argues that faculty of color from various groups (African American, Hispanic, American Indian, and Asian American) have interlocking experiences.[1] First, faculty of color often describe their experience of campus climate with phrases and words such as marginalization, otherness, or living in two worlds. The net result is occupational stress or taxation. Occupational stress is often experienced as long-term chronic stress which has implications for job performance and satisfaction, and work/family spill-over effects.[2]

Second, the tenure and promotion process, daunting under any circumstance, is made more difficult when pursued in such a climate. Faculty of color have long been perceived as publishing less than their white colleagues, a presumption that has been challenged by recent research.[3] While the data indicate that this thinking is not supported, it is important to note that perceptions become reality when attitudes and actions develop from those perceptions. This effect can contribute to sustaining a culture which understands faculty of color to be less productive in scholarship, and in turn, create tensions in how faculty of color are seen by majority faculty and students. Additionally, faculty of color are more likely to invest in community service and research activities that benefit communities of color, and spend more time in informal student contact, mentoring, and advising. In many colleges and universities, these priorities may weaken a bid for tenure or promotion.

Third, faculty of color report that racism and sexism create double binds for female faculty of color. Fourth, teaching is a major arena of difference between faculty of color and white faculty. Faculty of color face stronger challenges in earning student trust and respect, and often have to manage issues of race and ethnicity regardless of the subject matter of the course.

Job-satisfaction studies follow these descriptions of work experiences. A national survey showed that faculty of color were less satisfied with nearly every aspect of their jobs: compensation, rank and tenure, lack of recognition and appreciation, autonomy, job security, and opportunity to develop new ideas.[4] Job satisfaction is also linked to

1   Christine Stanley, "An Overview of the Literature," in *Faculty of Color Teaching in Predominantly White Colleges and Universities*, ed. Christine Stanley (Boston: Anker Publishing, 2006), 1-29.

2   D. H. Olsen and K. L. Stewart, "Family Systems and Health Behaviors," in *New Directions in Health Psychology Assessment. Series in Applied Psychology: Social Issues and Questions*, ed. H. E. Schroeder (Washington, DC: Hemisphere, 1991), 27-32; K. L. Stewart, *Stresses and Adaptation: A Multisystem Model of Individual, Couple, Family, and Work Systems* (Dissertation Abstracts International-A, 49 [08], 1989), P. Voydanoff, "Work Demands and Work-to-Family and Family-to-Work Conflict: Direct and Indirect Relationships," *Journal of Family Issues* 26 (2005): 707-726.

3   R. T. Blackburn, S. Wenzel, and J. P. Bieber, "Minority vs. Majority Faculty Publication Performance: A Research Note," *Review of Higher Education* 17 (1994): 217-282.

4   H. S. Astin, A. L. Antonio, C. M. Cress, and A. W. Astin. *Race and Ethnicity in the American Professoriate* (Los Angeles: Higher Education Research Institute, 1997).

campus climate.[5] Faculty of color report that they need to prove themselves repeatedly, that students question their credentials, that their credentials are sometimes ignored, that their skin color and ethnic features are sometimes emphasized over scholarly achievements, that they are often valued as "token" representatives of their race/ethnic group or of diversity as a whole, and that they feel generally unwelcome.

Beverly Absher surveyed 1212 CCCU faculty members using a modified version of the instrument used in the *American Faculty Poll*.[6] The three most important areas that determined job satisfaction for both female faculty and faculty of color were flexibility, security, and environment. Flexibility refers to work schedules that allow some independence and ability to accommodate family needs. Security refers to fairness in promotion and tenure processes, competitive salary, and adequate benefits. Environment refers to campus climate: meaningful work, time and resources to pursue scholarship, healthy relationships with colleagues, and a strong reputation of one's department and college or university. Absher argues that "a competitive salary and a more flexible work schedule with time for scholarly pursuits and a clear path for advancement and tenure, would go a long way in attracting and retaining minority faculty."[7]

The CCCU conducted a faculty survey in 1998 that was part of the *Taking Values Seriously* project.[8] Of 3144 faculty surveyed, 96.4% were white and 3.6% were faculty of color. This survey found statistically significant differences between white faculty and faculty of color on several dimensions. Faculty of color were more likely to have doctorates, but fewer were tenured. (They were more likely to have been recently hired as well.) Faculty of color were more likely to have personal goals including the following: to become an authority in one's field, to influence the political structure, to influence social values, and to help promote racial understanding. Accordingly, CCCU faculty of color reported more interest in research than their white counterparts. White faculty were more oriented toward teaching, whereas faculty of color valued a balance of research and teaching. Nevertheless, faculty of color spent more time advising students. With respect to campus climate, faculty of color were less satisfied than white faculty with salary, benefits, job security, relationships with administration, and overall job satisfaction.

In addition to these challenges, many of which are common in the academy, CCCU schools may face unique challenges. Lisa McMinn describes a structural tension for Christian colleges and universities that need to maintain their evangelical enclave (which, for most, is historically white) and also need to adapt to a broader academic environment that is pluralistic and accepting of diversity.[9] Evangelical colleges developed strategies for

5   C. S. Turner and S. L. Myers, Jr., *Faculty of Color in Academe: Bittersweet Success* (Needam Heights, Md.: Allyn and Bacon, 2000).

6   Beverly Absher, "Attraction and Retention of Females and Minorities in Christian Higher Education," *Journal of Research on Christian Education* 18 (2009): 160-189.

7   Ibid., 184.

8   Council for Christian Colleges and Universities, "Racial Issues in the CCU Faculty," 2004. http://www.cccu.org/professional_development/resource_library/racial_issues_in_the_cccu_faculty (accessed February 28, 2010)

9   Lisa McMinn, "Enclave Adaptation, Multiculturalism and Evangelical Christian Colleges," *Research on Christian Higher Education* 5 (1998): 23-52.

resisting secularization, but those very strategies of religious boundary maintenance and successful student recruitment may hamper their cultivation of multicultural sensitivity. Indeed, an analysis of the mission statements of 107 CCCU member institutions showed that the most common words in institutional missions were education, Christian, service, society, life, and academics.[10] There were no institutional missions with an explicit concern for diversity, though diversity could be a part of service, society, or life. A 2009 "Top Ten Issues" list issued by CCCU President Paul Corts describes the most important issues facing Christian higher education, but carries no mention of diversity other than as a pressure that may be recast as an opportunity: "Religious, demographic, economic, political, social and cultural phenomena are putting significant pressure on our institutions to adapt and change very rapidly or be marginalized as irrelevant: such challenges offer enormous opportunities."[11] There is no question that diversity is a value in the broader academy, though progress is needed to attain and sustain it. Within the CCCU, however, it is unclear how strongly or consistently diversity is valued across the theologically and denominationally diverse institutions.

Findings from the Joeckel/Chesnes Survey

Nieves described the difficulties in extracting statistically significant findings from these data. With a sample size of 1907, faculty of color represented only 114 respondents, and of those 114, thirty-eight described themselves as "Other" (twenty-nine were Black, twenty-four Asian and twenty-three Hispanic; FSQ 3). In analyzing the data, we used correlational analysis to establish predictive significance for some variables, compared percentages between groups (although these findings cannot claim statistical significance because of the disparity in number between majority faculty and faculty of color), and report some open-ended narrative responses. Our findings focus on campus climate, scholarship, and salary.

With respect to campus climate, faculty of color and white faculty agreed on a number of important issues. Majority faculty and faculty of color both agreed that when religious hypocrisy among faculty is a problem (in responses to FSQ 92), there is a stronger perception that conflict was not charitably resolved, that a spirit of charity and humility was weaker among faculty and administration, that conflict between faculty and administration was not charitably resolved, that there was a sense that administration was not doing a good job running the institution, and that the administration worked in less of a Christ-like manner (Table 1). Majority faculty and faculty of color agreed that when morale among faculty is good, then conflict was charitably resolved, a spirit of charity and humility also existed among faulty and administration, conflict between faculty and administration was also charitably resolved, there was a sense that

---

10   Michael Firman and Krista Merrick Gilson, "Mission Statement Analysis of CCCU Member Institutions," *Christian Higher Education* 9 (2010): 60-70.

11   Paul Corts, "Top Ten Issues," Council for Christian Colleges and Universities, 2009. http://www.cccu.org/professional_development/resource_library/top_ten_issues_in_christian_higher_education (accessed March 1, 2010).

administration was doing a good job running institution, and the perception is that administration works in a Christ-like manner (Table 2).

It is important to note that even when faculty of color and white faculty share common perceptions, they are different, at the group level, in their length of experience at colleges. Faculty of color often have less experience in these contexts, as 56% of faculty of color are newcomers to CCCU institutions compared with 30% of majority faculty having reported that they taught in a CCCU college or university for 0-5 years. When examining longer length of service, only 10% of minority faculty compared with 32% of majority faculty had experience of sixteen or more years teaching at a CCCU institution (Table 3).

With respect to scholarship, faculty of color have stronger concerns than white faculty. More faculty of color (77%) have a Ph.D. or an Ed.D., compared with 70% of whites. Thirty percent of faculty of color have published a book, in contrast with 24% of white faculty. Seventy-one percent of faculty of color have published in a peer-reviewed journal, compared with 61% of whites. Forty-six percent of faculty of color who published a book also presented 1-2 papers at conferences in the past two years, compared with 39% of whites who published books and presented 1-2 papers in the past two years. Interestingly, more white faculty, 70%, perceive their institution as a place of rigorous intellectual activity compared with 65.6% of faculty of color (Table 4).

Faculty of color are more likely to report that they took a job in Christian higher education because of a desire to integrate faith and learning (40%), which can include scholarship, and only 35% took their position out of a commitment to Christian higher education. More white faculty (45%) took their position out of a commitment to Christian higher education, and 29% because it was an opportunity to integrate faith and learning. Furthermore, this difference in commitment to Christian higher education as a motivation for entering the workplace mirrors the large disparity in perception amongst faculty of color and white faculty regarding the administration's performance of its work in a Christ-like manner. More white faculty, 72%, compared with 61% faculty of color, perceived a Christ-like work performance from the administration. Further, climate factors include the disparity reported in perception between faculty of color and majority faculty regarding religious hypocrisy among faculty. Thirty percent of white faculty strongly disagree that religious hypocrisy is a problem, whereas fewer faculty of color, 18%, strongly disagree that religious hypocrisy among faculty is a problem (Table 5).

Despite their stronger commitment to scholarship, faculty of color teach more courses. Forty-eight percent of white faculty teach 1-3 classes per semester or trimester and 52% teach four or more. For faculty of color, 43% teach 1-3 classes per semester or trimester, and 57% teach four or more. Fifty-two percent of faculty of color strongly agreed that they would welcome a course-load reduction for the express purpose of spending more time doing research, compared with 37% of white faculty (Table 5). In a narrative comment, one faculty of color expressed the most difficult part of teaching at a Christian college: "not having sufficient time for research and yet being expected to keep up scholarly pursuits." Surprisingly, then, majority faculty data indicated an inverse relationship between the need for course reduction and the quality of the work environment. Specifically, when white faculty welcomed course-load reduction to do more research there was less agreement that conflict among faculty was charitably resolved, decreased belief that a spirit of humility and charity between faculty and administration exists, a decreased belief that the administration is doing a good job at running the institution, and a decreased belief that the administration performs its work in a Christ-like manner. Interestingly, there was no relationship with desire for course-load reduction and any of these variables for faculty of color.

For faculty of all races and ethnicities, correlational analysis showed that when they perceived their college/university as a place of rigorous intellectual activity, they also perceived that morale is good and that religious hypocrisy is not a problem among faculty (Table 6).

The Joeckel/Chesnes survey was not focused on job satisfaction, as some of the surveys covered in the literature were. Open-ended responses raise a concern related to job satisfaction, however. Fourteen open-ended responses reported that the most difficult part about being a professor at a Christian university is the pay. Typical comments read, "supporting a family on the pay," or "bad pay." Others reflected negatively on the relationship between pay to workload: "Ratio of the workload (high) and salary (low)," or "overworked and underpayed [sic]."

Discussion

Our findings reinforce studies that more comprehensively assessed the perceptions of faculty of color at predominantly white academic institutions. Job-satisfaction concerns related to the ratio of workload to salary, teaching load, and insufficient support for research are reflected in other literature about Christian colleges and universities and the academy in general. Our findings bolster Absher's recommendation that institutions resource faculty of color to achieve their scholarly goals. Faculty of color are, as a group, well-credentialed, published, and wanting to do more scholarship, yet they have heavier teaching loads and spend more time formally and informally advising students. At both the institutional and departmental levels, there is a need for policies that implement equity in course loads, advising loads, including recognition of informal advising, faculty sponsorship of student activities, and committee service. Along with policy, attention should be given to social norms and communication patterns that could reduce the felt need to accept extra institutional service as a way of supporting diversity goals, or of securing promotion and tenure.

Campus climate issues for CCCU institutions seem less negative than those described by Stanley for secular campuses. Our findings show that faculty of color and white faculty have relatively positive perceptions of campus climate in ways that interrelate faculty morale, perceptions of administration, and the spiritual qualities of institutions. As CCCU institutions apply these findings, then, it is important not to separate out faculty of color as a single group (they represent many races and ethnicities) nor as a group entirely separate from whites. Institutional endeavors that strengthen the integrity and humility of policy-making, administration, and conflict resolution will benefit faculty of all races and ethnicities, and may link to positive perceptions in other arenas.

One important area of difference was the greater likelihood that faculty of color have chosen to work at a Christian college or university because of the opportunity to integrate faith and learning, whereas white faculty are more likely to be at the institution out of a commitment to Christian higher education. For example, a white faculty member may have attended a Christian college, or have family connections to a Christian college, or their church or denomination may be associated with a Christian college. These sorts of connections foster an attachment to Christian higher education as an educational niche that supports particular Christian traditions. Faculty of color may perceive opportunities for expressing and cultivating their Christian commitments in teaching and scholarship at a Christian college, but may not have personal or historical ties to Christian colleges, and so may not be focused on Christian higher education in and of itself. An understanding of this difference may help address the tension between the need to preserve institutional identity (which is often racially white) and to broaden multicultural inclusion. Articulating identity and mission in terms of preserving historic tradition and integrating faith with intellect may make Christian colleges appear compelling, both to those who originate in a denominational or religious tradition and those who join the tradition for professional reasons.

One area for future research is to better understand faculty of color by group. Stanley emphasizes that faculty of color have interrelated concerns and common experiences at predominantly white colleges and universities, but it is also important to understand the experiences, perceptions, and opinions of specific groups. International faculty, for instance, have experiences and perceptions influenced by their place of origin and how that place of origin is perceived by majority faculty and students. Asian American, Hispanic, Native American, and African American faculty will also vary based on both their personal and collective experiences, and the ways in which each American ethnicity is viewed by majority people.

Another area for future research is to study the commitment of CCCU institutions to diversity. As Nieves documents, faculty diversity has increased for the CCCU as a whole, but a closer analysis may show growth in diversity for some regions, denominations, traditions, or specific colleges, and stability or even decline in others. The CCCU itself has offered support for racial, ethnic, and gender diversity on campuses by sponsoring conferences, offering leadership development opportunities, and networking scholars and administrators. As Nieves notes, these initiatives are not always sustained at optimal levels. Reasons for commitment or resistance to diversity will vary across CCCU schools, and those variables would shed light on how diversity is understood, valued, and articulated at various institutions and by the CCCU itself.

The call for more research can be never-ending. A more pressing invitation is to act on what we already know.

Table 1: Zero-order correlations between the perception of religious hypocrisy in faculty and campus-climate questions sorted by majority (N = 1799) and minority (N = 108) identification.

Conflict among faculty is charitably resolved:	
Majority faculty	Minority faculty
-0.443 (p<0.001)	-0.428 (p<0.001)
A spirit of humility and charity between faculty and administration exists:	
Majority faculty	Minority faculty
-0.348 (p<0.001)	-0.489 (p<0.001)
Conflict between faculty and administration is charitable resolved:	
Majority faculty	Minority faculty
-0.358 (p<0.001)	-0.458 (p<0.001)
The administration at my institution is doing a good job of funning the institution:	
Majority faculty	Minority faculty
-0.276 (p<0.001)	-0.434 (p<0.001)
The administration at my institution performs its work in a Christ-like manner:	
Majority faculty	Minority faculty
-0.314 (p<0.001)	-0.497 (p<0.001)

Table 2: Zero-order correlations between the perception of good morale in faculty and campus-climate questions sorted by majority (N = 1799) and minority (N = 108) identification.

Conflict among faculty is charitably resolved:	
Majority faculty	Minority faculty
0.485 (p<0.001)	0.536 (p<0.001)
A spirit of humility and charity between faculty and administration exists:	
Majority faculty	Minority faculty
0.702 (p<0.001)	0.683 (p<0.001)
Conflict between faculty and administration is charitable resolved:	
Majority faculty	Minority faculty
0.695 (p<0.001)	0.675 (p<0.001)
The administration at my institution is doing a good job of funning the institution:	
Majority faculty	Minority faculty
0.738 (p<0.001)	0.728 (p<0.001)
The administration at my institution performs its work in a Christ-like manner:	
Majority faculty	Minority faculty
0.685 (p<0.001)	0.708 (p<0.001)

Table 3: Length of tenure at the current institution of a faculty member sorted by majority (N = 1799) and minority (N = 108) identification. Values are in percent.

	Majority	Minority
0 – 5 years	30.3	55.4
6 – 10 years	25.1	25
11 – 15 years	12.7	9.8
16 or more years	32	9.8

Table 4: Academic achievements in faculty, sorted by majority (N = 1799) and minority (N = 108) identification. Values are in percent.

	Majority	Minority
Possess a terminal degree	70.2	76.8
Published a book	23.8	29.5
Published in a peer-reviewed/refereed journal	60.8	71.4
Has published a book and has presented 1-2 papers in past 2 years	38.8	45.5
Somewhat or strongly agrees that their institution is a place of rigorous intellectual activity	70	65.6

Table 5: Faculty responses, sorted by majority (N = 1799) and minority (N = 108) identification. Values are in percent.

	Majority	Minority
Why did you take a job in Christian Higher Education?		
Commitment to Christian Higher Ed	45.2	35.2
Opportunity to integrate faith and learning	28.7	39.8
Agreement with the statement "The administration at my institution performs its work in a Christ-like manner"	72.1	61
Strong disagreement with the statement "Religious hypocrisy among faculty is a problem at my college/ university".	30.1	17.9
Number of classes taught per semester		
Less than three	48	42.7
Four or more	52	57.3
Strong agreement with the statement "I would welcome a course load reduction for the express purpose of spending more time doing research."	36.4	52.1

Table 6: Zero-order correlations between the perception of their institution as a place of rigorous intellectual activity and faculty morale and hypocrisy sorted by majority (N = 1799) and minority (N = 108) identification.

Morale among faculty at my institution is good	
Majority faculty	Minority faculty
0.403 (p<0.001)	0.396 (p<0.001)
Religious hypocrisy among faculty is a problem at my institution.	
Majority faculty	Minority faculty
-0.250 (p<0.001)	-0.255 (p<0.001)

BIBLICAL MULTICULTURALISM

Moving Forward in Deed and in Truth

TERRIEL BYRD AND OLGA RYBALKINA

Over fifty years have passed since the May 17, 1954, landmark decision of Brown v. the Board of Education was handed down. This legislation concluded that racially separate and unequal schools were illegal. However, since the early Civil Rights movement of the 1950s and 1960s, questions continue to be asked regarding diversity within America's educational landscape and specifically on the campuses of its private Christian colleges and universities. The purpose of this essay is to provide both theological and cultural reflections on several of the insights and themes revealed in the two preceding essays of this section.

In "Race and Ethnicity in CCCU Schools: Rhetoric and Reality," Alvaro Nieves probes the perceptions and/or misperceptions between majority and minority groups in academia. In "Understanding CCCU Faculty of Color," Jenell Williams Paris and Michelle Knights build upon Nieves's work while extending the conversation further, particularly by the use of data in the area of the responses given by faculty of color.

In this third essay, the pastor, professor, and author of a recently published book addressing racial separation in the Christian life of America (Byrd) joins the student-development professional (Rybalkina) to discuss theological, social, and academic issues related to multiculturalism. Reflections offered in this essay have emerged as a result of an earnest theological inquiry in relation to diversity and multiculturalism, as well as active engagement in the labor of multicultural education and reconciliation. The final part of the essay contains practical recommendations based on the biblical framework for understanding and acting upon diversity issues in the Christian university setting.

Historical Developments

In 1991, Nicholas Wolterstorff observed, "The Christian church is probably the most ethnically diverse grouping on earth; very few ethnic groups are not represented in

Christ's Body. Yet of almost all of those ethnic groups it is true that if a member of the group attended one of the colleges belonging to the Christian College Coalition, he or she would feel alien—and worse, would typically experience discrimination."[1] Based upon results from the Joeckel/Chesnes survey, this sad commentary still appears to be applicable to the perceived state of Christian colleges and universities. Such a statement, however, must be considered within the context of both past and present reality. We must acknowledge the progress made by many Christian colleges and universities. As Nieves chronicles, since the late 1990s the CCCU has been seeking ways to enhance diversity and fulfill the Christian mandate of racial reconciliation at the college level, and the numbers bear out that an increase of people of color has occurred on CCCU campuses

In July 2001, the CCCU sponsored a conference dubbed the "Consultation on Racial Harmony." The three-day event, held in northern Virginia, included twenty-seven educators from diverse ethnic backgrounds who spent two days in strategic consultation addressing some of the most critical issues of race relations in higher education. The CCCU's initiative was particularly significant because these discussions were taking place among leaders of private Christian colleges and universities. Reverend David Anderson, president of BridgeLeader Network and author of *Letters Across the Divide*, facilitated the forum. Anderson outlined a clear biblical mandate stressing the importance of multicultural ministries in both the church and the college campus community. At that time, CCCU President Bob Andringa proposed two goals for the Racial Harmony Consultation: 1) offering personal growth and development to provide leadership in the area of racial harmony and educational diversity; 2) identifying areas of consensus about how the Council and its campuses can advance in reflecting the biblical mandate for unity and the educational advantages of diversity. The Consultation on Racial Harmony demonstrated a sincere desire to challenge CCCU educators to think more deeply about ways in which they, and the institutions they represent, could more collectively and positively address the issue of race in higher education.

In February 2002, the CCCU's Commission for Advancing Intercultural Competencies mandated that "the Council develop a broader, biblically-based, holistic approach to help faculty, administrators and students understand more deeply the principle of 'loving our neighbor.'"[2] The timing could not be more critical in light of emerging research consistently revealing that "white and non-white faculty and students are in agreement that racism still exists and members of both groups recognize the problem within their campus communities."[3] Ten years later, we can recognize many notable examples demonstrating the progress made on many Christian campuses across the United States. Regretfully, at the same time, research data from this and other projects

---

1 Nicholas Wolterstorff, Foreword to *Ethnic-Minorities and Evangelical Christian Colleges*, ed. D. John Lee (New York: University Press of America, 1991), 11.

2 Bob Andringa, "Commission on Intercultural Competencies Holds First Meeting," Council for Christian Colleges & Universities, *CCCU Advance* (Winter 2002-2003): 10.

3 Alvaro Nieves, "Race and Ethnicity in CCCU Schools: Rhetoric and Reality," 207.

suggest that racism or passive ignorance continues to negatively impact the lives of minority students, faculty, and staff.

Navigating the Postmodern Discourse

The opening statement of Allan Bloom's book, *The Closing of the American Mind*, reads: "There is one thing a professor can be absolutely certain of: almost every student entering the university believes, or says he believes, that truth is relative."[4] One of the many challenges faced by those who seek to advance diversity at many evangelical colleges is the perception that multiculturalism is primarily linked to some anti-Christian view of pluralism, postmodernism, and their language of tolerance and moral relativism. The title of Dennis McCallum's edited volume, *The Death of Truth: Responding to Multiculturalism, the Rejection of Reason and the New Postmodern Diversity,*[5] suggests precisely this. Indeed, cautious reasoning is necessary, for, as Kraft puts it, "it is an unfortunate fact that many uninformed people, in the name of cultural relativism, have turned to a moral or ethical relativism."[6] The classic "culture wars" debate is often evoked, which immediately creates barriers against meaningful dialogue. Nieves cites the comment from a professor of color responding to a survey question: "Trying to extricate a student's faith from socio-political assumptions makes life difficult for all."[7] He cites another respondent who noted the difficulty of "working to fight against common cultural Christian beliefs among white, evangelical Americans."[8] It appears the tension is between two different perceptions of Christian beliefs. "The postmodern understanding of truth leads postmoderns to be less concerned than their forebears to think systematically or logically. Postmoderrns feel comfortable mixing elements of what have traditionally been considered incompatible belief systems."[9] It is extremely difficult to engage in productive discussions about inclusiveness, tolerance, and multiculturalism when such terms inscribed in common cultural beliefs are viewed as code for moral relativism and anti-foundationalism in the context of a postmodernism worldview. "Most postmoderns make the leap of believing that this plurality of truths can exist alongside one another. The Postmodern consciousness, therefore, entails a radical kind of relativism and pluralism."[10] Christian educators must emphasize the value of diversity within the biblical context. As Martin Marty notes, "It is hard to look at the varieties of multicultural expressions in America without seeing their enriching potential, the possibility of their being able to enhance the lives of those in other subcultures."[11] For such an enhancement to be fully realized in the context of

---

4 Allan Bloom, *The Closing of the American Mind* (New York: Simon & Schuster, 1987), 25.

5 Dennis McCallum, ed., *The Death of Truth: Responding to Multiculturalism, the Rejection of Reason and the New Postmodern Diversity* (Minneapolis: Bethany House Publishers, 1996).

6 Charles Kraft, *Christianity in Culture* (Maryknoll, N.Y.: Orbis Books, 1995), 50.

7 Nieves, 207.

8 Ibid.

9 Stanley J. Grenz, *A Primer on Postmodernism* (Grand Rapids, Mich.: Eerdmans, 1996), 15.

10 Ibid, 14.

11 David A. Hoekema and Bobby Fong, eds., *Christianity and Culture in the CrossFire* (Grand Rapids/ Cambridge: Eerdmans, 1997), 18.

evangelical Christianity, it is therefore enormously important to emphasis the biblical foundation of multiculturalism and embrace truth as God's construction (Matt.24:35). Anything less is a betrayal of the biblical mandate of Christian unity and wholeness.

Where We Are Today

According to Emerson and Smith's work, *Divided by Faith: Evangelical Religion and the Problem of Race in America,* "Groups that stress tolerance, openness to diversity, and inclusiveness typically lack the ability to have strong comparison groups by which to define their boundaries . . . . In sum, groups that are more capable of constructing distinct identity boundaries, short of becoming genuinely countercultural, produce stronger collective identities."[12] Thus it is difficult to cultivate change when the change is perceived to be a threat to the group's very identity. We need a paradigm shift away from the socio-political, racialized theories of identity to the biblical mandate for a multi-cultural community as the authentic representation of the family of God. Most Christian schools are closely connected to Christian denominations. Non-denominational institutions reflect the racial and ethnic composition of their local church memberships. Martin Luther King, Jr. said: "Unfortunately, most of the major denominations still practice segregation in local churches, hospitals, schools, and other church institutions. It is appalling that the most segregated hour of Christian America is eleven o'clock on Sunday morning, the same hour when many are standing to sing: 'In Christ There Is No East Nor West.'"[13] The church must be viewed from outside a trajectory of the limitations of demographical and geographical boundaries. The kingdom is made up of "a great multitude that no one [can] count, from every nation, from all tribes and peoples and languages, standing before the throne . . ." (Revelation 7:9). It goes without saying that these Christian institutions should be motivated by a higher calling, a calling rooted in a belief that Christ has called us to racial reconciliation and justice. The Council has demonstrated at times a level of good intention on this issue.

A concluding statement in Paris and Knights's essay prompts action: "The call for more research can be never-ending. A more pressing invitation is to act on what we already know."[14] So what do we know? We know that while the numbers of minority or underrepresented faculty and students have expanded, enhancing the social climate on many Christian campuses, the situation has yet to reach a desired state of harmony and reconciliation that both faculty and students expect: a state of harmony and reconciliation to erase perceptual disparities in their experiences as scholars, learners, and members of the college community.

Minority faculty and students have similar concerns related to being representatives of a small population on campus. This status creates a sense of alienation, a burden

---

12   Michael O. Emerson and Christian Smith, *Divided by Faith: Evangelical Religion and the Problem of Race in America* (New York: Oxford University Press, 2000), 143.

13   Martin Luther King, Jr. T*he Martin Luther King, Jr. Companion: Quotations from the Speeches, Essays and Books of Martin Luther King, Jr.*, ed. Coretta Scott King (New York: St. Martin's Press, 1993), 27.

14   Jenell Williams Paris and Michelle Knights, "Understanding CCCU Faculty of Color," 217.

to prove one's worth under the pressure of existing stereotypes. For faculty, as offered in Paris and Knights's essay, this burden may lie in a real or perceived reality related to "compensation, rank and tenure, lack of recognition, appreciation, autonomy, job security, and opportunity to develop new ideas."[15] For students, the challenge often lies in academic and social dimensions of college life. One of the student participants in a qualitative study in progress conducted by Rybalkina shares, "When I first came to this [small Christian] university, I felt very left out. At home I had people from all races, but on this campus, I was only with Black people, this is the norm here."[16] Facing prejudice and misconceptions and experiencing alienation are common to more minority students on our Christian campuses than we educators want to admit.

The majority of qualitative comments gathered from the Joeckel/Chesnes survey that touch on issues of multiculturalism are offered by minority faculty and students. Nieves contends that this pattern "is consistent with the tendency of majority group members not having to face such issues on a regular basis. Many, if not most, minority faculty are aware of facing these issues on a daily basis."[17] Personal experience and struggles lead to the greater sense of commitment to the work of reconciliation among minority faculty, both through scholarship and engagement in campus life. Similarly, in our work with college students we have observed more passion and enthusiasm toward racial understanding and harmony demonstrated by students of color. Our fundamental belief upon which we will reflect follows this principle: a work of reconciliation should not be a mission for few, but a mandate for all members of the community, an essential dimension of spiritual growth and tangible practice of Christian life.

Biblical Mandate

When the apostle Paul wrote to the church of Thessalonica, the letter is addressed to the church, not to an individual—the implication being that the church must seek to work in community. Some issues can only be resolved by the collective church. Paul begins his letter to the Thessalonica church with unmixed praise, "remembering before our God and our Father your work of faith and labor of love, and steadfast hope in our Lord Jesus Christ" (1 Thessalonians 1:1-3; NRSV). Paul picks out three great ingredients of the Christian life which must be present if true reconciliation is to occur. First, in order for reconciliation to move beyond mere rhetoric, it must become work, which is inspired by faith. And the work ideally must be done by all members of the CCCU family, not just a few who see themselves as advocates of reconciliation.

Second, there is labor which is prompted by love. Love takes us higher than prejudice and racism. "As Christians, our hope of a heavenly home is certainly not to be understood as 'two homes, one white and the other black.' Let us all read again the words

---

15 Ibid., 212.

16 Olga Rybalkina, "Black, White, His? Psychosocial and Theological Aspects of Identity," paper presented at the Christians on Diversity in the Academy annual national conference, Azusa Pacific University, California, March 24-26, 2010.

17 Nieves, 207.

of our Lord. 'Your will be done on earth as in heaven.' Here on earth is a good place to begin practicing what we surely await in heaven"[18] The work of racial reconciliation and justice begins here on earth.

Finally, we need patience made possible by hope (1 Thessalonians 1:3). It may be said that the authentic work of justice is the ability to give the gift of hope to the hopeless. The concept of racial reconciliation must be the vision of hope for all Christians and especially for those who have been charged to impart knowledge and wisdom to generations of young people who will carry on the legacy of Christ's kingdom here on earth.

A Dimension of Spiritual Growth

Multiculturalism for its own sake is an empty and even dangerous goal if pursued outside of the worshipful acknowledgement of God, when we aim "our heart away from the Creator to some aspect of the creation as if it were God."[19] As Berger and Cleveland observe, "secular approaches to 'diversity' and 'unity in diversity' have unintentionally idolized race and the system of racialization. Vocational ministry to and with 'others' remains marred by the pride, judgments, and condemnation found in tribalism, rather than the unity of the Spirit."[20] We must with humble acknowledgement recognize our sheer dependence upon one another if we wish to grow and become spiritually mature.

The Christian academy must be concerned about the community dimensions of its spiritual life and spiritual growth, which reflects the diversity in God's kingdom. Administering and teaching in the Christian academy is more than simply the imparting of knowledge. An epistemology must be rooted and grounded in an authentic transformation as interpreted in the context of the biblical, multicultural metanarrative of the Christian faith. This inclusive faith provides the foundation for the integration of theory and practice, resulting in kingdom building for God's glory. Jesus demonstrated the most effective approach to spiritual growth and the integration of faith and learning when he selected the twelve disciples, that diverse band of followers from different walks and stations in life, ranging from a former tax collector, Matthew, to Simon, a political zealot. He taught them by precept and by example. This integration of faith and learning within a community of faith takes into account a rich social, cultural, and religious context. The spiritual dimension of faith and learning can only be realized in the holistic context that demonstrates concern for the united body of Christ. Martin Luther King, Jr. once stated, "I can never be what I ought to be until you are what you ought to be . . . . "[21] Furthermore, we can never compartmentalize the academic world from the religious/spiritual sphere of life experiences; rather, we must find ways to live out

---

18   Terriel R. Byrd, *I Shall Not Be Moved: Racial Separation in Christian Worship* (Lanham, Md.: University Press of America, 2007), 55.

19   James Smith, *Desiring the Kingdom: Worship, Worldview, and Cultural Formation* (Grand Rapids, Mich.: Baker Academic, 2009), 85.

20   Tamara Cleveland and Daniel Berger, "A Kingdom Divided: A Seminary Professor and Student Respond to Racialization and Its Impact in Evangelical Higher Education," paper presented at the Christians on Diversity in the Academy annual national conference, Azusa Pacific University, California, March 24-26, 2010.

21   Martin Luther King, Jr., *The Measure of a Man* (Minneapolis: Fortress Press, 2001), 45-46.

a Christian worldview while examining many complex social and philosophical issues, without compromising objective academic standards of excellence.

The Practice of Christian Life

Biblical multiculturalism begins by affirming the authority of Scripture and the transforming work of the Holy Spirit in shaping the moral and spiritual ethic of the Christian academic community. That is to say, biblical multiculturalism should commit to the clear scriptural teachings on unity and oneness. The biblical concept of the Christian family as the body of Christ must be primary, over and above familial traditions or ethnic and cultural identities or perspectives of individuals or groups within the academy. This demonstrates and reflects a willingness to be submissive to the transforming power of God's Spirit (Romans 8:26-27; 12:1-5; 1 Corinthians 12:12-27; 2 Corinthians 5:14-21; Galatians 3:28; Ephesians 4:3-5; 4:10-16). The basic foundation undergirding biblical multiculturalism is the principle of unity and love within the context of a community of sisterhood and brotherhood as lived and taught by Jesus Christ (John 15:1-16; 1 Corinthian 13:13; 1 John 4:7-21).

In praxis, CCCU schools should seek to recruit qualified leaders who reflect sensitivity to issues of shared leadership and authority across ethnic and cultural lines. This means not merely recruiting or staffing as a politically correct notion, but recruiting those who understand the biblical mandate of inclusiveness and multiculturalism as a biblically sound practice. While we believe that the work of reconciliation should be recognized as the work for every member of the college community, we emphasize the importance of intentional leadership in this direction at the presidential and vice-presidential levels. While grass-root efforts may bring about the transformation of culture within the university setting, such efforts will be far more successful with the solid and active commitment from the college presidents, chief academic officers, and school deans. Professional development and peer accountability can be fostered by the CCCU through a consistent and purposeful appeal to the Christian college leaders.

Second, the commitment to biblical multiculturalism should be fostered among faculty. In a national study of faculty development needs, multiculturalism and diversity as related to teaching emerged as one of the eight top issues in the faculty development program.[22] Faculty need to be encouraged and equipped to be intentional in exploring a theology of integration. This intentionality should begin with the place of worship. For example, one demonstrative symbol of this resolve could be a willingness not only to visit other worship services across racial/ethnic lines, but also to participate in discussion groups addressing ways to remove barriers and build bridges of unity among Christian worshipers.

Third, biblical multiculturalism should encourage Bible colleges and seminaries to develop internship models for engaging their students across cultural and racial lines.

---

22 Mary Dean Sorcinelli, A. E. Eddy, and A. L. Beach, *Creating the Future of Faculty Development: Learning from the Past, Understanding the Present* (Bolton, Mass.: Anker Publishing Company, 2006).

Ministry students could spend (for credit) a semester working in a local, racially and ethnically diverse congregation, serving as youth pastors and in other ministry servant/ leadership roles. There could also be mentoring programs within racially and ethnically diverse churches that partner with the CCCU. These experiences could be both culturally enriching and spiritually beneficial.

Fourth, the vision of biblical multiculturalism should encourage Christian colleges and seminaries to further boost minority staff and faculty participation, as well as to encourage further development of culturally sensitive curriculum within those institutions. For example, the broader religious community needs to be aware of the uniqueness of, and contributions made by, the African/Latino/Asian American Christian community. This would include, but not be limited to, teaching in the areas of music history and styles, homiletical tradition, theological perspectives, leadership styles, church history, civil rights, and social-justice activities. Again, this information can be part of a means of educating the wider Christian community concerning these Christian faith traditions.

Fifth, inspired by biblical multiculturalism, we must encourage mainstream denominational and non-denominational Christian publishing organizations to be more culturally sensitive in their Christian educational materials. This involves the integration of ethnically diverse content into mainstream Christian educational curriculum. Presently, this ethnic content is often directed to specifically religious educational needs according to racial demographics. Ethnically diverse materials could be more broadly disseminated as a reflection of God's kingdom. Though many rural Christian communities may rarely see a black face, the Christian education literature that is used in these communities should reflect in some way that people of color are a part of the Christian family and are worthy of having their stories told and pictures seen by others than members of their own race. The same holds true in predominantly African American communities which rarely, in a religious setting, interact with white Christians.

Sixth, biblical multiculturalism should inspire Christian scholars to establish distinctly Christian perspectives on diversity as an alternative to secular approaches that are predominantly represented in today's literature, including the majority of textbooks used for courses addressing multicultural issues in pedagogy, psychology, social work, and other fields. As an example, in his recent presentation at the Christians on Diversity conference sponsored by Azusa Pacific University, Heekap Lee persuasively argued for the need for a biblical approach to multicultural education, contrasting it with the current perspective of polyculturalism and cultural relativism permeating the content of instruction today.[23]

A final and primary recommendation is to recognize biblical multiculturalism as an integrative goal of holistic student development of college students through both curricular and co-curricular programs, helping students recognize themselves as those "made in the image of God, united as a human race, divided by a fallen condition into

---

23   HeeKap Lee, "Biblical Foundation of Multiculturalism: What Does the Bible Say about Multicultural Education?" Paper presented at the Christians on Diversity in the Academy annual national conference, Azusa Pacific University, California, March 24-26, 2010.

ethnae who through Christ are co-equal citizens of the Kingdom and servants and stewards of the King."[24] Faculty and staff must be intentional about their commitment to work together to design academic and student-life curriculum. Academic curriculum should reflect biblical multiculturalism, which should then be integrated into the areas of spiritual discipleship, relational transformation, and experiential learning.

In conclusion, Nieves reminds us that there are plenty of "well-meaning people at all levels who sincerely recognize the need for greater diversity for spiritual, ethical, and practical reasons."[25] What is needed most to make further progress is the commitment of top leadership, intentionality at all levels, and an actual plan to move forward in deed and truth towards the Kingdom of God and for the glory of the King (Colossians 3:17).

---

24   Cleveland and Berger, "A Kingdom Divided.".

25   Nieves, 199.

Bibliography: Part Five

Absher, Beverly. "Attraction and Retention of Females and Minorities in Christian Higher Education." *Journal of Research on Christian Education* 18 (2009): 160-189.

Andringa, Robert. "Commission on Intercultural Competencies Holds First Meeting." *CCCU Advance* (Winter 2002-2003).

Astin, H. S., A. L. Antonio, C. M. Cress, and A. W. Astin. *Race and Ethnicity in the American Professoriate.* Los Angeles: Higher Education Research Institute, 1997.

Blackburn, R. T., S. Wenzel, and J. P. Bieber. "Minority vs. Majority Faculty Publication Performance: A Research Note." *Review of Higher Education* 17(1994): 217-282.

Bloom, Allan. *The Closing of the American Mind*. New York: Simon & Schuster, 1987.

Byrd, Terriel R. *I Shall Not Be Moved: Racial Separation in Christian Worship*. Lanham, Md.: University Press of America, 2007.

Corts, Paul. "Top Ten Issues." Council for Christian Colleges and Universities, 2009. http://www.cccu.org/professional_development/resource_library/top_ten_issues_ in_christian_higher_education (accessed March 1, 2010).

Cose, Ben. "Diversity Takes a Hit during Hard Times." *Chronicle of Higher Education*, October 18, 2009, B1.

Council for Christian Colleges and Universities. "Racial Issues in the CCCU Faculty," 2004. http://www.cccu.org/professional_development/resource_library/racial_issues_in_the _cccu_faculty (accessed February 28, 2010).

Emerson, Michael O. and Christian Smith. *Divided by Faith: Evangelical Religion and the Problem of Race in America*. New York: Oxford University Press, 2000.

Felder, Cain Hope, ed. *Stony the Road We Trod: African American Biblical Interpretation*. Minnesota: Augsburg Fortress, 1991.

Firman, Michael and Krista Merrick Gilson. "Mission Statement Analysis of CCCU Member Institutions." *Christian Higher Education* 9 (2010): 60-70.

Grenz, Stanley J. *A Primer on Postmodernism*. Grand Rapids, Mich.: Eerdmans, 1996.

Hacker, Andrew. *Two Nations: Black and White, Separate, Hostile, Unequal*. New York: Scribner, 2003.

Hoekema, David A. and Bobby Fong, eds. *Christianity and Culture in the CrossFire*. Grand Rapids, Mich.: Eerdmans, 1997.

King, Jr., Martin Luther. *The Martin Luther King, Jr. Companion: Quotations from the Speeches, Essays and Books of Martin Luther King, Jr.* Ed. Coretta Scott King. New York: St. Martin's Press, 1993.
_____. *The Measure of a Man*. Minneapolis: Fortress Press, 2001.

Kraft, Charles. *Christianity in Culture*. Maryknoll, N.Y.: Orbis Books, 1995.

Lee, D. John. *Ethnic-Minorities and Evangelical Christian Colleges*. New York: University Press of America, 1991.

McCallum, Dennis. *The Death of Truth: Responding to Multiculturalism, the Rejection of Reason and the New Postmodern Diversity*. Minneapolis: Bethany House, 1996.

McMinn, Lisa. "Enclave Adaptation, Multiculturalism and Evangelical Christian Colleges." *Research on Christian Higher Education* 5 (1998): 23-52.

Olsen, D. H. and K. L. Stewart. "Family Systems and Health Behaviors." In *New Directions in Health Psychology Assessment. Series in Applied Psychology: Social Issues and Questions,* 27-64. Edited by H. E. Schroeder. Washington, DC: Hemisphere, 1991.

Skipper, James K, Anthony L. Guenther, and Gilber Nass. "The Sacredness of .05: A Note Concerning the Uses of Statistical Levels of Significance in Social Science." *The American Sociologist* 2 (1967): 16-18.

Smith, James K. A. *Desiring the Kingdom: Worship, Worldview, and Cultural Formation*. Grand Rapids, Mich.: Baker Academic, 2007.

Stanley, Christine. "An Overview of the Literature," In *Faculty of Color Teaching in Predominantly White Colleges and Universities*, 1-29. Edited by Christine Stanley. Boston: Anker Publishing Company, 2006.

Stewart, K. L. *Stresses and Adaptation: A Multisystem Model of Individual, Couple, Family, and Work Systems.* Dissertation Abstracts International-A, 49(08), 1989.

Turner, C. S., and S. L. Myers, Jr. *Faculty of Color in Academe: Bittersweet Success.* Needam Heights, Mass.: Allyn and Bacon, 2000.

United States Kerner Commission, Report of the National Commission on Civil Disorders. Washington, D.C.: D.C. Government Printing Office, 1968.

Voydanoff, P. "Work Demands and Work-to-Family and Family-to-Work Conflict: Direct and Indirect Relationships." *Journal of Family Issues* 26 (2005): 707-726.

PART SIX

GENDER EQUITY

FINDING A HOME IN ACADEMIA

Gender Equity at CCCU Institutions

M. ELIZABETH LEWIS HALL

CHAPTER 16

"Even where no strict injustice is perpetrated against women, they are often plagued by a vague but persistent sense of *homelessness*. The social world which they inhabit is not constructed according to 'their measure'; it is a male world and they often feel as aliens in it."
—**Miroslav Volf**[1]

Gender equity has long been an elusive goal in the academy, where the academic structure of tenure, promotion, and university duties was initially constructed on the basis of men's careers and life cycles.[2] Gender inequity has significant consequences, not only for the women involved, but for female students who are not exposed to same-sex mentoring and role-modeling, and for institutions, which are deprived of the talent pool represented by women. In 2006, the American Association of University Professors (AAUP) issued a report on the state of gender equity in the academy and noted that the current state of affairs continues to reflect a series of accumulated disadvantages: "Women faculty are less likely than men to hold full-time positions. Women in those full-time positions are underrepresented in tenure-track positions, and have not attained senior faculty rank . . . at the same rates as men. At each full-time faculty rank, women earn less than

---

1 Miroslav Volf, *Exclusion and Embrace: A Theological Exploration of Identity, Otherness, and Reconciliation* (Nashville: Abingdon Press, 1996), 184.

2 J. Bickel, "Scenarios for Success: Enhancing Women Physicians' Professional Advancement," *Western Journal of Medicine* 162 (1995): 165-169.

men . . . ."[3] And while it might be assumed that these trends would correct themselves over time, the data do not support this assumption: Female salaries in 2005-06 showed that for full professors, women earned 88 cents to each dollar earned by men and 93 cents to the dollar for associate and assistant professors. These numbers were lower than they were thirty years previously, when they were 90 and 96 cents, respectively.

Contributors to Gender Inequity

In recent years, research has helped clarify the factors that contribute to gender inequity in the academic context as well as those that do not. Among factors that do not appear to currently contribute to the lack of gender equity is a lack of qualified applicants. In 2007, women earned 45.5 percent of doctorates.[4] While percentages vary among academic areas, faculty hiring has failed to reflect the percentage of women graduating in any given field.

Another potential culprit that has been discredited is that gender inequity simply reflects women's choice to stay home or work part-time, perhaps because of family responsibilities. While this certainly may be the case for some women, overall trends suggest that this is not generally the case. For example, it is noteworthy that women have achieved parity at institutions granting associate degrees, but are most underrepresented at universities that award doctorates.[5] This pattern suggests that choice is not a primary factor and that institutional variables contribute to the current situation of inequity. In addition, choice does not explain lower percentages of women in tenure-track positions, nor salary inequities when rank is held constant.

Other discredited theories have suggested that gender differences in salary are due to the concentration of women in disciplines with lower-paying labor markets and in institutions with higher teaching loads, and to gender disparities in publications. Each of these factors contributes some variance to salary inequality. However, each may also reflect inequality in itself. For example, women are underrepresented in the hard sciences, but this is at least partially due to the fact that the professional climate is demonstrably chillier to women in these environments. They have little-to-no mentoring for crucial career advancement, and consequently, there are high drop-out rates for women in these fields.[6] While women on average spend more time teaching than do men and less time on research,[7] it is unclear whether this is due to personal preferences or to the fact that women are overrepresented in two-year institutions where more teaching is required and where research is not as large a component of the job. In addition, these factors simply do not explain all of the inequities in salaries. Recent studies that take

---

3   M. S. West and J. W. Curtis, "AAUP Faculty Gender Equity Indicators 2006" (American Association of University Professors, 2006), 6.

4   V. Welch, Jr., "Doctorate Recipients from United States Universities: Selected Tables 2007" (Chicago: National Opinion Research Center. Retrieved September 20, 2009: http://www.norc.org/SED.htm)

5   West and Curtis, "AAUP Faculty Gender Equity Indicators 2006," 7.

6   B. M. Vetter, *What Is Holding up the Glass Ceiling?: Barriers to Women in the Science and Engineering Workforce* (Occasional Paper 92-3. Washington, D.C.: Commission on Professionals in Science and Technology, 1992).

7   J. Glazer-Raymo, *Shattering the Myths: Women in Academe* (Baltimore: Johns Hopkins University Press, 1999).

into account all of these variables continue to find an "unexplained" disadvantage of several percentage points in average salaries.[8]

Finally, the idea that women's failure to advance in rank or leadership responsibilities simply reflects gender differences in aspirations has also been discredited. Shultz, Montoya, and Briere[9] actually found that more women (88%) than men (77%) in their faculty sample indicated a desire to advance in rank, tenure, or position in their fields.

In contrast, other factors have emerged as significant contributors to inequity. One of these is difficulty in balancing career goals with family responsibilities. While this can be a challenge for both men and women, the evidence suggests that it disproportionately impacts women. For example, Shultz, Montoya, and Briere[10] found that more women than men faculty reported personal obstacles to academic advancement and that family responsibilities were the most often cited obstacles to achieving their goals. Consequently, institutions desiring to support women faculty often implement "family-friendly" policies and practices to minimize these obstacles for women and for the increasing number of men shouldering heavy family responsibilities.

Factors associated with the academic environment have also emerged more clearly as significant contributors to inequity. Deficits theory, first articulated by Sonnert and Holton,[11] posits that structural obstacles in the workplace climate (legal, political, and social), as well as more specific negative experiences (such as gender discrimination and sexual harassment), hinder the success of women faculty. In other words, the deficit model posits that "women are treated differently in science" (or in academia), and the difference model says "women act differently in science" (or, again, in academia).[12] Research supports the deficits theory, demonstrating that difficulties in advancement appear to be primarily due to "formal and informal structural mechanisms (e.g., discrimination, limited networking) that provide female scientists with fewer opportunities and more obstacles in their career paths, leading to lowered success, satisfaction, and retention."[13]

Gender Inequity in Christian Academia

The research cited above has largely been conducted in secular institutions. Women working in Christian academic settings, such as those represented by CCCU institutions, are also influenced by factors emerging from the Christian subculture in these settings, and some of these characteristics moderate the factors described above. What is different about these Christian settings? Research shows that prescribed gender roles

8 West & Curtis, "AAUP Faculty Gender Equity Indicators 2006."

9 E. L. Shultz, A. L. Montoya, and P. M. Briere, "Perceptions of Institutional Climate," *U.S. Department of Education Educational Resources Information Center (ERIC)* ED353234 (1992).

10 Ibid.

11 Gerhard Sonnert and Gerald Holton, *Who Succeeds in Science?: The Gender Dimension* (New Brunswick, N.J.: Rutgers University Press, 1995). See also Gerhard Sonnert and Gerald Holton, "Career Patterns of Women and Men in the Sciences," *American Scientist* 84 (1986): 63-71.

12 Sonnert and Holton, *Who Succeeds in Science?*, 9.

13 Isis H. Settles, L. M. Cortina, J. Malley, and A. J. Stewart, "The Climate for Women in Academic Science: The Good, the Bad, and the Changeable," *Psychology of Women Quarterly* 30 (2006): 47-58.

are prevalent in evangelical samples.[14] While it would be misleading to suggest that all evangelicals think similarly about gender, given the diversity of perspectives on gender represented in evangelical Christianity,[15] research has consistently shown that individuals identifying with evangelicalism or similar forms of conservative Christianity tend to be more traditional in their gender schemas than the general population. In addition, for largely historical reasons, gender is "a central organizing principle and a core symbolic system in this subculture."[16] Evangelicals tend to be quite passionate about their views on gender roles, contributing to the salience of gender issues in this context.

Evangelical Christians are also more conservative politically than the general population. Over the years, various studies have found connections between evangelicalism and support for Republican candidates as well as support for conservative social policies (e.g, abortion, women's rights).[17] These political and social preferences seem to have crystallized with the 1980 elections and probably had their origin in debates over school prayer and abortion. In recent years, this conservatism has also been manifest in non-social issues (e.g., issues related to economic security and national defense), suggesting an evangelical embrace of conservative ideology in general.

How do these characteristics of the evangelical subculture affect the experiences of women in evangelical institutions? They are more likely to encounter traditional gender schemas reflected in interactions and in very small differences in treatment—"micro-inequities"—that, over time, accumulate to disadvantage and discourage women.[18] Several studies have documented these micro-inequities in evangelical academic institutions, noting issues such as unfriendly attitudes from male colleagues and students,[19] difficulties in hiring and in tenure review,[20] subtle disrespect from students and difficulties in collegiality, discrimination and exposure to negative comments about women, less influence in decision-making, feeling they were evaluated more stringently than

---

14   John. P. Bartkowski, "One Step Forward, One Step Back: Progressive Traditionalism and the Negotiation of Domestic Labor in Evangelical Families," *Gender Issues* 17 (1999): 37-61. See also Bartkowski, *Remaking the Godly Marriage: Gender Negotiation in Evangelical Families* (New Brunswick, N.J.: Rutgers University Press, 2001), 69-86. Also see Sally K. Gallagher and Christian Smith, "Symbolic Traditionalism and Pragmatic Egalitarianism: Contemporary Evangelicals, Families, and Gender," *Gender & Society* 13 (1999): 211-233.

15   Sally K. Gallagher, "Where Are the Antifeminist Evangelicals?: Evangelical Identity, Subcultural Location, and Attitudes toward Feminism," *Gender and Society* 18 (2004): 451-472. See also David A. Gay, Christopher G. Ellison, and Daniel A. Powers, "In Search of Denominational Subcultures: Religious Affiliation and 'Pro-Family' Issues Revisited," *Review of Religious Research* 38 (1996): 3-17.

16   Julie Ingersoll, *Evangelical Christian Women: War Stories in the Gender Battles* (New York: New York University Press, 2003), 16.

17   For a review, see Howard Gold and Gina E. Russell, "The Rising Influence of Evangelicalism in American Political Behavior, 1980-2004," *Social Science Journal* 44 (2007): 554-562.

18   Beth B. Haslett and Susan Lipman, "Micro Inequities: Up Close and Personal," in *Subtle Sexism: Current Practice and Prospects for Change*, ed. Nijole V. Benokraitis (Thousand Oaks, Ca.: Sage, 1997), 34-53. See also Settles, Cortina, Malley, and Stewart, "The Climate for Women in Academic Science."

19   Marti Watson Garlett, "Waiting in the Wings: Women of God in the Evangelical Academy," unpublished dissertation, Claremont Graduate School of Education, Claremont, CA (1997). See also Marti Watson Garlett, "Female Faculty on the Fringe: Theologizing Sexism in the Evangelical Academy," *Research on Christian Higher Education* 4 (1997): 69-97.

20   Julie Ingersoll, *Evangelical Christian Women*, 70-91. See also Debra L. Sequeira, Thomas Trzyna, Martin L. Abbott, and Delbert S. McHenry, "'The Kingdom Has Not Yet Come': Coping With Micro-Inequities Within a Christian University," *Research on Christian Higher Education* 2 (1995): 1-35.

the males, and feeling uninformed about resources and advancement.[21] Many of these experiences were tied to patriarchal religious beliefs by the participants.[22] Furthermore, research on encountering discriminatory gender-based actions and comments in a CCCU institution shows that when these experiences are attributed to the Christian belief system of the perpetrator, the negative effects of these experiences are intensified.[23]

Women in the evangelical subculture may also have more internalization of traditional gender expectations, which place high priority on marriage, childrearing, and homemaking. If this is the case, and in contrast to secular institutions, women at Christian institutions may be less likely to pursue postgraduate degrees or aspire to academic careers.[24] They may also face increased difficulty with respect to work-family balance if they feel internal and/or external pressures to meet traditional standards of childcare and housekeeping.[25] Consistent with this view, Sequeira, Trzyna, Abbott, and McHenry[26] found that female faculty in their Christian university pursued their terminal degrees more intermittently than the males because of family concerns. Ingersoll,[27] in her qualitative study of evangelical women, noted that women in Christian higher education face a double-bind in which these women must model "good Christian character," including Christian ideals of domesticity and "feminine" character traits such as humility and selflessness, while at the same time being competent academicians, which often requires assertiveness and self-confidence. Walker[28] confirmed the experience of being in a double-bind in her study of Christian female faculty. And while the evangelical subculture is generally pro-family, this does not always translate into support for working mothers. Two separate studies on female Christian academicians revealed that when evangelical institutions did not support the women's attempts at work-family balance, this led to attrition or distress.[29] This internalization of traditional gender expectations

21 M. Elizabeth Lewis Hall, Shelly Cunningham, and Brad Christerson, "Biola University Gender Climate Study" (La Mirada, Ca.: Biola University (Spring, 2008).

22 Sequeira, Trzyna, Abbott, and McHenry, "The Kingdom Has Not Yet Come"; Ingersoll, *Evangelical Christian Women.*

23 M. Elizabeth Lewis Hall, Brad Christerson, and Shelly Cunningham, "Sanctified Sexism: Gender Harassment in Evangelical Universities," *Psychology of Women Quarterly* 34 (2010):181-185.

24 Colleen Warner Colaner and Steven M. Giles, "The Baby Blanket or the Briefcase: The Impact of Evangelical Gender Role Ideologies on Career and Mothering Aspirations of Female Evangelical College Students," *Sex Roles* 58 (2008): 526-534; Colleen Warner Colaner and Susan C Warner, "The Effect of Egalitarian and Complementarian Gender Role Attitudes on Career Aspirations in Evangelical Female Undergraduate College Students," *Journal of Psychology & Theology* 33 (2005): 224-229.

25 Christopher G. Ellison and John P. Bartkowski, "Conservative Protestantism and the Division of Household Labor among Married Couples," *Journal of Family Issues* 23 (2002): 95-985; M. Elizabeth Lewis Hall, Tamara L. Anderson, and Michele M. Willingham, "Diapers, Dissertations, and Other Holy Things: The Experiences of Mothers Working in Christian Academia," *Christian Higher Education* 3 (2004): 41-60; Cynthia Neal Kimball, Terri Watson, Sally Schwer Canning, and Joan Laidig Brady, "Missing Voices: Professional Challenges for Academic Women," *Journal of Psychology and Christianity* 20 (2001): 132-144.

26 Sequeira, Trzyna, Abbott, and McHenry, "The Kingdom Has Not Yet Come."

27 Ingersoll, *Evangelical Christian Women,* 27, 79-80.

28 Juanie N. Walker, "Pragmatic Paradoxes of Gender and Authority at a Christian University: Ethnography and Analysis of Female Academicians' Narratives," *Research on Christian Higher Education* 8 (2001): 19-42.

29 Hall, Anderson, and Willingham, "Diapers, Dissertations, and Other Holy Things"; Sequeira, Trzyna, Abbott, and McHenry, "The Kingdom Has Not Yet Come."

could be reflected in a paucity of eligible applicants for academic jobs and in increased instability in the female work force.

The Joeckel/Chesnes Survey

The data set showcased in the present book provides further opportunity to explore the contributors to gender inequity in Christian academia. In this essay, a number of questions about the experience of women faculty in CCCU schools will be asked:

1. How well-represented are females? How do women on campus compare to men?
2. How do female scholarly accomplishments compare to those of males? What are some contributors to productivity?
3. How does the women's perception of gender equity on campus compare to that of men? What contributes to perceptions of gender equity for women?

Gender Representation and Comparisons

CCCU data for 2003 indicate that 34.56 percent of full-time faculty are women, compared to 65.44 percent of men. This represents less than a 1 percent increase from 1998, when women constituted 33.80 percent of full-time faculty. Nationwide, the average of full-time female faculty in all baccalaureate institutions is 41.9 percent.[30] This indicates that CCCU schools lag far behind the national average in terms of percentage of women. In the present sample, 37.7 percent of the sample were women and 62.3 percent were men, closely approximating the CCCU numbers and suggesting that the current sample is representative.

The current data set does not allow for other important comparisons of gender equity, including rank or earning comparisons. However, the data do allow us to compare women and men on a number of other indicators. Statistical comparisons (see *Statistical Details* section at end of the chapter) indicated that women do not differ from men in their ethnic composition, but on average they have been at their institutions less time, are less likely to have a doctorate, have been Christians for a slightly shorter time, and attend church less often. Women are also more likely to be Democrats and to consider themselves more liberal theologically.

The present questionnaire also contained a large number of items asking for perceptions of the academic environment and opinions on a number of subjects ranging from student regulations to environmental concerns. In order to reduce the data to a smaller set of variables, a factor analysis was conducted on all of these items (questions 14-85, and 88-102; see *Statistical Details* for details). The resulting factors led to the creation of ten scales: Conservatism/Liberalism, Academic Climate, Climate Change, Theological Fit, Environmental Concerns, Integration of Faith and Learning, Diversity Satisfaction,

---

30   West and Curtis, "AAUP Faculty Gender Equity Indicators 2006."

Theological Flexibility, University Regulations, and Academic Freedom. Scores on each of these scales were calculated for each participant.

Gender comparisons were then run on each of these new scales (*Statistical Details*). Although men and women do not differ significantly from each other in their perception of the academic climate, in their degree of concern for the environment, in their commitment to the integration of faith and learning, and in their perception of the university regulations for students, they do differ significantly in a number of other ways. Women are significantly more liberal than are the men across a range of theological, political, and social issues, and are more likely to believe that human activity is producing climate change. They are less likely to be comfortable with their institution's faith statement and are less open to change in their theological positions. They are less satisfied with diversity issues at their institution, including the diversity of the student body and the gender equality of female students and faculty, and less satisfied with academic freedom at their institutions.

Productivity

Regarding productivity, women do not differ from men in the quantity of essays/papers presented at conferences over the past two years, but they are less likely to have published a book or a peer-reviewed article (*Statistical Details*). What might account for the differences in publication productivity between men and women? Two logistic regressions (one for books, and one for articles) were run to see whether number of years at their current institution (a proxy for time since graduation) and degree earned might account for the differences in publications between men and women, given that women on average had been at their institutions less time and were less likely to hold a doctorate. Both of these variables accounted for some of the gender differences in publications, but not all. In other words, it would appear that part of the reason women faculty are not as well-published as male faculty is that they have not been at their institutions as long (possibly indicating more recent graduation dates) and have a smaller percentage of doctorates.

What factors contribute to productivity among the women? In order to explore this question, two logistic regressions were again run, but with only the female participants. Years at their institution and degree earned were again entered, along with the ten scales (using gender equity instead of the diversity-satisfaction scale). The results indicated that women who had been at their institutions longer, who had earned a doctorate, and who reported higher degrees of integration of faith and learning were more likely to have published a book. Degree earned was the only variable to predict publication of an article; women who had earned a doctorate were more likely to have published.

Gender Equity

Two items addressed gender equity. These were averaged, and gender comparisons showed that women were much less likely to perceive gender equity in their institutions than were the men (*Statistical Details*). Two multiple regressions were run on the women's data in order to determine whether any of the demographic or attitudinal/perceptual data predicted gender equity. The first multiple regression examined the contributions of the demographic data, including years at their institution, ethnicity, political affiliation, self-identification as theologically conservative or liberal, highest degree earned, length of time as a Christian, frequency of church attendance, publication of a book or peer-reviewed article, and frequency of conference presentations over the past two years. The results indicated that women who considered themselves more theologically liberal, who had been Christians longer, who had presented more papers at conferences over the past two years, and who were Democrats were less satisfied with gender equity at their institutions.

The second multiple regression considered the relationship between the attitudinal/perceptual variables as reflected in the scales, including Conservatism/Liberalism, Academic Climate, Climate Change, Theological Fit, Environmental Concerns, Integration of Faith and Learning, Theological Flexibility, University Regulations, and Academic Freedom. Diversity Satisfaction was not included in the analyses since two of its items were the items used in the gender-equity outcome measure. The results indicated that women who were more liberal across a number of theological, social, and political issues, who expressed more dissatisfaction with the overall academic climate, and who perceived less academic freedom were less satisfied with the gender equity of their institutions.

Conclusion

The findings presented above suggest that CCCU schools have a long way to go in achieving gender equity. In fact, the data show that numerically, gender equity is a greater problem than in secular institutions. Women in CCCU schools are underrepresented when compared to national averages. The findings further suggest that gender norms in the conservative Christian community may contribute to gender inequity. Earlier it was suggested that the influence of traditional gender stereotypes may lead to certain outcomes, such as smaller percentages of women seeking postgraduate degrees, smaller numbers of women seeking careers in academia, and greater job instability due to family demands. The underrepresentation of women, the decreased likelihood of having a doctorate in comparison to men, and the smaller amount of time in their present institutions found in the present sample are all consistent with this assumption.

Whether these findings reflect the internalized norms regarding gender in the women themselves resulting in a reduced pipeline for hiring, the limiting structure of opportunity in which career decisions are made (such as lack of support for graduate training and limited options for work/family balance),[31] or hiring/advancement discrimination on the part of the institutions cannot be determined from these data. Furthermore, in the absence of comparative data from secular sources in the present sample, it is unclear whether evangelical gender norms might contribute to limited structures of opportunity and hiring/

---

31 Bartkowski, "One Step Forward, One Step Back," 8-9.

advancement discrimination above and beyond the problems clearly documented in secular academia. However, it is worth noting that female representation is clearly worse than in secular institutions and that the disparity in highest degree earned is not found in secular institutions. Furthermore, Christerson, Hall, and Cunningham[32] compared an evangelical college to a secular college in the same geographic location and found that the discrepancies between men and women in rank, resources received, and satisfaction with aspects of the university climate were significantly greater at the evangelical college. These results suggest that the gender norms of the evangelical subculture do contribute to the disparities noted in the Joeckel/Chesnes survey.

However, the gender norms of the evangelical subculture do not tell the whole story. The data also suggest that other aspects of the Christian subculture of the academic institutions may result in women feeling out of place. Simply put, women may be less conservative than the surrounding institutional climate, which may lead to a sense of not fitting in. In addition, women are a minority and have been at their institutions less time. Consequently, they may feel less of a sense of influence on the academic climate of the institution and, in fact, they report being less satisfied with academic freedom at their institutions than do the men, suggesting negative experiences in expressing their perspectives. Furthermore, the data show that even within the female sample these variables were related to perceptions of gender equity. Women who were more liberal theologically, who were Democrats, who were more liberal across a number of theological, political, and social areas, and who perceived less academic freedom were, in fact, less satisfied with the gender equity of their institutions. In summary, the less the women fit in with conservative evangelical norms, the more dissatisfied they were.

Why might it be the case that women do not experience a good fit with the conservative and gender-related subcultural norms of their institutions? In the developmental sequence that leads to an academic career, evangelical women experience a number of formative influences that do not affect men. For men, higher education and academic careers are consistent with the normative gender roles advocated in the evangelical subculture; these aspirations are consistent with the breadwinner role. In contrast, women who end up in academic careers must fight subcultural expectations in order to arrive at their goals.[33] In a subculture that prioritizes marriage, childrearing, and homemaking, academic women choose educational and employment paths that are often in tension with these aims. This self-selection process may result in an overrepresentation of women who do not conform to subcultural norms. In addition, because of their gender-related experiences, they may also be more likely to critically examine the assumptions of the evangelical subculture, including traditional roles for women in the church and in the home, as well as normative Christian views with respect to politics, the environment, and social issues. While male academics may be fairly representative of the general evangelical population (or perhaps only slightly more liberal, given research findings that higher

32   Christerson, Hall, and Cunningham, "The Gender Dynamics of an Evangelical University."

33   Colaner and Giles, "The Baby Blanket or the Briefcase"; Colaner and Warner, "The Effect of Egalitarian and Complementarian Gender Role Attitudes on Career Aspirations."

educational achievements correlate with liberalism), female academics are not. And the subsample of evangelical women resulting from this unique selection process may often find themselves at odds with the predominant evangelical subculture.

Finally, the fact that women are in a minority in their academic settings is worth mentioning. Research has demonstrated that being in the minority has significant effects on workplace experiences. One of the most frequently reported problems faced by women who are in the minority (as well as by ethnic minorities) is their social isolation and limited access to informal interaction networks.[34] In addition to the important benefits of social support and friendship, this also places women at a disadvantage because they are cut off from informational resources that are critical for job effectiveness and career advancement, such as information about promotion strategies, funding opportunities, and publication collaboration. In a qualitative study at an evangelical university, Christersen, Hall, and Cunningham[35] found that the most commonly cited difficulty among female faculty respondents was exclusion from male social groups. The interviews further revealed the women's perception that male faculty were worried that too much interaction would result in the impression of an inappropriate relationship. This finding suggests that the social isolation experienced in academia in general may be accentuated by the evangelical subculture, which is profoundly gendered.[36]

In brief, academic women do not fit prevailing gender norms, they do not fit with prevailing conservative norms in theological, political, and social areas, and they do not fit socially because of their minority status. The findings of the Joeckel/Chesnes survey are consistent with another study at a CCCU institution, which found that male faculty reported a significantly higher sense of "fitting in" than the female faculty.[37] Person-environment fit is a predominant theory in organizational psychology. It refers to "various dimensions of compatibility between the characteristics of individuals and the attributes of their work environments."[38] Furthermore, the compatibility has to do with the individual's subjective experience; it is the *perceived* similarity between the person and the environment that matters.[39] Studies suggest that person-environment fit is related to a number of organizational variables, including job satisfaction, performance, organization commitment, turnover, and psychological and physical well-being.[40] Consequently, addressing women faculty's sense of fit with the institution has consequences, not only

---

34   Herminia Ibarra, "Personal Networks of Women and Minorities in Management: A Conceptual Framework," *Academy of Management Review* 18 (1993): 56-87.

35   Christerson, Hall, and Cunningham, "The Gender Dynamics of an Evangelical University."

36   Ingersoll, *Evangelical Christian Women,* 107.

37   Hall, Cunningham, and Christerson, "Biola University Gender Climate Study."

38   Jennifer A. Lindholm, "Perceived Organizational Fit: Nurturing the Minds, Hearts, and Personal Ambitions of University Faculty," *Review of Higher Education* 27 (2003): 125-149, 127.

39   J. R. Edwards, D. M. Cable, I. O. Williamson, L. S. Lambert, and A. J. Shipp, "The Phenomenology of Fit: Linking the Person and Environment to the Subjective Experience of Person-Environment Fit," *Journal of Applied Psychology* 91 (2006): 802-827.

40   Ibid.

for their personal well-being and vitality, but for the effectiveness of their academic units and, ultimately, the well-being of their colleges or universities.[41]

One aspect of person-environment fit has to do with person-culture fit, that is, "the match between the organization's existing cultural characteristics (norms and values) and the individual's values."[42] Research suggests that gender norms are part of this person-environment fit.[43] A group's level of acceptance of non-normative gender-related behavior influences fit; when individuals feel accepted, they experience more fit. In addition, when an individual's gender orientation is congruent with the collective gender orientation, there is likely to be a stronger perceived person-group fit. Research suggests that gender-diverse groups tend to be more open to both nontraditional and traditional gender-related behavior, suggesting the importance of increasing the numbers of women in CCCU schools.

How can CCCU institutions help women find their way home in Christian academia? How can women establish a sense of space, a home within the university where they feel comfortable, respected, and appreciated? The answers are, by necessity, complex and multifaceted. Research stemming from a person-environment fit framework suggests the importance of having a few "like-minded" institutional peers who share similar worldview, values, and approaches to research, teaching, and service, or who provide intellectual stimulation.[44] Although these types of interpersonal connections may occur within departments, many women (and minority) faculty find them in campus organizations outside of their departments. This suggests the importance of organized units where women can connect, such as faculty women's retreats, women's centers, same-sex mentoring, and other organized groups of women.

The results of the Joeckel/Chesnes survey also suggest the importance of academic freedom in helping women feel a better sense of fit. Even where administrators are supportive of the expression of a variety of positions on controversial topics, this support may be negated by the lack of obvious manifestations of this support. For example, do student campus organizations reflect a diversity of positions on certain topics such as politics or women's issues? Do speakers invited on campus for chapels or other public forums express a variety of perspectives, or are they unilaterally conservative? Is the educational philosophy aimed at challenging students and encouraging their ability to think, or is education a process of "filling in the blanks" with the "right" answers?

Another obvious intervention is to increase the representation of women among the faculty and to support their advancement efforts so that they are also represented in higher ranks and at the highest levels of administration. Underrepresentation often occurs because of faculty hiring practices. Going through "usual networks" may result

---

41 Lindholm, "Perceived Organizational Fit."

42 Hassan I. Ballout, "Career Success: The Effects of Human Capital Person-Environment Fit and Organizational Support," *Journal of Managerial Psychology* 22 (2007): 741-765, 752.

43 Angela M. Young and David Hurlic, "Gender Enactment at Work: The Importance of Gender and Gender-Related Behavior to Person-Organizational Fit and Career Decisions," *Journal of Managerial Psychology* 22 (2007): 168-187.

44 Ibid.

in more of the same types of candidates—men. In addition, research shows that once recruitment has occurred, largely unconscious biases in the search process tend to advantage white men.[45] Consequently, hiring processes must be carefully examined in order to facilitate the hiring of qualified faculty women.

Finally, attempts must be made to address the general climate issues that allow for "micro-inequities" to accumulate, disadvantaging women. Changing a climate is very difficult, but inroads can be made using a strategy that Meyerson and Fletcher[46] call the "small wins" approach. The small-wins strategy aims at producing incremental changes by challenging biases that are so entrenched in the system that they are not even noticed until they are gone. This process involves diagnosis of the problem, often through interviews or focus groups, followed by experimentation in which small initiatives attempt to eradicate inequity-producing processes. Over time, these small changes accumulate—in fact, they tend to snowball—to solve problematic aspects of the work climate.

Our Christian heritage contains a wealth of resources that could be invoked in addressing gender inequality, foremost of which are the concepts of love of neighbor, compassion, justice, and putting the needs of others before one's own needs. Ongoing attention to this problem, combined with research and training, can draw on that legacy in addressing existing challenges for female faculty in CCCU institutions. Our educational institutions play a crucial role in transmitting the values of our evangelical subculture to the next generation. Addressing gender inequity in our institutions can have positive consequences for women far beyond the boundaries of our campuses.

---

45   Mary Ann Danowitz Sagaria, "An Exploratory Model of Filtering in Administrative Searches: Toward Counter-Hegemonic Discourses," *Journal of Higher Education* 73 (2002): 677-710.

46   Debra E. Meyerson and Joyce K. Fletcher, "A Modest Manifesto for Shattering the Glass Ceiling," *Harvard Business Review* (January-February 2000): 126-136.

Statistical Details

Factor Analysis and Scale Construction

In order to reduce the large number of items to a smaller set of variables, a factor analysis was conducted on all of the attitudinal and perceptual variables (questions 14-85, and 88-102). Principle-components analysis using varimax rotation was used because the primary purpose was to identify and compute composite scores for the factors underlying the questionnaire. Given the large number of variables produced, an eigen-value cutoff of 1.5 percent was chosen, resulting in ten theoretically interpretable factors. The eigen values showed that the first factor explained 15.23 percent of the variance, the second, 7.71 percent of the variance, the third, 3.45 percent, the fourth, 2.54 percent, the fifth, 2.06 percent, and the remaining variables, under 2 percent of the variance. All items loaded on their respective factors at .5 or above.

Following are the ten resulting scales, with the items loading on each. Items followed by (R) were reverse scored, and scores created for each participant by creating averages for each scale.

Conservatism/Liberalism: 36, 39, 40, 51(R), 52, 62(R), 63, 65(R), 66(R), 67(R), 70(R), 71, 72, 73, 76, 77. High scores represent more liberal views across a variety of theological, political, and social issues (e.g., inerrancy, abortion, war in Iraq, homosexuality); low scores represent more conservative views.

Academic Climate: 79, 80, 81, 82, 83, 84, 85, 95, 96. High scores represent dissatisfaction with the academic climate.

Climate Change: 53, 54, 55, 56. Lower scores represent the belief that human activity is producing climate change.

Theological Fit: 22, 23(R). Low scores represent a higher sense of fit with the institution's faith statement.

Environmental Concerns: 58, 59, 60, 61. Lower scores represent higher degrees of concern for the environment.

Integration of Faith and Learning: 15, 18, 19, 42. Lower scores represent higher degrees of integration of faith and learning.

Diversity Satisfaction: 88, 89, 90. Low scores represent higher degrees of satisfaction with racial and gender concerns.

Theological Flexibility: 30, 31. Low scores represent greater willingness to change theological views.

University Regulations: 46, 47, 48, 49. Low scores represent greater satisfaction with university regulations for students.

Academic Freedom: 96, 97, 98(R). Low scores represent greater satisfaction with academic freedom at their institution.

Gender Comparisons on Demographic Data and Scales

Item/Scale	M	F	t	df
				Mean
Years at institution	2.52 (1.23)	2.27[a] (1.20)	4.21**	1905
Theologically conservative/liberal	2.21 (1.09)	2.58 (1.23)	-6.91**	1905
Length of time as Christian	5.89 (.51)	5.83[a] (.59)	2.53*	1905
Church attendance	1.68 (.74)	1.84 (.80)	-4.35**	1905
Conference presentation	2.00 (1.08)	1.94 (1.06)	1.24	1905
Courses per semester	2.55 (.92)	2.39 (.95)	3.38**	1729
Conservatism/Liberalism	2.48 (.85)	2.63 (.90)	-3.79**	1838
Academic Climate	2.24 (.87)	2.24 (.87)	-.26	1742
Climate Change	2.62 (1.11)	2.29 (.93)	6.52**	1795
Theological Fit	1.92 (.94)	2.03 (.99)	-2.52*	1861
Environmental Concerns	1.91 (.62)	1.86 (.58)	1.63	1799
Integration of Faith and Learning	1.68 (.67)	1.72 (.60)	-1.30	1869
Diversity Satisfaction	2.24 (.87)	2.74 (1.02)	-10.79**	1739
Theological Flexibility	3.09 (1.13)	3.30 (1.09)	-3.96**	1841
University Regulations	2.28 (1.08)	2.24 (1.11)	.76	1803
Academic Freedom	2.13 (.95)	2.28 (.93)	-3.25**	1740
Gender Equity	1.76 (.95)	2.43 (1.18)	-12.95**	1738

Note. * p < .05 ** p < .001 Standard deviations appear in parentheses below means.
[a] Numbers represent five-year groupings.

Item/Scale	M	F	X^2	df
			Frequency	
Ethnicity			5.26	4
Caucasian	1121 (1118.2)	674 (676.8)		
Black	16	12		

	(17.4)	(10.6)		
Asian	11	12		
	(14.3)	(8.7)		
Hispanic	11	9		
	(12.5)	(7.5)		
Other	26	12		
	(23.7)	(14.3)		
Political affiliation			28.93*	3
Democrat	214	197		
	(256)	(155)		
Republican	555	322		
	(546.3)	(330.7)		
Independent	325	146		
	(293.4)	(177.6)		
Other	92	54		
	(91)	(55)		
Highest degree earned			61.22*	2
Doctorate	905	439		
	(837.1)	(506.9)		
Master's	213	242		
	(283.4)	(171.6)		
Other	66	36		
	(63.5)	(38.5)		
Published book			50.13*	1
Yes	350	109		
	(285.9)	(173.1)		
No	838	610		
	(902.1)	(545.9)		
Published article			53.71*	1
Yes	805	366		
	(729.5)	(441.5)		
No	383	353		
	(458.5)	(277.5)		

Note. * p < .001 Expected frequency, in percent, appears in parentheses below percentages.

Productivity

Two logit regressions were used to estimate whether gender would predict publication of a book and publication of an article, taking into account length of time at institution and degree earned. Logit regressions were used because the dependent variables are discrete; the value is 1 if the individual has published a book/article, and 0 if he or she has not published a book/article. Length of time at institution and degree earned were entered in the first step and gender in the second. Models were significant for both publishing a book (X^2 [3] = 162.40, $p < .001$) and publishing an article (X^2 [3] = 350.30, $p < .001$). The results indicated that length of time at institution, degree earned, and gender each significantly predicted publication of a book; degree earned and gender predicted publication of a journal article.

In addition, two logit regressions were run with gender as the only predictors in order to compare the odds ratio without accounting for years at institution and degree earned, with the odds ratio taking these two variables into account. For publication of a book, the odds ratio for gender was 2.34. For publication of an article, the odds ratio was 2.03. Both of these numbers are lower when years at institution and degree earned are included in the model (see tables below).

Summary of Logistic Regression Analysis Predicting Publication of a Book

Variable	B	SE B	Odds ratio	Wald statistic
Time at institution	.29	.05	1.34	38.25*
Degree earned	1.25	.18	3.49	50.50*
Gender	.65	.13	1.91	25.39*

* p < .001

Summary of Logistic Regression Analysis Predicting Publication of an Article

Variable	B	SE B	Odds ratio	Wald statisti
Time at institution	.09	.05	1.09	3.57
Degree earned	1.98	.12	7.25	253.54*
Gender	.49	.11	1.63	19.08*

* p < .001

Two additional logit regressions were run with only the female sample, in order to explore predictors of publication. Years at institution, degree earned, and the ten scales were all entered in one step for each of the two regressions. Models were significant for both publishing a book (X^2 [12] = 35.66, $p < .001$) and publishing an article (X^2 [12] = 126.65, $p < .001$). The results indicated that length of time at institution, degree earned, and integration of faith and learning each significantly predicted publication of a book; only degree earned predicted publication of a journal article.

Summary of Logistic Regression Analysis for Female Faculty Predicting Publication of a Book

Variable	B	SE B	Odds ratio	Wald statistic
Time at institution	.23	.10	1.26	5.54*
Degree earned	.93	.28	2.53	10.64***
Conservatism/Liberalism	.20	.18	1.22	1.17
Academic Climate	.01	.17	1.01	.01
Climate Change	-.20	.16	.81	1.55
Theological Fit	-.08	.14	.93	.29
Environmental Concerns	.22	.22	1.24	.92
Integration of Faith and Learning	-.52	.23	.60	5.14*
Theological Flexibility	.12	.11	1.13	1.28
University Regulations	.05	.12	1.05	.15

Academic Freedom	-.01	.15	.99	.00
Gender Equity	.11	.12	1.12	.94

* p < .05
** p < .01
*** p < .001

Summary of Logistic Regression Analysis for Female Faculty Predicting Publication of an Article

Variable	B	SE B	Odds ratio	Wald statistic
Time at institution	.03	.08	1.03	.15
Degree earned	1.90	.20	6.70	90.46***
Conservatism/Liberalism	.14	.15	1.15	.93
Academic Climate	.02	.14	1.02	.03
Climate Change	-.19	.12	.83	2.43
Theological Fit	-.09	.16	.91	.66
Environmental Concerns	.00	.18	1.00	.00
Integration of Faith and Learning	-.21	.16	.81	1.71
Theological Flexibility	.07	.09	1.07	.60
University Regulations	-.05	.09	.95	.30
Academic Freedom	.22	.12	1.25	3.38
Gender Equity	.03	.10	1.03	.07

* $p < .001$

Gender Equity

To examine the effects of the demographic, attitudinal, and perceptual variables on perceptions of gender equity, two multiple regressions were run. In the first multiple regression, all demographic variables (years at their institution, ethnicity, political affiliation, self-identification as theologically conservative or liberal, highest degree earned, length of time as a Christian, frequency of church attendance, publication of a book or peer-reviewed article, and frequency of conference presentations over the past two years) were entered simultaneously. In the second multiple regression, all attitudinal and perceptual variables (Conservatism/Liberalism, Academic Climate, Climate Change, Theological Fit, Environmental Concerns, Integration of Faith and Learning, Theological Flexibility, University Regulations, and Academic Freedom; Diversity Satisfaction was not included in the analyses since two of its items were the items used in the gender equity measure) were entered simultaneously.

The multiple regression predicting Gender Equity on the basis of demographic variables indicated a significant linear relationship ($F(10, 435) = 7.81, p < .001; R = .39; R^2 = .15$; *Adjusted R^2* = .13). Political affiliation, self-identification as theologically conservative or liberal, length of time as a Christian, and frequency of conference presentations in the past two years significantly predicted Gender Equity, with all variables accounting for 15% of the variance. The multiple regression predicting Gender Equity on the basis of attitudinal and perceptual variables was also significant ($F(9, 623) = 36.45, p < .001$;

$R = .59$; $R^2 = .35$; *Adjusted* $R^2 = .34$). Conservatism/Liberalism, Academic Climate, and Academic Freedom significantly predicted Gender Equity, with all variables accounting for 35% of the variance.

Multiple Regression Analyses of Demographic and Attitudinal/Perceptual Variables on Gender Equity

Scale	Variable	B	SE B	β	sr
Gender Equity	Years at institution	-.08	.04	-.08	-.08
	Ethnicity	.22	.25	.04	.04
	Political affiliation	-.31	.15	-.13*	-.09
	Theologically conservative/				
	liberal	.23	.06	.24***	.17
	Highest degree earned	-.11	.12	-.05	-.04
	Length of time as Christian	.23	.10	.10*	.10
	Church attendance	.04	.07	.03	.03
	Published book	-.13	.15	-.04	-.04
	Published article	.05	.12	.02	.02
	Conference presentation	.11	.05	.10*	.09
Gender Equity	Conservatism/Liberalism	.12	.06	.09*	.07
	Academic Climate	.58	.05	.43***	.36
	Climate Change	-.10	.05	-.08	-.06
	Theological Fit	.07	.05	.06	.05
	Environmental Concerns	-.04	.07	-.02	-.02
	Integration of Faith and Learning	-.01	.07	-.00	-.00
	Theological Flexibility	-.07	.04	-.06	-.06
	University Regulations	-.00	.04	-.00	-.00
	Academic Freedom	.14	.05	.11**	.09

* p < .05
** p < .01
*** p < .001

ARE WE DOOMED?

Why Christian Colleges and Universities Must Lead on the Issue of Gender Equity and Why They Don't

BETTINA TATE PEDERSEN AND ALLYSON JULE

All academia has recognized for several decades now the importance of addressing issues of diversity and inclusion. One of the issues that the Joeckel/Chesnes survey of CCCU institutions seeks to explore is how faculty view specific issues, including gender issues in Christian higher education, particularly in the CCCU. M. Elizabeth Lewis Hall's article on gender equity in this collection explores the broad question of gender equity by looking at female representation among the faculty in CCCU institutions (37.7 percent are women compared to 62.3 percent men), female scholarly accomplishments compared to those of males, and male and female perceptions of gender equity on CCCU campuses (FSQs 2, 11, 12, 13, 89, and 90). Much of what she has examined in the survey data bears out the near truisms that have emerged in the larger conversation on gender equity in academia in the last forty years, thus suggesting that the conditions in Christian higher education are not so different from those in secular academia concerning gender equity. Indeed, her analysis suggests that the situation in the CCCU is yet more conservative than in secular institutions; that is, gender equity does not exist.

It is clear that gender equity conditions matter as a broad feature of human rights, but within a Christian context, the issue of human rights—as grounded in the redemption offered in Jesus Christ and including gender equity—was one we had hoped to see functioning differently.

We understand that many in the CCCU may not see issues of human rights and Christ's redemption as necessarily linked or compatible, but we begin from the position that they may be and even must be viewed as such. Further, the ways in which gender equity brings into fuller incarnation the redemption of Christ elevates the importance of addressing these issues within Christian higher education. As Lesly Massey rightly observes in his *Women in the Church*, "[Jesus] spoke out against social injustice and moral evil of every description,"[1] and as Hall notes in her article, "Our Christian heritage contains a wealth of resources that could be invoked in addressing gender inequality, foremost of which are the concepts of love of neighbor, compassion, justice, and putting the needs of others before one's own needs."[2]

While the reasons for persistent gender inequity in secular academia have been largely identified as systemic, these same reasons may not be as easily acknowledged as systemic within Christian higher education because of the underlying religious influences that are both perceived and represented by too many as God-ordained and divinely appointed. Julie Ingersoll's study, *Evangelical Christian Women: War Stories in the Gender Battles*, notes that "undermining the clear-cut divisions between masculinity and femininity is threatening because it undermines the very order of the universe itself."[3] Longstanding differences between what masculinity and femininity have been constructed to mean are taken as divine givens and therefore understood to be sacred tenets not to be interrogated or dismantled. We have argued elsewhere that these differences do indeed rest, not on divine decree or intention, but on the underlying religious influences systemic to Christian higher education.[4] We argue here that these religious influences express themselves in the political and theological views of faculty in Christian higher education and in the CCCU in particular, and that they are potent forces in shaping gender inequity in the CCCU. Our chapter focuses, then, on these political and theological influences which we believe can be seen in the survey data and which underlie and shape perceptions of and responses to gender issues among CCCU faculty.

Often these political and theological influences begin from the point of view that Christian faith, expressed in its divinely ordained tenets, is potentially threatened by an intellectualism characterized by open inquiry that many fear will dismantle faith by critiquing its tenets regarding gender. Once put into place, this critique will take Christian institutions and individuals on a descent into secularization. This skepticism about the effects of open inquiry is particularly acute when gender is the focus of the inquiry, and this skepticism has been rendered especially hostile as cultural forces have reductively coalesced around a limited range of positions and issues involving gender. Indeed, this survey data would seem to illustrate Ingersoll's claim that "anti-feminism may be the dominant perspective in this conservative Christian subculture," even though she notes that Christian feminists or biblical feminists have resisted this perspective for several decades now.[5] Our starting point aligns with this resistance to anti-feminism. We take the view that a Christian commitment and a feminist commitment are not only compatible, but are essential "though often marked with struggle, pain, and ambiguity."[6]

---

1 Lesly F. Massey, *Women in the Church* (Jefferson, N.C.: McFarland and Company, 2002), 9.

2 Hall, "Finding a Home in Academia," 246.

3 Julie Ingersoll, *Evangelical Christian Women: War Stories in the Gender Battles* (New York: New York University Press, 2003), 29.

4 Allyson Jule and Bettina Tate Pedersen, *Being Feminist, Being Christian: Essays from Academia* (New York: Palgrave, 2006), 1-58.

5 Ingersoll, *Evangelical Christian Women*, 2

6 Jule and Pedersen, *Being Feminist, Being Christian*, 5.

If Christian academics and institutions are engaged in an open intellectual inquiry that leads to a critique of existing conditions of gender inequity, then we cannot resist such a critique as well as its implications for change. Rather, we can and must accept it as a call to a greater participation in the redemption of Christ and the creation of conditions that contribute to the full flourishing of women and men in our institutions and in the world. It is our view that only if and when Christian higher education can be viewed as not fundamentally in conflict with the intellectual life, and more specifically with the intellectual discourse on gender, can gender equity happen in the CCCU. But it is precisely the rigidity of traditional views on gender arising from conservative biblical interpretations and from a firm commitment to biblical inerrancy that present formidable barriers to open intellectual discourse and inquiry on gender (Table 2).

Limitation of the Survey

We would have hoped for deeper questions concerning gender equity in the survey so that the data from the questions themselves could have clearly revealed why gender equity is not more fully addressed and realized in CCCU schools.[7] As is, we see an expected pattern of responses confirming that most faculty members in CCCU schools are happy with the status quo.[8] We do not know if representations of women in positions of leadership (or other gender issues such as inclusive language policies, flexible maternity/paternity leave policies, on-site child care programs and facilities, wage equity, promotion and tenure equity, women preachers in chapels, sexual-harassment education and institution-wide policies, accommodation for pregnant students, etc.) matter deeply or if gender inequity is viewed as all that important an issue to Christian faith or to creating a particular kind of Christian climate. A few people (a few women) mentioned gender inequity explicitly, but not very many at all. The vast majority, regardless of gender, expressed concerns about workload or managing expectations, and while these concerns may very well be connected to gender inequity, it is difficult to ascertain a connection from the survey data on these issues.

Clearly, a consciousness regarding gender inequities has not reached a critical tipping point, and we are saddened by this. We see an apathy which suggests little is possible regarding full gender inclusion. Besides, we cannot detect from the data if a connection has been made at all between gender inequity and the climate and attitudes which allow it. The gender inequity that Hall maps out in the previous chapter (that the

7 It would have been interesting for the survey to have organized questions explicitly around a consideration of gender issues. As the survey was organized, the "gender" questions were simply located within the stream of the survey's 106 questions. It may be argued that the choice not to clearly identify a section of the survey as devoted to gender issues aimed to elicit responses that were less artificial or guarded, but given that we had to rely so heavily on the anecdotal comments rather than the "gender questions" responses to reveal more specific and honest assessments of gender issues, we are not confident that the survey successfully queried its respondents about the depth and breadth of gender equity in CCCU institutions.

8 We want to note additionally, and perhaps hopefully, that of the 9594 email invitations that were sent out, 8853 reached viable email accounts (739 bounced) and only 1907 faculty responses were received (~21.5 percent); thus, the sampling represented by this survey data is small. Further, while the scope of the Joeckel/Chesnes survey was admittedly only CCCU institutions, not all Christian colleges and universities in North America are members of the CCCU.

CCCU has more men than women, that more men produce academic work, and that more women than men see the inequities) has not yet been destabilized by those who do see the significance of full inclusion to the integrity of Christianity itself, let alone to Christian institutions. Where the survey data show the greatest indication of views and experience divergent from the "status quo" pattern is in the anecdotal comments to FSQ 104 and FSQ 106 (Table 4).[9] As anecdotal material, it is much harder to render uniform, but these comments at least begin to suggest a counter-narrative to the status quo that remains dominant in CCCU institutions. This counter-narrative coalesces around three themes—biblical interpretation, academic freedom, and an evangelical homogeneity (or climate).

Theology and Biblical Interpretation

It is our view that there exists very little difference between male and female faculty responses to questions of theology and biblical interpretation (authority and inerrancy). Most respondents agreed or strongly agreed with evangelical attitudes to such positions. Marginally more men (21.8 percent) than women (16.8 percent) expressed doubts about their faith in response to the FSQ 37 statement, "I have had more doubts about my faith over the past year" (Table 1). However, this leaves almost 80 percent of both sexes not having more doubts. In addition, in response to FSQ 39 and FSQ 40 ("Answers to more questions are primarily black and white, not shades of gray" and "Truth is absolute, not relative."), more men than women agreed. Given that more men agreed with these statements, it seems possible to suggest that they are more certain about their sense of morality and truth than are women faculty and, conversely, that more women faculty experience less certainty about these matters. We see these gendered patterns in response as minor, though we see the responses to the three statements taken together as revealing little doubt and much certainty about theology and biblical interpretation among the majority of CCCU faculty surveyed here, regardless of gender. But the majority of questions on the survey provided little or no room for explanation, nor did they expressly clarify definitions of terms used in the statements: for example, "doubts" mean what, exactly, and are those doubts connected to issues of gender or gender equity?

Of the 106 survey statements, only five asked for fuller written responses; yet, it was these written responses we found to be more helpful in understanding faculty experiences and positions concerning biblical and theological views and their intersection with issues of gender inequity. We explored these responses as those made by female and male respondents.

---

9   FSQ 104, "Do you believe the education that students receive at a Christian college/university is superior to that at a secular/state school? Why or why not?" and FSQ 106, "What is the most difficult part about being a professor at a Christian university?"

Female Faculty Responses:
Comments concerning Issues of Theology and Biblical Interpretation

"Hitting the wall of Christian cliché theology that prevents reasoned or critical thinking from being pursued."

"I find myself continually brought up short by people who think that it is blasphemous to actually read and interpret the Bible, to allow your mind to enjoy the images and texts and to attentively consider all the nuances of language and the ramifications of the analogies."

"Staying objective when faced with different belief systems."

"Reconciling a Christian world view with course material (literature) that, by nature, reflects life as it is in the sinful and secular world. Also, it is a challenge to instruct students who have very narrow views."

"Students who are so afraid of discovery of ideas that might call into question aspects of their faith beliefs."

"Sometimes there is a feeling that everything needs to be taught in line with a specific, possibly narrow-minded, interpretation of what Christianity is and is not."

"Students who use their faith as a shield against thinking rather than to enhance their interaction with the world."

"Dealing with the presuppositions of students who are unwilling to be open-minded about new ideas or ideas contrary to their own. In essence, many students come with their minds already made up, and they are unwilling to test their presuppositions or question anything they already believe."

"Getting the students to think beyond their Sunday School boundaries and pat Sunday School answers. This particular aspect of dealing with students is one of the most difficult parts."

"It is the pharisaical attitudes of fellow faculty members who assume to know Truth and are quick to judge and criticize those of us who admit to struggling to reconcile conflicts between what we observe and what the Scriptures say. It is difficult to respect (and earn the respect of) colleagues who are very vocal in their criticisms, drowning out the voices of those of us who attempt to model Christian curiosity."

"Students who see the world in black and white and therefore judge me."

"Challenging the narrow minds of Christian conservatism."

"The kind of 'litmus tests' naive students tend to apply to professors' and each other's faith: the pervasiveness of oversimplified ideas that become faith tests and a faith discourse deeply implicated in the national politics of the so-called 'Christian right.'"

"Dealing with foreclosure in students from extremely conservative or sheltered backgrounds."

"The most difficult part about being a professor at a Christian university is always having to hide any beliefs that are a little more liberal than is official policy at the institution, for example, re: abortion, homosexuality, dancing."

"Working with fundamentalist faculty and students for whom truth is absolute."

Male Faculty Responses:
Comments concerning Issues of Theology and Biblical Interpretation

"Dealing with biblical literalists."

"The most difficult part is struggling against the anti-intellectual bias of contemporary Christianity. This fear of thinking is a reaction against the anti-religious bias of contemporary secularism."

"Opening closed minds and filling them with a love of learning—be it from a bad conservative background that discourages free inquiry or from the lack of curiosity and the utterly pragmatic bent bred into today's coddled youth."

"Balancing the rational with the spiritual in ways that don't upset the constituency."

"Witnessing the chilling effects of authoritarian conservatism."

"Narrow mindedness and background of the students. Inability to address issues outside of initial beliefs."

"Ultra conservative students' reluctance to consider alternative ways of thinking."

"Encouraging a critical engagement with matters of religion among students, faculty, and administration is difficult when reinforcement of existing belief is more highly valued."

"Wondering how open your students are to diverse theological perspectives."

"The tightrope someone in our department (Religion) must walk with respect to the various constituencies."

"Dealing with fundamentalists."

"Fundamentalists who make Christianity look ridiculous."

"The assumption that we all believe exactly the same way."

"A lack of tolerance of different perspectives, all of which may be legitimately held by sincere, knowledgeable Christians".

"Working to fight against common cultural Christian beliefs among white, evangelical Americans."

"Attitude of unquestioned acceptance of traditional answers to large questions."

"Being true to Scripture while relating properly to the culture."

"Dealing with religious fundamentalism in students and administrators."

While the statistical tally of FSQ 32, FSQ 33, and FSQ 36 shows that a majority of the faculty surveyed accept biblical authority and inerrancy, these anecdotal comments to FSQ106 (Table 4) would seem to point to a dissatisfaction sometimes potentially, sometimes implicitly, and sometimes explicitly linked to gender but not captured in the gradated response options of the questions. These comments indicate the presence of an emerging culture of resistance that could challenge received notions about the Bible or biblical inerrancy and could, in turn, lead to greater exploration of gender issues in CCCU institutions. Further, it is our view that the entrenched attitudes of a literalist and inerrantist interpretation of Scripture, which are strongly felt and insisted upon by the CCCU community, constitute a formidable barrier to discussing whether or not gender equity exists in CCCU institutions, let alone to establishing commitments, policies, and climates that bring it into being.

Academic Freedom

Here again the majority of respondents indicated that they felt they had academic freedom in their CCCU institutions in direct response to FSQ 96, "I possess academic freedom at my college/university," but the tally of responses to FSQ 96 taken together with the anecdotal comments to FSQ 106 indicated a wide variance in the interpretation/understanding of which "freedoms" respondents were thought to have (Table 4). Of great concern to us as feminist scholars is the freedom women in particular feel on CCCU campuses to voice opinions on any and all matters, but especially on matters relating directly to gender equity. Faculty comments that indicated they did not feel free to discuss topics considered taboo to an evangelical Christian culture are particularly significant here. Many of these subjects were the very ones that would have to be included in an open inquiry about gender equity: topics such as feminism, sex, women in leadership at all levels, glass ceilings, pay equity, women in historically masculine disciplines such as biblical studies or preaching (including preaching in campus chapel services). Thus on the one hand, the survey data overtly report that academic freedom exists, while on the other hand, the anecdotal comments suggest only certain kinds exist—and they are not those vital to identifying gender inequity and working toward eradicating it.

We believe the survey used for analysis here offers limited qualitative data with which to work. We see a story left untold about the lived experiences of women in positions of power within evangelical communities. Thankfully there are other qualitative studies emerging which explore more deeply the often painful experiences within Christian higher education and we direct our readers to explore those counter-hegemonic narratives.[10] Nevertheless, there are some patterns exposed in the present survey which we believe are worth highlighting.

According to the questionnaire, it is fair to say that the average CCCU faculty member is male. This average faculty member usually votes Republican, is comfortable with the institution's faith statement and its Christian identity. He is more likely to strongly agree with biblical inerrancy and view premarital sexual intercourse as wrong. He sees the morale at work as good and views the campus as racially diverse (which few are). He thinks the female faculty and female students are treated equally to the males, and he ultimately considers himself as possessing academic freedom. His female contemporary is not as content as he is (Table 2). The responses to the relevant questions and isolates bear this out. The sampling of comments below expresses concern with limited academic freedom often associated with controversial subjects (which could include matters of gender equity and/or sexuality):

Female Faculty Responses:
Comments concerning a Sense of Academic Freedom

> *"I am less conservative in my beliefs than many of my students and do not always feel comfortable in discussions about social and moral issues."*

> *"Some views are less tolerated than others, particularly political views."*

> *"Two things—feeling like I have to tiptoe around sensitive topics, often having to do with sex or evolution. Or worse, over-explain. So in teaching I can cover the concept, but have to be concerned that they will misunderstand that in presenting secular viewpoints to educate them they mistake this for my viewpoint and think I don't hold to Christian values."*

> *"Some ideas, concepts, events are 'outside' the religious box and don't nicely fit into any kind of integration attempt. There is an expectation of some faculty and students that everything should have a verse to support it or it's bad, or secular, which means it is not to be discussed. The environment here can be too sheltered from the real world to the detriment of the student's education."*

> *"Constituencies that want to control what is presented to students for analysis and evaluation."*

> *"Others—faculty, students and administrators all assume you think and believe a particular way."*

---

10   Ingersoll, *Evangelical Christian Women;* Nicola Hoggard Creegan and Christine C. Pohl, *Living on the Boundaries: Evangelical Women, Feminism and the Theological Academy* (Downers Grove, Ill.: InterVarsity Press, 2005); Serena Jones, *Feminist Theory and Christian Theology: Cartographies of Grace,* Guides to Theological Inquiry Series (Minneapolis: Fortress Press, 2000).

"Limits on topics, 'safe' films, etc., even though our school is one of the better ones, you still know you can be opening up a can of worms if one of your students decides to complain."

"The most difficult part of teaching at a Christian college is feeling the need to preface readings (in my discipline of Literature) with numerous disclaimers."

"The perception of it being a step below a state school. I also get discouraged by how there are some topics that the students have been sheltered form—I teach Human Sexuality. I also think some students are afraid of questioning the things they have been taught their whole life."

"Being somewhat liberal . . . the fear of saying something or revealing a belief that will not be considered acceptable."

"Fear of 'offending' someone (either faculty or student)."

"The taboos relating to various issues of inquiry and discussion."

"Being careful about how I discuss some issues."

"Superior's support in presenting challenging philosophies and ideas that are subtly opposed to the faith."

"Self-censorship on cultural issues when my students and their parents hold very strong opinions with which I do not agree."

"The need to censor what I say about the questions I have and the books I read. There are certain things I cannot bring to class because they might offend conservative parents of our students."

"Working with narrow minded individuals."

"Discussing controversial subjects opposed by the religious right."

"The most difficult part about being a professor at a Christian university is always having to hide any beliefs that are a little more liberal than is official policy at the institution, for example re: abortion, homosexuality, dancing."

Male Faculty Responses:
Comments concerning a Sense of Academic Freedom

"The issue of academic freedom and the time and funds for adequate research."

"Balancing the rational with the spiritual in ways that don't upset the constituency."

"Not sure how honest the students can be with us since we are a Christian school. Can they truly share their thoughts, beliefs?"

"Limitations of openness of thought and expression of ideas that do not conform to doctrine."

"Having to pretend to believe things that I really don't."

"Probably living in a fish bowl. You have considerably less freedom than many secular professors, but not necessarily less freedom than other Christians teaching in secular institutions."

"At times, efforts to maintain academic integrity are at odds with the beliefs and practices of the Christian constituency. Walking this tightrope is difficult."

"Having to walk so carefully around complex and difficult issues without pushing too hard on what is typically accepted by the evangelical world."

"Closed minded students who seem to think that some subjects are 'off limits.'"

"Academic freedom being subject to a conservative board of trustees."

"Not being able to discuss more controversial subjects for fear of offending a student."

"The homogeneity of the students sometimes puts a damper on exploring issues."

"We don't tell the truth, conflict is buried, the real mission of the university is 'don't rock the boat.'"

"Limiting academic freedom"

"Receiving complaints from parents, pastors and other constituents about ideas presented in class."

"Closed-mindedness by students, faculty, administration and staff."

"Being limited in some of the aspects of my work that I can teach. Certain portions of Art and Photographic History must be left behind."

"Dealing with sensitive or controversial subjects."

"The anti-intellectualism that evangelical schools often suffer from."

"Inability to freely express my liberal (and vital) faith to students and colleagues without fear of harsh scrutiny and dire consequences."

"The most challenging thing is to train students to open up to all points of view and think critically so they can own an informed faith system, while at the same time trying to nurture their faith in Christ and have them grow in love for God, all creatures, and creation."

While the actual responses to the survey questions dealing with academic freedom (FSQ 96, FSQ 97, and FSQ 98) suggest that a majority of respondents feel they have academic freedom, many of the comments to FSQ 106 suggest otherwise (Table 4). This observation taken together with the discrepancies over how respondents identified "free-doms" leaves us with the apparent reality that some respondents understood "freedom" to mean "freedom to express their Christian faith" and others thought "freedom" to mean "freedom to express or address controversial subjects," many of which included connections to subjects related to gender. Parker Palmer attends to the importance of difference in our Christian communities, calling us to open our discourse to honest inquiry: "We live in this world together, and we must mind the difference. So the truth in the gospel tradition is to be spoken and lived in community, and tested in a continuing communal process of dissent and consent."[11] Kim Phipps, current president of Messiah College, one of the schools in the CCCU, understands the culture of Christian higher education well, and of the CCCU in particular. As one of the few women presidents of CCCU institutions, her acknowledgement of the need for open inquiry and discourse on matters of gender, toward which there appears to be strong resistance in many CCCU schools, carries particular weight: "without recognition of conflict, reconciliation is impossible."[12] It appears in the anecdotal data of this survey that much work remains to be done to bring the conflict over gender inequity in the CCCU into consciousness.

Evangelical Sub-cultural Homogeneity (Climate)

On reviewing the faculty comments to the survey, it is impossible not to see the close connection of Republicanism and CCCU faculty. Most respondents of either sex identify themselves as Republican (46.8 percent of the men who responded to the survey and 44.9 percent of the women) though more women than men self-identify as Democrat (18 percent of the men and 27.5 percent of the women; Table 2 and Table 3). Considering the significantly greater numbers of men as faculty, this is no small detail: the Democratic Party and the positions on issues typically taken by Democrats are underrepresented. Also of note is the self-identified politics of the student respondents: 8.7 percent of male students and 13.5 percent of female students identify themselves as Democrat. Because of the very low numbers of young men at CCCU schools (a trend consistent with secular academia as well), the chances of ever meeting a male Democrat student are quite small (Table 3).

We also noticed some additional patterns in the written responses to the two key questions: FSQ 104 and FSQ 106. FSQ 104 ("Do you believe the education students receive at a Christian college/university is superior to that at a secular/state school? Why or why not?) elicited responses that varied widely and no distinct view aligned with either sex. Some said yes; some said no; most said that it depends on the institution. Often those who responded "yes" included some explanation that their "yes" meant they could discuss Christianity or Christian issues explicitly at their CCCU institutions which they

---

11   Parker Palmer, "Toward a Spirituality of Higher Education," in *Faithful Learning and the Christian Scholarly Vocation*, ed. Douglas V. Henry and Bob R. Agee (Grand Rapids, Mich.: Eerdmans , 2003), 82.

12   Kim Phipps, "Epilogue: Campus Climate and Christian Scholarship," in *Scholarship and Christian Faith: Enlarging the Conversation*, ed. Douglas Jacobsen and Rhonda Husted Jacobsen (Oxford: Oxford University Press, 2004), 174.

indicated/believed they could not do at secular institutions. The most interesting comment along this line of explanation came from a man (#1575): "Yes, insofar as they are at liberty to study seriously Christian issues; not insofar as certain topics are taboo—like sex and feminism." No woman made explicit mention of gender, sex, or feminism. The most aggressively negative comment concerning feminist thinking also came from a man (#209) who said, "Politically correct thinking at secular institutions, shaped by Marxist critique of justice and radical feminism, limits the ability to think and create workable solutions to human problems."

In response to FSQ 106 ("What is the most difficult part about being a professor at a Christian university?"), more men than women mention the lower pay as the most difficult part of their job. More women mention the expectations and workload. One woman (#314) wrote, "I like being a professor here. There is a glass ceiling for women though. Men rule while women do an overwhelming amount of the work." Women also mention the climate as the most difficult part about being a professor at a Christian institution. One woman (#57) wrote, "Having no sense of community." She goes on to articulate the better sense of community she felt at a state university, a sense of community that highlights the lack of "gender bias" as a part of that sense of community: "Having no sense of community—neither academic nor Christian support—very, very different than working at a secular or state university where I had lots of collegial relationships with both Christians and non-Christians—significantly experienced community, encouragement, vigorous debate, respect for differing views, accountability and support from fellow Christian colleagues. No gender bias either!!" Woman #172 wrote, "It is also hard to be a female at a denominational school that denies that women can serve the church according to gifts not plumbing." Woman #179 wrote, "The traditional views of women in leadership—it is a barrier to be overcome here. Not all men or women (both faculty and students) welcome it." Woman #658 wrote, "Being a woman and seeing the hypocrisy run rampant around me." Woman #1403 wrote, "I am a female Bible professor . . . enough said . . ." and woman #1482 wrote succinctly, "being a woman." Women also mention issues of lack of respect and a general sense of "nervousness" that they may be misunderstood or even reported by students if they don't tow the party line. Few mention pay. Needless to say, no men at all mentioned "being a man" as the most difficult part of his job. Only one man (#1072) mentions that his own progressive views on women and leadership are problematic for him. In short, only a few women (six out of the 550 women who responded to this question) identify their sex/gender as the issue. Clearly this is not many at all; however, that so many others mention climate and other more typical complaints of women, such as workload and living up to expectations, does suggest a troubling reality for female faculty within the CCCU. Not one woman suggested the converse—that she feels a full flourishing of her gifts and calling as either a burgeoning possibility or an accomplished reality. The comments below would seem to suggest that more women faculty express concerns with climate issues than do men faculty.

Female Faculty Responses:
Concerning the Workplace Environment

"The climate"

"Dealing with power struggles between the 'bucks' and the 'does.'"

"Being a female Roman Catholic—I often feel disrespected, unappreciated and unheard by certain individuals."

"Finding a way to respectfully engage with practices or beliefs that treat people disrespectfully (e.g. treating women as less valuable than men)."

"[P]erhaps the most difficult is the over-working of professors (class loads, university-sponsored exracurriculars, committees) under the guise of 'ministry,' with the unstated implication that to refuse to take on one of these tasks is not doing one's part to serve the students or be part of the Great Commission."

"Repressive atmosphere of group think. That dissent of any sort or questioning of some sort is viewed as dangerous."

"The closed environment, lack of openness to others with different ideas and opinions."

"The expectation that all of my beliefs are the same as others (evolution). I also find people expect me to be a Republican."

"I think that faculty aren't as conservative as the Board or the administrators so that leads to some tension—but it's mostly handled gracefully on both ends."

"Potentially being perceived as having the thoughts and stances representative of all Christian faculty members."

"The narrow and rigid ideological framework—suspicious of the world and even ideas themselves—that most students bring to their university education makes the difficult task of teaching them even more difficult. It becomes a delicate and high-stakes balance of helping them maintain/preserve their faith while simultaneously helping them open their worldview up to new ideas and ways of thinking as educated persons."

"Some entering students are extremely conservative and defensive, willing to judge peers and faculty on little information. They don't question their own assumptions enough, and many prefer an authoritarian classroom model."

Male Faculty Responses:
Concerning the Workplace Environment

> *"Low pay and dismal benefits, especially to families. Christian Colleges and Universities are without a doubt the most family unfriendly places to work in academia."*

> *"The tension between strong faith and social tolerance."*

> *"We have a culture of non-confrontation, based on a somewhat twisted understanding of a Christian community, so that academic and moral issues about which there is debate cannot be addressed in public without garnering the 'don't rock the boat' response from other faculty."*

> *"The conservatism of the other faculty members."*

> *"The frequent assumption of politically right politics being shared by all."*

> *"Dealing with right-wing politics."*

> *"Bridging the gap between Christian Republicans and Christian Democrats."*

Conclusion

Redemptive social justice is the point of the gospel. Scripture itself repeatedly states that true religion, which is always aimed at the redemption Jesus seeks to bring to the world, may be measured by the way it treats the most marginalized and oppressed.[13] "Because Christianity has its ultimate source in the mind and ministry of Jesus Christ," Massey reminds us, "[Jesus'] own attitude toward women has critical significance in evaluating church doctrines and tradition today."[14] Marginalizing women in the CCCU *may* not be the most egregious form of gender discrimination in the world but it is most certainly placed on the continuum of sexism in the world, and thus part of the global crisis of sexist oppression. The fact that it is still easier to recognize egregious forms of sexism "out there" rather than the more subtle ones close to home indicates that we still have a long way to go toward improving gender equity in CCCU institutions. The few indications of dissatisfaction with gender issues, gender equity, and climate do not represent any serious challenge to the status quo because there is overwhelming job satisfaction. In addition, one of the problems we have with qualitative research, like this survey, is that the emphasis is placed on equity and balancing. We do not think that either alone will solve the deeper, more profound and spiritual brokenness that underlies all our gender relations. Goals for achieving more equitable arrangements are important, and we do not mean to say anything otherwise here, but our vision is for more than equity and balance. We are longing for a full celebration of woman in all her uniqueness, capacity,

---

13 James 1:27, Matthew 25:36, Isaiah 58:7 and 16:4, Ezekiel 18:7, Hebrews 13:12.

14 Massey, *Women in the Church*, 16.

potential, and humanness, and for a reconfigured celebration of man on grounds that do not enable his flourishing at the expense of women.

The question the CCCU (as a national organization or as individual member institutions) is not asking is why do our theological beliefs and understanding of biblical interpretation, our notions of academic freedom or our anti-intellectualism, and our homogeneity and the current gender climate or inequity go together. As Parker Palmer proclaims, "At its deepest reaches, the gospel is a way of knowing, and if we cannot recover that way of knowing, I do not really think we can do Christian higher education or form our students in a Christian ethic."[15] To understand the gospel as a way of knowing and not merely a way of doing calls us to an intellectual endeavor to seek out the inequities and injustices surrounding gender, to acknowledge that they do in fact exist within our Christian communities and institutions, and to refuse to tolerate them any longer. To this end the CCCU could establish an office of gender issues at the national headquarters in Washington, DC so that addressing gender issues becomes one of the CCCU's paramount goals. (Individual CCCU institutions could do so for their own campuses as well.) The CCCU could use its website to offer resources on best practices for achieving gender equity[16]; it could offer contacts to universities that have established policies for achieving greater consciousness about gender inequity and greater policies toward eliminating it (like policies on university-wide inclusive language use, equity in pay/promotion/tenure, exemplary maternity/paternity leaves, etc.); it could establish annual conferences on gender issues rather than occasional sessions or conferences; it could expand all effective existing programs and initiatives that address gender issues; and at the very least it could commission annual, biannual, or five-year studies by recognized gender issue scholars within Christian higher education (perhaps similar to *Shining Lights and Widening Horizons: A History of the Council for Christian Colleges & Universities, 2001-2006*[17]), to deeply study the state of gender equity in the CCCU; it could establish a listserv expressly for the purposes of discussion of gender issues in Christian higher education. To do anything less, to be content with the way things are in our CCCU institutions, is not a response that will produce a different gender reality in the CCCU. As is, we're doomed to gender inequity in the CCCU. It is only if and when we are prepared to examine our theology and our understanding of our faith and liberation that gender equity has a chance.

---

15   Palmer, "Toward a Spirituality," 81.

16   Paula J. Caplan, *Lifting a Ton of Feathers: A Woman's Guide to Surviving in the Academic World* (Toronto: University of Toronto Press, 1995), 161-72. Her chapter eight, "Check-list for Woman-Positive Institutions," is particularly helpful in offering concrete measures and practices for indentifying and creating institutional climates that enable women academics to flourish.

17   James A. Patterson, *Shining Lights and Widening Horizons: A History of the Council for Christian Colleges & Universities, 2001-2006* (Washington, D.C.: Council for Christian Colleges and Universities, 2006).

Table1: Comparative responses of faculty in percent to questions regarding faith, morality, and truth.

FSQ37 Respondents who somewhat or strongly agree with the statement "I have had doubts about my faith over the past year."	
Total (1831)	20
Male (1142)	21.8
Female (689)	16.8
FSQ39 Respondents who somewhat or strongly agree with the statement "Answers to moral questions are primarily black and white, not shades of gray."	
Total (1816)	30.1
Male (1135)	32.6
Female (681)	28
FSQ40 Respondents who somewhat or strongly agree with the statement "Truth is absolute, not relative."	
Total (1813)	69.7
Male (1133)	73.9
Female (680)	62.8

Table2: Comparative responses of faculty in percent to questions regarding political orientation, faith, morality, and campus climate.

FSQ4 Respondents who self-identified as "Republican" as their political affiliation.	
Total (1907)	46.1
Male (1188)	46.8
Female (719)	44.9
FSQ22 Respondents who somewhat or strongly agree with the statement "I am comfortable affirming my college/university's faith statement."	
Total (1856)	90.2
Male (1154)	91.2
Female (702)	88.6
FSQ36 Respondents who strongly agree with the statement "I believe in biblical inerrancy."	
Total (1825)	39.5
Male (1142)	40.5
Female (683)	37.8
FSQ76 Respondents who strongly agree with the statement "Premarital sexual intercourse is wrong."	
Total (1758)	72.9
Male (1103)	75.7
Female (655)	68.1
FSQ85 Respondents who somewhat or strongly disagree with the statement "Morale among faculty at my college/university is good."	
Total (1736)	25.3
Male (1094)	25.0
Female (642)	26.0

FSQ88 Respondents who somewhat or strongly disagree with the statement "The student body at my college/university is racially diverse."	
Total (1729)	55.1
Male (1089)	53.7
Female (640)	57.4
FSQ89 Respondents who somewhat or strongly agree with the statement "Female faculty at my college/university are treated equally to male faculty."	
Total (1729)	68.4
Male (1089)	76.7
Female (640)	54.3
FSQ90 Respondents who somewhat or strongly agree with the statement "Female students at my college/university are treated equally to male students."	
Total (1733)	80.9
Male (1094)	87.4
Female (639)	69.9

Table3: Comparative responses of faculty and students in percent to the question "What is your political affiliation?"

Faculty FSQ4	All (1907)	Male (1188)	Female (719)
Democrat	21.6	18	27.5
Republican	46.1	46.8	44.9
Independent	24.8	27.5	20.2
Other	7.7	7.8	7.5
Students SSQ4	**All (2389)**	**Male (665)**	**Female (1724)**
Democrat	12.2	8.7	13.5
Republican	63	62.5	63.1
Independent	12.2	13.4	11.7
Other	12.7	15.4	11.7

HOLDING ON TO
THE TRADITIONS OF MEN

Christianity, Gender,
and the Academy

JENNIFER MCKINNEY

Women have come a long way in the process of formal education from the nineteenth century when they were thought to be naturally less intelligent than men, too physically delicate to stand the rigors of education, or too likely to become like men—coarse, vulgar, and loud.[1] Today women comprise more than half of all college graduates, and while this represents progress, women are still underrepresented in graduate education, as college faculty, and as college administrators.[2] For the women who do find a home in academia, they experience a glass ceiling—fewer tenure-track positions, lower pay, lower rank, and often heightened expectations as "female" faculty.[3] These realities are disturbingly familiar to those who study gender in higher education, perhaps even more so to the women who experience them every day.

Yet in *The Rise of Christianity* Rodney Stark reports that in its first five centuries, "Christianity was unusually appealing" to the women who flocked to it because they were accorded substantially higher status than anywhere else in the classical world.[4] These early Christian women held positions of leadership, honor, and authority within the church—far more than their pagan or Jewish sisters. When Christianity became the dominant faith of the empire, however, "the roles open to women became far more limited."[5]

---

1 Florence Howe, *Myths of Coeducation* (Bloomington: Indiana University Press, 1984). See also Claire M. Renzetti and Daniel J. Curran, *Women, Men, and Society* (San Francisco: Allyn and Bacon, 2003).

2 As a group, women have fared far better in advancing in education than racial and ethnic minorities. See Renzetti and Curren, *Women, Men, and Society*.

3 JoAnn Miller and Marilyn Chamberlin, "Women Are Teachers, Men Are Professors," *Teaching Sociology* 28 (2000): 283-298.

4 Rodney Stark, *The Rise of Christianity: How the Obscure, Marginal Jesus Movement Became the Dominant Religious Force in the Western World in a Few Centuries* (Princeton: Princeton University Press, 1996), 95.

5 Ibid, 108.

Becoming an official religion changes the impact of Christianity. Over time, Christianity is itself transformed to reflect the values and practices of the larger culture. Rather than being a counter-cultural movement, correcting the inequalities of the larger culture, Christianity itself begins to perpetuate the same inequalities. In the previous essays, M. Elizabeth Lewis Hall and Bettina Tate Pedersen and Allyson Jule demonstrate that, far from the flush of early Christianity, women are limited in roles and status in the American academy, including CCCU colleges and universities. But being driven by a Christian mission, shouldn't CCCU schools look different than their secular counterparts? In looking at CCCU faculty percep-tions of a variety of topics, Joeckel and Chesnes' data show cleavages in faculty responses by gender, reinforcing what is already well-documented in the research literature—persistent patterns of gender inequality remain a fundamental characteristic of CCCU schools. While CCCU schools aspire to be defined by their Christian mission, unfortunately they are also defined by their unconscious commitments to gender inequality.

Why is this so? The underlying reason is that American Christianity is a social insti-tution that, in many ways, has become so assimilated to American standards of thinking and living that it often unreflectively adopts American cultural patterns. These American values are then recast as distinctive elements of Christianity. Sociologist Richard Perkins, a former CCCU faculty member, writes that, "Evangelicalism has become imbued with a number of cultural traits that aren't the least bit biblical, but are solidly middle-American."[6] In the case of higher education, CCCU schools have unwittingly adopted two sets of American traditions about gender. In part they have borrowed contemporary gender patterns from secular higher education. And in part they have retained gender ideas broadly held in the evangelical subculture. These evangelical ideals frequently origi-nate in cultural movements outside of the church. Once these ideals and practices are institutionalized within the larger culture, American Christians legitimate them—after the fact—through scriptures that align with current practices. Assimilating to these larger social structures indelibly impacts how and what gets done in CCCU institutions regarding gender.

Social Structures of Gender Inequality in Higher Education

Gender is, by definition, socially structured.[7] Social structures pattern our behavior into rules and routines clustered around "appropriate" activities. Amidst these normalizing structures, social institutions absorb these rules and routines, giving them a legitimating ideology that proclaims the rightness and necessity of how and why their arrangements, practices, and social relationships look a particular way.[8] Social psychologists Cecilia Ridgeway and Shelley Correll explain that, as a social institution, gender is a "system

---

6   Richard Perkins, *Looking Both Ways: Exploring the Interface between Christianity and Sociology* (Grand Rapids, Mich.: Baker Book House, 1987), 169.

7   Social scientists distinguish sex from gender, using "sex" to refer to the biological characteristics distinguish-ing females and males (emphasizing anatomy, physiology, hormones, and reproductive systems), and "gender" to refer to the social, cultural, and psychological traits linked to females and males through particular social contexts (gender is what is learned and changes over time within and across cultures).

8   Patricia Yancy Martin, "Gender as Social Institution," *Social Forces* 82 (2004): 1249-1273.

of social practices for constituting people as two significantly different categories, men and women, and organizing social relationships of inequality on the basis of that difference."[9] Categorizing women and men into such distinctive groups and awarding different human traits to each (e.g., women are nurturing, men are aggressive) is so routine it is rendered an invisible and natural process.[10] Seen in this way, all other social institutions have embedded gender biases that are legitimated through the processes of the society as a whole.

Hall's chapter demonstrates how female professors throughout the American academy continue to labor under "a series of accumulated disadvantages."[11] Despite the desire for full equality and near parity in qualified applicants, women hold fewer full-time positions, have lower rank, and are paid less for equal rank than men. The single greatest cause of this persistent inequality is the disproportionate pull of family responsibilities on women and the unwillingness of the academic workplace to adjust to this.[12] There will be no workplace gender equity if the workplace is structured in a way that accommodates men better than women. The evidence indicates that higher education generally has failed to implement "policies and practices that minimize obstacles for women."[13]

As a social institution, Christianity is not exempt from being organized by these gender biases, nor is it exempt from legitimating them and subsequently perpetuating them. On gender issues CCCU schools, in general, have uncritically adopted the workplace practices of secular academia. They incorporate language of gender equality in their hiring statements and set up sexual harassment processes to prevent the most egregious kind of abuses, but leave unchanged hiring assumptions, workload, and promotion and tenure structures that have kept women from achieving equality in the secular workplace.[14] The most recent survey of church-related schools on rank and salary from the Association of American University Professors (AAUP) shows a gender gap in both the secular and church-related academy—one that has remained unchanged for more than a decade.[15] In church-related institutions male faculty make up more than half of all assistant, associate, and professor ranks, compared to just over a third of women in these positions.[16] Even

---

9   Cecilia Ridgeway and Shelley J. Correll, "Unpacking the Gender System: A Theoretical Perspective on Gender Beliefs and Social Relationships," *Gender & Society* 18 (2004): 510.

10   Issues of a binary gender system also impact the approximately four percent of people in a population born neither male nor female. See Ann Fausto-Sterling, "The Five Sexes: Why Male and Female Are Not Enough," *The Sciences* (March/April 1993: 20-24).

11   M. Elizabeth Lewis Hall, "Finding a Home in Academia: Gender Equity at CCCU Institutions," 235.

12   Hall, "Finding a Home in Academia," 237. See also Maike Ingrid Philipsen, *Challenges of the Faculty Career for Women: Success and Sacrifice* (San Francisco: Jossey-Bass, 2008); M. A. Mason, M. Goulden, and M. Wolfinger, "Babies Matter," in S. J. Bracken, K. D. Allen, and D. R. Dean, eds., *The Balancing Act: Gendered Perspectives in Faculty Roles and Work Lives* (Sterling, Va.: Stylus, 2006).

13   Hall, "Finding a Home in Academia," 237.

14   A recent cross-national study of scientists in academia confirms that men's salaries range anywhere from 18-40 percent higher than women's and that the gender disparities actually grow over the course of their careers. See Gene Russo, "For Love and Money," *Nature* 465 (June 2010), 1104-1107.

15   Renzetti and Curran, *Women, Men, and Society*.

16   The most notable divergence in rank is between female (8 percent) and male (21 percent) full professors. See the American Association of University Professors, "Distribution of Faculty, by Rank, Gender, Category, and

when controlling for rank within church-related institutions, male faculty earn higher salaries than female faculty.[17] Christian colleges and universities could achieve gender equality by implementing gender equitable and family-friendly practices that are substantially different than those at secular institutions—fulfilling a mission that is distinctly Christian. Yet CCCU schools, as a whole, do not seem to be moving in this direction.

Evangelical Social Attitudes and Evangelical Higher Education

CCCU colleges and universities have also incorporated another set of traditions that impede progress toward gender equality. As Hall notes, national surveys have consistently found that evangelicals are more likely than other Americans to prescribe social roles by gender.[18] This is not, contrary to popular belief, because of anything in the Bible.[19] It is because the birth of neo-evangelicalism coincided with the institutionalization of the American middle-class gender norms of the "long decade" of the 1950s.[20] This breadwinner/homemaker gender structure was then reified as a Christian absolute using Scripture to support this borrowed cultural tradition.

When analyzed as a social institution, we can clearly see when and why Christianity absorbs and adapts to changes within other American institutions.[21] In the colonial and early American agrarian economy, the labor of women as well as men was essential to survival. Though these households were not bastions of egalitarianism, the power shared between women and men was much more equitable because of their economic interdependence; the productive labor of both women and men was necessary, and thus more equally valued. Throughout the nineteenth century, however, with the rise of Industrialization, productive labor was increasingly replaced by waged labor. While

---

Affiliation, 2009-10 (Percent)" in *The Annual Report on the Economic Status of the Profession, 2009-10*, <http://www.aaup.org/NR/rdonlyres/E070FD4B-A560-4470-A4E0-72ABB563C690/0/Table12.pdf> retrieved May 15, 2010.

17   American Association of University Professors, "Average Salary for Men and Women Faculty, by Category, Affiliation, and Academic Rank, 2009-10 (Percent)" in *The Annual Report on the Economic Status of the Profession, 2009-10*, <http://www.aaup.org/NR/rdonlyres/478F4364-233A-4F7C-91A3-D022B0DF1DED/0/Table5.pdf > retrieved May 15, 2010.

18   Hall, "Finding a Home in Academia," 238. See also Sally K. Gallagher. *Evangelical Identity and Gendered Family Life* (New Brunswick, N.J.: Rutgers University Press, 2003); R. Marie Griffith, *God's Daughters: Evangelical Women and the Power of Submission* (Berkeley: University of California Press, 2000); Michael Kimmel, *Manhood in America: A Cultural History* (New York: Oxford University Press, 2006).

19   Pedersen and Jule are right to be concerned about literalist interpretations of the Bible and their impact on attitudes toward gender in CCCU institutions. Biblical inerrancy's justification of separate roles for women and men is also something that shifts and is a symptom of the larger problem of assimilating to a secular gender structure. See Julie Ingersoll, *Evangelical Christian Women: War Stories in the Gender Battles* (New York: New York University Press, 2003).

20   Stephanie Coontz, *Marriage, a History: How Love Conquered Marriage* (New York: Penguin Books, 2006); Cherlin, *The Marriage-Go-Round* (New York: Vintage Books, 2009). See also Gallagher, *Evangelical Identity and Gendered Family Life*; Griffith, *God's Daughters: Evangelical Women and the Power of Submission*; Kimmel, *Manhood in America*; and Bart Landry, *Black Working Wives: Pioneers of the American Family Revolution* (Berkeley, Ca.: University of California Press, 2000).

21   Apart from gender, the same process can be seen with slavery and Christianity. Emerson and Smith write that for early Christians the original unwritten rule was that by accepting Christ the slave was freed from both sin and slavery. But when Christians realized a cheap (free) labor source may be crucial to economic survival, an ideology developed that rationalized why accepting Christ didn't mean being free from slavery. Perkins adds that over a period of time the ideology became so normalized that even within a democracy slavery was scripturally justified, coexisting with Christianity for years. See Michael O. Emerson and Christian Smith, *Divided by Faith: Evangelical Religion and the Problem of Race in America* (New York: Oxford University Press, 2000); Perkins, *Looking Both Ways*.

families struggled to produce goods at home and earn money in the paid labor force, adolescents and men left home to earn money, while women and younger children stayed behind in the family farm to produce the goods that could not be purchased. Whereas men were initially ridiculed for abandoning their "God-given" role at home to work in waged labor,[22] over time a new gender structure developed. The new structure constructed "separate spheres" for women and men, valuing men for their success in the marketplace (spawning the "cult of the self-made man") and valuing women for their place in the home (spawning the "cult of domesticity").[23] This shift toward a breadwinner/homemaker ideology, predicated on changing economic conditions, became the gender status quo. Adjusting to these new social arrangements, American Christians began to legitimate this organization of breadwinner/homemaker as God-ordained,[24] even though this new family form could be attained only by upper-middle class white families[25] until the 1950s post-War economic boom.[26]

In her work on gender, family life, and evangelicalism, sociologist Sally K. Gallagher writes about how evangelical gender norms emulated the cultural ideal of husbands' breadwinning and wives' homemaking in the 1950s. Yet by the 1970s, with the economic boom exhausted, middle class women who had previously enjoyed sufficient class advantage to remain at home now found themselves going to work in order to pay for goods deemed necessary for a middle-class lifestyle.[27] Today evangelical women are employed at similar rates as the general population, their median household incomes mirroring that of other Americans.[28] Yet evangelicals still espouse a highly gendered division of labor.

As a result of the discrepancy between lived reality and religious gender ideals, the language of breadwinner evolved into the language of "headship," meaning man as spiritual leader and final authority in the home. For women, the language of homemaker shifted to the language of "submission"—wives being submissive to their husbands.[29] This resulted in an institutionalized rhetoric of male headship and authority that was "articulated in hundreds of books, through thousands of radio broadcasts, and in millions of pulpits and Sunday school classes every week all over the country."[30] Though

---

22 Stephanie Coontz, *The Way We Never Were: American Families and the Nostalgia Trap* (New York: Basic Books, 2000).

23 Ibid; Coontz, *Marriage, a History*; Gallagher, *Evangelical Identity and Gendered Family Life*; Kimmel, *Manhood in America;* Landry, *Black Working Wives*.

24 Social values often follow social reorganization. Once economic conditions created a separate spheres ideology, American Christians could find scriptural precedent for this type of social organization, for example, 1 Corinthians 11:3. For Black Christians, with a gender ideology focusing on career, family involvement, and community uplift for women and men, there was also scriptural precedent, for example, Galatians 3:28.

25 For most Americans the breadwinner/homemaker ideal could only remain that—an abstract ideal. Working class and immigrant whites could not afford to live this lifestyle. Black women and men were actively excluded from this lifestyle, creating a competing gender ideology that emphasized career, family involvement, and community uplift. This alternative gender ideology for Black women and men was also legitimated by Christian Scriptures. See Landry, *Black Working Wives.*

26 Cherlin, *The Marriage-Go-Round;* Coontz, *The Way We Never Were*; Landry, *Black Working Wives*.

27 Gallagher, *Evangelical Identity and Gendered Family Life.*

28 Ibid.

29 Ibid.

30 Ibid, 179.

evangelical Christians adopt a gender ideology of headship/submission, in practical terms many live within more equitable or egalitarian relationships. This forces them to work very hard to put together the disparate ideals of a "natural" and gendered division of labor with their lived experience.[31]

When social structures adopt new ideologies, individuals are apt to internalize them even though many cannot truly live up to them.[32] This gender ideology serves to maintain the idea of separate spheres for women and men, where women's worth is founded in their familial relationships and men's worth is founded in their success in the marketplace.[33] When women transgress this ideology by participating in the paid labor force, they are still evaluated (internally and externally) on the basis of their family relationships, impacting their ability to achieve equality in the academy.[34] Hall's essay observes that "women in the evangelical subculture may also have more internalization of traditional gender expectations, which place high priority on marriage, childrearing, and homemaking."[35] Because of this, not only does the gender structure serve as a barrier to women entering the professoriate, once women surmount these barriers they are more likely than their male counterparts to experience a work-family tension, negatively impacting their positions.[36]

It is not, however, just women who internalize these ideals. Gender is a stratified system allocating privilege to some (men), while disadvantaging others (women). Overwhelmingly, men do not believe they have gender, seeing "gender" as synonymous with "women." In comparing racial privilege to gender privilege, Peggy McIntosh writes that even if men are willing to accede that women are disadvantaged, they are far less willing to concede that, by default, men are privileged. Men are unwilling to grant that they benefit from a system where they receive awards they have not earned.[37] Yet even when men are aware of their privilege and do not seek to have it bestowed, it still operates across social structures because the entire society operates under the assumption of gender as a central organizing principle[38]—where men are accorded higher status, are seen as more generally competent, and are evaluated more leniently.[39] Most members of a society operate within these invisible social structures, including Christians. These gender ideologies then bleed over into the Christian academy, lowering the rates at which women enter the

---

31 Ibid. See also Judith Stacey, *Brave New Families: Stories of Domestic Upheaval in Late Twentieth Century America* (New York: Basic Books, 1990).

32 Barbara Risman, "Gender as Social Structure: Theory Wrestling with Activism," *Gender & Society* 18 (2004): 429-450.

33 Mary Blair-Loy, *Competing Devotions: Career and Family among Women Executives* (Cambridge, Mass.: Harvard University Press, 2003).

34 This evaluation of women in relation to their families impacts women across all social categories, not just Christian women. See Blair-Loy, *Competing Devotions*.

35 Hall, "Finding a Home in Academia," 239.

36 Philipsen, *Challenges of the Faculty Career for Women: Success and Sacrifice*. See also Mason, Goulden, and Wolfinger, "Babies Matter."

37 Peggy McIntosh, "Unpacking the Invisible Knapsack," in *Race, Class, and Gender in the United States: An Integrated Study*, ed. Paula S. Rothenberg (New York: Worth Publishers, 2004).

38 Not all males are accorded the same status; race, social class, and sexual orientation also impact privilege. See Kimmel, *Manhood in America*; R. W. Connell, *Masculinities* (Berkeley: University of California Press, 2005).

39 Ridgeway and Correll, "Unpacking the Gender System."

professoriate, solidifying obstacles borrowed from the secular academy, and blinding male academics (as well as many female academics) to the depth of gender inequalities at evangelical institutions.

Perceptions of Faculty Gender Equity at CCCU schools

So how do we measure the extent to which these gender ideologies impact faculty at CCCU schools? Several elements of the Joeckel/Chesnes survey suggest that evangelical gender ideologies subtly shape the perceptions of faculty at CCCU schools.[40] One survey item directly measured faculty perception of male/female faculty equality, asking if female faculty were treated equally vis-à-vis their male counterparts within their CCCU institutions. Though a majority of both male and female faculty agree that men and women are treated equally, there is a significant and strong divergence between them (see Table 1). Fully 77 percent of male faculty agree that female faculty at their institutions are treated equally to male faculty. Yet just over half of female faculty (54 percent) agree that female and male faculty are treated equally. In fact, four times as many female faculty (12 percent) as male faculty (3 percent) strongly disagree that female and male faculty are treated equally. The statistically significant relationship between gender and attitudes toward faculty being treated equally showed the strongest divergence between women and men of all analyses, even when controlling for political affiliation, church attendance, belief in biblical inerrancy, and theological conservativeness/liberalness. Gender remained the strongest predictor of whether or not faculty felt that women and men were treated equally at their institutions, with women being significantly more likely to believe women and men are not treated equally. These data underscore the idea that men are much less likely to perceive gender inequalities.

Three other indicators in the survey tell us something about faculty perceptions of how gender operates in the context of CCCU schools. These three questions asked faculty whether or not they agreed with women having the right to become pastors,[41] if approaches to their disciplines were shaped by their gender, and whether or not faculty felt hesitant to address certain important issues in class because of teaching at a Christian college/university.

In responding to the statement, "Women should have the right to become pastors," a revealing 29 percent of faculty either disagree (21 percent) or are undecided (8 percent) that women have the right to become pastors (FSQ 70). Not surprisingly, there is a significant disparity between men's and women's responses (see Table 2). More than one in three male faculty (34 percent) could not agree with the idea that women should have the same opportunity as men to be pastors. This response shows how strongly the evangelical gender ideology of separate roles operates in the evangelical academic world. Significant numbers of CCCU faculty—more than a third of men and 20 percent of women—believe

---

40   Joeckel and Chesnes took a census of CCCU faculty, sending emails to 9,594 faculty. With a response rate of just 22 percent, however, we cannot interpret the data as being representative of CCCU faculty as a whole.

41   The language of "rights" is problematic because rights are a matter for the institution of government (specifically democracy), rather than religion. This language may have impacted faculty responses.

that women should not have access to the most visible leadership role in organized Christianity, solely because they are women. This demonstrates that underneath a veneer of equality, substantial numbers of men and women believe that there is something so fundamentally different about men and women that their gender should influence their social roles, career tracks, and God's ability to call them into particular vocations.

The next question asked respondents whether they agree that, "My approach to my discipline is shaped by my gender" (FSQ 41). Female faculty are more than twice as likely as their male peers to strongly agree that their approach to their discipline is shaped by their gender (see Table 3). Such a startling discrepancy between women's and men's perceptions illustrates that men are significantly less likely to see gender at work in how they think about their disciplines. For men, gender and the consequences of gendered inequalities tend to be masked, negatively impacting efforts to create gender equality.

One last question indirectly measures the context of gender within CCCU schools. Faculty were asked if they are "hesitant to address certain important issues in class because I teach at a Christian college or university" (FSQ 90). A statistically significant relationship exists between gender and whether or not faculty feel hesitant to address certain issues (see Table 4). A majority of both female and male faculty disagree that they are hesitant to address important issues because of teaching at a Christian institution. Yet male faculty (72 percent) are significantly more likely to disagree than their female colleagues (63 percent disagreed), and female faculty are significantly more likely to agree that they are hesitant to address certain important issues in class because of teaching at a Christian institution.

These data raise several issues. The first is that women and men within CCCU institutions are not experiencing the same things. All of these analyses specify statistically significant relationships between gender and faculty perception, showing a sharp divergence of opinion or practice by gender. Both women and men have, to some extent, normalized a gendered structure; but women, much more so than men, see inequalities at work. That such substantial numbers of women and men believe women do not have the right to become pastors, that gender doesn't impact approaches to their disciplines, and that gender impacts what gets taught in a CCCU context confirms that, albeit invisible, the gender structure is pervasive as both a social structure and as individual preference.

The data from this survey demonstrate how difficult it will be to address the persistent, documented issues of gender inequality within the CCCU. More than three-quarters of men do not see gender inequality within the CCCU as a problem at their institutions. Since men have higher rank and salary than women, they are more likely to be in positions of authority with the power to enact change; however, they do not tend to see gender inequalities. Women, on the other hand, who are far more likely to perceive gender inequality at their institutions, are far less likely to hold positions with the power to initiate change.

There's another problem at work here with considerable implications beyond the experience of faculty in CCCU institutions. Gender as a social institution is not just about how faculty interact with each other or the institution as a whole. Having assimilated to the larger cultural gender structure and successfully legitimating these inequalities as God-ordained practices, we model these inequalities in our classrooms, perpetuating them by teaching them to new generations of students

Perceptions of Student Gender Equality at CCCU schools

Our internalized and unequal gender expectations bleed into the academy. We unconsciously build them into our institutional behavior patterns and thereby make them concrete and central to everyday interactions. This impacts what we teach and model to our students regarding gender norms. Though the research is clear that daily classroom interaction is fraught with gender inequalities, one of the great ironies of gender bias is that it mostly goes unnoticed by educators who are personally committed to fairness.[42] Unfortunately, being committed to fairness does not neutralize the inequalities that surround educators, nor the inequalities that they perpetuate.

Research shows that female students, unlike male students, lose ground the longer they stay in school.[43] They endure a host of micro-inequalities. Though gender inequalities abound at all levels of education, research shows the greatest imbalance at the college level where male students are accorded higher status[44]—even when objective measures of performance show no difference between women and men.[45] Female students are more likely to be interrupted by teachers (and male students) and are taken less seriously than males in their comments. Professors consistently use sex-stereotyped examples in class and refer to males as "men" and females as "girls." Feedback given to male students more often revolves around their academic and intellectual ability, while feedback given to female students more often centers on their physical appearance, classroom etiquette, and personality attributes.[46]

The Joeckel/Chesnes survey specifically asked CCCU faculty their perceptions regarding student gender equality at their institutions (FSQ 90). Though a majority of both male and female faculty agree that female and male students are treated equally, nearly two-thirds (63 percent) of men strongly agree that male and female students are treated equally, whereas only a little over one-third (37 percent) of women strongly agree that female and male students are treated equally (see Table 5). Nearly three times as many female as male faculty strongly disagree that students are treated equally.

We have, however, more data than on attitudes of student equality. Joeckel and Chesnes administered a companion survey to CCCU students, asking three questions relating to gender equity. Students were asked whether or not they felt that male and female students in their colleges are treated equally. Similar to the faculty responses, there was a significant relationship between gender and whether or not students believed

42 Myra Sadker and David Sadker, *Failing at Fairness: How Our Schools Cheat Girls* (New York: Scribner, 1995).

43 Myra Sadker, David Sadker, Lynn Fox, and Melinda Salata, "Gender Equity in the Classroom: The Unfinished Agenda," in *The Gendered Society Reader,* edited by Michael S. Kimmel with Amy Aronson (New York: Oxford University Press, 2003).

44 Ibid.

45 Shelley J. Correll, "Constraints into Preferences: Gender, Status, and Emerging Career Aspirations," *American Sociological Review* 69 (2004): 93-113. See also Sadker and Sadker, *Failing at Fairness.*

46 Bernice R. Sandler, *The Campus Climate Revisited: Chilly for Women Faculty, Administrators, and Graduate Students* (Washington, D.C.: Project on the Status and Education of Women, 1986). See also Renzetti and Curren, *Women, Men, and Society.*

men and women are treated equally (see Table 6). Sixty-three percent of the male students strongly agree that male and female students are treated equally, whereas 52 percent of female students strongly agree. What may be more interesting, however, is that a clear majority of students (80 percent of female and 83 percent of male students) agree that the sexes are treated equally within their institutions, indicating that overall, female and male students also may not see systemic inequalities.

The second question regarding gender elicited quite an interesting response. Again like the faculty, students were asked whether or not women should have the right to become pastors. Though there was not a statistically significant difference between female and male students and their attitudes toward women becoming pastors, what is striking is that roughly 56 percent of both female and male students—just over half— agree that women should have the right to become pastors (see Table 7).[47] This is a conspicuous difference from the approximately 77 percent of faculty who agree that women should have the right to become pastors. What is even more noteworthy is that slightly more female students disagree that women should have the right to become pastors (30 percent of female students versus 28 percent of male students). Like the faculty, a significant number of CCCU students believe that women and men are so different that they should not have equal access to the same pastoral opportunities.

Finally, the survey asked whether or not students felt they have a professor who they identify as a mentor (SSQ 20). Since women are underrepresented in places of authority in academia, we would expect that female students are less likely to feel that they have a mentor. The survey responses bore this out. Female students are significantly less likely than male students to strongly agree that they have a professor who served as a mentor (see Table 8). Two processes may be at work here. Because women are underrepresented in academia, they are more likely to serve on committees and do administrative work. Women are also spending more time doing household and childcare labor. These commitments may create a campus environment where female faculty are less visible or less available to mentor students. Less access and visibility may unintentionally reproduce the gender-segregated academy, impacting female students' choices of classes, majors, and/or careers.

Conclusion

As we look at faculty perceptions of gender equity within CCCU institutions, it is important to remember that our current ideals of gender—even within the Christian community— have not always been thus. Gender, as a social institution, changes; it is not a transhistorical process.[48] When shifts in the larger culture take place, social institutions adapt, respond-

---

47   That female and male students do not have significantly different attitudes about equality within their schools may be a more disturbing phenomenon, indicating that CCCU females and males have equally assimilated to the prevailing gender ideology. In their work on Christian university student perceptions of gender, Gallagher and Wood noted a significant discrepancy between female and male attitudes of gender, with male students more likely than their female counterparts to accept "traditional" gender roles. See Sally K. Gallagher and Sabrina L. Wood, "Godly Manhood Going Wild?: Transformations in Conservative Protestant Masculinity," *Sociology of Religion* 66 (2005): 135-159.

48   Martin, "Gender as Social Institution"; Connell, *Masculinities*; Kimmel, *Manhood in America*.

ing to new needs and demands. Americans in general, and Christians in particular, have trouble seeing the impact of larger social structures and forces in our lives. Unfortunately, that leaves Christians vulnerable to adapting to the American status quo, without even recognizing that our American beliefs and practices necessarily shape or even subvert our Christian beliefs and practices. Much of what American Christians believe about gender is tied to a 1950s secular cultural model that has been scripturally justified, subordinating the message of the gospel in favor of the interests of the status quo. This shapes how we think, what we model, and what we teach within the Christian academy.

In her essay Hall states that gender equity has been an elusive goal for the CCCU; however, one must wonder if it has been a goal at all. The essays presented here chronicle the substantial evidence that gender disparities exist in both the secular academy and within CCCU institutions. It is clear that gender segregation is stubbornly resilient and persistent.[49] Having incorporated divisions of gender into our faith, we not only constrain ourselves, we subsequently constrain what our students deem as appropriate or even possible vocations, based on their gender. It is easy to see what leads Pedersen and Jule to conclude that "we are doomed."

Yet this I call to mind, and therefore I have hope (Lamentations 3:21). The CCCU has a mandate for a Christian vision, relying on the example of Jesus Christ who redeems all social systems. Because Christ presented the same content in the same form to both women and men, never relegated women to only the domestic sphere, and fully incorporated women into his ministry,[50] we ought to critically examine our gender commitments. Jesus saw how social structures distorted religious thought and practices, consistently dismissing the cultural commitments that religious elites mistook for faith commitments.[51] In Mark 7:8 Jesus tells religious leaders that they have "let go the commands of God and are holding on to human traditions." (The NIV states they are holding on to "the traditions of men.") Paul tells us to no longer be conformed to this world, but to be transformed by the renewing of our minds (Romans 12:1-2). We must take these directives seriously in order to model a truer Christian reality, by learning how to detach ourselves from cultural commitments that do not model the life to which Jesus calls us.

Gender equity is not just a job for women, but for all followers of Jesus. The CCCU must strive to restructure policies that value whole people as women, men, parents, and workers. The only way to do this is to stop legitimating historical, secular constructs as Christian and to create models of higher education and gender that reflect the glory of a risen and redeeming Christ. Religion has an amazing potential to mitigate gender inequality. But until we recognize that much of American Christianity is an appropriation of middle-class American ideology, we may, in fact, be doomed.

---

49   Correll, "Constraints into Preferences."

50   Kevin Neuhouser, "Why I Am a Feminist," *The Falcon* 81:26 (October 4, 2006) <http://www.thefalconon-line.com/article.php?id=5149> retrieved May 15, 2010.

51   For example, in Matthew 23 Jesus rebukes religious leaders, calling them "blind guides" for mistaking their religious rules and practices as righteous; Mark 2-3 Jesus breaks the religious rules for fasting, as well as gleaning and healing on the Sabbath.

Table 1: Faculty Response to "Female faculty at my college/university are treated equally to male faculty" by sex in percentages.

	Sex [a]	
	Male	Female
Strongly agree	47.3%	23.8%
Somewhat agree	29.4%	30.5%
Neutral	8.7%	10.5%
Somewhat disagree	11.9%	23.3%
Strongly Disagree	2.7%	12.0%
p=0.000 [b] Cramer's V=0.294 [c]		

Table 2: Faculty Response to "Women should have the right to become pastors" by sex in percentages.

	Sex [a]	
	Male	Female
Strongly agree	49.7%	62.7%
Somewhat agree	16.7%	16.2%
Neutral	8.7%	6.1%
Somewhat disagree	11.0%	8.1%
Strongly Disagree	14.0%	7.0%
p=0.000 [b] Cramer's V=0.146 [c]		

Table 3: Faculty Response to "My approach to my discipline is shaped by my gender" by sex in percentages.

	Sex [a]	
	Male	Female
Strongly agree	6.0%	13.8%
Somewhat agree	31.5%	42.6%
Neutral	17.0%	13.3%
Somewhat disagree	18.8%	15.2%
Strongly Disagree	26.6%	15.1%
p=0.000 [b] Cramer's V=0.204 [c]		

Table 4: Faculty Response to "I am hesitant to address certain important issues in class because I teach at a Christian college/university" by sex in percentages.

	Sex[a]	
	Male	Female
Strongly agree	5.8%	5.3%
Somewhat agree	16.5%	22.3%
Neutral	6.1%	9.2%
Somewhat disagree	27.7%	28.9%
Strongly Disagree	44.0%	34.3%
p=0.000[b] Cramer's V=0.113[c]		

Table 5: Faculty Response to "Female students at my college/university are treated equally to male students" by sex in percentages.

	Sex[a]	
	Male	Female
Strongly agree	62.9%	37.3%
Somewhat agree	24.5%	32.6%
Neutral	5.7%	11.2%
Somewhat disagree	4.9%	14.5%
Strongly Disagree	2.0%	4.4%
p=0.000[b] Cramer's V=0.272[c]		

Table 6: Student Response to "Female students at my college/university are treated equally to male students" by sex in percentages.

	Sex[a]	
	Male	Female
Strongly agree	62.8%	51.9%
Somewhat agree	19.7%	28.3%
Neutral	9.9%	12.4%
Somewhat disagree	5.1%	6.1%
Strongly Disagree	2.4%	1.4%
p=0.000[b] Cramer's V=0.113[c]		

Table 7: Student Response to "Women should have the right to become pastors" by sex in percentages.

	Sex [a]	
	Male	Female
Strongly agree	39.7%	38.1%
Somewhat agree	16.9%	18.3%
Neutral	15.4%	13.4%
Somewhat disagree	11.6%	13.6%
Strongly Disagree	16.3%	16.5%
p=0.504 [b] Cramer's V=0.039 [c]		

Table 8: Student Response to "There is a professor at my college/university whom I identify as a mentor" by sex in percentages.

	Sex [a]	
	Male	Female
Strongly agree	28.0%	22.0%
Somewhat agree	26.4%	29.8%
Neutral	25.8%	27.7%
Somewhat disagree	10.3%	12.1%
Strongly Disagree	9.5%	8.4%
p=0.023 [b] Cramer's V=0.070 [c]		

a   Though the survey question asked faculty about their gender, the category responses of "male" and "female" are denotations of sex; gender categories include "man" and "woman."

b   A probability equal or less than 0.05 illustrates a statistically significant relationship between variables.

c   Cramer's V measures the strength of association between two categorical variables. Generally speaking, a Cramer's V>0.250 is considered a "strong" association, Cramer's V<0.100 is considered a "weak" association, and Cramer's V>0.100 and <0.250 is considered "moderate".

Bibliography: Part Six

Ballout, Hassan I. "Career Success: The Effects of Human Capital Person-Environment Fit and Organizational Support." *Journal of Managerial Psychology* 22 (2007): 741-765.

Bartkowski, John P. "One Step Forward, One Step Back: Progressive Traditionalism and the Negotiation of Domestic Labor in Evangelical Families." *Gender Issues* 17 (1999): 37-61.

———, *Remaking the Godly Marriage: Gender Negotiation in Evangelical Families*. New Brunswick, N.J.: Rutgers University Press, 2001.

Bickel, J. "Scenarios for Success: Enhancing Women Physicians' Professional Advancement." *Western Journal of Medicine* 162 (1995): 165-169.

Caplan, Paula J. *Lifting a Ton of Feathers: A Woman's Guide to Surviving in the Academic World*. Toronto: University of Toronto Press, 1994.

Christerson, Brad, M. Elizabeth Lewis Hall, and Shelly Cunningham. "The Gender Dynamics of an Evangelical University." Unpublished manuscript (2008).

Colaner, Colleen Warner and Steven M. Giles. "The Baby Blanket or the Briefcase: The Impact of Evangelical Gender Role Ideologies on Career and Mothering Aspirations of Female Evangelical College Students." *Sex Roles* 58 (2008): 526-534.

Colaner, Colleen Warner and Susan C. Warner. "The Effect of Egalitarian and Complementarian Gender Role Attitudes on Career Aspirations in Evangelical Female Undergraduate College Students." *Journal of Psychology & Theology* 33 (2005): 224-229.

Creegan, Nicola Hoggard and Christine C. Pohl. *Living on the Boundaries: Evangelical Women, Feminism and the Theological Academy*. Downers Grove, Ill.: InterVarsity Press, 2005.

Edwards, J. R., D. M. Cable, I. O. Williamson, L. S. Lambert, and A. J. Shipp. "The Phenomenology of Fit: Linking the Person and Environment to the Subjective Experience of Person-Environment Fit." *Journal of Applied Psychology* 91 (2006): 802-827.

Ellison, Christopher G., and John P. Bartkowski. "Conservative Protestantism and the Division of Household Labor among Married Couples." *Journal of Family Issues* 23 (2002): 95-985.

Gallagher, Sally K. "Where Are the Antifeminist Evangelicals?: Evangelical Identity, Subcultural Location, and Attitudes toward Feminism." *Gender and Society* 18 (2004): 451-472.

Gallagher, Sally K. and Christian Smith. "Symbolic Traditionalism and Pragmatic Egalitarianism: Contemporary Evangelicals, Families, and Gender." *Gender & Society* 13 (1999): 211-233.

Garlett, Marti Watson. "Female Faculty on the Fringe: Theologizing Sexism in the Evangelical Academy." *Research on Christian Higher Education* 4 (1997): 69-97.

———, "Waiting in the Wings: Women of God in the Evangelical Academy." Unpublished dissertation, Claremont Graduate School of Education, Claremont, CA (1997).

Gay, David A., Christopher G. Ellison, and Daniel A. Powers. "In Search of Denominational Subcultures: Religious Affiliation and 'Pro-Family' Issues Revisited." *Review of Religious Research* 38 (1996): 3-17.

Glazer-Raymo, J. *Shattering the Myths: Women in Academe*. Baltimore, Md.: Johns Hopkins University Press, 1999.

Gold, Howard and Gina E. Russell. "The Rising Influence of Evangelicalism in American Political Behavior, 1980-2004." *Social Science Journal* 44 (2007): 554-562.

Hall, M. Elizabeth Lewis, Tamara L. Anderson, and Michele M. Willingham. "Diapers, Dissertations, and Other Holy Things: The Experiences of Mothers Working in Christian Academia." *Christian Higher Education* 3 (2004): 41-60.

Hall, M. Elizabeth Lewis, Brad Christerson, and Shelly Cunningham. "Sanctified Sexism: Gender Harassment in Evangelical Universities." *Psychology of Women Quarterly* 34 (2010):181-185.

Hall, M. Elizabeth Lewis, Shelly Cunningham, and Brad Christerson. "Biola University Gender Climate Study." La Mirada, Ca.: Biola University (Spring, 2008).

Haslett, Beth B. and Susan Lipman. "Micro Inequities: Up Close and Personal," In *Subtle Sexism: Current Practice and Prospects for Change*, 34-53. Edited by Nijole V. Benokraitis. Thousand Oaks, Ca.: Sage, 1997.

Ibarra, Herminia. "Personal Networks of Women and Minorities in Management: A Conceptual Framework." *Academy of Management Review* 18 (1993): 56-87.

Ingersoll, Julie. *Evangelical Christian Women: War Stories in the Gender Battles.* New York: New York University Press, 2003.

Jones, Serena. *Feminist Theory and Christian Theology: Cartographies of Grace.* Guides to Theological Inquiry Series. Minneapolis: Fortress Press, 2000.

Jule, Allyson and Bettina Tate Pedersen, ed. *Being Feminist, Being Christian: Essays from Academia.* New York: Palgrave Macmillan, 2006.

Kimball, Cynthia Neal, Terri Watson, Sally Schwer Canning, and Joan Laidig Brady. "Missing Voices: Professional Challenges for Academic Women." *Journal of Psychology and Christianity* 20 (2001): 132-144.

Lindholm, Jennifer A. "Perceived Organizational Fit: Nurturing the Minds, Hearts, and Personal Ambitions of University Faculty." *Review of Higher Education* 27 (2003): 125-149.

Massey, Lesly F. *Women in the Church.* Jefferson, N.C.: McFarland and Company Inc., 2002.

Meyerson, Debra E. and Joyce K. Fletcher. "A Modest Manifesto for Shattering the Glass Ceiling." *Harvard Business Review* (January-February 2000): 126-136.

Palmer, Parker J. "Toward a Spirituality of Higher Education." In *Faithful Learning and the Christian Scholarly Vocation,*75-87. Edited by Douglas V. Henry and Bob R. Agee. Grand Rapids, Mich.: Eerdmans, 2003.

Patterson, James A. *Shining Lights and Widening Horizons: A History of the Council for Christian Colleges & Universities, 2001-2006.* Washington, DC: Council for Christian Colleges and Universities, 2006.

Phipps, Kim. "Epilogue: Campus Climate and Christian Scholarship." In *Scholarship and Christian Faith: Enlarging the Conversation,* 171-183. Edited by Douglas Jacobsen and Rhonda Husted Jacobsen. Oxford, UK: Oxford University Press, 2004.

Sagaria, Mary Ann Danowitz. "An Exploratory Model of Filtering in Administrative Searches: Toward Counter-Hegemonic Discourses." *Journal of Higher Education* 73 (2002): 677-710.

Sequeira, Debra, Thomas Trzyna, Martin L. Abbott, and Delbert S. McHenry. "'The Kingdom Has Not Yet Come': Coping With MicroInequities Within a Christian University." *Research on Christian Higher Education* 2 (1995): 1-35.

Settles, Isis H., L. M. Cortina, J. Malley, and A. J. Stewart. "The Climate for Women in Academic Science: The Good, the Bad, and the Changeable." *Psychology of Women Quarterly* 30 (2006): 47-58.

Shultz, E. L., A. L. Montoya, and P. M. Briere. "Perceptions of Institutional Climate." *U.S. Department of Education Educational Resources Information Center (ERIC)* ED353234. (1992).

Sonnert, Gerhard and Gerald Holton. *Who Succeeds in Science?: The Gender Dimension.* New Brunswick, N.J.: Rutgers University Press, 1995.

_____, "Career Patterns of Women and Men in the Sciences." *American Scientist* 84 (1986): 63-71.

Vetter, B. M. *What Is Holding up the Glass Ceiling?: Barriers to Women in the Science and Engineering Workforce.* Occasional Paper 92-3. Washington, D.C.: Commission on Professionals in Science and Technology, 1992.

Volf, Miroslav. *Exclusion and Embrace: A Theological Exploration of Identity, Otherness, and Reconciliation.* Nashville: Abingdon Press, 1996.

Walker, Juanie N. "Pragmatic Paradoxes of Gender and Authority at a Christian University: Ethnography and Analysis of Female Academicians' Narratives." *Research on Christian Higher Education* 8 (2001): 19-42.

Welch, V., Jr. "Doctorate Recipients from United States Universities: Selected Tables 2007." *Chicago: National Opinion Research Center.* Retrieved September 20, 2009: http://www.norc.org/SED.htm

West, M. S. and J. W. Curtis. "AAUP Faculty Gender Equity Indicators 2006." American Association of University Professors (2006).

Young, Angela M. and David Hurlic. "Gender Enactment at Work: The Importance of Gender and Gender-Related Behavior to Person-Organizational Fit and Career Decisions." *Journal of Managerial Psychology* 22 (2007): 168-187.

PART SEVEN

EVOLUTION AND
THE SCIENCE CLASSROOM

DECONSTRUCTING THE SECOND PILLAR OF ANTIEVOLUTIONISM IN CHRISTIAN HIGHER EDUCATION

THOMAS C. CHESNES

CHAPTER 19

> If they [infidels] find a Christian mistaken in a field which they themselves know well and hear him maintaining his foolish opinions about Scripture, how are they going to believe those books in matters concerning the resurrection of the dead, the hope for eternal life, and the kingdom of Heaven, when they think their pages are full of falsehoods on facts which they themselves have learnt from experience and reason? Reckless and incompetent expounders of Holy Scripture bring untold trouble and sorrow on their wiser brethren . . . .[1]

—**St. Augustine of Hippo, 416 CE**

The modern evolutionary synthesis has widespread acceptance by the vast majority of working biologists, underlies and unifies all of the sub-disciplines of the biological sciences,[2] and is supported overwhelmingly by the federal courts.[3] Still, the topic remains a contentious subject among many Christians. Opposition to the scientific merit of evolution is often based primarily on philosophical grounds, portraying evolution as a threat to Christian faith. If students see the acceptance of evolution as being incompatible with Christianity, as well as presuming that evolution is a false or atheistic theory, students of the CCCU may be less likely to critically evaluate the scientific evidence.

---

1 St. Augustine, *On the Literal Meaning of Genesis,* trans. John Hammond Taylor (New York: Newman, 1982), Book 1, Chapter 19.

2 Donald Kennedy, "Breakthrough of the Year," *Science* 310 (2005): 1,869.

3 Notably Epperson v. Arkansas, 1968, Edwards V. Aguillard, 1987, and Kitzmiller v. Dover Area School Board, 2005.

289

The historical basis for antievolutionism in modern society has been described as resting on three pillars: the claim that evolution is a theory in crisis, that evolution is incompatible with Christianity, and that both evolution and opposing views should be taught in classrooms (regardless of scientific merit).[4] A major hurdle to teaching evolution in Christian higher education is the widespread adherence to the second pillar: the perceived incongruity between Christian faith and evolutionary theory. In fact, the Joeckel/Chesnes survey finds that 66.5 percent of sampled students somewhat or strongly disagreed with the statement, "The theory of evolution is compatible with Christianity" (SSQ 39). Approximately 35 percent of faculty also disagree with this statement (FSQ 51).

The belief in the incompatibility between Christianity and evolutionary theory, especially among students, remains significant despite the publication of recent works by a number of Christian scholars who illustrate how the scientific principles and theological worldviews can coexist.[5] Students are often surprised to learn that there is an "accommodationist" or complementary view between science and religion. They are even more surprised that the proponents are committed Christians.

Many students enter the academy viewing the interface between Christianity and evolution within the framework of a conflict model, forcing the individual into an "either/or" decision: on one hand, to believe in a strongly supported biological theory which excludes the need for a personal, loving creator or, on the other hand, to reject evolutionary theory (which underlies all biological sciences) in order to maintain belief in the existence of God and biblical truth. As with most cases, the thoughtful middle ground is drowned out in the debate, but this complementary position can only be fleshed out when the scientific and philosophical components of the theory are separated. The complementary position weakens the second pillar of antievolutionism, yet is less subscribed to than the conflict model among students in Christian institutions.

As stated before, the roots of opposition to evolution are often based on philosophical or theological considerations. Firstly, an evolutionary view of natural history is seen by many as a contradiction to a literalistic interpretation of Genesis. Belief in biblical inerrancy is a strong correlate to denying the compatibility between evolution and Christianity (as will be expanded upon later). In addition, annotations within study Bibles have been noted as conveyances for antievolutionary sentiment, attaching to Scripture the annotator's philosophical interpretation of science.[6]

The teaching of evolution is also often framed in the rhetoric or context of holy war, sometimes linking the scientific theory to spiritual battles between angels and demons

4 Eugenie Scott and Glenn Branch, "Antievolutionism: Changes and Continuities," *BioScience* 53 (2003): 282-285.

5 Notable examples include Francis Collins, *The Language of God* (New York: Free Press, 2006). See also Darrel Falk, *Coming to Peace with Science* (Downers Grove, Ill.: InterVarsity Press, 2004) and Kenneth Miller, *Finding Darwin's God* (New York: Harper Perennial, 2007).

6 Brian J. Alters and Sandra M. Alters, *Defending Evolution* (Sudbury, Mass.: Jones and Bartlett, 2001), 69 -74.

for the souls and minds of students.[7] It is obvious that when given the choice within these terms, students whose personal faith and relationship with God are priorities will opt to the side of light rather than darkness. This associated metaphysical conflict is a significant barrier for the science educator. Consider this free response from a CCCU student:

> It is not that I am closed minded to the subject [evolution], but growing up in a Christian home and environment, going to church, youth group, and a Christian school, it has been literally preached and drilled into my head that evolution is a crazy impossible notion. I have been told repeatedly that people will try to change my viewpoint on evolution because it is such an accepted theory in our world today . . . . because of the way I have been raised, my faith plays a huge part in why I don't believe in evolution.

Further, some individuals fear that the acceptance of evolutionary theory will lead to undesirable societal consequences. Belief in evolutionary theory has been associated with a host of immoral excesses such as unrestrained aggression, promiscuity, and the dissolution of the family.[8] In a 2003 study, selfishness and racism, as well as a decreased spirituality, sense of purpose, and self determination, were perceived by college students as societal impacts of accepting the theory.[9] Belief in biological evolution is often cited as a precursor to eugenics, Social Darwinist ideology, and the Nazi Holocaust.[10]

To bolster philosophical and theological opposition to evolution, numerous seemingly scientific objections are often given, such as those involving moon dust,[11] the second law of thermodynamics[12], the coexistence of human and dinosaur tracks,[13] and many of the so-called "icons" of evolution.[14] Most have been thoroughly refuted in the scientific literature and have become ineffective as serious arguments against the theory. Despite refutation by the scientific community, it is not uncommon to encounter these questions in the science classroom.

Intelligent Design is often proposed as a valid scientific alternative to evolution, and is seen as such by both the majority of sampled students and faculty in the Joeckel/ Chesnes survey, with 57.1 percent and 54 percent supporting Intelligent Design, respectively (SSQ 40, FSQ 52). Although Intelligent Design is presented to the public as a

---

7   Frances R. A. Paterson and Lawrence F. Rossow, "Chained to the Devil's Throne: Evolution and Creation Science as Religio-Political Issue," *American Biology Teacher* 61 (1999): 358-364.

8   Eileen Barker, "Does It Matter How We Got Here? Dangers Perceived in Literalism and Evolutionism," *Zygon* 22 (1987): 213-225.

9   Sarah K. Brem, Michael Ranney, and Jennifer Schindel, "Perceived Consequences of Evolution: College Students Perceive Negative Personal and Social Impact in Evolutionary Theory," *Science Education* 87 (2003): 181-206.

10   Jerry Bergman, "Darwinism and the Nazi Race Holocaust," *Creation Ex Nihilo Technical Journal* 13 (1999): 101-111.

11   Andrew A. Snelling and David Rush, "Moon Dust and the Age of the Solar System," *Creation Ex Nihilo Technical Journal* 7 (1993): 2-42.

12   Daniel F. Styer, "Entropy and Evolution," *American Journal of Physics* 76 (2008): 1,031-1,033. See also Emory F. Bunn "Evolution and the Second Law of Thermodynamics," *American Journal of Physics* 77 (2009): 922-925.

13   Ronnie J. Hastings, "The Rise and Fall of the Paluxy Mantracks," *Perspectives on Science and Christian Faith* 40 (1988): 144-154.

14   Kevin Padian and Alan D. Gishlick, "The Talented Mr. Wells," *Quarterly Review of Biology* 77 (2002): 33-37.

scientific model,[15] the program has failed to produce output which would be considered "scientific." Design theory provides no testable or falsifiable hypothesis,[16] makes no testable predictions, and suggests no new avenues for research.[17] Intelligent Design advocates have produced no peer-review articles providing rigorous accounts (by experimentation or calculation) of how the intelligent design of any biological system occurred.[18] As a result, the United States Federal Court determined that Intelligent Design is not a legitimate science.[19] Regardless, design theory persists as a valid alternative to the majority of the faithful.

In the Joeckel/Chesnes survey, theological self-identification was a strong predictor of whether one will accept design theory as a valid alternative to evolution. Those who self-identified as "strongly conservative" in their theological beliefs were also more likely to believe in biblical inerrancy (r= .55, p<0.001) and that the Bible is the only authoritative source of information about God (r= .43, p<0.001). Acceptance of Intelligent Design as a valid alternative to evolution was greatest among students and faculty who self identified as theologically conservative (Table 1). Likewise, this group in both students and faculty was also most likely to disagree that Christianity was compatible with evolution (Table 2).

As expected, students in a natural science major were most likely to find evolution to be compatible with Christian faith (Table 3a) and less accepting of Intelligent Design as a valid alternative, although still a majority (Table 3b). Faculty in the social sciences see the greatest compatibility between Christianity and evolution, followed by natural science faculty (Table 4a). The natural science faculty were the only group in which a majority did not view Intelligent Design as a valid alternative to evolution (Table 4b). Interestingly, social science faculty were most likely to find compatibility between Christianity and evolution while their students were the least likely. Health science faculty found the least compatibility between evolution and their faith, despite the important role evolutionary theory plays in medical science and human health, especially regarding patterns of disease, pharmaceuticals, genomics, and biotechnology.[20]

Home-schooled students and those who attended Christian high schools more commonly disagreed with the notion of compatibility between faith and evolution than their counterparts from public and private nonreligious high schools (Table 5). In addition, home- and Christian-school graduates were significantly more likely to accept Intelligent Design as a valid alternative.

---

15   Thomas Woodward, *Darwin Strikes Back: Defending the Science of Intelligent Design* (Grand Rapids, Mich.: Baker Books, 2006).

16   Ted Peters and Martinez Hewlett, *Can You Believe in God and Evolution? A Guide for the Perplexed* (Nashville: Abingdon Press, 2006), 50. See also Elliott Sober, "What Is Wrong with Intelligent Design?" *Quarterly Review of Biology* 82 (2007): 3-8.

17   Kenneth R. Miller, *Only a Theory: Evolution and the Battle for America's Soul* (New York: Viking, 2008), p. 86.

18   Kitzmiller v. Dover Area School District, Trial transcript: Day 12, Morning session, Part 1. Cross examination of Michael Behe.

19   Judge John E. Jones III, Memorandum Opinion, Kitzmiller v. Dover Area School District, 64.

20   J. J. Bull and H. A. Wichman, "Applied Evolution," *Annual Review of Ecology and Systematics* 32 (2001): 183-218. See also Anusuya Chinsamy and Eva Plaganyi, "Accepting Evolution," *Evolution* 62 (2007): 248-254.

In general, as students mature and move through the collegiate ranks, they tend to be more open toward the idea of compatibility between Christianity and evolutionary theory (Table 6). While 76 percent of freshmen disagree that compatibility is possible, only 57 percent of seniors disagree. A similar trend is seen in the length of tenure of faculty (Table 7). Over 38 percent of new faculty disagreed with the concept of compatibility; faculty with tenures of sixteen years or more at their institution showed only 30 percent disagreement.[21]

This increased openness with time spent in Christian higher education may be due to what Arthur Holmes considers a Christian college distinctive: the *active* integration of faith and learning.[22] He explains, "The Christian college will not settle for a militant polemic against secular learning and science and culture, as if there were a great gulf fixed between the secular and the sacred. All truth is God's truth, no matter where it is found, and we can thank him for it all."[23] Although this is the ideal, it is likely that this attitude may not be manifested in all CCCU classrooms. This active integration, however, requires a deeper understanding of theology, hermeneutics, critical thinking, and epistemology, characteristics hopefully developed during the course of one's Christian higher education. In addition, the student may also gain a better understanding of the mechanisms of science, including its limitations, its provisional nature, and the process of peer review. One can move beyond simplistic explanations and truly integrate the complexity of God's special revelation in Scripture and general revelation in nature. This can be a hurdle for many of our students, but with faculty fostering the understanding that "all truth is God's truth," this complexity can be embraced and play an important part of the educational process.

Unfortunately, this is not always the case. In *The Scandal of the Evangelical Mind*, Mark Noll writes, "For deeply embedded historical reasons, evangelical thinking about science is still a shadow of what God, nature and the Christian faith deserve."[24] Too often, the subject of evolution in the classroom has been glazed over, formally discounted before being presented, or avoided altogether. To the chagrin of some students, evolution is covered more extensively than expected. Consider the variety of free responses from CCCU students:

> *"We flew through evolution in a matter of 30 minutes because of some of the parents."*

> *"I learned the basics of evolution such as the big bang and how Darwin claims he has proof towards his theory, but on the other hand all my teachers had the ability to inform us that this theory is all wrong and that the bible states that God is the creator of the world and so on."*

---

21   Admittedly these data are snapshot; cohorts were not followed longitudinally.

22   Arthur F. Holmes, *The Idea of a Christian College*, revised edition (Grand Rapids, Mich.: Eerdmans, 1987), 6.

23   Ibid., 7.

24   Mark Noll, *The Scandal of the Evangelical Mind* (Grand Rapids, Mich.: Eerdmans, 1994), 233.

"On the acedemic [sic] level, professors are less intimidating because they are not trying to brainwash students into believing evolution, or Global Warming, they simply want to teach."

"Professors are wishy-washy when it comes to talk about evolution and whether or not they believe in it."

"Even at a Christian school evolution is taught as rule not as a theory which is just what i would get at a secular school. part of why i came here was to not have evolution taught to me as a rule but here i am getting exactly what i would be at a secular school. to be honest i don't really consider my school to be Christian"

". . . it is easy to have the nagging fear that I am not being given a fair look at certain things that are considered opposed to Christianity. Am I being given a fair look at Evolution? Was I given a fair explanation of Existential philosophy? If I were to debate a person on this topic, would I find that I am uninformed on a topic I thought I knew a great deal about?"

Students come into the Christian academy with diverse expectations on the treatment of evolution in their science classes. For some, presenting evolutionary theory without dismissing its validity is seen as a betrayal of the school's Christian mission. Others may suspect their science education is deficient because of a perceived incomplete treatment of the subject. In any given classroom, a biology professor teaching evolution may be simultaneously viewed as subversive to his or her faith by some or his or her academic discipline by others.

The perception that evolutionary theory and Christian faith are incompatible is extremely bothersome to many biology faculty in CCCU institutions, as expressed from the faculty free response questions:

"I am a biologist and my department strongly supports the teaching of evolution to biology majors. Sometimes it is difficult to explain this stand to Christians who are not scientists and to non-academicians."

"I teach evolution. So I find the most difficult part is to justify my faith to students, sometimes faculty, that are not open-minded enough to recognize the compatibility of science and faith."

"I never had a problem with parents or upper administration until I came here and openly expressed my views that I'm a firm proponent of evolution (yes, we evolved from apes). Students have much less problems accepting my views than 'grown ups' I'm sorry to say."

As seen in Table 4a, the majority of Christian faculty with advanced degrees in the biological sciences believe Christianity to be compatible with evolution. Simply put, they believe both accounts of reality to be "true." Their Christian belief, a theistic philosophy, is not mutually exclusive to their understanding of evolution, a scientific explanation.

Their reasons for Christian belief are varied. Their reasons for evolutionary belief are based on scientific evidence and data. As Richard T. Wright states in *Biology Through the Eyes of Faith* (a book published for the CCCU), "No one should accept evolutionary reasoning without examining the evidence, but be advised: the evidence is strong, and it is convincing."[25]

Evolutionary theory has had great pragmatic success—such as in biotechnology, agriculture applications, and pharmaceutical and medical protocols.[26] It unifies the biological subdisciplines and has immense explanatory power. Support from findings in both the fossil and molecular record provides further evidence of the predicted evolutionary processes. As I tell my Biology II students, "If evolution did not occur, for some reason God made it look like it did." Certainly there are gaps in our knowledge and the fossil record, there are valid scientific controversies, and advocates do often overstate their case. However, the data in support of evolutionary theory far outweigh the data to the contrary. When objectively studied, the data are overwhelming. Not to include evolution in the biology curriculum is to commit academic fraud.

Some fear that, by making disbelief in evolutionary theory a litmus test for Christian orthodoxy, it will in effect drive many away from faith. Saint Augustine addressed this issue nearly 1,600 years ago. When Scripture is misinterpreted and contradicts knowledge gained by reason, it will result in "... people outside the household of faith thinking our sacred writers held such opinions, and, to the great loss of those whose salvation we are concerned, the writers of Scripture are criticized as unlearned men . . . ."[27] More recently, Denis Lamoureux describes his concern for the potential pastoral fallout by Christians exposed to an education in evolution. He states, "Will Christians, who have been indoctrinated into anti-evolutionary models like ID Theory, lose their faith once they see and grasp the indubitable evolutionary evidence? It is for this reason that the church must develop a thoroughly Christian approach to evolution."[28] An additional, and equally unsettling, fallout could be a reduction in the number of Christians involved in science. Christian students may avoid the sciences altogether because of preconceived incongruities with their faith. They may also be unprepared for entrance exams and graduate programs if their biological undergraduate training is deficient.

These negative consequences can be stemmed by a proper treatment of evolutionary theory in the Christian academy. A first step should be to diffuse the culture-war implications associated with evolution. This can only be done by disassociating the philosophical extensions of theory from the scientific. Philosophical worldviews and scientific explanations are not mutually exclusive. Practicing methodological naturalism

25   Richard T. Wright, *Biology Through the Eyes of Faith*, revised and updated (San Francisco: HarperCollins 2003), 144.

26   Michael Antolin and Joan Herbers, "Evolution's Struggle for Existence in America's Public Schools," *Evolution* 55 (2001): 2379-2388.

27   St. Augustine, *On the Literal Meaning of Genesis*, trans. John Hammond Taylor (New York: Newman, 1982), Book 1, Chapter 19.

28   Denis O. Lamoureux, "Gaps, Design, & 'Theistic' Evolution: A Counter Reply to Robert A. Larmer," *Christian Scholar's Review* 37 (2007):101-116.

in science does not commit the Christian to metaphysical naturalism in philosophy.[29] Students should understand that atheism is not a prerequisite for belief in evolutionary theory. Science cannot assess the metaphysical; it cannot be used to prove or disprove the existence of God. Doing so is a violation of science's domain. It is simply outside of its limits.

The majority of the burden, however, lies on the science faculty. In addition to the formidable theological barriers, many students have a poor understanding of science, its vocabulary (i.e. theory and law), and in particular the basic tenets of evolutionary biology.[30] Because they fail to understand the basic mechanisms of evolution, they fail to appreciate how empirical evidence relates to the claims put forth by evolutionary theory.[31] Further, science educators should communicate what exactly science is and what it is not. This can be achieved by an emphasis on the limits of science, especially of how these limits are often violated when scientific propositions metamorphose into philosophical claims—claims which are unwarranted and pose an unnecessary threat to one's Christian faith.

---

29   Patrick McDonald and Nivaldo J. Tro, "In Defense of Methodological Naturalism," *Christian Scholar's Review* 38 (2009): 201-230.

30   Anne Sinclair and Murray Patton Pendarvis, "Evolution vs. Conservative Religious Beliefs," *Journal of College Science Teaching* 27(1997): 167-170.

31   Tania Lombrozo, Andrew Shtulman, and Michael Weisberg, "The Intelligent Design Controversy: Lessons from Psychology and Education," *Trends in Cognitive Sciences* 10 (2006): 56-57.

Table 1: Percent agreement by CCCU students and faculty with the statement "Intelligent Design is a valid alternative to the theory of evolution."

Theological Self Identification	Student	N	Faculty	N
Strongly Conservative	81.9%	(319)	78.2%	(404)
Somewhat Conservative	75.2%	(1001)	81.3%	(836)
Neutral	58.2%	(444)	37.6%	(188)
Somewhat Liberal	61.9%	(333)	31.2%	(305)
Strongly Liberal	50.9%	(72)	10%	(63)
Not a Christian	33.3%	(26)	n/a	(0)

Table 2: Percent disagreement by CCCU students and faculty with the statement, "The theory of evolution is compatible with Christianity."

Theological Self Identification	Student	N	Faculty	N
Strongly Conservative	87.1%	(319)	68.5%	(404)
Somewhat Conservative	73.5%	(1001)	35.4%	(836)
Neutral	59.0%	(444)	16.0%	(188)
Somewhat Liberal	44.0%	(333)	7.9%	(305)
Strongly Liberal	30.6%	(72)	1.6%	(63)
Not a Christian	53.8%	(26)	n/a	(0)

Table 3: a) Disagreement of CCCU students with the statement "The theory of evolution is compatible with Christianity," sorted by academic major; b) Agreement of CCCU students with the statement "Intelligent Design is a valid alternative to the theory of evolution" sorted by academic major.

a)	Major	N	Evo Disagree
	Natural Sciences	(110)	50.0%
	Arts	(96)	60.2%
	Communication	(105)	62.2%
	Humanities	(97)	63.7%
	Education	(375)	66.6%
	Health Sciences	(312)	67.3%
	Business	(375)	67.4%
	Religion/Theology/Bible	(197)	68.3%
	Social Sciences	(332)	68.4%
b)	Major	N	ID Agree
	Natural Sciences	(110)	61.5%
	Health Sciences	(312)	63.8%
	Arts	(96)	67.1%
	Business	(375)	67.4%

	Social Sciences	(332)	67.8%
	Education	(375)	69.5%
	Communication	(105)	74.3%
	Religion/Theology/Bible	(197)	75.5%
	Humanities	(97)	77.2%

Table 4: a) Disagreement of CCCU faculty with the statement "The theory of evolution is compatible with Christianity," sorted by academic discipline; b) Agreement of CCCU faculty with the statement "Intelligent Design is a valid alternative to the theory of evolution," sorted by academic discipline.

a)	Discipline	N	Evo Disagree
	Social Sciences	(237)	24.9%
	Natural Sciences	(312)	27.4%
	Humanities	(319)	27.9%
	Arts	(172)	29.6%
	Religion/Theology/Bible	(185)	32.7%
	Communication	(73)	38.2%
	Education	(236)	45.5%
	Business	(159)	48.0%
	Health Sciences	(131)	56.8%
b)	Discipline	N	ID Agree
	Natural Sciences	(312)	42.5%
	Humanities	(319)	51.3%
	Arts	(172)	51.9%
	Social Sciences	(237)	53.6%
	Business	(159)	57.6%
	Health Sciences	(131)	58.7%
	Education	(236)	60.8%
	Religion/Theology/Bible	(185)	60.8%
	Communication	(73)	62.7%

Table 5: Disagreement with the statement "The theory of evolution is compatible with Christianity" and agreement with the statement "Intelligent Design is a valid alternative to the theory of evolution," by CCCU students sorted by high school education.

High School	Evo Disagree	ID Agree
Public High School (1533)	62.2%	66.2%
Non-Christian Private (27)	63.0%	61.9%
Christian School (485)	74.8%	77.2%
Home School (150)	84.7%	81.3%

Table 6: Disagreement with the statement "The theory of evolution is compatible with Christianity," and agreement with the statement "Intelligent Design is a valid alternative to the theory of evolution," by CCCU students sorted by class rank.

Class Rank	Evo Disagree	ID Agree
Freshman (550)	76.0%	71.9%
Sophomore (482)	68.5%	71.2%
Junior (504)	64.9%	66.6%
Senior (546)	57.1%	72.8%

Table 7: Disagreement with the statement "The theory of evolution is compatible with Christianity," and agreement with the statement "Intelligent Design is a valid alternative to the theory of evolution," by CCCU faculty sorted by length of tenure at institution.

Length of Tenure at Institution	Evo Disagree	ID Agree
0 - 5 yrs (566)	38.7%	57.7%
6 - 10 yrs (448)	36.8%	59.9%
11-15 yrs (223)	35.4%	53.8%
16 + yrs (556)	30.0%	51.5%

INHERITED BELIEFS AND EVOLVED BRAINS

A CCCU Challenge

HOWARD J. VAN TILL

CHAPTER 20

> Once introduced into a population, belief in the existence of a supreme god with properties such as being superknowing, superpowerful, and immortal is highly contagious and a hard habit to break. The way our minds are constructed and develop [as the outcome of biological evolution] make these beliefs very attractive.[1] —**Justin L. Barrett**

Christianity and Evolution: Incompatible or Complementary?

Supported by data from the Joeckel/Chesnes survey, Thomas Chesnes noted in the previous essay that approximately two-thirds of CCCU students and one-third of CCCU faculty members believe that Christianity and evolution are incompatible, thereby forcing an "either/or" type of decision (FSQ 51, SSQ 39). In his judgment, this belief has substantial consequences and effectively functions as "The Second Pillar of Antievolutionism in Christian Education." Furthermore, he found it noteworthy that the antievolutionism that grows out of this belief persists "despite the publication of recent works by a number of Christian scholars" who find their commitment to Christianity and their acceptance of evolutionary principles to be *complementary*—that is, they allow the possibility of *compatible* answers to questions appropriately addressed to either Christian theology or the natural sciences.

Scholars who find Christianity and evolution compatible must, of course, believe that each of them can be rightly understood in a way that leaves ample room for the

---

1 Justin L. Barrett, *Why Would Anyone Believe in God?* (Lanham, Md.: AltaVista Press, 2004), viii.

other to contribute answers to certain questions that are considered essential to its perspective; that is, scientists and Christians must agree not to offer conflicting answers to the same questions.

The natural sciences, for instance, must define "evolution" in a way that does *not* categorically rule out the belief that the universe is a creation that was given its being (everything that it is, and everything that it is equipped to do) by a Creator. With that understanding, I shall in the remainder of this essay use the word "evolution" to mean the idea, developed by the natural sciences, that the formational history of the entire universe (including life on Earth) can be understood as the outcome of "natural" processes (that is, processes made possible by the capabilities and potentialities inherent in the natural world). Note carefully: this does *not* preclude a role for divine creative action; it says only that the Creator's will for the formation of physical structures and of living creatures could be achieved without *one particular style* of divine action—that is, without irruptive, supernatural acts (acts that overpower nature) of form-imposing intervention (sometimes called acts of *special creation* when each biological *species* is envisioned as having been independently formed by God). In like manner, when a Christian scholar argues for complementarity, Christianity must be understood in a way that does *not* require its followers to read the biblical creation narratives in a woodenly literalistic fashion; that is, such narratives need not be read as chronicles of successive divine acts of supernatural, form-imposing intervention.

So, are Christianity and evolution compatible or not? They certainly can be, provided that each is understood in the manner just suggested. In fact, that was precisely the way I settled the matter in my own mind and in my teaching at a CCCU institution for over thirty years.[2] I began with the traditional Christian belief that the entire universe—everything that it is, and everything that it is capable of doing—is not self-existent, but has its being as a gift from its Creator. From that it follows that every one of its "natural" formational capabilities is—without exception—a God-given "gift of being." How could it be that the natural formational capabilities of the universe are so remarkably fruitful as to make possible the evolution of the most mind-boggling array of physical structures and living creatures that have ever existed? That could be the case, I argued, only as the consequence of the astounding creativity and limitless generosity of the Creator. God was not only sufficiently creative to conceive of a world that would evolve by employing its wealth of natural capabilities; God was also sufficiently generous to gift the Creation with all of the formational capabilities needed to make evolution possible. Even though I might now find it fruitful to explore additional ways of reconciling evolution and religious worldviews, I still see this "Fully-Gifted Creation Perspective" as the best approach for persons holding to a traditional Christian theology.[3]

---

2 For a sample of this integrated approach to science and religion, see Howard J. Van Till, *The Fourth Day: What the Bible and the Heavens Are Telling Us about the Creation* (Grand Rapids, Mich.: Eerdmans, 1986).

3 For more detailed developments of this perspective, see my chapter, "The Fully Gifted Creation," in J. P. Moreland and John Mark Reynolds, editors, *Three Views on Creation and Evolution* (Grand Rapids, Mich.: Zondervan, 1999), 161-218, and also my chapter, "Is the Universe Capable of Evolving?" in Keith B. Miller, editor, *Perspectives on an Evolving Creation* (Grand Rapids, Mich.: Eerdmans, 2003), 313-334.

What Is the Source of the Incompatibility Judgment?

The fact that two-thirds of the CCCU students polled by Joeckel and Chesnes considered evolution *not* to be compatible with Christianity immediately raises the question, Why is that so? What led the majority of students to this antievolutionary stance? Did they do the requisite homework and familiarize themselves with the relevant scientific evidence? Did they reach this conclusion on the basis of a technical competence in the evaluation of scientific theories? I must admit that I have deep doubts concerning these scenarios.

My own inclination is to focus instead on the strong influence that parents, teachers, and preachers have had on the beliefs that students bring to their experience at CCCU institutions. In fact, I need look no further than my own personal experience to gain a sense of the powerful influence of the "received view," the set of beliefs that we inherited from our family, our church and, in my own case, attendance at a Christian day school for twelve years before setting foot on the campus of a Christian college. Years of immersion in a consistently religious environment have inevitable consequences. There is no way to avoid them. Recall the words of the CCCU student response cited by Chesnes:

> It is not that I am closed minded to the subject [evolution], but growing up
> in a Christian home and environment, going to church, youth group and a
> Christian school, it has literally been preached and drilled into my head that
> evolution is a crazy impossible notion. . . . [B]ecause of the way I have been
> raised, my faith plays a huge part in why I don't believe evolution.

A "huge part"? Indubitably. And I would not be at all surprised to find that, in this case, "huge" constituted something in the vicinity of 100 percent.

Now, is there anything odd or out of place about this state of affairs? No, I think not. Inheriting beliefs about all manner of things—not just religious beliefs, but beliefs about anything imaginable—is as normal and predictable as anything can be. Knowing of this familiar cognitive effect, Christians take the education of their children seriously in both home and church. And many of us are familiar with Christian communities that go the extra mile and invest huge amounts of money and effort to set up systems of Christian day schools to make sure that their children inherit the approved belief system.

Why do people do that? We could, of course, craft a purely religion-based answer in familiar scriptural language. Speaking about children, parents are urged to "bring them up in the training and instruction of the Lord" and to "Train a child in the way he should go, and when he is old he will not turn from it" (excerpted from Ephesians 6:4 and Proverbs 22:6, NIV).

But the phenomenon of conditioning children to hold certain communally held beliefs is not at all unique to the Christian faith. It is not even unique to religion in general. It is the standard practice of almost any community. It is fundamental to the dynamics of human group behavior; it is an integral part of being a member of a family, a clan, a social coalition, a tribe. And social coalitions—tribes—built on the foundation of communally held *religious* beliefs appear to be exceptionally strong and to have an overwhelming impact on human belief and behavior. Watch the evening news on television or read the daily newspaper and note how many of the major events of the day are rooted in the actions and interactions—sometimes commendably compassionate, sometimes deplorably abusive and destructive—of persons who are acting out their deep sense of identity with one of the world's historic religions.

It is, consequently, inevitable that students arrive on campus with a set of inherited beliefs, including beliefs that are religiously significant. In my judgment, it is clear from the Joeckel/Chesnes survey that the majority of CCCU students come with the inherited belief that the concept of evolution is incompatible with their commitment to Christianity. Whether that stance is packaged with the belief (a) that Christianity necessarily entails the concept of special creation or (b) that the concept of evolution necessarily rules out the idea that the universe is God's creation, the second pillar of antievolution—the belief that Christianity and evolution are incompatible—is an issue that CCCU faculty members need to place on the table for open examination by persons who are qualified to deal with it.

Is Intelligent Design a Valid Scientific Alternative to Evolution?

Antievolution sentiments come in a variety of flavors. Several decades ago, the chief critics of the evolutionary paradigm were the proponents of young-earth special creationism. One of their goals was to get a perspective called "Creation-Science"—a package of purported empirical evidences that the age of the universe was in the ballpark of six-thousand to ten-thousand years and that the formation of certain species required supernatural acts of special creation—into the public school science classroom.

That strategy ended in disaster, of course. It was obvious to knowledgeable observers that Creation-Science was little more than a ruse, a primitive ploy for slipping religious dogma into the science classroom thinly disguised as a scientific theory. Not only did it fail the test as credible science, but it also gave religion a black eye for its mischievous use of dubious tactics.

But recently there has appeared a new movement (ID) that calls for the inclusion of a concept that its proponents have named "Intelligent Design Theory" as an alternative to evolution in the science classroom. From the Joeckel/Chesnes survey it appears that a majority of CCCU students and faculty consider ID to be both acceptable to Christianity and a valid alternative to the theory of evolution (FSQ 52, SSQ 40). With admirable candor, however, 18.4 percent of the students and 3.2 percent of the faculty admitted that they did not know what ID is (FSQ 52). Having engaged this movement's literature and leadership for nearly two decades, and having discussed its tenets and its claims with audiences at numerous CCCU institutions, I strongly suspect that the actual percentages are much higher than those reported in the survey. In my judgment, there is still a great deal of misunderstanding with regard to what constitutes the actual tenets of ID and whether or not ID theorists have actually demonstrated anything of scientific merit. This is not the place for a full-scale critique of the ID program, but since the survey did make reference to it, let us examine its fundamentals.

Stated as succinctly as possible, I see the main tenets of ID theory to be these:

1. The universe fails to possess the requisite natural formational capabilities to make possible the evolution of all biotic structures and life-forms by the exercise of its natural capabilities (a belief held in common with special creationism).

2. This failure is empirically detectable. Certain biotic structures are demonstrably too "complex" to have formed naturally.

3. Consequently, it must be the case that these biotic structures were assembled for the first time (complete with the necessary genetic information to ensure their propagation in future generations) in a non-natural manner by some unknown, unembodied Agent—called the "Intelligent Designer"—that possesses both the ability and the desire to exercise form-imposing power over the natural world.

My evaluation of the ID hypothesis, as set forth in the above tenets and in numerous publications by ID proponents, has led me to a conclusion essentially the same as expressed by Chesnes in the previous chapter. The first of these tenets is nothing more than an *ad hoc* presumption, one that could be confirmed only if we had a *complete* knowledge of the universe, which we do not have. The second is simply false. To say that a biotic structure is too "complex"—in the specific and unconventional manner that ID proponents define and use the term "complex"—requires the determination of a numerical probability value that is flatly impossible to compute. That leaves the third tenet—a postulate built on the presumption that the first two are valid—without any support.[4]

In my judgment, the most that ID proponents can truthfully claim is something like this: If science cannot at this time offer a complete and detailed step-by-step explanation for how biotic structure X (the bacterial flagellum is ID's favorite example) came to be assembled solely by known natural causes, then it is *logically permissible* to posit that the assembling of X required one or more episodes of non-natural, form-imposing action by an agent we choose to call the "Intelligent Designer."

That may be a true statement, but it is neither a new discovery nor a scientific advance. A proposition may be both *logically permissible* and *of no explanatory value*. As some playful critics have pointed out, exactly the same logic as employed by ID allows one to posit that X was assembled by an agent called the "Flying Spaghetti Monster."

But the name "Intelligent Designer" (a name undoubtedly chosen for its religious attractiveness) deserves further attention. Taken at face value, it suggests that this agent's primary action is to *design* something, where, in common parlance, to *design* something is an act of the mind—the act of intentionally planning something for the accomplishment of a purpose. But nearly all of the evidential argumentation by proponents of ID is concerned, not with mental action, but with a hand-like action of *assembling* something

---

4 A brief version of my evaluation of some features of the ID rhetoric can be found as a chapter in Richard F. Carlson, editor, *Science and Christianity: Four Views* (Downers Grove, Ill.: InterVarsity Press, 2000), 188-194. For a much more detailed evaluation, see Howard J. Van Till, "Are Bacterial Flagella Intelligently Designed? Reflections on the Rhetoric of the Modern ID Movement," *Science and Christian Belief* 15 (2003): 117-140.

that (according to ID rhetoric) could not have come to be assembled by natural processes alone. So, as puzzling as it may seem, Intelligent Design theory is not about *design* at all. It is about how some biotic structures may have gotten *assembled*—perhaps by the hidden hand-like action of an unidentified, unembodied agent with power over the natural world. That being the case, perhaps the Intelligent Designer should be re-named the "Surreptitious Assembler."

CCCU faculty members, especially those teaching one of the natural sciences, need to be prepared to guide their students in the evaluation of ID claims. Yes, the rhetoric may be religiously attractive so that it resonates with inherited beliefs, but the ID movement has so far produced nothing of scientific relevance regarding the credibility or empirical warrant of evolution as it is understood within the scientific community.

Some Positive Goals for CCCU Science Faculty

What can CCCU science faculty do to help students come to (1) a well-informed point of view regarding the scientific concept of evolution and (2) a well-reasoned position regarding the relationship of evolution and Christianity? In harmony with the sentiments expressed by Chesnes in the previous chapter, I would list the following:

- Distinguish between (a) the historic Christian concept of a Creator as the *giver of being* to a creation and (b) the special creationist idea that the primary action of a Creator is to *impose new forms* on the raw materials of a creation that is not equipped to actualize these forms by the use of its God-given formational capabilities.[5]
- Distinguish the scientific concept of evolution from various anti-theistic metaphysical commitments preached by some vocal, self-appointed spokespersons for the evolutionary paradigm.
- Inform students that the concept of evolution is not a "crazy impossible notion" but a carefully crafted scientific paradigm that enjoys a vast and diverse array of empirical support.
- Inform students of the manner in which several Christians have come to rest comfortably with the idea that Christianity and evolution (as each is understood by these persons) are compatible.

This list may seem rather straightforward and obvious, but if students come to a CCCU institution with a strong inherited belief in some form of special creationism, then CCCU faculty members can expect to encounter substantial resistance to their efforts to open students' minds to the option of seeing evolution as compatible with Christianity. Even if the students do not resist, their parents and other influential supporters of the college/university may nonetheless offer vocal criticism or threaten to withhold support. And

---

5   It is common in contemporary Christian circles to assume that the concept of special creation is rooted in Scripture. But science historian (and Evangelical Christian) Richard P. Aulie has argued that this concept is more closely related to the ideas of Plato and Aristotle, especially their notion of the fixity of species. For the development of this argument, see Richard P. Aulie, "The Doctrine of Special Creation," *American Biology Teacher* 34 (1972): 11-23.

if these persons are members of a board of trustees, the pressures may be exceedingly difficult to bear. In extreme cases, careers may be put on the chopping block.

Given that situation, some college/university supporters might advise faculty members to be pragmatic and just avoid the whole topic. But, as Chesnes stated clearly, "Not to include evolution in the biology curriculum is to commit academic fraud." That stance resonates with the strategy adopted by a friend who teaches biology at a CCCU college. When confronted with the suggestion that he should avoid some controversial topic he responds with an animated and forceful, "But we're a university!"

Right, and what does it mean to say so? It means that our first responsibility is to educate, to "lead out," to lead students out of sheltered environments and into new intellectual territories by promoting good questions and showing, by example, how honest answers can be constructed. That being the case, then a CCCU institution should never allow itself to be reduced by external pressure to an indoctrination center for the preservation of unexamined dogma. How can an inherited belief be respected if it cannot even be examined? How can a heritage be honored if it is treated as if it were too fragile to survive critical evaluation?

But Is Compatibility Our Final Answer?

So far in this chapter I have maintained a positive attitude toward Chesnes' goal of countering the antievolution bias that the majority of CCCU students inherited from their home environments. And since the belief that Christianity and evolution are not compatible is the "second pillar" of that negative attitude, I have great sympathy for the strategy of promoting the idea that Christianity and evolution are not incompatible, but complementary. That is, in fact, the way that I approached the issue most of my career. In lighter moments I call it the "Can we all just get along here?" approach.

But is "compatible and complementary" the final answer to the question, What is the relationship of Christianity and the evolutionary paradigm? At the risk of making some members of the CCCU community uneasy, I am going to close this brief chapter with a few comments regarding what I believe will become the next, and very challenging, episode in the ongoing interaction of science and religion—comments dealing with the application of scientific methodology to an examination of the phenomenon of religious belief itself. That is why I quoted a brief excerpt from the work of cognitive scientist Justin L. Barrett at the beginning of this chapter.

Framing a Tough Question

I shall begin with a reminder of what evolution entails. If evolutionary biologists are correct—and I certainly believe that they are on this matter—then the bodies that we inherited from ancestors of long ago are bodies that are loaded with diverse traits that gave those ancestors the ability to survive in the challenging environments of their distant past.

Yes, that is obvious enough, but it is not only our *bodies* that evolved. Our *brains* are equally the product of our evolutionary development. The brains we inherited from ancestors of long ago—the brains that support and shape all of our mental processes, including the cognitive processes that generate our beliefs—also have structures and capabilities that demonstrated *survival value* in the face of challenges met in the distant past. What our brains are able and prone to do today is what they needed to do in order to survive yesterday.

But that raises a substantive challenge: The evolved human brain is made of the same "dust" as the evolved body. The human brain, consequently, like the human body, is optimized for *survival*—for the reproductive success of our species. Having survived, however, we humans now want something more, something unique to the cognitive bent of our species; we want knowledge. We want to grasp *truth*. We want to know true things about our world, about ourselves, about the ultimate mystery of our existence. And, since our inherited worldviews focus a great deal of attention on these profound matters, this means that we want to know whether or not our inherited beliefs are *warranted* (supported by substantive evidence and sound reasoning).

How can we learn about these deep matters? By using our mental capacities, I presume. But here is the tough question that we now face: How can we be sure that a brain tuned by evolution for survival will be able to tell the difference between *comforting illusions* and *what is actually true*?

Where to Look for an Answer

My training in physics provides me with a useful strategy for exploring certain restricted kinds of questions, but it is clear that I must look to other disciplines for information and theorizing that are relevant to the difficult question just posed. The people I have found most helpful in satisfying my curiosity on these matters are researchers working in a relatively new field called the *cognitive science of religion*.[6]

Cognitive science investigates the mental processes by which we come to know or believe something about the world. The cognitive science of religion applies its tools for investigation and theorizing to the phenomenon of religious beliefs and practices. Its goal is not to determine whether any particular religious belief is true or false, but only to find out how humans arrive at religious beliefs and why people participate in religious practices.

---

6 Persons working in this area of cognitive science include Justin L. Barrett, Pascal Boyer, Todd Tremlin, Scott Atran, Ilkka Pysiäinen, E. Thomas Lawson, Harvey Whitehouse, D. Jason Slone, and many others. I would recommend that persons who wish to be introduced to this area of investigation by authors favorably inclined toward religion begin with Justin L. Barrett, *Why Would Anyone Believe in God?* (Lanham, Md.: AltaMira Press, 2004), perhaps followed with Todd Tremlin, *Minds and Gods: The Cognitive Foundations of Religion* (New York: Oxford University Press, 2006) or Jeffrey Schloss and Michael Murray, editors, *The Believing Primate: Scientific, Philosophical, and Theological Reflections on the Origin of Religion* (New York: Oxford University Press, 2008). For a very different religious perspective, see Pascal Boyer, *Religion Explained: The Evolutionary Origins of Religious Thought* (New York: Basic Books, 2001).

The Naturalness of Religion Thesis

One thing that cognitive science researchers have learned is that having religious beliefs is a nearly universal human phenomenon—almost every human being holds some sort of religious beliefs. Call this the *naturalness of religion* thesis. The particular beliefs vary greatly from person to person, or from tribe to tribe, but the general phenomenon of having religious beliefs is as common and natural as breathing. The following are examples of this line of thought as expressed by two scholars in the cognitive science of religion (both of whom happen to be graduates of a CCCU institution). "My point . . . is fairly simple: widespread belief in God arises from the operation of natural processes of the human mind in ordinary human environments. Belief in God does not amount to anything strange or peculiar; on the contrary, such belief is nearly inevitable."[7] "Explaining why people believe in gods requires first explaining the way people think. Describing the nature and variety of god concepts and their place in religious systems requires first describing the structure and function of the brain. Understanding the origin and persistence of [mental images of] supernatural beings requires first understanding the evolved human mind."[8] Cognitive science sees the natural human proclivity for religious belief as the byproduct of a particular brain function that was, and continues to be, essential to our survival—the detection of *agents* (where "agents" are beings that have intentions and the ability to carry them out).

To illustrate the importance of having an agent-detection system, suppose you were walking alone in a remote and unfamiliar wilderness location. As you walk through a wooded region, you hear the snap of a twig or a small branch. The sound seems to be coming from a location behind you. Startled, your intuitive response is to suspect the presence of an agent and to initiate appropriate action—quickly. After all, that snapping sound might signal the approach of a hungry predator.

Overreaction turns out to be good for survival. Even if further and more leisurely reflective analysis reveals that the sound you heard was caused by a harmless falling branch, no problem. Under-reaction, however, could be lethal. Failure to detect a prowling tiger could mean "you're lunch." Better to be safe than sorry.

So, the normal human brain has been equipped by evolution with a mental module that Justin Barrett calls a Hypersensitive Agency Detection Device—HADD (where "hypersensitive" means "prone to overreact"). HADD's job is to alert us to the possible presence of agents whose actions may affect us, either positively or negatively.

Now, suppose that a normal human mind, equipped with HADD, formulates a profound question such as, Why is there a universe? HADD's contribution is to posit a responsible agent—*maybe our universe is here by the intentional action of some agent.* Think of the universe as an effect, and of some intentionally acting agent as its cause. Perhaps, but the familiar cast of conventional agents to whom we might appeal—embodied

---

7 Barrett, *Why Would Anyone Believe in God?*, 122.

8 Tremlin, 6.

agents like tigers or other humans—doesn't seem up to the task of bringing universes into existence.

Okay, then why not posit (as the normal human brain seems inclined to do) the existence of a more capable agent, one equipped with whatever additional qualities or powers are needed—say, an unembodied supernatural, person-like agent, a Spirit, a Creator, "God"? And while we are at it, why not propose that this personal God-Agent is also in charge of establishing universal moral principles and of holding humans accountable for their behavior?

If cognitive science researchers are correct, that is the way the human mind works. We are naturally prone to posit the existence of agents whose intentional and purposeful actions provide attractive explanations for things that would otherwise be unexplainable. And the rest, most cognitive scientists say, is history—a fascinating history of humanly crafted myths that vary from tribe to tribe and from century to century, a rich history of imaginative narratives that function as "storied theologies" in which "God" is assigned the role of a superhuman or supernatural agent whose intentional actions account for some of the most profound features of the human experience. These are the storied theologies that form the core of our inherited system of religious beliefs.

But Are These Inherited Beliefs Justified?

So, cognitive science concludes that the phenomenon of holding some set of religious beliefs is as natural as natural can be. But the naturalness of religious belief in general tells us nothing about the *truth or falsehood* of any particular religious belief. So, we are back to the question posed earlier: How can we be sure that a brain tuned by evolution for survival will be able to tell the difference between comforting illusions and enduring truths? Or, to state it differently: How well can *evolved minds* be expected to evaluate the truth-content of *inherited beliefs*?[9]

These are not easy questions to deal with. Neither are they attractive questions that will be welcomed by anyone who prefers to leave inherited beliefs unexamined, thereby avoiding both the discomforts of controversy and the bumps and bruises of tribal denunciation or institutional censure. Others would argue that these questions ought to be sidelined, not because they are difficult or disturbing, but because they miss the central point of religion—it is not about what we *know* to be certain; it is about how we *live* to be compassionate. Still others, speaking as disinterested observers, might agree that corporate religion is not an effective institution for crafting enduring truths; on the contrary, they would argue, it is an adaptive social coalition whose principal survival benefit in the modern environment is the emotional security gained by strong group identity. And if these observers are correct, should not questions regarding the warrant for specific inherited beliefs be welcomed in the pursuit of truth?

---

9   For a friendly exchange on questions of this sort, see Justin L. Barrett, "Is the Spell Really Broken? Bio-psychological Explanations of Religion and Theistic Belief," *Theology and Science* 5 (2007): 57-72, followed by Howard J. Van Till, "How Firm a Foundation? A Response to Justin L. Barrett's 'Is the Spell Really Broken?'" *Theology and Science* 6 (2008): 341-349.

Whether welcomed or not, however, questions about the justification of inherited religious beliefs and the mental capacities of the evolved human mind will persist. They are important questions and CCCU institutions will need to deal with them forthrightly and courageously. Many interesting answers have yet to be framed and tested. My best wishes to all who stand ready and willing to contribute.

CHAPTER 21

EVOLUTION AND CHRISTIAN FAITH

RICHARD G. COLLING

The shouting all around us makes it hard to hear. But the voice of God is different than other sounds. It can be heard over the din that drowns out all else. Even when it is not shouting. Even if it is just a whisper. Whether revealed through scripture or coded in our DNA, the softest whisper still inspires and transforms over chaos and confusion . . . when it is speaking the truth. —**Richard Colling**

Michael (not his real name) looked across my office desk, discouraged and visibly shaken. As if I were his last spiritual lifeline, his eyes, filled with confusion, pleaded with me to reassure him that what he was learning in his biology classes about evolution was not really true.

Michael was a sophomore biology student. He came to us—as many students from the mid-western United States—from a strong Christian-fundamentalist family. All of his life he was told that evolution was a "lie of Satan," starkly incompatible with Scripture and the Christian faith. The passionate anti-evolution teachers during Michael's formative years were the people he loved and trusted most: his parents and pastors. And their vocal confidence and insistent denial of evolution left no doubt that they regarded evolution as a litmus-test issue of Christian orthodoxy. One was either in or out—no middle ground whatsoever.

My heart ached as he related his story. Both his parents and pastors had recently informed him that if he accepted evolution he could neither be a Christian nor a part of the church fellowship. Emotionally and spiritually cut off, he broke into a soft sob as the agonizing spiritual pain and rejection overcame him.

Michael was an inquisitive and bright college student. He simply could not comprehend why acceptance within his faith community required him to check his God-given intellect at the door of the church. As a Christian biology faculty member for many years, I had seen this troubling scenario play out many times before in the lives of other students. Michael was at a crisis point. He was almost persuaded to unbelief, but not by science or evolution. Rather it was the insistent scientifically uninformed teaching and judgmental spirit of his religious mentors precipitating his faith crisis.

We talked for a long while that afternoon and several times during the semester. I prayed with him, each time encouraging him to hold fast to his faith—explaining that many Christians, including myself, saw no conflict with evolution and the Christian faith. Nevertheless, at the end of the term, Michael transferred to a nearby state university. The last I inquired, he had apparently abandoned the Christian faith altogether.

Unfortunately, Michael's harrowing experience with these apparently well-intentioned, but misguided Christians is far too common, prompting many to regard Christianity as a non-viable option.

Is all Truth God's Truth?

According to the Joeckel/Chesnes survey, 66.5 percent of CCCU students and 35 percent of CCCU faculty share the view of Michael's religious mentors that evolution is incompatible with the Christian faith (FSQ 51 and SSQ 39). This finding should concern all believers because the either/or proposition carries with it an inherent hazard seemingly unrecognized by its anti-evolution proponents.

Of course, if evolution truly is a figment of biologists' imaginations, this either/or proposition functions just fine: God's supernatural role, along with the Christian faith, is safe from the perceived lethal talons of science. But what if evolution is real? Indeed, the Human Genome Project, completed in 2003, along with genetic analysis of the DNA of numerous other species has changed everything in this regard. More on this later.

So the relevant questions appear rather straightforward. Is the anti-evolution cohort of the Christian community right: Is evolution really Satan's lie? Does evolution truly preclude belief in God and exhibit incompatibility with the Christian faith? Significantly, who framed the question of God and science in this either/or manner anyway? And finally, why does it matter? It seems to me that, for a Christian, addressing these questions matters for at least three reasons:

Truth: As a matter of basic scriptural principle, to the best of one's ability, Christians are obligated to speak the transparent truth. Being scientifically uninformed is categorically no excuse for blindly or intentionally perpetuating false information. Such conduct cannot possibly honor God. It is far better to simply acknowledge those things one does not know than to claim a self-anointed religious or scriptural authority paradigm to justify speaking—or tolerating—falsehood.

Credibility: One of my biology faculty colleagues, Aggie Posthumus, aptly notes that, "What you allow, you teach." In this context, when a vocal Christian minority requires that the facts of biology be disregarded, yet the larger Christian community fails to immediately confront and assertively disown such a position, it paints all Christians as out of touch with reality. As a consequence, the spiritual witness of Christians in general is eroded and the credibility of Christians to engage in *any* issue is called into question. After all, if Christians refuse to acknowledge obvious physical/biological realities, why should anyone trust them to render reasonable analyses on spiritual or other issues? This incremental under-the-radar trend toward cultural irrelevance should be profoundly troubling to all Christians. Even as I write this chapter, for the first time in American history, it appears that Christian Protestants will soon no longer be represented on the United States Supreme Court. Coincidence or case in point?

Love and Compassion: As Michael's experience illustrates, believers *and unbelievers* who understand and accept evolution find it hard to comprehend the suspicion and hostility directed toward them by Christians who portray them as enemies of the faith. Such unfair and harsh judgment—especially when done in the name of God—does not honor God or draw people to the Christian faith. Instead, it alienates them. Scripture tells us that Christians should be known for their love and compassion, and for their openness to new revelation, inspiration, and learning. Indeed, Jesus modeled these concepts for us to emulate. In this light, how can the judgmental spirit directed toward those who accept evolution possibly be justified by those who call themselves followers of Christ?

Danger and Opportunity

Herein, then, lies perhaps one of the greatest challenges for the Christian community— defining a pivotal and crucial point in the modern history of the Christian faith. For if evolution is real, describing a continuum of life over many millions of years, and if Christians truly believe the Bible, uniformly embracing the biblical maxims that God is the creator and all truth is God's truth, *the only logical and viable faith-preserving position for Christians is that evolution must be seen as part of God's wondrous creative plan.*

This understanding raises a difficult question that many in the Christian community may not be ready to hear: By their continued adamant denial of well-established evolutionary processes and the continued framing of evolution in an either/or format in opposition to God, are literalist Christians unintentionally fortifying the atheist's case against God?

In light of the physical reality of evolution, the self-defeating and destructive theological consequences of a literalist "incompatibility" position are indeed profound: *Denial of evolution ultimately reduces to denial of God and his almighty creative acts.*

Thus, in an unfortunate and evidently unforeseen twist of irony, the literalist anti-evolution Christians, while claiming to speak *for* God, actually find themselves speaking *against* belief in God. Marching hand-in-hand with outspoken atheistic scientists like Richard Dawkins, they proclaim the exact same scientifically unfounded message that evolution and belief in God are incompatible. In doing so, anti-evolution Christians have unwittingly adopted and vocally embraced an atheistic position as a fundamental tenet of the faith—utterly failing to recognize that this either/or proposition virtually guarantees that as scientific understanding regarding evolution continues to advance,

God's role as creator and sustainer of life is slowly but surely erased. Nothing like painting oneself into a corner! Everyone knows that in a courtroom setting, an attorney who successfully frames the opening arguments will eventually win the case. I have never understood why Christians so naively and eagerly agreed to play by the atheist's rules regarding evolution. Surely we can do better!

Nevertheless, for better or worse, here we find ourselves at the dawn of the twenty-first century in a society driven by advances and understanding in science and technology. The human genome—the letter-by-letter codebook of human life—simultaneously reveals both magnificent and messy secrets of our evolutionary past at unimaginable levels of precision. These revelations are real and concrete physical realities: indisputable facts. They can no longer be denied or ignored by Christians without risking a slow, but certain cultural irrelevance.

Therefore, if Christians truly believe that the Christian faith has something of priceless and eternal value to offer the people of the world, it seems crucial that these scientific realities be courageously addressed with honest and open resolve. Indeed, I would think that Christian leaders would be eager to begin.

A Potential Leadership Role for CCCU Member Institutions

Thomas Chesnes, in the first essay of this section, "Deconstructing the Second Pillar of Anti-evolutionism in Christian Higher Education," quotes Arthur Holmes regarding evolution, "The Christian college will not settle for a militant polemic against secular learning and science and culture, as if there were a great gulf fixed between the secular and the sacred. All truth is God's truth, no matter where it is found, and we can thank him for it all." Chesnes correctly points out that this wonderful ideal is not always manifested at all CCCU member institutions—to the shame of Christian-college administrators who fail to provide a "safe" environment for discussion of these controversial issues. Nevertheless, Holmes's statement is an honorable standard to which Christian colleges must aspire. Biology and the Bible need never be at war, and the risk of losing the next generation is becoming too great to ignore.

Profound confusion and misinformation seemingly overwhelm efforts to achieve a positive faith-affirming détente between evolution and the Christian faith. For this reason, the journey will require courageous and steadfast leadership. But positive transformational change *is* attainable if education is afforded a high priority. In this context, CCCU institutions can indeed play a leading role by redefining terms, exposing flawed atheistic assumptions, promoting knowledge and understanding, dispelling fear, and most importantly, articulating a reasoned theological perspective of evolution that establishes a permanent place for God and the Christian faith in the intellectual discussions of the culture. Hand in hand, I believe Christian leaders and CCCU member institutions *can* effectively—and redemptively—accomplish this peace mission. In doing so, they will render an invaluable service to God and the Christian faith.

A Vision for the Road Ahead

Having spent the first pages of this essay describing the hazards and liabilities inherent in the foundational underpinnings of the "Second Pillar of Anti-evolutionism in Christian Higher Education" addressed in the Joeckel/Chesnes survey of Christian Colleges, I would like to devote the remainder of this essay to providing some foundational background information about science and evolution, and also to offer insights and perspectives that could help CCCU member institutions regarding positive future actions.

Dynamics and Challenges of Teaching Evolution —Precise Definitions, Emotions, and Scientific Facts

A functionally viable framework for reconciling evolution with the Christian faith must start with a scientifically accurate and philosophically appropriate understanding of evolution itself. But learning is not completely a function of the cognitive/analytical parts of the brain: Language and emotions play important roles! And when it comes to evolution, emotional fervor runs high. Therefore, if we legitimately claim the badge of bona fide Christian educators, we must *unapologetically* speak the truth of science, but we must also do so with a sensitive, loving, and accepting spirit.

When my book, *Random Designer*, was published,[1] a National Public Radio interviewer asked an intriguing question: "What is the greatest challenge you experience in teaching evolution at a Christian college?" I told her that the greatest challenge had nothing to do with teaching evolution per se: Evolution is what it is. Rather, my greatest challenge was to sensitively listen to and gauge my students' backgrounds so that I could effectively reassure them that new understandings in science need never threaten their faith.

In a large and diverse classroom of general-education students, this is no small undertaking. For students coming from very conservative Christian backgrounds where evolution is routinely pronounced as evil, the challenge is to speak the truth about evolution while simultaneously encouraging and affirming them in their faith. For non-believers, the task is different, but equally important: to encourage them to keep an open mind, perhaps even to give this God thing a second look. When successful in striking just the right balance—speaking the truth in love while also recognizing and affirming all individuals where they are in their spiritual and intellectual journey—something magical happens. The preconditioned division and suspicion they brought to the classroom begin to melt away, replaced by understanding and acceptance.

Coming to Terms with Terms

Evolution is easily one of the most misunderstood scientific concepts in the general culture, a fact that greatly amplifies the confusion and angst regarding its compatibility with the Christian faith. The unfortunate reality is that words like randomness, evolution, and

---

1 Richard Colling, *Random Designer: Created from Chaos to Connect with the Creator* (Bourbonnias, Ill.: Browning Press, 2004).

mutation positively drip with ambiguity—frequently poorly defined and easily misunderstood. Therefore, it is essential that these terms be precisely defined and understood by all parties.

A few years ago, I met with some clergy leaders to describe my book and explain my views on evolution. During the course of the inquisition, I was asked if evolution was true. My response was, "Yes, yes, no, and maybe—it depends on how one defines evolution." I expanded on the idea.

- If evolution is used in the generic sense such as, "The university has evolved over the years," the answer is "yes."
- If evolution is used strictly to describe the biological/genetic mechanisms by which all life is related, the answer is also an unambiguous "yes."
- If evolution is defined in the context of secular atheism (and as we have seen, literalist anti-evolution Christians) that insists that evolution precludes the existence of God and is incompatible with Christian faith, the answer is an emphatic "no."
- Finally, if evolution is defined as the means by which the first living cells (known to have inhabited the Earth several billions of years ago) were created, the answer is a definite "maybe." The truth is that while evolution well explains biological development and speciation events, the mechanism(s) responsible for the appearance of the first life forms is still a mystery.

I had hoped that these nuanced, yet important distinctions would be helpful to the clergy leaders. Unfortunately, the judgmental, anti-evolution, literalist mindset permeated the room, and having already reached their conclusions regarding evolution and those who teach it, I honestly do not think they were even listening.

Overcoming Emotional Obstacles to Learning about Evolution

Another significant obstacle to understanding evolution and mapping a path to peace is that, in addition to being poorly defined, words such as mutation and evolution often carry enormous negative emotional baggage. When using such emotionally charged words, the consequences for relationships can be disastrous as well-meaning, good people talk right past one another and misunderstanding, confusion, and agitation escalate. Emotions are powerful because they typically (at least initially, until we have counted to ten!) overwhelm rationality. After all, I doubt you would take it kindly if someone called you a mutant! Thus, it is important to recognize that using seemingly counter-intuitive, emotionally laden concepts like random and evolution in our references to God represents a formidable emotional challenge for many, despite the fact that when properly understood, these concepts are indeed inherently compatible with one another.

What Is Evolution Anyway? Our Perspective Determines Our Destiny

A few years ago, I presented two papers at the Wesleyan Theological Society science/religion conference at Duke University. During the discussion period, a respected university theologian made what was to me a most startling and puzzling pronouncement. He said, in essence, that evolution dictated death, dying, and suffering, and that it must be considered in this context when discussing its theological implications. The unmistakable inference was that this person believed evolution was something bad. I have since learned that this view is also widely held by many Christian pastors and religious leaders.

It was an epiphany, one of those special moments when a complex problem is comprehended in a completely new way. I suddenly realized that if just one small (but hugely significant!) scientific misconception could be corrected, an entirely new and much more productive path forward might be possible.

So let's be perfectly clear: Does evolution dictate death and suffering? Emphatically no! Simply put, this idea is just completely wrong. In fact, it is precisely the opposite: Evolution functions proactively—and redemptively—to preserve life and health, not to detract from or destroy it!

The genetics driving this redemptive feature of evolution are a bit beyond the scope of this essay, but perhaps an analogy will suffice for the present. One of my sons is a police patrol officer. In preparation for duty, each day he dons his bullet-proof vest. Police statistics say that it is highly unlikely that the vest will actually ever be needed, even over his entire career in law-enforcement. However, I must confess that I am very glad that he conscientiously takes this protective precaution—just in case! Evolution functions in a similar manner, proactively (and continuously) duplicating, reorganizing, and modifying genes in our DNA. These new versions of genes can then serve as life-saving backups when essential functional genes are occasionally damaged or destroyed. In this way, they provide critical protection and resilience for life just as the bullet-proof vest—just in case!

The accuracy or inaccuracy of our perspective determines our destiny. If the underlying assumptions and understandings of evolution are plainly wrong, productive outcomes are unlikely. Thus if the Christian community truly desires to find compatibility between evolution and the Christian faith, a scientifically sound understanding of evolution is a necessary pre-requisite. Perhaps this more accurate redemptive perspective regarding evolution can be useful in this regard.

The Genetic Evidence Demonstrating Evolution

Until the late 1990s much of the evidence of evolution came from rare and sometimes confusing fossil records embedded in different geological strata dispersed all over the world. However, recent advances in molecular biology—especially in the field of genetics—have changed everything. These advances culminated in 2003 with the completion of the Human Genome Project, an international endeavor spearheaded by Francis Collins, a Christian, author of *The Language of God*, and co-founder of the Biologos Foundation, an organization committed to seeking harmony between science and faith.

The human genome is a 3.1 billion-letter linear digital DNA directory of humanity. This directory is unlocking the secrets of humanity's present and past genetic connections with all other life at unimaginable levels of detail and precision. This is not your mother or father's gap-laden fossil record; rather, it is an exquisitely detailed map of our entire evolutionary history! The actual genetic concepts and corresponding data are exceedingly complex, yet also very intelligible to the trained molecular-geneticist. I will summarize several of the distinctive categories.

Analysis of Chromosome Rearrangements

When individual chromosomes in different species are compared, it becomes apparent that some species share common breakage and fusion patterns. Breaks and fusions in the chromosomes are not mysteries, but well-understood genetic events that occur, albeit relatively rarely, in all advanced life forms. Like assembling a jigsaw puzzle in which every piece fits "just right," defining the locations of common breakages or fusions in different species allows geneticists to decipher the chronological relationships between these species. Numerous cases have been documented, but a most noteworthy example is human chromosome two which is the unmistakable fusion product of two ape chromosomes[2]. Since chromosomes are inherited only through the parental line, this physical reality unequivocally demonstrates common ancestry between humans and the ape line.

Gene Duplications—New Gene Assemblies

Gene duplications within DNA occur with relatively high frequency. Typically the resulting spare copies of genes are simply redundant, but occasionally they, either alone or in combination with other genes, give rise to new biological functions. An interesting example is color vision in primates in which the duplication of the opsin gene bestows color vision to the ape line, including humans[3]. Once again, since such genetic traits are passed only from parents to offspring, by identifying the precise location and inheritance of such changes in human DNA compared to DNA from related species, geneticists are able to firmly establish chronological evolutionary relationships.

Pseudogenes

Duplicated genes occasionally experience very specific mutations that render them inactive. These inactivated genes are called pseudogenes and, once established, they are permanently retained as residual "baggage" within our DNA, inherited uniformly from parents to the offspring in each succeeding generation. Humans possess thousands of these mutated inactive genes. In addition, and highly relevant to this type of evolutionary

2 J. W. Ido, A. Baldini, D. C. Ward, S. T. Reeders, and R. A. Wells, "Origin of Human Chromosome: An Ancestral Telomere-Telomere Fusion," *Proceedings of the National Academy of Sciences USA*, 88.20 (1991): 9051-5. See also De Pontbriand, et. al., "Synteny Comparison between Apes and Human Using Fin-mapping of the Genome," *Genomics* 80 (2002): 395. Also David L. Wilcox, "Establishing Adam: Recent Evidences for a Late-Date Adam (AMH@100,000 BP)," *Perspectives on Science and Christian Belief*, 56 (2004): 49-53.

3 See K. S. Dulai, M. von Dornum, J. Mollon, , and D. Hunt, "The Evolution of Trichromatic Colour Vision by Opsin Gene Duplication in New World and Old World Primates," *Genome Research* 9 (1999): 629.

genetic analysis, each pseudogene typically exhibits a unique inactivating mutation that endows it with a precise one-of-a-kind "fingerprint" all its own—a sort of evidence within the evidence. The presence, in different species, of identical pseudogenes located at precisely the same location *and* bearing the exact same inactivating mutation (fingerprint) establishes a common evolutionary heritage between these species.[4]

HERVs and Parasitic Kin

Our DNA is being overrun by parasites. It's true! That is the bad news. The good news is that humanity is, but for individual rare (and tragic) exceptions, dealing with these genomic DNA parasites rather well. These virus-like pieces of DNA, numbering in the millions, never leave our cells and literally pepper our DNA. One group of parasites, the human endogenous retroviruses (HERV), appears to be kin to the HIV-AIDS virus. A key characteristic of these DNA parasites is their ability to conservatively replicate in our cells (that is, to make a copy of the parasitic DNA while leaving the original copy intact). The copied DNA piece is then free to randomly insert itself into a brand new location and once this new insertion event has occurred, the precise position in the DNA is permanently fixed. Both the original *and* new parasite DNA are then faithfully transmitted to succeeding generations. These distinctive features of random insertion and permanent fixation provide geneticists a powerful tool to explore evolutionary relationships between species. If two different species possess the same parasitic DNA piece located in the exact same position in their DNA, common ancestry is conclusively established. This field is still young, but already numerous examples have been described that demonstrate common evolutionary connections between apes and humans as well as other species of animals.[5]

These genetic concepts are complex, but it is important to note that complexity does not equate to uncertainty. The data described here are indisputable physical realities of God's creation—facts. Unfortunately, most of this genetic information is not widely known. In addition, in my experience, the receptivity index toward learning about such things among Christians is disappointingly low—even among leaders of Christian institutions of higher learning. For example, a Christian university theologian informed me—in no uncertain terms—that the genetic data described here which establishes our evolutionary heritage need not be taken seriously by Christians because the scientists doing the studies possessed "fallen" minds. Therefore, the conclusions the scientists reached need not, and could not, be taken seriously. He also made it abundantly clear

4   See Y. Gilad, O. Man, S. Paabo, and D. Lancet, "Human Specific Loss of Olfactory Receptor Genes," *Proceedings of the National Academy of Sciences USA* 100 (2003): 3324. See also A. Goldberg, et al., "Adaptive Evolution of Cytochrome Cosidase Subunit VIII in Anthropoid Apes," *Proceedings of the National Academy of Sciences USA* 100 (2003): 5873.

5   H. H Kazazian, "Mobile Elements: Drivers of Genome Evolution," *Science* 303 (2004): 1626. See also A. Salem, et. al., "Alu Elements and Hominid Phylogentics," *Proceedings of the National Academy of Sciences USA* 100 (2003):12787. See also J. W. Tomas, et. al., "Comparative Analysis of Multi-species Sequences from Targeted Genome Regions," *Nature* 424 (2003): 788. Finally, see L. Zhu, et. al., "Examination of Sequence Homology between Human Chromosome 20 and the Mouse Genome: Intense Conservation of Many Genomic Elements," *Human Genetics* 113 (2003): 60.

that my confidence in these things placed me outside acceptable Christian boundaries for a Christian university professor.

The medieval silence-the-messenger mentality is still alive and well among American Christians. Biology and religion faculty members at Christian institutions still come under pressure and/or attack if they publicly acknowledge evolution or point out the error and counterproductive consequences of the anti-evolution literalist's positions.

A Michigan pastor and long-time friend, Reverend Jerry Batterbee, related that the evangelical response of many of his Midwestern pastoral peers to evolution was, "We sure hope evolution isn't true, but if it is, let's make sure no one finds out about it." Aldous Huxley once said: "Facts do not cease to exist because they are ignored."[6] Surely Christian leaders can do better.

Prophets Without Honor—An Invitation

Family is everything. As Howard Van Till notes in the preceding chapter, "Inherited Beliefs and Evolved Brains: A CCCU Challenge," people predictably will do all in their power to safeguard their families (or tribe) from harm. Indeed, what father or mother, upon learning of a potential danger to the family, would not take immediate and decisive action to proactively warn the family members and institute whatever measures necessary to help them prepare and confront the danger looming ahead? It is the reasonable, responsible, and right thing to do.

As a microbiologist and Christian educator, I have had a front-row seat over the past three decades as the genetic data (God's data) unequivocally demonstrating the reality of evolution has become known. I recognized early on that continued denial of this growing body of scientific evidence by Christians was a recipe for cultural and spiritual irrelevance. Because I care for my Christian family, I attempted to gently warn the leaders—particularly in my own denomination—of the impending danger of the anti-evolution mindset. Believing that education and honest, open intellectual discussion of topics like evolution provided the best possible resolution, I wrote *Random Designer*, a book designed to promote compatibility between science and faith to Christians and also non-believers. In addition, I repeatedly offered to meet with pastors and church/university leaders, individually or in small groups, to update them on the latest scientific findings relating to evolution and to offer assistance in devising strategies to help them develop theological frameworks that would be faithful to the science *and* faithful to the faith. The responses I received were, "No, it is better to let sleeping dogs lie," and "Your message of compatibility between science and Christian faith is unwelcome in the churches." Unjustified personal and professional attacks on my scholarship and Christian character soon followed.

What you allow, you teach. When leaders of Christian academic institutions value and support the voices of scientific ignorance, fear, power, and money—voices that seek to squelch and intimidate the voices of truth regarding God's magnificent creation—they

6 A. Huxley, *Proper Studies* (London: Chatto and Windus, 1927).

not only betray God; they erode the grand mission of Christian higher education. In addition, they broadcast the unmistakable message to the rest of the world that Christians are insecure in their faith and lack credible answers to the secular atheistic voices of science and culture. Are they right about Christians? Time will tell.

It is time to put an end to the false and destructive idea that God must be limited to a seventeenth-century understanding of science, and also the atheistic canard that God must be somehow divorced from his created order. I believe Christian higher education—beginning with CCCU member institutions—offers the best avenue to successfully achieve this goal. However, courageous, committed, and knowledgeable leadership is needed from three key groups.

- *Courageous Christian Leaders.* University administrators and boards of trustees are the essential catalysts: No meaningful discussion or progress can occur until explicit permission is granted from these key people. They must view their job as standing resolutely for education, facts, and truth. They must openly encourage discussions between qualified Christian biologists and religious leaders with an unwavering commitment to find common ground and bring peace to the division and discord. They must also nurture safe intellectual environments where the science of evolution as well as relevant theological/religious questions can be freely discussed in the classroom and beyond. Anti-evolution literalists will most certainly object and likely even issue ultimatums. How should the leaders respond? It is one thing to be tolerant of different views, but when the position of vocal Christians is 1) at odds with established facts and truth, 2) denies God's creative genius, 3) embraces the fundamental (and flawed) argument of atheistic scientists *against* belief in God, and 4) unfairly and harshly judges all other Christian brethren as outside the boundaries of the faith, one has to ask, "Will the real Christian leaders please stand up?" Courage indeed!
- *Courageous, knowledgeable biology faculty*. Biologists are needed who understand the latest genetic data, are effective communicators of complex scientific concepts to people with limited scientific backgrounds, and are willing to endure personal attack and vilification by the anti-evolution crowd. Input from physical science faculty could also be valuable. These science educators would simply serve as resource people to bring/keep religious leaders and theologians up to speed on the latest scientific knowledge relating to evolution.
- *Courageous religion faculty* These individuals must be genuine scholars of Scripture, theology, and the Christian faith – committed to expanding and/or modifying traditional Christian theology in ways that promote compatibility with new scientific discoveries. To successfully accomplish this task, they must also possess a basic understanding of evolution and how life truly

works. Ultimately, these professionals are key to the success or failure of this overall peace mission. As a professional and sacred trust, I sincerely hope they will respond to the call.

Christian scholars involved in these discussions must be unconditionally protected from "administrative drift." Weak institutional leaders often talk a good game, giving the appearance of public support, but actions are another thing altogether. When the anti-evolution literalists wear them down with threats to restrict donations, to stop sending students to the university, or demand that faculty members be disciplined, restricted, or fired for teaching evolution, a different leader often emerges, and truth and integrity become casualties. While such conduct should never take place at Christian institutions, sadly, it does indeed occur. Appeasement of ignorance is a lazy form of leadership. It betrays the truth and erodes the Christian faith in subtle, yet insidious ways as onlookers realize that even in Christian circles money and personal-power politics trump truth, integrity, and genuine education.

If any of these three groups of people fail in their respective responsibilities, the entire message of compatibility between evolution and the Christian faith is likely doomed—at least in this generation. Yet failure is not an option. In light of the indisputable evidence establishing evolution's reality, if Christians persist in their claims that evolution is incompatible with the Christian faith, *it is they themselves who are pronouncing the verdict against God and, by extension, the Christian faith.* That is why it is crucial that Christian leaders rise to the occasion and articulate a more positive, faith-affirming resolution.

The challenge is not for the faint of heart. Jesus said a prophet is without honor in his home country. Christian leaders and faculty members with the courage to address the evolution issue honestly and openly will quickly come to understand Jesus' words on a very personal level. However, the next generation is looking for us to be salt and light—to be credible witnesses of the world as it is, as well as the God and faith that we claim. Given this biblical command, can we do any less?

In 2 Timothy 1:7 (NIV), the apostle Paul writes, "For God has not given us a spirit of fear, but of power, love and a sound mind." The truth is that a mature faith has nothing to fear from science. Evolution, properly defined and understood, should never be viewed as being at odds with the Christian faith. An unequivocal public affirmation of this truth from the Christian community—especially the Christian theological leadership—is long overdue. CCCU member institutions have a grand opportunity to play a transformational role in articulating a grander narrative of God. Therefore, I invite all CCCU member institutions to join the effort. Michael and thousands of others like him are depending on us.

Bibliography: Part Seven

Alters, Brian J. and Sandra M. Alters. *Defending Evolution: A Guide to the Creation/Evolution Controversy.* Sudbury, Mass.: Jones and Bartlett, 2001.

Antolin, Michael and Joan Herbers. "Evolution's Struggle for Existence in America's Public Schools." *Evolution* 55 (2001): 2,379-2,388.

Augustine. *On the Literal Meaning of Genesis.* Translated by J. H. Taylor. New York: Newman Press, 1982.

Aulie, Richard P. "The Doctrine of Special Creation." *American Biology Teacher* 34 (1972): 11-23.

Barker, Eileen. "Does It Matter How We Got Here? Dangers Perceived in Literalism and Evolutionism." *Zygon* 22 (1987): 213-225.

Barrett, Justin L. *Why Would Anyone Believe in God?* Lanham, Md.: AltaMira Press, 2004

Barrett, Justin L. "Is the Spell Really Broken? Bio-psychological Explanations of Religion and Theistic Belief," *Theology and Science* 5 (2007): 57-72.

Bergman, Jerry. "Darwinism and the Nazi race Holocaust." *Creation Ex Nihilo Technical Journal* 13 (1999): 101-111.

Boyer, Pascal. *Religion Explained: The Evolutionary Origins of Religious Thought.* New York: Basic Books, 2001.

Bumm, Emory F. "Evolution and the Second Law of Thermodynamics." *American Journal of Physics* 77 (2009): 922-925.

Brem, Sarah K., Michael Ranney, and Jennifer Schindel. "Perceived Consequences of Evolution: College Students Perceive Negative Personal and Social Impact in Evolutionary Theory." *Science Education* 87 (2003): 181-206.

Bull, J. J. and H. A. Wichman. "Applied Evolution." *Annual Review of Ecology and Systematics* 32 (2001): 183-218.

Carlson, Richard F., editor. *Science and Christianity: Four Views.* Downers Grove, Ill.: InterVarsity Press, 2000.

Chinsamy, Anusuya and Eva Plaganyi. "Accepting Evolution." *Evolution* 62 (2007): 248-254.

Colling, Richard. *Random Designer: Created from Chaos to Connect with the Creator.* Bourbonnias, Ill.: Browning Press, 2004.

Collins, Francis. *The Language of God: A Scientist Presents Evidence for Belief.* New York: Free Press, 2006.

De Pontbriand, A., Wang X-P, Cavaloc Y., et. al. "Synteny Comparison between Apes and Human Using Fin-mapping of the Genome." *Genomics* 80 (2002): 395.

Dulai, K. S., M. von Dornum, J. D. Mollon, and D. M. Hunt, "The Evolution of Trichromatic Colour Vision by Opsin Gene Duplication in New World and Old World Primates." *Genome Research* 9 (1999): 629.

Falk, Darrel. *Coming to Peace with Science; Bridging the Worlds between Faith and Biology.* Downers Grove, Ill.: InterVarsity Press, 2004.

Gilad, Y, O. Man, S. Paabo, and D. Lancet. "Human Specific Loss of Olfactory Receptor Genes." *Proceedings of the National Academy of Sciences* USA, 100 (2003): 3324.

Goldberg A., D. E. Wildman, T. R. Schmidt, M. Huttemann, M. Goodman, M. Weiss, and L. Grossman. "Adaptive Evolution of Cytochrome c Osidase Subunit VIII in Anthropoid Apes." *Proceedings of the National Academy of Sciences* USA, 100 (2003): 5873.

Hastings, Ronnie J. "The Rise and Fall of the Paluxy Mantracks." *Perspectives on Science and Christian Faith* 40 (1988): 144-154.

Holmes, Arthur F. *The Idea of a Christian College.* Revised edition. Grand Rapids, Mich.: Eerdmans, 1987.

Ido, J. W., A. Baldini, D. C. Ward, S. T. Reeders, and R. A. Wells. "Origin of Human Chromosome: An Ancestral Telomere-Telomere Fusion." *Proceedings of the National Academy of Sciences* USA, 88, No. 20 (1991): 9051-9055.

Jones, III, Judge John E. Memorandum Opinion, *Kitzmiller v. Dover,* Federal Case 4;04-cv-02688-JEJ Document 342, 2005.

Kazazian, H. H. "Mobile Elements: Drivers of Genome Evolution." *Science* 303 (2004): 1626.

Kennedy, Donald. "Breakthrough of the Year." *Science* 310 (2005): 1,869.

Lamoureux, Denis O. "Gaps, Design, & 'Theistic' Evolution: A Counter Reply to Robert A. Larmer." *Christian Scholar's Review* 37 (2007): 101-116.

Lombrozo, Tania, Andrew Shtulman, and Michael Weisberg. "The Intelligent Design Controversy: Lessons from Psychology and Education." *Trends in Cognitive Sciences* 10 (2006): 56-57.

McDonald, Patrick and Nivaldo J. Tro. "In Defense of Methodological Naturalism." *Christian Scholar's Review* 38 (2009): 201-230.

Miller, Kenneth R. *Finding Darwin's God: A Scientist's Search for Common Ground between God and Evolution.* New York: Harper Perennial, 2007.

_____. *Only a Theory: Evolution and the Battle for America's Soul.* New York: Viking, 2008.

Noll, Mark. *The Scandal of the Evangelical Mind.* Grand Rapids, Mich.: Eerdmans, 1994.

Padian, Kevin and Alan D. Gishlick. "The Talented Mr. Wells." *Quarterly Review of Biology* 77 (2002): 33-37.

Paterson, Frances R. A. and Lawrence F. Rossow. "'Chained to the Devil's Throne': Evolution and Creation Science as Religio-Political Issue." *American Biology Teacher* 61 (1999): 358-364

Peters, Ted and Martinez Hewlett. *Can You Believe in God and Evolution? A Guide for the Perplexed.* Nashville: Abingdon Press, 2006.

Salem, A. H., D. A. Ray, J. Xing, P. A. Callinan, J. S. Myers, D. J. Hedges, R. K. Garber, Witherspoon, DJ, Jorde, LB, and MA Batzer "Alu elements and hominid phylogentics. *Proceedings of the National Academy of Sciences* USA (2003):12787.

Schloss, Jeffrey and Michael Murray, editors. *The Believing Primate: Scientific, Philosophical, and Theological Reflections on the Origin of Religion.* New York: Oxford University Press, 2008.

Scott, Eugenie and Glenn Branch. "Antievolutionism: Changes and Continuities." *BioScience* 53 (2003): 282-285.

Sinclair, Anne and Murray Patton Pendarvis. "Evolution vs. Conservative Religious Beliefs." *Journal of College Science Teaching* 27 (1997): 167-170.

Snelling, Andrew A. and David Rush. "Moon Dust and the Age of the Solar System." *Creation Ex Nihilo Technical Journal* 7 (1993): 2-42.

Sober, Elliott . "What Is Wrong with Intelligent Design?" *Quarterly Review of Biology* 82 (2007): 3-8.

Styer, Daniel F. "Entropy and Evolution." *American Journal of Physics* 76 (2008): 1031-1033.

Tomas, J. W., J. W. Touchman, R. W. Blakesley, et. al. "Comparative Analysis of Multi-species Sequences from Targeted Genome Regions." *Nature* 424 (2003): 788.

Tremlin, Todd. *Minds and Gods: The Cognitive Foundations of Religion.* New York: Oxford University Press, 2006.

Van Till, Howard J. *The Fourth Day: What the Bible and the Heavens Are Telling Us about the Creation.* Grand Rapids, Mich.: Eerdmans, 1986.

_____. "The Fully Gifted Creation." In J. P. Moreland and John Mark Reynolds, editors, *Three Views on Creation and Evolution, 161-218.* Grand Rapids, Mich.: Zondervan , 1999.

_____. "Is the Universe Capable of Evolving?" In Keith B. Miller, editor, *Perspectives on an Evolving Creation, 313-334.* Grand Rapids, Mich.: Eerdmans , 2003.

_____. "Are Bacterial Flagella Intelligently Designed? Reflections on the Rhetoric of the Modern ID Movement." *Science and Christian Belief* 15 (2003) 117-140.

_____. "How Firm a Foundation? A Response to Justin L. Barrett's 'Is the Spell Really Broken?'" *Theology and Science* 6 (2008): 341-349.

Wilcox, David L. "Establishing Adam: Recent Evidences for a Late-Date Adam (AMH@100,000 BP)." *Perspectives on Science and Christian Belief*, 56 (2004):49-53.

Woodward, Thomas. *Darwin Strikes Back: Defending the Science of Intelligent Design.* Grand Rapids, Mich.: Baker Books, 2006.

Wright, Richard T. *Biology Through the Eyes of Faith.* Revised and Updated. San Francisco: HarperCollins, 2003.

Zhu L, Swengold GD and MF Seldin "Examination of sequence homology between human chromosome 20 and the mouse genome:intense conservation of many genomic elements. *Human Genetics* 113 (2003): 60.

CONCLUSION

MOVING UP
THE SLIPPERY SLOPE

GEORGE M. MARSDEN

CHAPTER 22

s this fascinating volume helps confirm, evangelical higher education has experienced a renaissance in recent decades. Scholarship that is self-identified as "Christian"[1] has become a considerable industry and is at least making a mark in the academic mainstream. Many excellent evangelical graduate students have been earning their doctorates and as a result evangelical colleges of the CCCU types have enjoyed a wonderful buyer's market in hiring new faculty. Happily, student enrollments have kept pace with this surge so that, on the whole, CCCU schools have been growing in size as well as in stature relative to other colleges and universities.

Even in the midst of all this success, evangelical higher education is characteristically beset by anxieties. Many of these anxieties fall into one of two categories. The most influential of these sets of anxieties are the worries that the college will lose its Christian moorings and slide into secularism as has happened to so many colleges and universities that were founded by Christians. These worries are probably most often found among trustees, administrators, donors, and church constituencies, though something like a quarter of faculty members (according to the survey) share a concern over the inroads of secularism at their schools (FSQ 20). The counter-anxiety is that efforts to maintain a particular identity may become oppressive, stifling, and counter-productive, or at least that they may inhibit healthy Christian growth. These concerns are found among another minority of faculty at the opposite end of the spectrum of opinions and are among the concerns that are especially highlighted in this volume.

Apparently my own work helped give shape to some of the current forms of the first set of anxieties—that is, the worries that schools will lose their Christian identity—so I

---

1 "Christian" is used as an adjective this way mainly by evangelical and Reformed Christians and seldom by Roman Catholics or mainline Protestants.

think I should try to set the record straight on what I actually think regarding that issue. In a couple of the essays in this volume my work, especially *The Soul of the American University: From Protestant Establishment to Established Disbelief* (1994), is associated with the "slippery slope" worry that CCCU schools are liable to slide into secularism if they relax their guard. Joe Ricke remarks that my views have "taken on a second life in the CCCU." He goes on to say that "The fear of 'the slippery slope to secularization' (and related concerns) has come to motivate not only much of our theorizing but also our new faculty orientation, faculty development, and self-definitions (in catalogs, promotional materials, mission statements, and, now, even academic-freedom statements)." The editors of this volume, Samuel Joeckel and Thomas Chesnes, devote their essay to an analysis of the role of fears of the slippery slope and they particularly deplore the way such fears may stifle intellectual inquiry and due regard for diversity of thought. My essay supplements theirs with some historical analysis and offers my own version of what might be a balanced approach.

It is easy to understand why people concerned about retaining the Christian identities of CCCU schools would utilize *The Soul of the American University* in the way that they do. The idea of a "slippery slope" was around long before my book and was a standard way of justifying doctrinal and behavioral safeguards in Christian higher education. The standard rhetoric was that Harvard and almost every major American school had been founded by Christians but had lost its faith. Strongly anchored Christian colleges were therefore necessary to combat secularism. Although my book was concerned with the mainstream academy and was an attempt to provide nuance for a complex history, *The Soul of the American University* also provided weight and documentation for the already existing standard story used by the defenders of Christian higher education.

In fact, I do not think that the patterns that dominate the story in *The Soul of the American University* are applicable to the current state of the great majority of CCCU schools. Let me explain why. The central story line of *The Soul of the American University* concerns the dominant American culture that was predominantly Protestant in its religious affiliation. At the beginning of the history in the American colonies the assumptions about religion and culture, and particularly about religion and education, were those of Christendom. Protestant religion was assumed to have an official public role in education, including higher education. Even into the nineteenth century, religious and government agencies often cooperated in founding and maintaining colleges and universities. These Protestant schools had little of what we would call intentional integration of faith and learning, but more often supplemented secular subjects (as the classics or sciences) with some Christian teaching and required chapel. The process that is often described as secularization, beginning with the rise of the modern universities after the Civil War, is more precisely understood as that of differentiation of the disciplines and the privatization of religion, especially of particular theological teachings. Mainline Protestantism also became more inclusive, particularly of liberal outlooks that focused on morality above doctrine.

As universities and most of their disciplines came to be defined increasingly by natural scientific models that effectively excluded religious concerns, mainstream Protestants could always point to hundreds of their smaller colleges that still provided required chapel, requirements in Bible and theology, and more protected communities. During the course of the twentieth century, however, most of these schools lost whatever sectarian edge they had and their denominational identities faded. Mainstream Protestant educators had one foot in the dominant American public culture and the other foot in their denominational heritage and had long assumed that these two should not be in essential conflict. During the first half of the century they could usually depend on self-selection to provide sympathetic Protestant faculty without imposing strict denominational or creedal tests. By the latter decades of the century denominational support for such colleges waned and faculty became diverse. Such schools still had religion faculties, but for the rest of the curriculum they followed university practices that emphasized scientific standards and inclusivism, and treated religious belief as essentially a private option, even if an encouraged one. This drift away of mainstream Protestant colleges and universities from most aspects of their former distinct religious identities is what people have in mind when they talk about "the slippery slope."

"The slippery slope," though perhaps not the most felicitous image, does certainly point to a historical reality and suggests what may be a future danger, but the implication of an imminent peril of a slide into apostasy and secularism does not describe the current position of the great majority CCCU schools. Lots of things in contemporary culture do exert a sort of gravitational pull away from the particulars of more traditional evangelical faiths and in the direction of more secular or at least religiously liberal outlooks. But if we employ such an imagery of a slope with secularism at the bottom, we should also recognize that most CCCU schools are firmly anchored on it and negotiating it via a sort of cog railroad or funicular with elaborate precautions already in place to prevent any sudden slippage. Perhaps it may be debated whether they are moving up or down this slope (that will depend on one's standards of measurement) but in most cases the chances of any extended slide or free fall are slight.

One cannot rule out the possibility, of course, that some CCCU schools may lose their evangelical identity during the next decades. Strong religious movements have a tendency to lose their sectarian edges over the course of generations. And not all of the more than one hundred CCCU colleges and universities fit the same pattern. Some have something closer to a mainline Protestant heritage, and there are other important differences among their religious affiliations, so that there may be significant exceptions to every generalization. Nonetheless, to the extent that we can generalize, it is important to observe that most of the CCCU schools have histories over the past century that are in some relevant ways almost the opposite of histories of most mainline Protestant colleges and universities that are described in *The Soul of the American University.*

The baseline for the secularization of most of the mainline Protestant (Congregational/United Church of Christ, Presbyterian, Episcopal, Methodist, American [or Northern] Baptist, Disciples, and the like) colleges and universities was an American culture in which Protestantism was regarded as the default religion. Although some of these schools had been founded with a sectarian identity, by the late nineteenth and early twentieth century the more common pattern was more like that of the new Methodist universities (Vanderbilt, Northwestern, Syracuse, Southern California, and Duke) that aspired to be both deeply religious and to play a leadership role in shaping mainstream American culture. To be a good Christian and to be a good American were pretty much the same thing. American culture was, of course, permeated by evils: personal vices to be avoided and social wrongs to be corrected. But in most respects (beyond opportunities for worship and added theological beliefs), a Christian point of view need not be any different from that of a virtuous humanist.

Now consider the baseline for most CCCU schools. Most of them and their supporting religious constituencies were shaped by the legacy of the fundamentalist controversies beginning in the 1920s, which helped to indelibly imprint on them a sectarian sense of being outsiders to the cultural mainstream. That sectarian sense included opposition to liberal Protestantism or what they saw as "culture Protestantism." In most cases this attitude of being different was related to a conversionist brand of evangelicalism that emphasized both radical personal transformation and purity and also the importance of affiliating with properly "pure" communities of fellow believers who followed correct fundamental doctrines. Such communities often thrived on emphasizing how they differed both from secular outlooks and other brands of Christianity. In some cases ethno-religious heritages and/or confessional traditions sharpened the sense of the virtues of being different. In the white American South, the experience was somewhat different since evangelical religion was still pervasive in the surrounding culture. But pure southern evangelicalism could gain resonance by emphasizing its differences from northern liberalism—as symbolized, for instance, by biological evolution. It is true, of course, as I have often pointed out in writing about fundamentalism, that the sectarian sensibilities of such groups were always selective and often paradoxically mixed with a sense of being cultural insiders. Fundamentalists and their evangelical heirs might sing "I am a stranger here within a foreign land," but also proudly proclaim themselves as "one-hundred percent Americans" and be deeply infected by unexamined assumptions of the surrounding culture. Still, despite such inconsistencies, a sectarian sense of being different was an essential to the ethos that shaped the background of most (even if not all) CCCU schools.

Next consider the characteristic patterns of change for these schools over the past sixty years. Around 1950 most of the CCCU schools that then existed were Bible colleges or highly sectarian liberal arts schools. Typically they defined themselves by strict and usually fundamentalistic doctrinal tests for faculty and strict behavior restrictions for everyone, including prohibitions of movie going, theatre attendance, smoking, drinking, dancing, and card playing. Over the decades these schools have changed remarkably. Some people (such as fundamentalist observers) would describe these changes as secularization. Most of those associated with those schools do not see it as anything of the sort. Rather, they see it as a maturing of deep evangelical commitment and as a matter of growing in Christian understanding. They may have given up some of the older gatekeeping tests, but one thing that has not been given up is commitment to gate keeping.

Nowhere is that more clear than in the process of faculty hiring, which in my view is the crucial issue in keeping a distinct identity. Fifty or sixty years ago faculty had to give evidence of personal faith in Jesus Christ, but the typical tests administered in faculty hiring may have included, in addition to basic evangelical doctrinal commitments, belief in the inerrancy of the Bible, rejection of biological evolution, and a premillennial understanding of Christ's second coming. Today, basic evangelical doctrinal commitment and evidence of personal faith in Jesus Christ are still required, but one of the most characteristic tests in hiring is whether the candidate is willing to engage in the integration of faith and learning in his or her discipline. What has happened is that, rather than having simply given up some of the old tests (to the extent they have been given up) of difference, CCCU schools have built a sense of difference into the very fabric of the academic enterprise. Teaching at a Christian college is expected to mean that one is exploring the issue of what difference Christianity makes to one's academic discipline and the way it might help shape the lives of one's students. Thus CCCU colleges have attacked the dualism between matters of faith (explicit Bible teaching and doctrine) and academic work, a dualism that was a significant factor in making mainline Protestant colleges susceptible to drift into secularism through most of the curriculum even while they kept a Christian option on the side.

With the question of "what difference does a robust Christian perspective make for education" as an ever-present component of the enterprise (even if that difference is not always apparent in a fair number of areas), former Bible colleges and strictly sectarian liberal arts colleges have been able to modify some of the traditional gate-keeping tests without such changes threatening to send the school free-wheeling downhill into secularism. Though fundamentalists would think otherwise, these changes have not typically sent schools sliding steadily into theological liberalism either (as the Joeckel/ Chesnes surveys confirm). Typically the arguments for adjusting creedal or behavior tests have been that the new standards would be more consistent with classic evangelical Christian orthodoxy, as opposed, for instance, to the standards of classic early twentieth-century fundamentalism. Such changes have not been at all like those typical of mainline Protestant colleges in the twentieth century, which typically moved from a mix of orthodoxy and Protestant liberalism to becoming increasingly inclusive and arguing that, after all, the spirit of Christianity was more essential than the letter.

Questions of academic freedom at CCCU colleges ought to be understood in the light of this history. The larger setting is that CCCU schools presently appear to have a good thing going and so the question is how to preserve that and continue to grow. Crucial to the histories and the health of the schools as Christian institutions is that they continue to have some definite boundaries. The specifics of these differ from school to school and from tradition to tradition and the history demonstrates that these are somewhat adjustable without losing essential identity. Nevertheless, adjusting boundaries is very different from dismantling them. By the same standard, so long as there are some definite and generally well-accepted boundaries, as there seem to be at most CCCU schools, then there should be room for some flexibility regarding academic freedom within commitment to those boundaries, rather than creating an atmosphere of strictly patrolling the borders.

Apparently the atmosphere surrounding such issues is not bad at most of the schools, since about 85 percent of faculty respondents agree at least somewhat with the statement "I possess academic freedom at my college/university," while only about 10 percent disagree (FSQ 96). More remarkable is that over half agree in some measure with the statement that "Professors at Christian institutions have more freedom to discuss issues and ask questions than do professors at secular institutions" (FSQ 97). I was a bit bemused to see that Professor Ricke refers to this as "The Marsden Effect," since I am not sure how I would have answered that question. My first instinct is to say that academic freedom is somewhat more limited at CCCU schools than at secular institutions. I have indeed made the argument that it is misleading to argue that Christian schools lack academic freedom just because they have some definite boundaries on what may be taught, since all school have such boundaries. But it would seem to me that at Christian schools one has not only most of the boundaries commonly found in secular schools (one cannot make racist or sexist remarks or deny the Holocaust, for instance) but also a considerable number of additional limitations defined by the specifics of the religious tradition. It is true that, while there is room in the mainstream academy for some Christian perspectives, some *types* of religious discourse (e. g. proselytizing or appealing to the authority of Scripture) would be out of bounds. So there is a significant tradeoff.[2] In any case, I think the broad point stands that all schools have their boundaries and the practical questions regarding academic freedom have to do with the atmosphere and expectations for faculty members when they enter territory close to those limits.

For the sake of simplicity, I think we can say that there have been two major poles in dealing with academic-freedom issues at Christian colleges and universities: these are the "defender of the faith" model and what Anthony Diekema has called in *Academic Freedom and Christian Scholarship* (Eerdmans, 2000) the covenantal model. Probably at most CCCU schools there has been a mix of these two approaches, but generally speaking the "defender of the faith" approach was more common a couple of generations ago when the typical scenario would be that if a faculty member appeared to be too close to transgressing a border he or she might be sharply reined in by presidential authority. My guess is that today something like the covenantal model is far more common. The ideal is that once faculty members have signed on to the standards of the school and have become part of a covenanted, cooperative, and worshipping academic community, the default position regarding teaching about controversial issues would be trust. As a covenanted *academic* community, one of the goals is to cultivate among students habits of asking questions about what difference their faith should make for understanding

---

2 I suspect that the high agreement with the statement in FSQ 97 has to do with the ambiguity of the wording so that most respondents were interpreting "discuss issues and ask questions" to refer to some issues relating to the Bible or theology and their discipline or related moral questions and were not thinking much about restrictions at their own colleges regarding points of view that they themselves would not want to endorse anyway. Furthermore, they are free to discuss and ask questions about many anti-Christian views, even if they are not free to *advocate* those views.

all of reality and in shaping their life choices. They should also be learning how to find models for answering those questions informed by the best in their faith tradition as well as other scholarship and intelligence. But it is especially important in Christian colleges, where a recognized drawback is that students may become too "sheltered" from alien ideas, that teaching and learning be not simply indoctrination and that there should be genuine openness to taking alternative points of view seriously. Hence it seems especially important to cultivate covenanted trust of the teacher's discretion as much as possible. At the same time, of course, it needs to be recognized that covenants do have terms (and that schools have covenants with their churches, their constituencies, and their students) and so there are limits which will need to be enforced by due procedure appropriate to academic freedom cases at any other school. But the ideal is that such due process should also take place, as much as is possible, in an atmosphere of covenantal trust and mutuality.

For those who fall more on the "defender of the faith" end of the spectrum, the slippery-slope analogy has been especially popular. Evangelical sub-groups have often thrived on emphasizing the dangers of what they oppose and in providing clear black and white alternatives. In such a setting it has often been a persuasive argument to say that if a school gives up a strict interpretation of a doctrine or practice it will inevitably be launched down the road to secularism, as indeed happened to some mainline Protestant institutions. For those more on the covenantal end of the spectrum, which I would endorse, the emphasis will be more on growing and maturing (or moving up the slope, if you will) within the rich resources of historic Christianity (which should not be compromised and are inherently somewhat flexible) as a way of meeting the threat of secularism and retaining a positive witness. To use a biblical analogy, administrators who adopt the covenantal model should see their task as not like that of the servant who kept the master's money safe by burying it in the ground but rather as confidently continuing to build on the rich resources Christian colleges and universities have been given.

Having firm boundaries does not necessarily reduce academic rigor. There have been schools that are bounded by extensive creedal restrictions that have been academically rigorous and cultivated remarkable creativity within those bounds. There have also been religiously affiliated schools that put "freedom" as a highest value that have been intellectually shoddy. The relevant variables have more to do with historical traditions of intellectualism or anti-intellectualism than they have to do with how widely open a school is to any point of view. Sometimes, rigid boundaries are used to restrict inquiry and creativity. But even within relatively narrow boundaries a covenant atmosphere of trust can help generate a healthy atmosphere of rigorous and exciting intellectual inquiry, while an inquisitorial spirit can inhibit academic growth even within relative broad parameters.

A major means for overcoming the faith-based anti-intellectualism that has infected many evangelical groups has been to develop stronger emphases regarding the integration of faith and scholarship. CCCU schools have come a long way as scholarly communities in the past two generations and even a considerable way since Mark Noll wrote *The*

Scandal of the Evangelical Mind in the early 1990s. Most of them have had a considerable legacy of constituency suspicion of intellectual inquiry to overcome, but there are many signs of progress in countering simplistic anti-secularism with more sophisticated alternatives to secularism. It is encouraging to see, for instance, that the great majority of faculty respondents not only say that they "have a good idea of what is meant by the phrase 'the integration of faith and learning'" (FSQ 18) but also that "it is not difficult for me to integrate faith and learning in my discipline" (FSQ 19). I doubt if such results would have been nearly as high twenty years ago. Part of the issue is that "integration of faith and learning" has become something of a shibboleth at many CCCU schools in recent decades and is often a considerable factor in new faculty orientation. How deep the integration goes or how adequate it is has been a matter of some debate and new books on that topic keep appearing. Nevertheless, even if "integration" is sometimes affirmed mainly "in principle," it is an excellent principle to have around in Christian academic institutions that are concerned with building their identity and leadership in the midst of secular alternatives.

Another encouraging dimension of the survey regarding concern for "integration" is that one of the most frequent comments from faculty as to why they thought education at their school superior to that at secular schools is that they believed education at their school was "holistic," dealing with students' character and spiritual lives and not just their intellect.[3] That is significant since it is sometimes alleged that the prevailing integration model is too exclusively intellectual. While it is understandable why some might interpret some of the talk of integration as too intellectual, in fact I would think that few teachers at Christian colleges would think of their task as just intellectual as opposed to holistic or addressing matters of character and spiritual lives. It is true that there are many challenging intellectual issues involved in determining what differences Christian approaches should make in various disciplines, so that most—perhaps too much—writing and discussion regarding integration has been on the intellectual side. But the great strength of such discussions in the Christian college setting is that they are taking place in the context of an intentional Christian community in which one of the most widely understood goals is to provide a holistic educational and spiritual atmosphere. Discussions of the intellectual challenges regarding faith and learning are integrally linked to questions of the spiritual health of the community and of the individuals in it. So these are not competing concerns, but rather are complementary.

Still I agree with writers in this volume and of other works who emphasize addressing the holistic dimensions of the enterprise more fully. The central question is: what sort of community are we trying to create? And the crucial related question is: how might such a community best contribute to cultivating habits and practices of all kinds (spiritual, moral, and intellectual) that will best prepare students as they attempt to follow Christ in an extremely diverse and complex world? Nicholas Wolterstorff's phrase "educating for shalom" captures well at least one version of what such an emphasis might

---

3   Carol Woodfin mentions this as a very frequent sort of response to FSQ 104.

mean, though the implications of the ideal need to be collectively fleshed out.[4] How that is best done will vary among various faith traditions. However, one of the values of the CCCU is that it fosters intercommunication among representatives of various faith traditions so that they can learn from each other—for instance, Mennonite schools have led the way in developing service learning. Or schools shaped by classic evangelical heritages are often strong in cultivating strong personal commitment and devotional practices. Reformed schools are often strong on theory and on how best to constructively address aspects of mainstream culture. Some more eclectic thinkers, of whom James A. K. Smith is an influential recent representative, emphasize the importance of traditional liturgical practices in worship. One of the challenges in attempting to build healthy Christian communities that may include strong advocates of all these (and more) emphases is to find how to encourage all of them to flourish with mutual respect, recognizing that one approach does not fit all.

One principle seems clear, consistent with the theme of this volume. If the goal is to help shape mature Christians who can continue to grow as followers of Christ throughout their lives, then the most effective approaches, whether in scholarship or in spiritual and moral expectations, is to get beyond simplistic formulae that arm students with a set of black and white defenses against secularism and worldliness. Rather the goal should be to encourage students, as the CCCU colleges themselves seem to have been doing collectively in the past generation, to adopt firm habits and principles within strong commitment to a substantial Christian heritage so that they can respond and mature as they encounter new and often unforeseen challenges in the decades to come.

In emphasizing such approaches I do not want to minimize the dangers of secularism, or of giving up basic Christian teachings. I have spent much of my career trying to understand and analyze the subtle ways in which sub-Christian and anti-Christian motifs are built into the surrounding culture that we all take so much for granted and which shapes us. There is no doubt that religious people and institutions are constantly encountering something analogous to a gravitational pull to conform to the more secular cultural standards around them. My basic argument in this essay is based on the premise that institutions that successfully resist that cultural pull toward secularism must have traditions and mechanisms in place, especially regarding faculty hiring, to anchor them and to provide a counter pressure for developing positive Christian perspectives as alternatives to secularist views. If they have those, as I think most CCCU schools do, then they can have the flexibility to change with the culture in positive Christian ways. But that positive and hopeful assessment also presupposes that the sectarian sensibilities that schools have cultivated over the years and the mechanisms to preserve them be fine-tuned in response to on-going challenges, rather than be effectively abandoned. If they were abandoned, the pull of religious liberalism and secularism would eventually prevail. The image of the slippery slope contains an important element of truth. It is

---

4   Nicholas Wolterstorff, *Education for Shalom: Essays on Christian Higher Education* (Grand Rapids, Mich.: Eerdmans, 2004).

shorthand for a tendency to which any intense religious movement is likely to be prone after a number of generations and a phenomenon that has been especially conspicuous in the Western world in recent centuries. To point out that it is often misleading to use the metaphor to imply that one concession will start a landslide into secularism is not to say that vigilance regarding things essential should be neglected. Sometimes another metaphor, that of a backlash, is applicable to explain sizable abandonments of traditions in reaction to too-rigid defensiveness.

If there is a conspicuous weakness of the present volume it is that its commentators seem all to be on the progressive wing that emphasizes the virtues of more openness. The volume would be strengthened by hearing from representative CCCU faculty members or administrators who think that their schools need to do more to resist the inroads of secularism. Nonetheless, I am convinced that even for those who are most alert to such dangers and challenges, an historical perspective suggests that the most effective sorts of responses are along the line of building from the strength and momentum of recent decades, rather than being largely preoccupied with boundary maintenance. Secular drift is sometimes best forestalled by promoting positive Christianizing counter movements that require some flexibility.

Thinking about the issue of what sort of educational community a CCCU college or university should build is helped by asking the question: compared to what? My sense is that the relative gains of CCCU schools in recent decades have to do considerably with the perceived weaknesses of more secular educational institutions. CCCU schools are today correctly seen as offering what many people would perceive as a classic undergraduate education. They offer small communities in which the liberal arts have a prominent place but sciences and vocational skills are available as well with no sacrifice in quality compared with other private colleges or state schools. Moreover, they offer what is much more rare, a coherent interdisciplinary educational experience. In addition, with the maturing of discussions regarding integration of faith and learning, this coherence is built around an examined philosophy, even if it is one that does not always give all the answers.

Furthermore and not incidentally, CCCU schools offer this classic and coherent educational experience within an intentional Christian community that encourages worship and shared Christian practices. In a way that most American churches simply cannot do, Christian colleges provide a prolonged experience in which a basic message is that Christians are people who are in some sense set apart. There are, of course, lots of weaknesses and dangers in such communities and it is beyond my expertise to say how campus life should be best improved. But certainly it is clear that one purpose of such communities is to prepare the students for a lifetime of cultivating the habits of seeing themselves as in the world but not of it and of asking how their Christian commitments should intelligently be addressed to serving God and others in that world.

One of the great challenges facing most CCCU schools—and one that is not much directly addressed in this volume—is their relation to their supporting church communities. Although some of these schools are denominational, all of them in fact serve interdenominational church communities. They are dependent upon these various supporting church communities for their students and for their financial support. That means that school administrators are not free to act according to an abstract set of principles, but have always to be looking over their shoulders to assess what their constituencies think. Some constituencies are very strongly tied to symbolically powerful issues—creation science, for instance, or flashpoint political issues. That task of satisfying or placating these constituencies is complicated by the fact that various parts of their constituencies may hold opposing views on such issues. And as is clear from the surveys, not only do some faculty differ sharply from some constituents on such issues, but substantial numbers of faculty members differ with each other as well. So negotiating relationships to all these constituencies is no simple task.

Most CCCU schools are, in effect, para-church institutions. They build their own identities, but they are also intermeshed in a web of relationships with other church and para-church organizations that make up the complex entity of evangelicalism. Since these institutions are all voluntary, they are not easy to reform. In such a setting Christian colleges and universities might see their roles as to be that of gently guiding and reforming their supporting church communities by training laypeople (as well as clergy) who eventually can provide mature leadership in practicing the faith in an alien world. That process is a lengthy one. Christian colleges and universities should have room for prophetic people and should encourage prophetic ideals among both students and faculty. Some such people may help change the world. Yet in the short run, it is important to emphasize that the overall reforming influence of a school must be gentle, since it is, in fact, an historically embedded institution and practically speaking, the process of growth has to happen without alienating the supporting church communities.

Fifty years ago outsiders could view the predecessors of the CCCU schools as the last stands for dying sub-cultures[5]—views that the schools' defensive stances would have seemed to confirm. At that time "the secularization thesis," or the assumption that societies inevitably secularized as they modernize, prevailed among sociologists. Ironically, fundamentalists, who were resisting secularization, held a similar view regarding the likelihood of all but the most militant Christian institutions sliding into secularization. Today, by contrast, the secularization thesis is in disarray among sociologists and it is clear that evangelicalism is not going away in the United States. It is also clear that evangelical colleges and universities are flourishing. Even though they have changed dramatically in the past half-century, various secularizing trends that are indeed present have typically been offset by other Christianizing trends.

Finally, in thinking about how most effectively to set the tone for the mission of Christian colleges and universities, it may be helpful to consider their changing roles as contributors to the larger American society. Today in the public domain where diversity

---

5   Christopher Jencks and David Riesman in their classic study, *The Academic Revolution* (New York: Doubleday, 1968), described conservative faith-based colleges as "holdouts" (328) whose futures looked "bleak" and whose survival depended on social conditions that would continue to allow them to define themselves by their protests against mainstream cultural trends (333).

is such a great value there should be a strengthened rationale for Christian colleges and universities as means of strengthening American sub-communities. America has myriads of church-based sub-communities. If our public culture has genuinely moved beyond the melting-pot ideal to truly valuing diversity, then these sub-communities should be encouraged to have their own networks of institutions, including educational institutions. Such institutions, which almost always embody an ideal of serving the public welfare as well as promoting their own sectarian views, are arguably among the best resources for generating whatever social capital a democratic nation needs to survive.

Critics of the evangelical varieties of American sub-communities have long complained—often with justification—of their anti-intellectualism and the way that they can be swept by various populist fervors. In fact, because revivalist evangelicalism is so much dependent on a free-market religious economy, it is particularly susceptible to being shaped by strong leaders who promote simplistic either/or formulae that sell well. For that reason, such critics of evangelicalism, as well as evangelical educators themselves, should be enthusiastic about evangelicals building strong educational institutions that teach with enough nuance to avoid the lure of populist fervors. Such colleges and universities, whatever their imperfections, can contribute immensely to turning spiritually based enthusiasms toward thoughtful directions.

For evangelical educators themselves, these realities should enhance their sense of calling to serve Christ and his kingdom in ways that benefit both the church and the surrounding community. Evangelical Christianity has been one of the most remarkable and largest movements around the world in the past century. Its potentialities are truly immense. Because of its free-floating, religious free-market, populist character, however, it is also susceptible to all sorts of aberrations. Christian educational institutions can therefore play a vital role in helping to keep evangelicalism grounded in the larger traditions of Christian orthodoxies and to moderate some of the simplicities that inevitably characterize market-driven populist movements. One would hope that CCCU schools, with their relatively rich resources, would be the models for this worldwide educational enterprise. The Body of Christ has many parts and education is not always the most prominent, but it can be a vital part and hence can provide some followers of Christ with a high calling. If CCCU schools are going to meet that challenge, it will be done best by modeling how they themselves can grow and mature as Christian communities both firmly and confidently anchored in the best of the Christian heritage.

THE SECULAR CHALLENGES AND RESOURCES FOR ADDRESSING THEM

MARTIN E. MARTY

CHAPTER 23

First, a personal perspective

Invited to provide a concluding perspective by an outsider, which means someone not affiliated with Council for Christian Colleges and Universities schools, let me begin with a personal introduction, since readers may make some of their judgments based on awareness of my judgments, given their perspectives on my perspective. First off, my status as outsider is somewhat ambiguous, given the fact that I have so often been hosted at CCCU academies. Prompted by this assignment to be curious about the occasions, I found that through the years I have spoken at thirty-four schools on the "Members and Affiliates" list as of 2010, and that four of them risked an honorary doctorate on me.

What to do with "my kind"—we are legion—is a problem not only for us or CCCU schools but for that sector of American religion and culture usually code-named "evangelical." Often when invited to participate in evangelical gatherings, I have been introduced as "this year's non-evangelical . . . ." I then identify myself as (ordinarily) the only person in the room who belongs to a church body with the word "Evangelical" in its name, as in the "Evangelical Lutheran Church in America." As a Lutheran, I am heir to European church bodies that were more often called "Evangelical" than they were "Lutheran." Of course, the value in the identification depends upon how you define "evangelical" and how wide its borders may be. As CCCU leaders well know, many institutions of higher learning who are not (yet) members are committed to the values of the Council.

Further to advance the cause of providing credentials and identification, I have to add that my commitment to "Christian Colleges and Universities" is long-standing and firm. How to name them and how to describe their commitments and boundaries remain difficult. For twelve years I was on the Board of Regents, which I chaired for six years, at St. Olaf College in Minnesota. In its mission statement, which, I am confident, every regent could recite and sincerely profess commitment to whenever asked, the school defines itself as a "College of the Church, rooted in the Christian gospel . . . ." Interacting with a society described as "pluralist" and "secular," such a college—like all CCCU schools—struggles to keep on defining what its Christian commitment means. What this means for present purposes is that most of the questions and assessments in the Joeckel/Chesnes survey are not alien to many of us.

To cite all this is not to suggest that I picture that all readers are curious about these biographical details, but rather to stress that there can be no appraisal or counsel that is not colored by the perspectives we bring. What is true for CCCU "outsiders" is also true for CCCU "insiders," as I can testify from many hours of conversations over coffee or in conferences: that the denominational, confessional, environmental, or situational and experiential circumstances differ vastly among CCCU schools, as evidenced by the fact that leaders and members found a survey like this in the Joeckel-Chesnes program relevant and useful. Awareness of that complexity leads us all to be cautious in our generalizations of the sort that I shall now make, just as, more important, it might suggest coalitional and spiritual-kinship opportunities.

Second, some words about the survey instrument and the reported findings[1]

Just as there is no appraisal or report which is utterly unconditioned by personal experience and perspective, something we all learned in *Hermeneutics 101*, there is no way of undertaking a survey without having it reflect the curiosities and viewpoints of those who fashion it. Suppose, for instance, leaders of Catholic or Mainline Protestant "colleges and universities of the church" were to have to describe themselves as "theologically liberal or conservative" in their world of "in betweens," "both/ands," and paradoxes. Almost everywhere else, certainly in the secular academy, fewer than 22.4% would describe themselves as "strongly conservative" or fewer than 46% as "somewhat conservative." "Neutral" would likely prevail among more than the 10.8% in this survey (FSQ 5).

No doubt "biblical inerrancy" response rates would be one of the key indicators of difference from many CCCU schools and scholars. About 58% "strongly" or "somewhat" agree, when asked to declare themselves with respect to belief in "biblical inerrancy," though we visitors can testify to the fact that, in quite conservative campus circles, "inerrancy" falls short of concepts of biblical authority in its fuller scope (FSQ 36). Another example: a betting person would almost certainly envision a second survey ten years from now in which more than one-third would "strongly" or "somewhat" agree that "practicing homosexuals should be allowed membership in a Christian church" (FSQ 67). Similarly, those who observe trends as evangelicals reexamine their commitments would wager that in a few years the already strong opinion that "the evidence for human-induced climate

---

1   Even a concluding essay in a book rich in footnotes and scholarly apparatus should have at least one footnote. Here is mine, which has to do with genre. As I took notes on the chapters, I found many places which merit engagement in detail, but it would be difficult to begin to do this without exceeding the bounds of a concluding essay. What follows will be generalizations, but I think they are grounded in what I have read here.

change is convincing" will be stronger (FSQ 53). Evangelical campuses have become leaders in movements to protect the environment, seeing them as Christian responses to challenges. Still, in summary, these tabulations are no doubt rather accurate indicators of life on the CCCU campuses and the culture which supports them.

It is interesting to discern and grade what conservative Protestants are fighting about by noticing what does not get asked and what needs to be asked. Perhaps all faculty, students, alumni, and boards are so convinced and articulate about basic Christian doctrines that these would not define CCCU schools. For example, the issues of how the "human" and the "divine" in Jesus Christ are witnessed to and evident in such circles, favored though these questions of doctrinal import may be by theologians, would not be definers here. Yet almost no questions are more urgent in the Jewish-Christian or Jewish-Muslim dialogues and interactions than these. Surveys suggest that most Christians are unaware of or ignorant about these themes which occupied the churches for centuries in their struggles with non-Christians or among themselves—and which can hardly be described as settled yet. We are aware that there are also some new and intense debates about "free will," "predestination," and "divine foreknowledge" in evangelical circles. Such as these are not vivid markers and boundaries of Christian groups *vis-à-vis* non-Christians. Choices of what are considered to be relevant and even urgent would be similarly selective in Catholic, Orthodox, or Mainline Protestant academic circles.

On the relevance front, most questions which did eclipse concerns for classic Christian doctrines had to do with sexual issues. These may well have become the postmodern question which sucks up the doctrinal oxygen in the early twenty-first century. This is not the place to argue over CCCU evaluations of stem cell research, abortion, homosexuality, and sex education, but to point to the fact that in these cases the agenda for Christian higher education is more likely to be set by what is debated on "secular" televised talk shows and their radio counterparts, or electronic and digital transmissions. The topics presented in these forms of media reach the eyes, ears, and hearts more immediately and efficiently than do timeless Christian issues involving confrontations with Islam and other religions in this age of global interaction, suspicion, and more.

Transitioning to the chapter-themes: a word about tone

The fact that "secular" colleges and universities, their leaders and faculties and students, often dismiss or do not know or care about the academies and concerns of the CCCU schools is sufficiently based in observable reality that it merits inquiry, discussion, and response, and legitimately can be recognized as an agenda-setting issue. Lamenting the situation and criticizing the thoughtless outsider is, in my view, necessary, so long as it does not legitimate mean-spirited counter-sniping, defensiveness, paralysis, or unhelpful whining. Yes, that's it: whining. My study wall for years has borne a motto which helps guide my apportionment of time for themes of discussion or reading: No Whining.

No doubt the authors of the essays we have just read could have found plenty of excuse to whimper or whine, but for the most part they show that they find self-analysis, self-criticism, and careful analysis and criticism of the other more helpful. Any parents among them can testify to their own experiences with their children who whine. "Get out of here, please, get over your snit, pretty please, and then come back and we can do business!" Others condemned as I am to read the polemics of caucuses and interest groups in Christian denominations as these are reflected in their newsletters and journals will note that most of the editors and authors are simply crabby. "If only they would let this campus or church or nation be run the way I would run it, or as it would run itself if I were consulted, all would be well!"

Very little of such curmudgeonly attitudes shows up here. I believe that CCCU attitudes and approaches voiced by their scholars will get a better hearing as they get past whining. I like to commend that gripers study the prophecies in the Hebrew Scriptures, the sayings of Jesus, or the writings of Paul in efforts to find whining. These biblical figures could listen, criticize, analyze, prescribe, blast, and, yes, lament, but their responses are part of creative strategies, tactics which would have been thwarted and records of them hardly at home in the canon if they only mourned their place in the face of extraordinary contentions and ordinary daily living.

As someone who has spent most of his career *in partibus infidelium*, which is what Catholic hierarchs called the land of the unbelievers, but which to many of us means mainly the "other-believer" or the "half-believer" or the "multi-believer," I have often noted that informed critical witness can and does inspire dialogue and not dismissal. At the same time, complaints by evangelical carpers or their Catholic or Mainline Protestant counterparts about being wounded or misunderstood mean little in a world where almost all of us, including unbelievers, other-believers, half-believers, or multi-believers also have reason to whimper and whine or engage in the complementary acts of throwing tantrums.

The choice of 'secularization' as key—or code—word and theme

The attention which the contributors, beginning with the editors, pay to "secularization" is certainly appropiate, though it has limited usefulness and demands the rethinking some are giving it. One can define secularization in any number of ways. In this book it rarely means radical atheism or assured unbelief. What CCCU intellectuals want and need to face is more problematic than atheism. Every faculty in the Council can post any number of scholars who are able to handle the usual suspects—Dawkins and Hitchens and Harris and Company—with one power-pointing hand tied behind their backs. What is more perplexing is their confronting or, on better days, being confronted by those who are stirred from indifference by articulate and informed Christian scholars who are equipped with empirical data, some of it of the sort which grounds this book.

What becomes of the discussions if both partners (read: academic disciplines or projects as embodied by colleagues) are moved beyond indifference toward engagement? One dreams of more lively interactions of the sort numbers of Christian scholars have enjoyed in recent years. A person can begin by detailing the varieties of interests that "secularization" invites. Second that with reference to the fact that globally religion prospers against all odds. Although this fact may not convince others that Christianity is "true," it can open promising conversations.   As often pointed out, argument is based on having the answer in a disputed issue. The answer may come as a thesis, a hypothesis, a provocation, a resort to claimed possessions of absolutes. In the debates, the contender who holds the answer sets out to convince, convert, or defeat the other. The inhabitants *in partibus infidelium* are all prepared for such attempts. If a CCCU-inspired scholar chooses to come on to prove "the six-day creation" as a necessary corollary to taking the Genesis account of Creation seriously, all inquiry stops and the gray cloud of dismissal or the black cloud of scorn follows. If the Christian, grounded in faith, asks something like "How might we conceive of the origins and course of the universe(s)?" there will be a reshuffling of the "sides" in debate, a call upon a wider range of resources that are made available, and modesty in claims over the outcome. Odds are, there will then be future discussions which promise further outcomes.

The authors show awareness of the ambiguities associated with secularization and the secularization thesis. Their friendly neighborhood sociologist-colleagues, assuming these are up to date on the literature, will testify to the effect that the secularization thesis in its long-dominant unquestioned form has long been called into question, and has to be used with single-quotation marks and a knowing smile. Certainly such a thesis points to significant events and trends, but what these are and what each of them does to the thesis itself is regularly called into question. Behind this, also taken for granted in these chapters, is the assumption that secularization was and is a consequence and corollary of "the Enlightenment." But the Enlightenment is also being reappraised by historians, and it turns out, in many of its dimensions, to be quasi-religious in its undergirding philosophies, outlooks and intentions—along with its fashioning of rituals and practices which bear marks which were long associated with religions.

Not a few conservative Protestants have seen these questionings of secularization and the Enlightenment as opportunities to reset discussions of sorts often associated with the term "post-modern." Whatever else post-modernity is, it represents disaggregation, "coming apart," instability. Troubling though these may be, they at least allow for a fresh encounter between religion and the patterns of thought long called simply "secular." CCCU schools have many faculty members who can exploit these openings and opportunities. I read all but the most pessimistic chapters here as efforts to depict or propose such openings.

Comfort and stimulus from noticing the copings of others

To mention the ways advocates of the secularization-thesis and the Enlightenment are off-balance today might be to suggest a plausible occasion for *Schadenfreude*, rejoicing in the misfortunes of others. Certainly to engage in such is tempting if the Christians scholars simply want to act upon their impulses to resent the resenters of their Christian enterprise. Certainly, arrogant and unthinking dismissals of religion in all its forms set people up for a challenge if not a fall when their cultural, psychological, and intellectual foundations are called into question. At the same time, the post-modern situation is better viewed not as a time to rejoice in the assaults which those who devised, or for too long, have lived with the mixed blessings of modernity.

At the same time, some of the essays here reflect some of the isolation which authors of others in this same book decry. We hear something like, "We are alone." "Why don't others appreciate us?" Asking that question impels those who speak of isolation to look around and seek company among scholars and publics at large. If they take their own advice, they will see that they are not alone. Whoever inhabits halls of academe for any length of time knows how members of all the disciplines and professions so regularly complain that they meet silence, are dismissed as irrelevant, or are met with ignorant stares by those in such disciplines. Here it is impossible to serve as a partner-broker, but it is appropriate to point in several directions.

For example, the attempt to deal with rocks and rills (not simple slopes) of the secularization landscape in which we are all putatively sliding down does not occur only within the walls of academe. During the bumpy ride, with its downs and ups, it is valuable to look around at the larger scene and to determine that the other powers and structures are also shaped by this or that academic discipline and the prevailing assumptions of practitioners within each. Certainly the academy has culture-shaping power, but it is not unique and should not be granted inevitable superiority. Alongside it are other structures, such as those connected with entertainment, commerce, the arts, religion, politics, and public life. These are, for millions, bearers of the sacred, however tortured their place and expression may be.

To illustrate: many of the effects these authors associate with secular culture were not the result of purely secular and anti-sacred impulses. "The sacred" lives on in the experience of people individually and in groups. It serves to be analyzed, criticized, and exploited alongside classically religious effects. CCCU intellectuals are tempted to look out on how others have made their impacts as public intellectuals, or, better in this context, as public scholars. What has to be noted is that many of these make their impact outside the walls of academe. They are entrepreneurial, charismatic, news-making sorts who would be neglectful of students, if they had students. Scholar-teachers in all the disciplines in the academy interact with the worlds mediated by such public scholars, and one hopes that there will be more of them. But serving in the public-intellectual role may not be focal to their vocation. Pursuing it too avidly may lead to neglect of other responsibilities.

Add to this that some of the expression sought by numbers of authors in this collection are more readily attained through graduate universities than through undergraduate teaching. The reasons for this are simple: the graduate professor is called to be productive (of "new knowledge" as suggested in the pretentious, semi-fictional claim or assignment in many Ph.D. programs) and is more regularly expected or given incentive to issue forth in publications. Having been a pastor for a decade, I well learned that the calling prevented me from being as devoted to scholarly pursuits as my graduate professors had been. Desperate to keep up on what one must know, biblically, ethically, doctrinally, and pastorally in order to be a reasonably effective pastor, I read all that I could, attended conferences, went to graduate seminars, but could never pretend to be contributing to scholarship as conventionally pictured.

During thirty-five years of teaching in graduate schools I tried to teach undergraduates in every sixth course and found that the intellectual and temporal demands among them were more strenuous than were the advanced programs and projects under-taken with near-Ph.D.s. To illustrate: we gave strong incentives to and made strenuous demands, post-tenure, of professors at the college where I had been on the board and was for some months acting president. I became amazed at the ingenuity, consecration, learning, and focus of many of the professors there. But as they published and did not perish, they had to envy me, since all the while in graduate teaching situations I could enjoy an almost four-month summer without classroom duties, plus a quarter off for research every two years, and a teaching schedule they had to envy. If the authors would reassess the intellectual contributions that have a public dimension, they would find that the majority are graduate faculty or come from schools where sabbaticals come frequently and bounties come regularly.

More fruitful than just taking on the valuable and urgent short-range issue of taking on the culture within the various disciplines, one could look for more accent on long-range programs designed to help produce graduates who in the decades ahead, in politics, the arts, commerce, and education, could find appropriate ways to deal with secular-pluralist contexts. These CCCU schools give much attention to the question of how to preserve or, better, to enlarge upon Christian convictions in the academy, but they can also transfer these energies to help shape students who can continue the work beyond the academy.

I wonder whether the CCCU schools and their analysts and programmers, including some in this book, might be underselling their own achievements. The generation which came to maturity in the decades after World War II included an increasing number of scholars brought up in evangelicalism and its counterparts. However, for a variety of rea-sons, most of the scholars in it obscured their origins in, for example, fundamentalism and then spent much of their subsequent careers "taking revenge on their own spiritual past," as Max Scheler put it. It was a truism based on common observation that many of the foremost scholars in international relations, comparative literature, and anthro-pology were "missionary kids." They had acquired new missions as adults, in situations which did not allow them easily to celebrate or nurture their roots.

The generation (after "ours," I have to say) began to change and find a new place. More pioneers broke precedent by doing graduate work at the elite schools, and, while being transformed—isn't education supposed to transform people?—more of them stayed loyal and found new topics and approaches. A collection of philosophers in the American Philosophical Association wearied of being segregated or dismissed, and orga-nized a caucus which became among the largest and most animated in the Association at a time when language analysis and other anti-metaphysical assumptions were still simply ruling out religious concerns. The Modern Language Association as a whole may not have "got religion," but significant elements within it found a voice. In my own disci-pline, American Religious History, within one generation scholars at home in CCCU-type schools came to lead the discipline. Let me name a few: Mark Noll and George Marsden (who also contributes to this book), Edith Blumhofer, Grant Wacker, Harry Stout. I am not leading any Office of Inquisition or Doctrinal Affairs and so have not given them "faith tests," but I do know their cultural impact. Many of my own Ph.D. students came from these CCCU schools and their kin, and competed in prestigious graduate schools. So, a critic questions, they don't easily make a mark, and don't dominate? Who does?

Expressions of Christian intention in the larger societal context

Many of the CCCU colleges and universities that one comes across, as I have done when visiting as a lecturer, will impress for the ways in which they outstrip many other institutions in their contributions to inter-racial and inter-ethnic programs. Many of these Christian schools take on part of the mission which their church bodies or interest groups have supported, namely, education on other continents. Students exchanged in such programs contribute to the "multi-" situation of these schools which do not have extraordinary means of supporting foreign students. Is the larger public aware of the cosmopolitanism of these schools, which many dismiss as provincial? Having offered consolation for short-comings on other fronts, I have to add one here: producing within only a generation or two a complement of potential faculty members across the many disciplines is extremely difficult. Well-funded state and other secular schools also have difficulty achieving diversity of ethnic groups on faculties, and it should be noted that in some instances church-related academies do better than they in this "competition" for talent.

The difficult cases of anti-evolution and the sexual revolution

Any outsider like myself cannot bypass what may be the most troubling issue raised by these essays, an issue that is well-addressed by some authors and the people they quote. I refer to evolution. We recall that American Protestant fundamentalism rose in the century after 1859 mainly in response to "German" biblical criticism, progressivism in politics, social action, and philosophy, and Darwinian evolution. The first of these two are not fields which create the most scandal in the academy. Biblical higher criticism may be and is a problem in conservative churches, but the secular academy is generally unstirred. There are many ways to study texts, and the higher critical is one of them, in the eyes of most in universities. Meanwhile, over against progressivisms, fundamentalist scholars long reread the signs of the times as well as the Bible, and came up with a new round of apocalypticisms. When these loomed in politics, opponents responded politically. But they left end-of-the-world talk to Adventists, right-wing politicians, and folk religion. With evolution it was different.

As Professor Van Till and others here point out, evolutionary thinking is so integral to so many dimensions of scientific research and so rooted in the empirical situation that not to teach it, says the secular academy and say many Christians in it (and in select CCCU schools), is to prepare graduates unprepared for science. Anti-evolution is the one among all the scandals that reaches the world of cartoons, late-night comics, and mainstream church members, beginning with orthodox Roman Catholics, who have their own way of coming to terms with and then making use of evolution, and removed the predecessor "anti-" from the agenda. There is no way that I, a non-scientist, could talk anyone out of conventional anti-evolutionary thinking or into pro-evolutionary approaches. But I can make the common-sense observation that "Creation Research" and "Intelligent Design" did not find a durable base and place to serve as an alternative, and issues connected with evolution will stand in the way of interactions in the academy.

As for behavioral issues, one does not envy the administrators, chaplains, teachers, and counselors who set out counter-culturally to keep students from being absorbed into the sexual ethic, if one may call it that, in the terms of pop-culture. I read the chapter on that subject and came away with admiration for those in positions of responsibility who find ways to relate, and I will have interest in the progression of outcomes and gratitude that I am not placed where one must give counsel. The authors who pursue the issue of "control"—as in the case of *in loco parentis*—point to places and programs in which evangelicals do offer an alternative.

Some conclusions about conclusions

- I was surprised to see how neglected or besieged compulsory chapel attendance for students and expected attendance by faculty is. It's hard to see it survive at most schools and it is easy to see that something collegial (if not spiritual) will be lost if this marker of Christian participation weakens too much or fades.
- Assets of Christian education as practiced in these schools do not get advertised as much as they might be, even in these essays critical of defensiveness. Let me illustrate. At a gathering of academics from various schools in our metropolis a conversation developed in which someone from a state university said to a nationally recognized leader in one of the disciplines: "You are so published, so anthologized, so cross-referenced, that I would picture you'd be in demand at a state school like ours. Are you settling for being at a church-related school, or would you escape if you could?" Her answer: "I am right where I like to be. If we have some constraints, they are more or less of the sort typified by the phrase, 'You don't have the liberty to shout "Fire!" in a crowded theater.'" She went on: "Have you ever thought of this? I can assign texts by the great atheists and discuss atheism freely. In secular state schools, would I be so free to appraise the subject from so many angles?"
- Are CCCU colleges and universities to some extent intellectually sequestered because people in them believe "strange" and "other" things than are ordinarily represented in the mainstream? Maybe it is the *kind* of strange things that create the offense to others. Millions of faculty and students in Catholic schools believe all kinds of things about the "substance" of bread and wine in the Mass, or that Jesus is both human and divine and not just the 'nice guy' who taught well. Catholics offend when aspects of their sexual ethic get "imposed" by political interests, but it is not the transcendent

or supernatural aspects of Catholic living that create the problems. It is important to ask why something like anti-evolution teaching is a problem for the academy while many other doctrinal matters are not in the spotlight, or do not create scandal when they are.

- Where Christian schools choose to stress some counter-cultural aspects of their life and witness, and ours are cultures which ought to invite "countering," why should Christians be offended by the offended? In their tradition is a word of Jesus: "Woe to you, if all people speak well of you." Articulate believers do not have to go picking fights, but they should not be surprised if not everything they do fits the mainstream, if there is such place.

- One of the saddest revelations in the book has to do with administrators who were too inconsiderate, suspicious, or untrusting to circulate among the students one of the surveys on which the book is based. The authors had gone through proper channels and made no secret of the positive intent of what they were about. I should think that if there is an interest in presenting the best face possible on these more than one hundred institutions, leaders among them would take care to learn some etiquette and to foster and trust trust. Pardon my breach of etiquette for pointing this out.

- One of the best lines in the book is in the Joeckel-Chesnes essay: "Our argument . . . should not be taken as an indictment of conservatism . . . . Instead, [it] should be read as an admonition against the creation of a homogeneous academic culture that intimidates into silence those who disagree. When such a culture mobilizes the vigilance against secularization, intimidation and silence become more likely, threatening to stifle a thriving academic environment founded on open and honest conversation." That could serve as an epigraph for this book or a trigger for a good conference on the advantages of diversities of many sorts in CCCU schools.

- I read many paragraphs and even chapters in this book as implicit counsel, for example, in cases where there are discernments and definitions of secularization and how to meet its many varieties: "Be of good courage. Be not afraid. Be responsible, but be free." Such a message has value in secular schools too, which impose their own orthodoxies and stimulate timidity and fear.

- I end with a word of hope: that these chapters will provide a basis for discussion of its finding and the issues in CCCU schools and beyond them, and will contribute to the responsible growth of these schools. And I hope that those skeptical of the intent of the survey on which it is based will have been converted to see its value, which is significant.

APPENDIX

Faculty Survey Aggregate Data

FSQ 1: How many years have you taught at your college/university?

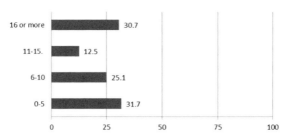

FSQ 2: What is your gender? (in percent, N = 1907)

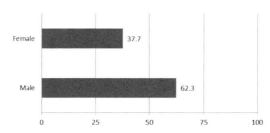

FSQ 3: What is your ethnicity? (in percent, N = 1907)

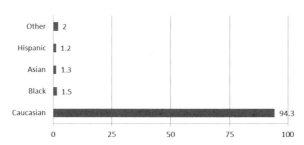

FSQ 4: What is your political affiliation? (in percent, N = 1907)

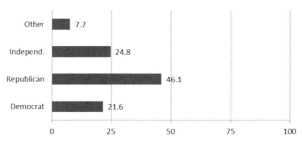

FSQ 5: Would you consider yourself to be theologically conservative or liberal? (in percent, N = 1907)

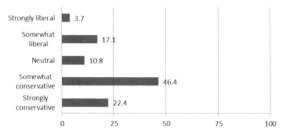

FSQ 6: Which of the following is the highest degree you received? (in percent, N = 1907)

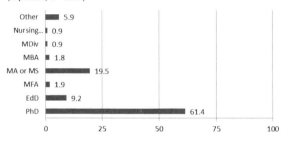

FSQ 7: How long have you been a Christian? (in percent, N = 1907)

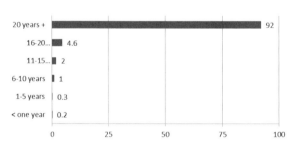

FSQ 8: How often, on average, do you attend church (excluding chapel at your college/university)? (in percent, N = 1907)

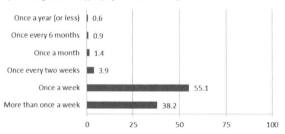

FSQ 9: To which religious denomination do you belong? (free response, N = 1907)

FSQ 10: To which religious denomination do you belong? (free response, N = 1907)

FSQ 11: I have written a published book.   (in percent, N = 1907)

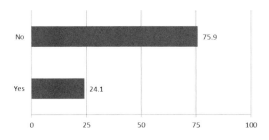

FSQ 12: I have written an article published in a refereed or peer-reviewed journal. (in percent, N = 1907)

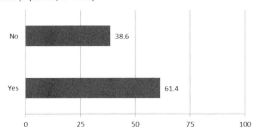

FSQ 13: How many essays/papers have you presented at conferences over the past two years?(in percent, N = 1907)

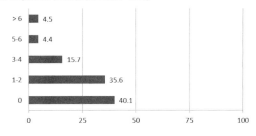

FSQ 14: Attending chapel at my college/university has enhanced my faith. (in percent, N = 1862)

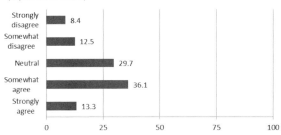

FSQ 15: The classes I've taught at this college/university have enhanced my faith. (in percent, N = 1869)

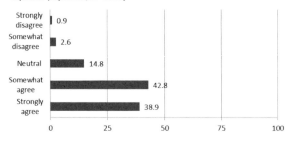

FSQ 16: Other faculty at this college/university have enhanced my faith. (in percent, N = 1869)

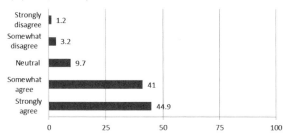

FSQ 17: As a result of the time I've spent at my college/university, my faith has: (in percent, N = 1862)

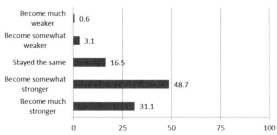

FSQ 18: I have a good idea of what is meant by the phrase, 'the integration of faith and learning.' (in percent, N = 1866)

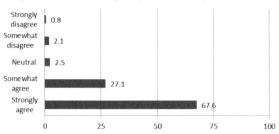

FSQ 19: It is not difficult for me to integrate faith and learning in my discipline. (in percent, N = 1862)

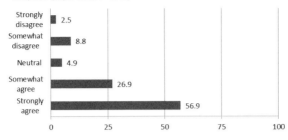

FSQ 20: My college/university has been negatively influenced by secularism. (in percent, N = 1855)

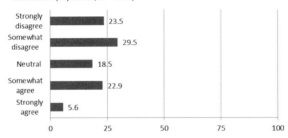

FSQ 21: Why did you take a job at a Christian college/university? (in percent, N = 1866)

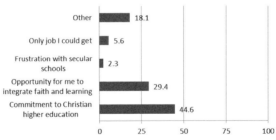

FSQ 22: I am comfortable affirming my college's/university's faith statement. (in percent, N = 1856)

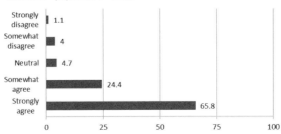

FSQ 23: I wish my college's/university's statement of faith were more generic and more broadly defined Christianity. (in percent, N = 1853)

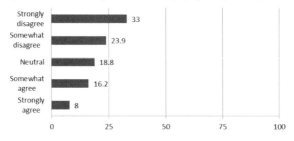

FSQ 24: If I no longer agreed with my college's/university's faith statement, I would leave. (in percent, N = 1854)

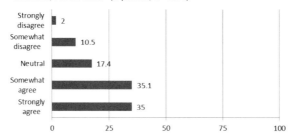

FSQ 25: My college/university should maintain its Christian identity. (in percent, N = 1861)

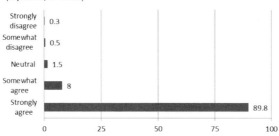

FSQ 26: Attending chapel should remain (or, if applicable, become) mandatory for faculty at my college/university. (in percent, N = 1852)

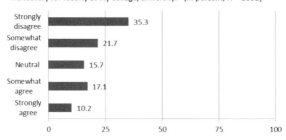

FSQ 27: My students are eager to learn and grow intellectually.
(in percent, N = 1864)

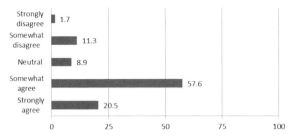

FSQ 28: My students would be willing to skip a class if it interfered with a
Bible study, missions trip meeting, or some other religious meeting held on
campus. (in percent, N = 1860)

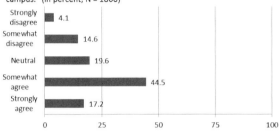

FSQ 29: Roman Catholics should not instruct at a Christian
college/university that has Protestant origins. (in percent, N = 1864)

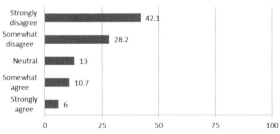

FSQ 30: My interpretation of the Bible has changed sometime within the
past year. (in percent, N = 1840)

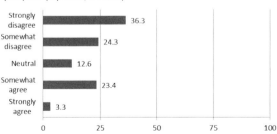

FSQ 31: It is possible that my interpretation of the Bible will change sometime in the future. (in percent, N = 1841)

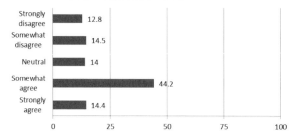

FSQ 32: The Bible is the only authoritative source of information about God. (in percent, N = 1833)

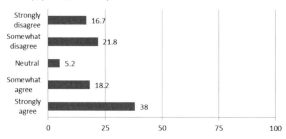

FSQ 33: I have had doubts over the past year about the Bible's authority. (in percent, N = 1833)

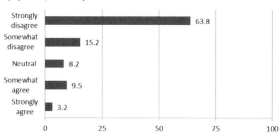

FSQ 34: It is acceptable to question the Bible. (in percent, N = 1825)

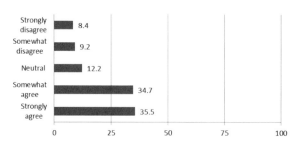

FSQ 35: Diversity of theological opinions among faculty and students is healthy for a Christian college/university.   (in percent, N = 1833)

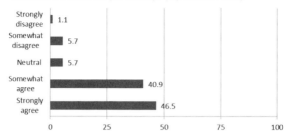

FSQ 36: I believe in biblical inerrancy.   (in percent, N = 1825)

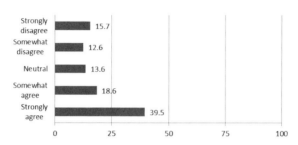

FSQ 37: I have had doubts about my faith over the past year. (in percent, N = 1831)

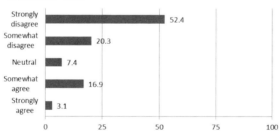

FSQ 38: Compared to my faith before graduate school, my faith after graduate school was: (in percent, N = 1831)

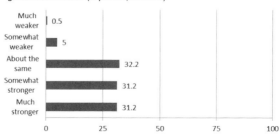

FSQ 39: Answers to moral questions are primarily black and white, not shades of gray. (in percent, N = 1816)

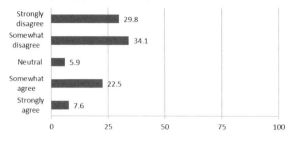

FSQ 40: Truth is absolute, not relative.   (in percent, N = 1813)

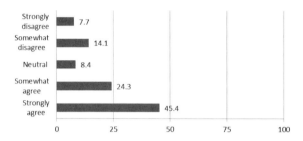

FSQ 41: My approach to my discipline is shaped by my gender. (in percent, N = 1821)

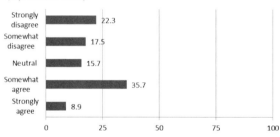

FSQ 42: My approach to my discipline is shaped by my religious beliefs. (in percent, N = 1825)

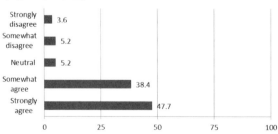

FSQ 43: Postmodernism can be compatible with Christianity.
(in percent, N = 1808)

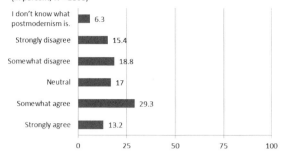

FSQ 44: What is your perception of the frequency with which students at
your college/university engage in binge drinking (five or more drinks on a
single occasion)?   (in percent, N = 1778)

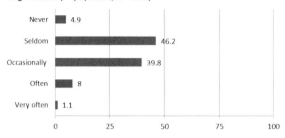

FSQ 45: What percentage of students at your college/university would you
estimate have had premarital sexual intercourse? (in percent, N = 1740)

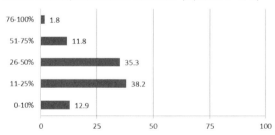

FSQ 46: My college's/university's rules for students regarding alcohol are
fair and reasonable.   (in percent, N = 1801)

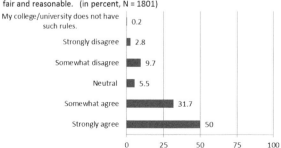

FSQ 47: My college's/university's rules for students regarding sex are fair and reasonable. (in percent, N = 1777)

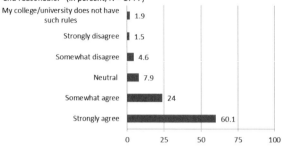

FSQ 48: My college's/university's rules for students regarding curfew are fair and reasonable. (in percent, N = 1769)

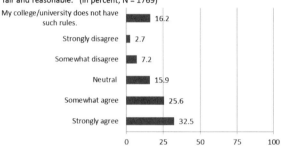

FSQ 49: My college's/university's rules for students regarding dress code are fair and reasonable. (in percent, N = 1782)

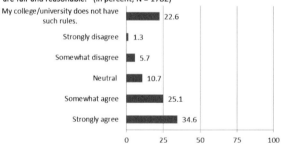

FSQ 50: Do you believe students at your college/university live sheltered lives? (in percent, N = 1809)

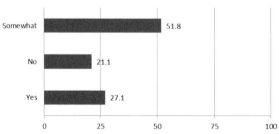

FSQ 51: The theory of evolution is compatible with Christianity.
(in percent, N = 1791)

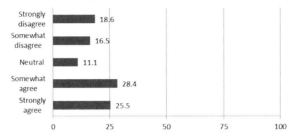

FSQ 52: Intelligent Design is a valid alternative to the theory of evolution.
(in percent, N = 1789)

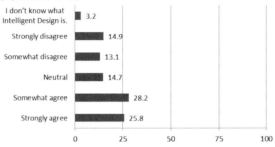

FSQ 53: The evidence for human-induced climate change is convincing.
(in percent, N = 1793)

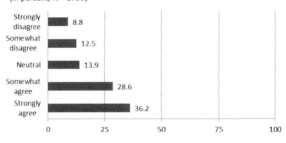

FSQ 54: Global climate change is significantly influenced by human
activities which produce greenhouse gases.   (in percent, N = 1788)

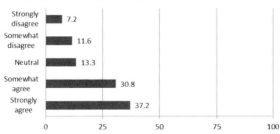

FSQ 55: In general, do you think that a rise in the world's temperature (caused by the "greenhouse effect") is: (in percent, N = 1769)

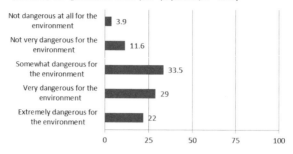

FSQ 56: Do you think that a rise in the world's temperature (caused by the "greenhouse effect") is: (in percent, N = 1772)

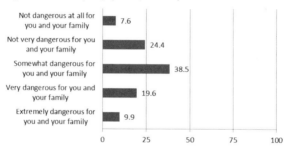

FSQ 57: It is just too difficult for someone like me to do much about the environment.(in percent, N = 1786)

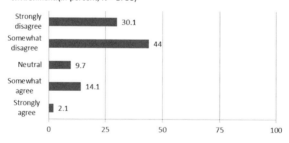

FSQ 58: I do what is right for the environment, even when it costs more money or takes more time.   (in percent, N = 1795)

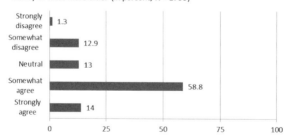

FSQ 59: How willing would you be to accept cuts in your standard of living in order to protect the environment? (in percent, N = 1786)

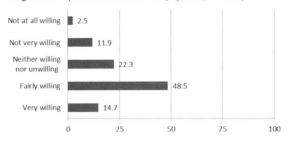

FSQ 60: I sort my garbage for the purpose of recycling. (in percent, N = 1796)

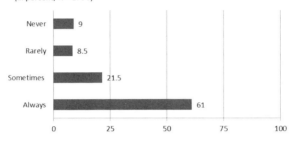

FSQ 61: It is important for Christians to care for the environment. (in percent, N = 1790)

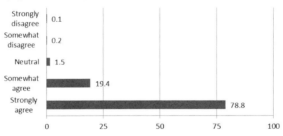

FSQ 62: Federal government agencies should provide funding for embryonic stem cell research. (in percent, N = 1789)

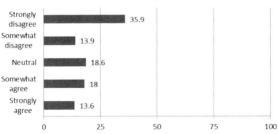

FSQ 63: I am morally opposed to embryonic stem cell research.
(in percent, N = 1781)

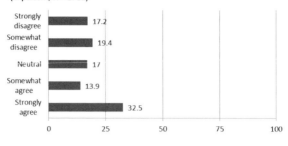

FSQ 64: People become homosexual because of : (in percent, N = 1862)

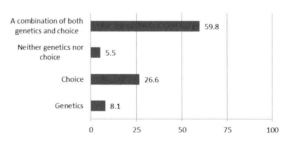

FSQ 65: Homosexuals should be given the right to marry.
(in percent, N = 1862)

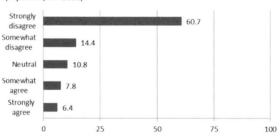

FSQ 66: Homosexuals should be given the right to form civil unions.
(in percent, N = 1760)

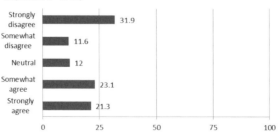

FSQ 67: Practicing homosexuals should be allowed membership in a Christian church.   (in percent, N = 1754)

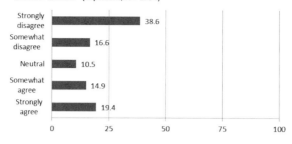

FSQ 68: Racial discrimination exists today.   (in percent, N = 1766)

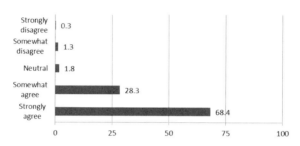

FSQ 69: Would you be uncomfortable if your neighbor were from a minority group?   (in percent, N = 1767)

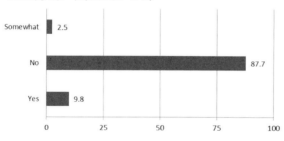

FSQ 70: Women should have the right to become pastors. (in percent, N = 1761)

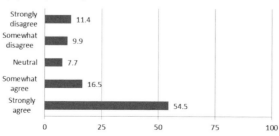

FSQ 71: Abortion is morally wrong.   (in percent, N = 1758)

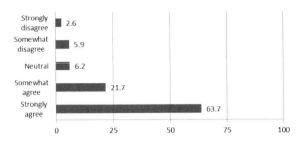

FSQ 72: Abortion should be made illegal in the United States.
(in percent, N = 1759)

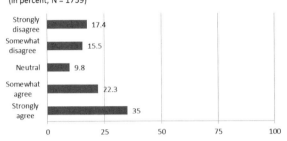

FSQ 73: I support the military campaign in Iraq.   (in percent, N = 1756)

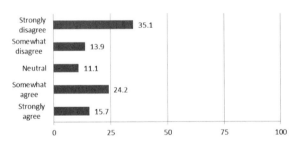

FSQ 74: The United States was founded as a Christian nation.
(in percent, N = 1755)

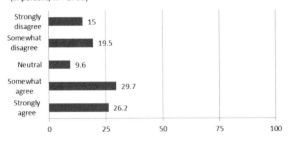

FSQ 75: I have experienced guilt because of my moral failings within the past year.   (in percent, N = 1757)

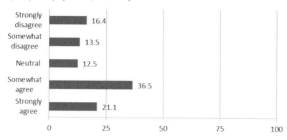

FSQ 76: Premarital sexual intercourse is wrong.   (in percent, N = 1758)

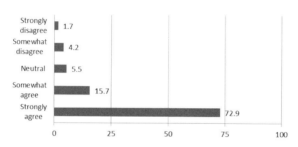

FSQ 77: I support abstinence-only sex education.   (in percent, N = 1754)

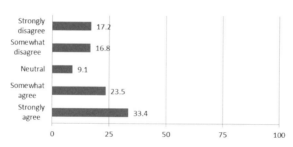

FSQ 78: It is morally wrong to watch an 'R-rated' film, even if you're 17 or older.   (in percent, N = 1752)

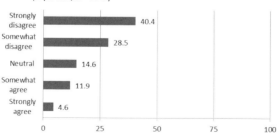

FSQ 79: A spirit of humility and charity exists among faculty at my
college/university.   (in percent, N = 1740)

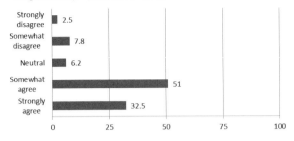

FSQ 80: Conflict among faculty at my college/university is charitably
resolved.   (in percent, N = 1737)

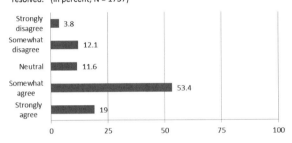

FSQ 81: A spirit of humility and charity between faculty and
administration exists at my college/university.   (in percent, N = 1740)

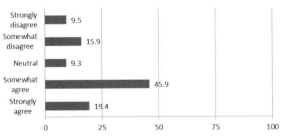

FSQ 82: Conflict between faculty and administration at my
college/university is charitably resolved.   (in percent, N = 1731)

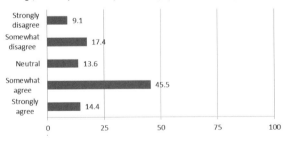

FSQ 83: The administration at my college/university is doing a good job of running the institution.   (in percent, N = 1737)

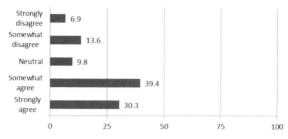

FSQ 84: The administration at my college/university performs its work in a Christ-like manner.   (in percent, N = 1736)

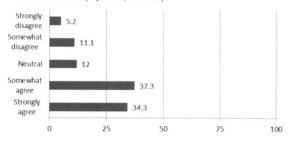

FSQ 85: Morale among faculty at my college/university is good. (in percent, N = 1736)

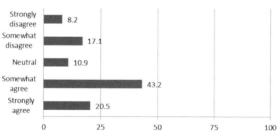

FSQ 86: How many courses do you typically teach each semester (or, if applicable, trimester)?   (in percent, N = 1731)

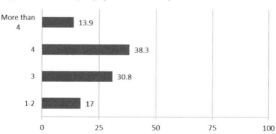

FSQ 87: I would welcome a course-load reduction for the express purpose of spending more time doing research. (in percent, N = 1729)

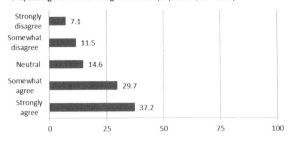

FSQ 88: The student body at my college/university is racially diverse. (in percent, N = 1729)

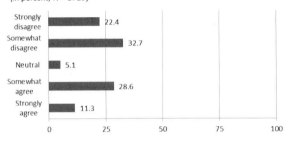

FSQ 89: Female faculty at my college/university are treated equally to male faculty. (in percent, N = 1729)

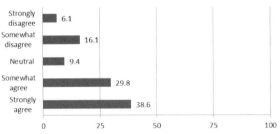

FSQ 90: Female students at my college/university are treated equally to male students. (in percent, N = 1733)

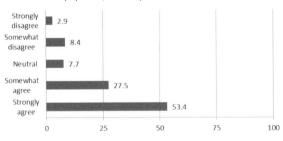

FSQ 91: My college/university is a place of vibrant spiritual activity.
(in percent, N = 1733)

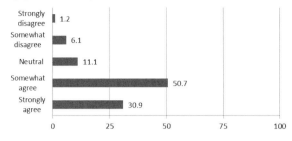

FSQ 92: Religious hypocrisy among faculty is a problem at my
college/university. (in percent, N = 1724)

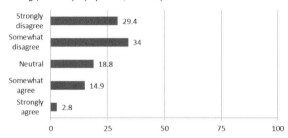

FSQ 93: Religious hypocrisy among students is a problem at my
college/university. (in percent, N = 1724)

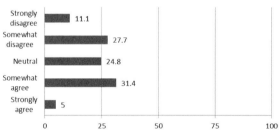

FSQ 94: My college/university is a place of rigorous intellectual activity.
(in percent, N = 1732)

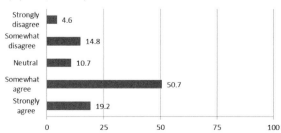

FSQ 95: I believe my college/university is following a course directed by God. (in percent, N = 1725)

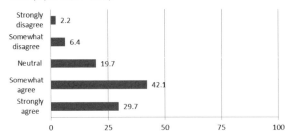

FSQ 96: I possess academic freedom at my college/university. (in percent, N = 1733)

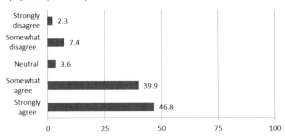

FSQ 97: Professors at Christian institutions have more freedom to discuss issues and ask questions than do professors at secular institutions. (in percent, N = 1862)

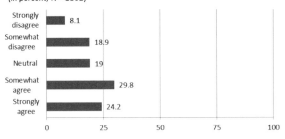

FSQ 98: I am hesitant to address certain important issues in class because I teach at a Christian college/university. (in percent, N = 1733)

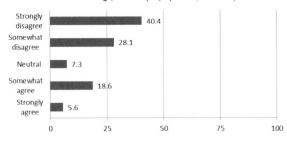

FSQ 99: The secular academy as a whole is dismissive of Christian scholarship.   (in percent, N = 1725)

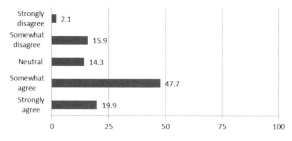

FSQ 100: I have had to (or will have to) compromise my faith to some degree in order to succeed in my research/scholarship. (in percent, N = 1862)

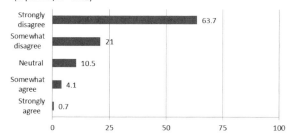

FSQ 101: The education I received at a secular college/university was good.   (in percent, N = 1738)

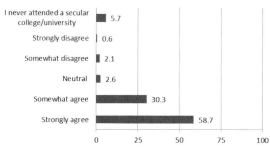

FSQ 102: My faith was ridiculed or rejected at the secular college/university I attended.   (in percent, N = 1737)

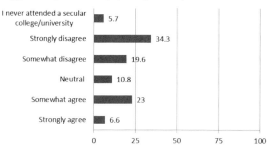

FSQ 103: From what college/university did you obtain your highest degree? (free response, N = 1639)

FSQ 104: Do you believe the education students receive at a Christian college/university is superior to that at a secular/state school? Why or why not? (free response, N = 1575)

FSQ 105: List two characteristics of the ideal or perfect student. (free response, N = 1588)

FSQ 106: What is the most difficult part about being a professor at a Christian university? (free response, N = 1512)

FSQ 107: What one piece of advice would you give to incoming freshmen at your college/university concerning academic life? (free response, N = 1514)

FSQ 108: What one piece of advice would you give to incoming freshmen at your college/university concerning religious life? (free response, N = 1502)

Student Survey Aggregate Data

SSQ 1: What is your gender? (in percent, N = 2388)

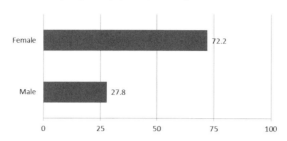

SSQ 2: What is your class ranking? (in percent, N = 2388)

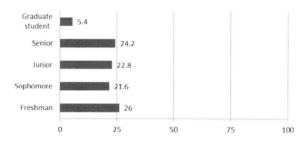

SSQ 3: To which of the following identities do you most identify?
(in percent, N = 2388)

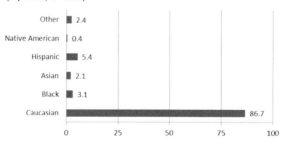

SSQ 4: What is your political affiliation? (in percent, N = 2388)

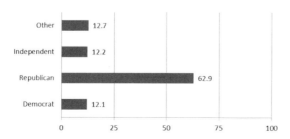

SSQ 5: What kind of high school did you attend?   (in percent, N = 2388)

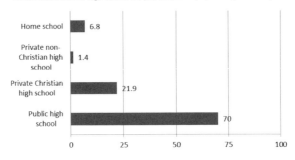

SSQ 6: How long have you been a Christian?   (in percent, N = 2388)

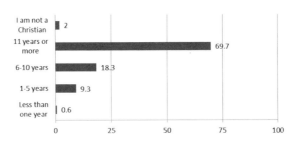

SSQ 7: What is your current GPA at your college/university? (If you are a Freshman, what was your unweighted GPA in high school?) (in percent, N = 2388)

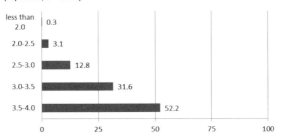

SSQ 8: What is your major? (free response, N = 2388)

SSQ 9: To which religious denomination do you belong? (Be as specific as possible--for example,   Southern Baptist.) (free response, N = 2388)

SSQ 10: Would you consider yourself to be theologically conservative or liberal? (in percent, N = 2388)

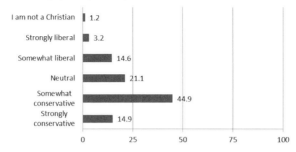

SSQ 11: My decision to attend a Christian college/university was a good decision.   (in percent, N = 2388)

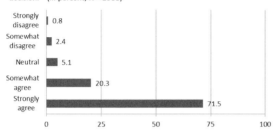

SSQ 12: What was the primary reason why you decided to attend your college/university? (in percent, N = 2388)

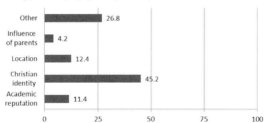

SSQ 13: Attending chapel at my college/university has enhanced my faith. (in percent, N = 2310)

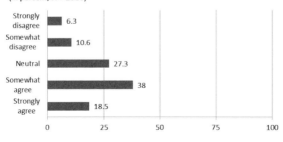

SSQ 14: The classes I've taken at this college/university have enhanced my faith.   (in percent, N = 2326)

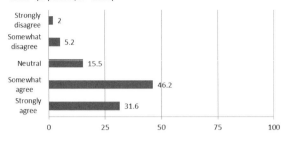

SSQ 15: The faculty at this college/university have enhanced my faith. (in percent, N = 2325)

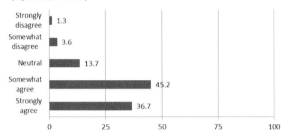

SSQ 16: As a result of the time I've spent at my college/university, my faith has: (in percent, N = 2322)

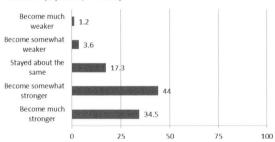

SSQ 17: I have a good idea of what is meant by the phrase, 'the integration of faith and learning.'   (in percent, N = 2319)

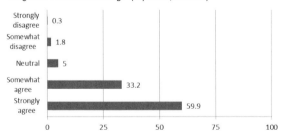

SSQ 18: I am eager to learn and grow intellectually during the time I spend at my college/university.   (in percent, N = 2329)

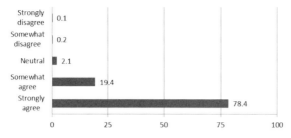

SSQ 19: I would be willing to skip a class if it interfered with a Bible study, a missions trip meeting, or some other religious meeting on campus. (in percent, N = 2327)

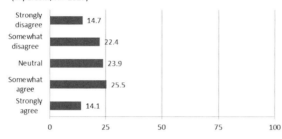

SSQ 20: There is a professor at my college/university whom I identify as a mentor.   (in percent, N = 2328)

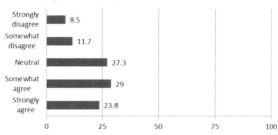

SSQ 21: My interpretation of the Bible has changed sometime within the past year.   (in percent, N = 2267)

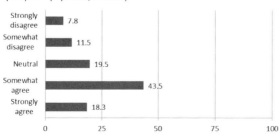

SSQ 22: It is possible that my interpretation of the Bible will change sometime in the future.   (in percent, N = 2265)

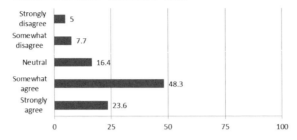

SSQ 23: The Bible is the only authoritative source of information about God.   (in percent, N = 2264)

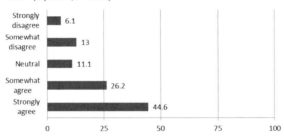

SSQ 24: I have had doubts over the past year about the Bible's authority. (in percent, N = 2267)

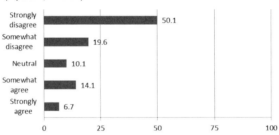

SSQ 25: It is acceptable to question the Bible.   (in percent, N = 2262)

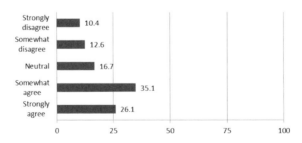

SSQ 26: Answers to moral questions are primarily black and white, not shades of gray.   (in percent, N = 2264)

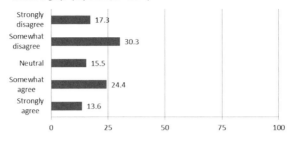

SSQ 27: I believe in biblical inerrancy.   (in percent, N = 2255)

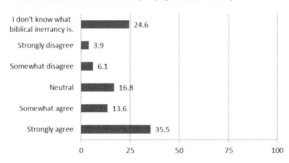

SSQ 28: Truth is absolute, not relative.   (in percent, N = 2263)

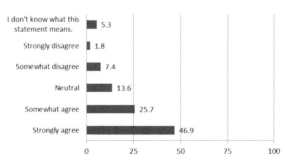

SSQ 29: Postmodernism can be compatible with Christianity. (in percent, N = 2261)

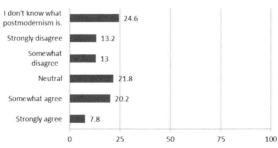

SSQ 30: Have you broken the rules regarding alcohol at your college/university?   (in percent, N = 2237)

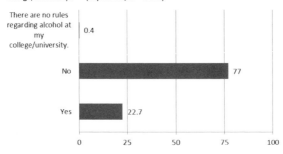

SSQ 31: Have you broken the rules regarding sex at your college/university?   (in percent, N = 2237)

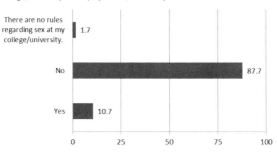

SSQ 32: Have you broken the rules regarding curfew at your college/university?   (in percent, N = 2239)

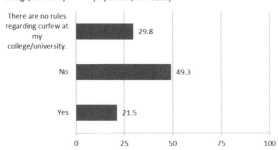

SSQ 33: Have you broken the dress-code rules at your college/university? (in percent, N = 2241)

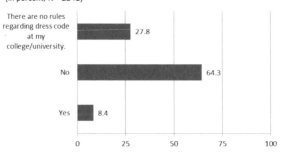

SSQ 34: Do you believe you live a sheltered life at your college/university?
(in percent, N = 2239)

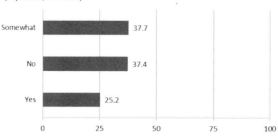

SSQ 35: Attending chapel should remain (or, if applicable, become)
mandatory for students at my college/university.   (in percent, N = 2236)

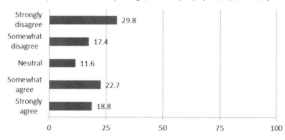

SSQ 36: Female students at my college/university are treated equally to
male students.   (in percent, N = 2244)

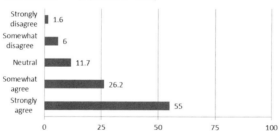

SSQ37: The student body at my college/university is racially diverse.
(in percent, N = 2241)

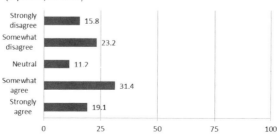

SSQ 38: Faculty at my college/university are racially diverse.
(in percent, N = 2242)

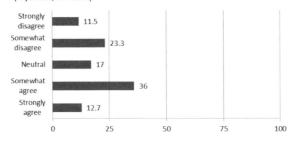

SSQ 39: The theory of evolution is compatible with Christianity.
(in percent, N = 2195)

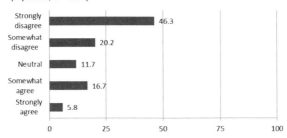

SSQ 40: Intelligent Design is a valid alternative to the theory of evolution.
(in percent, N = 2187)

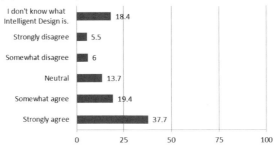

SSQ 41: It is important for Christians to care for the environment.
(in percent, N = 2188)

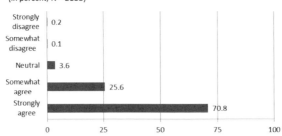

SSQ 42: The evidence for human-induced climate change is convincing.
(in percent, N =2184)

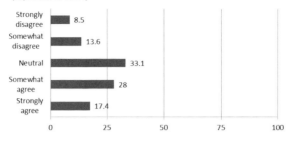

SSQ 43: Global climate change is significantly influenced by human
activities which produce greenhouse gases.   (in percent, N = 2188)

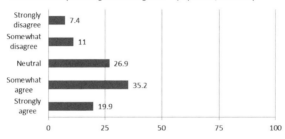

SSQ 44: It is just too difficult for someone like me to do much about the
environment.   (in percent, N = 2187)

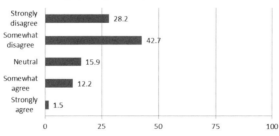

SSQ 45: I do what is right for the environment even when it costs more
money or takes more time.   (in percent, N = 2193)

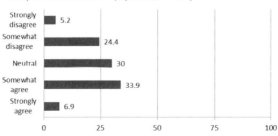

SSQ 46: How willing would you be to accept cuts in your standard of living in order to protect the environment?   (in percent, N = 2194)

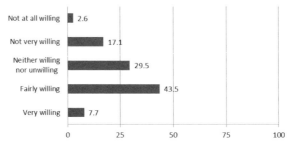

SSQ 47: I sort my garbage for the purpose of recycling. (in percent, N = 2198)

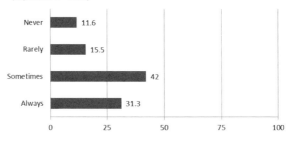

SSQ 48: Practicing homosexuals should be allowed membership in a Christian church.   (in percent, N = 2175)

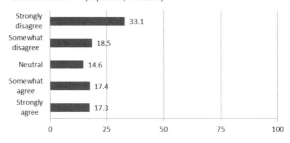

SSQ 49: Women should have the right to become pastors. (in percent, N =2175)

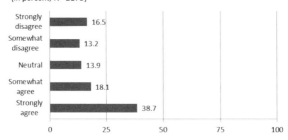

SSQ 50: Racial discrimination exists today.   (in percent, N = 2175)

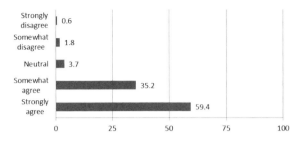

SSQ 51: Would you be uncomfortable if your neighbor were from a minority group?   (in percent, N = 2174)

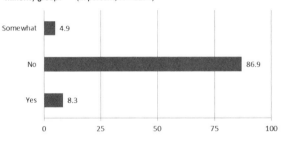

SSQ 52: Abortion is morally wrong.   (in percent, N = 2174)

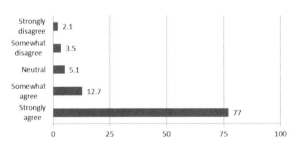

SSQ 53: I am morally opposed to embryonic stem cell research. (in percent, N = 1862)

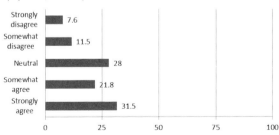

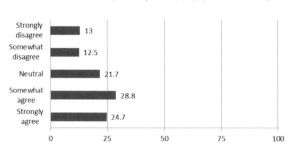

SSQ 54: I support the military campaign in Iraq.   (in percent, N = 2178)

SSQ 55: Do you believe the education you receive at a Christian college/university is superior to that at a secular/state school? Why or why not? (free response, N = 2050)

SSQ 56: What is the most difficult part about being a student at a Christian college/university? (free response, N = 2009)

CONTRIBUTORS

Wayne Barnard, Ph.D., worked in higher education for nineteen years, teaching undergraduate and graduate students at Abilene Christian University and serving as Associate Provost for Student Development and Dean of Campus Life. He now serves as Director of Student and Professional Programs for the International Justice Mission, a human rights agency that secures justice for victims of slavery, sexual exploitation, and other forms of violent oppression. Dr. Barnard holds a B.A. in Theology from Abilene Christian University, an M.A. in Marriage and Family Therapy from St. Mary's University, and a Ph.D. in Family Studies with a concentration in lifespan human development and college student development from Texas Woman's University.

Paul Blezien currently serves as the senior Vice President of William Jessup University in Rocklin, California. He has served there since 2004. Prior to that he was the Dean of Students at Northwestern College in Orange City, Iowa, and also held various posts within the University of Wisconsin system. He holds a doctorate from Azusa Pacific University, a master's degree from Ball State University and a bachelor's degree from the University of Wisconsin. He has contributed significantly to the research in faith-based higher education on the impact of short-term missions on college students.

Terriel R Byrd, Ph.D., is Professor of Christian Ministry Studies at Palm Beach Atlantic University. His publications and presentations include the *History of the First Black Church*, "The Non-African Perception of the African American Religious Experience," and "Interethnic Cultural Communication," presented at a meetings of the American Association of Behavioral Sciences and National Association of African-American Studies. His book, *I Shall Not Be Moved: Racial Separation in Christian Worship*, debuted on Amazon's "best new hot release" in the US, UK, and Canada. Byrd has served as Adjunct Professor of Homiletics for TCM International Institute in Hausa Edelweiss in Heilgenkreuz, Austria.

Thomas C Chesnes, Ph.D., Associate Professor of Biology at Palm Beach Atlantic University, has worked in estuaries, wetlands, and salt marshes throughout the southeastern United States, studying vertebrate, invertebrate, and plant species. He has researched, presented, and published work in a variety of areas including seagrass and invertebrate ecology, fisheries management, the invasive Burmese python in the Everglades, institutional sustainability, higher education, and the interface between science and religion. He has collaborated and coauthored works with undergraduate students in research, resulting in a number of peer-reviewed publications and professional presentations. He has recently published articles appearing in *Florida Scientist, North American Journal of Fisheries Management,* and *Biodiversity.*

Richard Colling, a Ph.D. microbiologist, served for twenty-eight years as Professor of Biology at Olivet Nazarene University—twenty-three years as chairman of the department. He left Christian higher education in 2009 amidst controversy surrounding his book *Random Designer*, a work promoting peace and harmony between science and faith.

Inspired by a deep love for students and a gift for communicating complex scientific concepts to general audiences, Colling believes that Biology and the Bible need never be at war and that open, honest inquiry nurtures a strong resilient faith. Colling's unique scientific perspective and strong personal faith offer a fresh new voice in the science-religion discussions.

April L Cunion, Psy.D., is an assistant professor at Regent University in Virginia Beach, Virginia. She is a licensed clinical psychologist with an emphasis on testing and assessment. Her research interests have largely addressed marriage and family issues with current research projects investigating emotional experiences of mothers, intensive mothering expectations, and prevalence rates of intimate partner violence following clinical intervention. She also has research interests in rural psychology and in the application of technological advances to better reach and serve rural populations clinically. She enjoys working collaboratively with her students and is the current advisor for both Regent University's Psi Chi group and the Undergraduate Psychology Club.

Elizabeth Lewis Hall, Ph.D., is Professor at Rosemead School of Psychology, where she teaches clinical and integration courses. In addition to teaching, she maintains a small clinical practice at the Biola Counseling Center in La Mirada, California. Her empirical research focuses on women's issues in the evangelical subculture and on the application of clinical psychology in the context of missions. In addition to publications in evangelical journals such as the *Journal of Psychology and Theology*, the *Journal of Psychology and Christianity*, and *Christian Scholar's Review*, she has contributed a Christian voice in secular venues such as *Mental Health, Religion and Culture*, *Sex Roles*, and *Psychology of Women Quarterly*.

David A Hoekema is Professor of Philosophy at Calvin College, where he has served as Academic Dean and Interim Vice President for Student Life. Previously he was Executive Director of the American Philosophical Association and taught at the University of Delaware and St. Olaf College. He received the B.A. from Calvin College and the Ph.D. from Princeton University. He serves as Publisher of *Christian Scholar's Review* and chairs the editorial board of *Soundings*. Publications include *Campus Rules and Moral Community* (Rowman and Littlefield,1994) and *Rights and Wrongs: Coercion, Punishment and the State* (Susquehanna University Press, 1986); with Bobby Fong he edited *Christianity and Culture in the Crossfire* (Eerdmans, 1997). Current research areas include political philosophy, philosophy of the arts, and the cultures and traditions of Africa.

Donald G Isaak is an associate dean of the College of Liberal Arts and Sciences at Azusa Pacific University. He earned his Ph.D. in geophysics at UCLA. Dr. Isaak has authored 50 scientific articles on mineral physics and Earth's deep interior. Prior to coming to APU, Dr. Isaak was at the Naval Research Laboratory, Washington, D.C., as a National Research Council Fellow. Among his most fulfilling life endeavors are ten years he and his family spent in West Africa during which he taught mathematics and physics in Nigerian secondary schools and served on the physics faculty at the University of Liberia.

Samuel Joeckel is Associate Professor of English and Honors Professor at Palm Beach Atlantic University. He has written on a wide range of subjects: eighteenth-century British literature, C.S. Lewis, humor theory, Christian higher education, and disability studies. His articles appear in *Christianity and Literature*, *Humor: International Journal of Humor Research*, *Christian Scholar's Review*, *SEVEN: An Anglo-American Literary Review*, *Christian Higher Education*, *Mythlore*, and *Sehnsucht: The C. S. Lewis Journal*. He served on the publications committee for the Conference on Christianity and Literature.

C Eric Jones is Associate Professor of Psychology and Director of Undergraduate Psychology at Regent University. He was previously the Associate Director and currently a board member of the Society for Christian Psychology. He earned his Ph.D. in experimental social psychology from Florida Atlantic University and his research interests include the effects of one's relationship with God on social cognition and social influence. More generally, he is engaged in using Christian understandings of human nature to articulate explanations for social thought and behavior. He is currently working on a Christian guide to the field of psychology for those graduating high school and entering college.

Allyson Jule, PhD, is Associate Professor of Education and Co-Director of the Gender Studies Institute at Trinity Western University in Langley, BC, Canada. She has particular research interests in the area of gender in the classroom, including gender at an intersection with religious identity. She is the author of *Sh-shushing the Girls* and *A Beginner's Guide to Language and Gender*. She is the editor of *Gender and the Language of Religion* and *Language and Religious Identity*, as well as co-editor of *Being Feminist, Being Christian* with Bettina Tate Pedersen. She has also written many articles which appear in *Gender and Education* and *Gender and Language* journals. Allyson Jule also serves on the Advisory Committee for the International Gender and Language Association (IGALA) and is the Media Reviews Editor for *Women and Language* journal.

Michelle V Knights, Ph.D., is Assistant Professor at Messiah College in Grantham, Pennsylvania, where she teaches in the Department of Human Development and Family Science. She has worked in higher education for twelve years and held various teaching and administrative positions with university systems in the USA and Canada. She earned a B.S. degree from York College, New York, and M.S. and Ph.D. degrees from the University of Delaware. Her empirical research focuses on development issues in children of disadvantaged backgrounds who experienced abuse and neglect.

George Marsden's best-known books are *The Soul of the American University*, *The Outrageous Idea of Christian Scholarship*, *Fundamentalism and American Culture*, and *Jonathan Edwards: A Life*. He received his Ph.D. from Yale, taught at Calvin College from 1965 to 1986, The Divinity School of Duke University from 1986 to 1992, and the

University of Notre Dame from 1992 to 2008. He has also been a visiting professor at the University of California at Berkeley, St. Andrews University, Scotland, and Harvard Divinity School. He is Francis A. McAnaney Professor of History Emeritus, University of Notre Dame. He resides in Grand Rapids, Michigan, and teaches part-time at Calvin College and Calvin Theological Seminary.

Martin E. Marty is the Fairfax M. Cone Distinguished Service Professor Emeritus at the University of Chicago. He taught in three faculties: Divinity School, History in the Social Sciences, and the Committee on the History of Culture in the Humanities. Through the decades he has participated in many campus ventures, has spoken at hundreds of them, and got a close-up view as Regent, Chair of the Board, and Interim President at St. Olaf College, which devotes much attention to the interplay of faith and learning, church and academy. He is the author of over fifty books, including the three-volume *Modern American Religion* (University of Chicago Press, 1997), *Education, Religion and the Common Good* (Jossey-Bass, 2000), and *Righteous Empire* (Harper & Row, 1977), which won the National Book Award.

Jennifer McKinney is Director of Women's Studies and Associate Professor of Sociology at Seattle Pacific University in Seattle, Washington. Jennifer's primary research focuses on American evangelical Christianity and how messages about gender and family are disseminated through evangelical megachurches. Jennifer's other research interests include how full-time ministry internships impact post-baccalaureates' evaluations of their call to ministry, as well as how evangelical movements within mainline denominations help to keep the mainline afloat. Jennifer has published in *The Sociological Quarterly*, the *Journal for the Scientific Study of Religion*, *The Journal of Youth Ministry*, and *Christianity Today*.

Alvaro L Nieves, Professor of Sociology, received the B.A. from the University of Miami, M.A. from the University of Kentucky and Ph.D. from Virginia Tech. Before joining the faculty at Wheaton College in 1983, he served as a Senior Research Scientist at Battelle, Pacific Northwest Laboratories in Richland, Washington. Since coming to Wheaton he served as Chair of the Department of Sociology and Anthropology from 1988 to 1994 and from 2006 to 2009. He teaches courses in Race and Ethnic Relations, Environmental Sociology, Demography, Statistics and Research Methods. He has also served as a consultant on work for the Department of Energy at Argonne National Laboratory. He recently served as the General Editor for the *Latino Heritage Bible* and as co-editor with Robert J. Priest of *This Side of Heaven: Race, Ethnicity and Christian Faith* (Oxford University Press). He and his wife Leslie Anne Nieves live in Warrenville, Illinois.

Philip Irving Mitchell is the director of the University Honors Program at Dallas Baptist University and associate professor of English. He has been twice nominated for Who's Who Among America's Teachers. His publications include essays in *Tolkien Studies*, *Christian Higher Education*, *The Journal of Christian Education and Behavior*, and contributions to *LOGOS: A Journal of Catholic Thought* and to *Approaches to Teaching* The Lord of the Rings (Norton). He is currently researching a book on G. K. Chesterton's responses to the nature of biography and history as part of a larger interest in twentieth-century British Christian responses to historiography.

Jenell Williams Paris is professor of anthropology at Messiah College in Grantham, PA. She has published four books: *Urban Disciples: A Beginner's Guide to Serving God in the City* (co-authored with Margot Owen Eyring, Judson, 2000); *Birth Control for Christians: Making Wise Choices* (Baker 2003); *Introducing Cultural Anthropology: A Christian Perspective* (co-authored with Brian M. Howell, Baker Academic, 2010); and *The End of Sexual Identity: Why Sex Is Too Important to Define Who We Are* (IVP, 2011).

Bettina Tate Pedersen is professor of literature at Point Loma Nazarene University where she teaches nineteenth- and twentieth-century British literature, women writers, and literary theory. She completed her doctorate at the University of Illinois, Urbana-Champaign. She is co-author/editor, with Allyson Jule, of *Being Feminist, Being Christian* (Palgrave 2006) and has published essays on nineteenth-century British and Canadian women writers and on teaching. She is currently at work on a book *Why Feminism Still Matters*, and two manuscripts of personal memoir. She lives with her spouse and two sons in San Diego, California.

Joe Ricke is professor of English at Taylor University, Upland, Indiana. He is a graduate of Nyack College (B.A.) and Rice University (M.A. and Ph.D.). His teaching and research interests include early drama (classical, medieval and early modern), Chaucer, medieval religious poetry, Shakespeare, early modern poetry, Christianity and literature, Lewis and Tolkien, and literary theory. He regularly performs and records in Middle English for The Chaucer Studio. He is also an actor, director, singer/songwriter, and poet. Recently, he contributed a chapter on the medieval dramatic shrew tradition to the forthcoming MLA volume, *Approaches to Teaching Taming of the Shrew*.

Daniel Russ is the Academic Dean and Director of the Center for Christian Studies at Gordon College where he also serves on the faculty. From 2002-2003 he was the Executive Director of Christians in the Visual Arts, an international arts organization that is housed at Gordon. He holds a B.A. in English from the University of Evansville, a M.A. in Biblical Studies from Dallas Theological Seminary, a M.A. in English from the University of Dallas, and a Ph.D. in Literature and Psychology from the University of Dallas. Dr. Russ has contributed to a number of books on classics, biblical studies, and cultural leadership, including *The Terrain of Comedy, The Epic Cosmos, Classic Texts and the Nature of Authority*, *The Tragic Abyss*, *An Invitation to the Classics*, and he co-authored an essay on "The Moral Imagination" published in *Christianity and the Soul of the University*. His book *Flesh-and-Blood Jesus: Learning to be Fully Human from the Son of Man* was published by Baker in 2008.

Olga Rybalkina serves as Director of International and Multicultural Programs and Assistant Professor of Education at Palm Beach Atlantic University. She received her

Ph.D. in higher education from the University of Toledo. Dr. Rybalkina's dissertation research on American and British higher education was recognized as the "Dissertation of the Year" from the Southern Association of Student Affairs Administrators. Dr. Rybalkina is the national chair for the international education knowledge community of the National Association of Student Affairs Administrators. Currently, she is engaged in research on the interrelation of spirituality and ethnicity in the identity-development process of Christian college students.

Allison Sanders graduated from Palm Beach Atlantic University with a major in English and a minor in Sociology in 2009. She then worked as a language assistant in Haute-Savoie, France. She will eventually complete a graduate degree related to language theory, and her main academic interests are within philology and the Enlightenment's influence on linguistic studies. Her graduation from a CCCU university for undergraduate studies has played an important role in her education as well as her conception of the educational process.

Edee Schulze has served in various student life capacities since 1987. After many years at Wheaton College, Edee transitioned in 2008 to take on the responsibilities of Vice President for Student Life at Bethel University (St Paul, Minnesota). Her research interests include women's issues in higher education (specifically the campus climate for women), moral and ethical development of college students and co-curricular learning experiences. Among other boards, she has served on the Executive Committee of the Association for Christians in Student Development and when she is not serving students, she works with children at risk in Latin America.

Howard J Van Till is Professor Emeritus of Physics and Astronomy at Calvin College, Grand Rapids, Michigan. A 1960 Calvin graduate, Van Till earned his Ph.D. in physics from Michigan State University in 1965. His current interests include the assessment of belief systems and the processes by which we construct them. Professor Van Till is a Founding Member of the International Society for Science and Religion and has served on the Executive Council of the American Scientific Affiliation and the Advisory Board of the John Templeton Foundation. He presently serves on the editorial boards of *Science and Christian Belief* and *Theology and Science*. His books include *The Fourth Day: What the Bible and the Heavens are Telling Us about the Creation* (Eerdmans, 1986) and a co-author of *Science Held Hostage: What's Wrong with Creation Science and Evolutionism* (IVP, 1988).

Susan Van Zanten earned her B.A. at Westmont College in 1978 and her Ph.D. from Emory University in 1982. She is the author of *A Story of South Africa: J. M. Coetzee's Fiction in Context* (Harvard, 1991) and *Truth and Reconciliation: The Confessional Mode in South African Literature* (Heinemann 2002). In addition, she coauthored, with Roger Lundin, *Literature Through the Eyes of Faith* (Harper, 1989), and is the editor of *Postcolonial Literature and the Biblical Call for Justice* (University Press of Mississippi, 1994). Susan served as the Director of the Center for Scholarship and Faculty Development at Seattle Pacific University for eight years, where she currently is professor of English.

David L Weeks, Ph.D., is a political science professor and dean of the College of Liberal Arts and Sciences at Azusa Pacific University. His academic interests include Christian liberal education, political philosophy, and American law and politics, especially the intersection of religion and politics. He has published articles on these topics in publications such as the *Journal of Church and State,* the *Christian Scholar's Review,* and the *International Encyclopedia of Political Science*. He also co-edited a book entitled *The Liberal Arts in Higher Education*. He has served as a Scholar-in-Residence at the Centre for Scholarship and Christianity in Oxford, England, a Salvatori Fellow in Washington, D.C., and has studied leadership at the Harvard Institute for Higher Education.

Carol Woodfin is associate professor of history at Hardin-Simmons University, Abilene, Texas. From 1993-2007 she taught at Palm Beach Atlantic University, West Palm Beach, Florida. She received her Ph.D. in history from Vanderbilt University, her M.A. in history from Wake Forest University, and her B.A. in history and political science from Hardin-Simmons University. She is the author of "Reluctant Democrats: The Protestant Women's Auxiliary and the German National Assembly Elections of 1919" (*Journal of the Historical Society*, 2004); "Founder, Professor, Dean, President: John D. W. Watts and the Baptist Theological Seminary, Ruschlikon, Switzerland" (*Perspectives in Religious Studies*, 2008), along with other articles and presentations on Baptist history, German Protestant women during the Weimar era, advising and mentoring undergraduate students, and microfinance in India.